reading research

ANTHOLOGY

The Why? of Reading Instruction

SECOND EDITION

ARENA PRESS   *Novato · California*

ARENA PRESS
20 Commercial Boulevard
Novato, California 94949-6191
800-422-7249
www.ATPub.com

CORE
5855 Christie Avenue, Suite A
Emeryville, California 94608
888-249-6155
www.corelearn.com

International Standard Book Number: 1-57128-207-6

10 09 08 07 06 05

15 14 13 12 11 10 09 08 07

 This icon indicates where a photograph or illustration was used in the original publication.

CREDITS

Editorial Director: Linda Gutlohn
Contributing Editors: Linda Diamond and B. J. Thorsnes
Book Design and Production: Lucy Nielsen
Permissions Editor: Veronica Oliva
Editorial Staff: Michael Cohen, Shelle Epton

ACKNOWLEDGMENTS

For each of the following selections, grateful acknowledgment is made for permission to adapt and/or reprint original or copyrighted material.

Allyn & Bacon: "Literature Circles, Book Clubs, and Literature Discussion Groups" by Nancy L. Roser, Susan Strecker, and Miriam G. Martinez. In *Promoting Literacy in Grades 4–9: A Handbook for Teachers and Administrators,* edited by Karen D. Wood and Thomas S. Dickinson. Copyright © 2000 by Allyn & Bacon. Reprinted by permission of the publisher.

American Educational Research Association: Excerpted from "A Cognitive Theory of Orthographic Transitioning: Predictable Errors in How Spanish-Speaking Children Spell English Words" by Olatokunbo S. Fashola, Priscilla A. Drum, Richard E. Mayer, and Sang-Jin Kang. In *American Educational Research Journal,* Vol. 33, No. 4, Winter 1996 issue. Copyright © 1996 by the American Educational Research Association. Adapted by permission of the publisher.

American Educator: "Getting at the Meaning: How To Help Students Unpack Difficult Text" by Isabel L. Beck, Margaret G.

McKeown, Rebecca L. Hamilton, and Linda Kucan. Reprinted with permission from the Spring/Summer 1998 issue of *American Educator,* the quarterly journal of the American Federation of Teachers and Isabel L. Beck. This material was originally published in and is adapted from *Questioning the Author: An Approach for Enhancing Student Engagement with Text.* Copyright © 1997 by the International Reading Association. "The Role of Decoding in Learning to Read" by Isabel L. Beck and Connie Juel. In S. Jay Samuels and Alan E. Farstrup (Eds.), *What Research Has to Say About Reading Instruction* (pp. 101–124). Reprinted with permission of Isabel L. Beck and the International Reading Association. All rights reserved. Page layouts reprinted with permission from the Summer 1995 issue of *American Educator,* the quarterly journal of the American Federation of Teachers.

American Psychological Association: Adapted from "Cross-Language Transfer of Phonological Awareness" by Aydin Y. Durgunoğlu, William E. Nagy, and Barbara J. Hancin-Bhatt. In *Journal of Educational Psychology,* 1993, Vol. 85, pp. 453–465. Copyright © 1993 by the American Psychological Association. Adapted with permission of the publisher. Adapted from "Reading Storybooks to Kindergartners Helps Them Learn New Vocabulary Words" by Claudia Robbins and Linnea C. Ehri. In *Journal of Educational Psychology,* 1994, Vol. 86, pp. 54–64. Copyright © 1994 by the American Psychological Association. Adapted with permission of the authors and the publisher.

Association for Supervision and Curriculum Development: "Learning About Learning to Read: A Conversation with Sally Shaywitz" by Marcia D'Arcangelo, *Educational Leadership,* October 1999, Vol. 57, No. 2, pp. 26–31. Reprinted with permission of the Association for Supervision and Curriculum Development. Copyright © 1999 by ASCD. All rights reserved. "Why Reading Is Not a Natural Process" by G. Reid Lyon. *Educational Leadership,* March 1998, Vol. 55, No. 6, pp. 14–18. Reprinted with permission of the Association for Supervision and Curriculum Development. Copyright © 1998 by ASCD. All rights reserved.

British Psychological Society: Excerpted from "Effective Academic Interventions in the United States: Evaluating and Enhancing the Acquisition of Early Reading Skills" by Roland H. Good III, Deborah C. Simmons, and Sylvia B. Smith. In *Educational and Child Psychology,* 1998, Vol. 15, No. 1. Reprinted with permission.

Brookline Books: Extract from "Language Development During Elementary School: The Gap Widens" in *Language and Reading Success* by Andrew Biemiller. (Cambridge, MA: Brookline Books, 1999), pp. 19–29. ISBN 1-57129-068-0. Used by permission of Brookline Books. A copy of this book can be obtained from Brookline Books, (800) 666-2665.

International Reading Association: Beck, Isabel L., and Juel, Connie. (1992). "The Role of Decoding in Learning to Read." In S. Jay Samuels and Alan E. Farstrup (Eds), *What Research Has to Say About Reading Instruction* (pp. 101–124. Reprinted by permission of Isabel L. Beck and the International Reading

(Continued on page 231)

CONTENTS

The Big Picture

Why Reading Is Not a Natural Process

by G. Reid Lyon

I am frequently asked why the National Institute of Child Health and Human Development (NICHD) conducts and supports research in reading, given that the NICHD is part of the National Institutes of Health, a federal agency that emphasizes basic biomedical science and health-related research. A primary answer is that learning to read is critical to a child's overall well-being. If a youngster does not learn to read in our literacy-driven society, hope for a fulfilling, productive life diminishes. In short, difficulties learning to read are not only an educational problem, they constitute a serious public health concern.

The NICHD has been studying normal reading development and reading difficulties for 35 years. NICHD-supported researchers have studied more than 10,000 children, published more than 2,500 articles, and written more than 50 books that present the results of 10 large-scale longitudinal studies and more than 1,500 smaller scale experimental and cross-sectional studies. Many of the longitudinal research sites initiated studies in the early 1980s with kindergarten children before they began their reading instruction and have studied the children over time.

Researchers have studied some children for 15 years, with several sites following the youngsters for at least 5 years. Additional research sites have joined within the past 3 years to investigate the effects of different reading instructional programs with kindergarten and first-grade children. At most research sites, multidisciplinary research teams study cognitive, linguistic, neurobiological, genetic, and instructional factors related to early reading development and reading difficulties.[1]

Reading Research and Scientific Tradition

The NICHD reading research has centered on three basic questions: (1) How do children learn to read English (and other languages)? What are the critical skills, abilities, environments, and instructional interactions that foster the fluent reading of text? (2) What skill deficits and environmental factors impede reading development? (3) For which children are which instructional approaches most beneficial, at which stages of reading development? Before summarizing findings related to these questions, I would like to explain the NICHD research process.

First, the NICHD reading research program is rooted in scientific tradition and the scientific method. The program rests on systematic, longitudinal, field-based investigations, cross-sectional studies, and laboratory-based experiments that are publicly verifiable and replicable. Second, the research integrates quantitative and qualitative methods to increase the richness, impact, and ecological validity of the data. However, using qualitative research methods requires the same scientific rigor employed in quantitative studies. Third, the NICHD reading research program is only one of many programs dedicated to understanding reading development and difficulties. The U.S. Department of Education's Office of Research and Improvement, the Office of Special Education Programs, and the Canadian Research Council have supported many outstanding reading researchers (see Adams 1990 for a research review).

From *Educational Leadership,* March 1998, Vol. 55, No. 6, pp. 14–18

The cumulative work of federally and privately funded researchers illuminates how children develop reading skills, why some children struggle to learn to read, and what can be done to help all readers reach proficiency. Although much remains to be learned, many findings have survived scrutiny, replication, and extension.

The Critical Role of Phonemic Awareness

How do children learn to read English? Reading is the product of decoding and comprehension (Gough et al. 1993). Although this sounds simple, learning to read is much tougher than people think. To learn to decode and read printed English, children must be aware that spoken words are composed of individual sound parts termed *phonemes*. This is what is meant by *phoneme awareness.*

Phoneme awareness and phonics are not the same. When educators assess phoneme awareness skills, they ask children to demonstrate knowledge of the sound structure of words *without any letters or written words present.* For example, "What word would be left if the /k/ sound were taken away from *cat*?" What sounds do you hear in the word *big*?" To assess phonics skills, they ask children to link sounds (phonemes) *with letters.* Thus, the development of phonics skills depends on the development of phoneme awareness.

Why is phoneme awareness critical in beginning reading, and why is it difficult for some children? Because to read an alphabetic language like English, children must know that written spellings systematically represent spoken sounds. When youngsters figure this out, either on their own or with direct instruction, they have acquired the alphabetic principle. However, if beginning readers have difficulty perceiving the sounds in spoken words—for example, if they cannot "hear" the /at/ sound in *fat* and *cat* and perceive that the difference lies in the first sound—they will have difficulty decoding or sounding out new words. In turn, developing reading fluency will be difficult, resulting in poor comprehension, limited

learning, and little enjoyment.

We are beginning to understand why many children have difficulty developing phoneme awareness. When we speak to one another, the individual sounds (phonemes) within the words are not consciously heard by the listener. Thus, no one ever receives any "natural" practice understanding that words are composed of smaller, abstract sound units.

For example, when one utters the word *bag*, the ear hears only one sound, not three (as in /b/-/a/-/g/). This is because when *bag* is spoken, the /a/ and /g/ phonemes are folded into the initial /b/ sound. Thus, the acoustic information presented to the ears reflects an overlapping bundle of sound, not three discrete sounds. This process ensures rapid, efficient communication. Consider the time it would take to have a conversation if each of the words we uttered were segmented into their underlying sound structure.

However, nature has provided a conundrum here: What is good for the listener is not so good for the beginning reader. Although spoken language is seamless, the beginning reader must detect the seams in speech, unglue the sounds from one another, and learn which sounds (phonemes) go with which letters. We now understand that specific systems in the brain recover sounds from spoken words, and just as in learning any skill, children understand phoneme awareness with different aptitudes and experiences.

Developing Automaticity and Understanding

In the initial stages of reading development, learning phoneme awareness and phonics skills *and* practicing these skills with texts is critical. Children must also acquire fluency and automaticity in decoding and word recognition. Consider that a reader has only so much attention and memory capacity. If beginning readers read the words in a laborious, inefficient manner, they cannot remember what they read, much less relate the ideas to their background knowledge. Thus, the ultimate goal of reading instruction—for children to understand and enjoy what they read—will not be achieved.

Reading research by NICHD and others reveals that "making meaning" requires more than phoneme awareness, phonics, and reading fluency, although these are necessary skills. Good comprehenders link the ideas presented in print to their own experiences. They have also developed the necessary vocabulary to make sense of the content being read. Good comprehenders have a knack for summarizing, predicting, and clarifying what they have read, and many are adept at asking themselves guide questions to enhance understanding.

Linguistic Gymnastics

Programmatic research over the past 35 years *has not* supported the view that reading development reflects a *natural process*—that children learn to read as they learn to speak, through natural exposure to a literate environment. Indeed, researchers have established that certain aspects of learning to read are highly unnatural. Consider the linguistic gymnastics involved in recovering phonemes from speech and applying them to letters and letter patterns. Unlike learning to speak, beginning readers must appreciate consciously what the symbols stand for in the writing system they learn (Liberman 1992).

Unfortunately for beginning readers, written alphabetic symbols are arbitrary and are created differently in different languages to represent spoken language elements that are themselves abstract. If learning to read were natural, there would not exist the substantial number of cultures that have yet to develop a written language, despite having a rich oral language. And, if learning to read unfolds naturally, why does our literate society have so many youngsters and adults who are illiterate?

Despite strong evidence to the contrary, many educators and researchers maintain the perspective that reading is an almost instinctive, natural process. They believe that explicit instruction in

phoneme awareness, phonics, structural analysis, and reading comprehension strategies is unnecessary because oral language skills provide the reader with a meaning-based structure for the decoding and recognition of unfamiliar words (Edelsky et al. 1991, Goodman 1996).

Scientific research, however, simply does not support the claim that context and authentic text are a proxy for decoding skills. To guess the pronunciation of words from context, the context must predict the words. But content words—the most important words for text comprehension—can be predicted from surrounding context only 10 to 20 percent of the time (Gough et al. 1981). Instead, the choice strategy for beginning readers is to decode letters to sounds in an increasingly complete and accurate manner (Adams 1990, Foorman et al. 1998).

Moreover, the view some whole language advocates hold that skilled readers gloss over the text, sampling only parts of words, and examining several lines of print to decode unfamiliar words, is not consistent with available data. Just and Carpenter (1987), among others, have demonstrated consistently that good readers rarely skip over words, and readers gaze directly at most content words. Indeed, in contrast to conventional wisdom, less-skilled readers depend on context for word-recognition. The word recognition processes of skilled readers are so automatic that they do not need to rely on context (Stanovich et al. 1981). Good readers employ context to aid overall comprehension, but not as an aid in the recognition of unfamiliar words. Whether we like it or not, an alphabetic cipher must be deciphered, and this requires robust decoding skills.

The scientific evidence that refutes the idea that learning to read is a *natural process* is of such magnitude that Stanovich (1994) wrote:

> That direct instruction in alphabetic coding facilitates early reading acquisition is one of the most well established conclusions in all of behavioral science. . . . The idea that learning to read is just like learning to speak is accepted by no responsible linguist, psychologist, or cognitive scientist in the research community (pp. 285–286).

Why Some Children Have Difficulties Learning to Read

Good readers are phonemically aware, understand the alphabetic principle, apply these skills in a rapid and fluent manner, possess strong vocabularies and syntactical and grammatical skills, and relate reading to their own experiences. Difficulties in any of these areas can impede reading development. Further, learning to read begins far before children enter formal schooling. Children who have stimulating literacy experiences from birth onward have an edge in vocabulary development, understanding the goals of reading, and developing an awareness of print and literacy concepts.

Conversely, the children who are most at risk for reading failure enter kindergarten and the elementary grades without these early experiences. Frequently, many poor readers have not consistently engaged in the language play that develops an awareness of sound structure and language patterns. They have limited exposure to bedtime and laptime reading. In short, children raised in poverty, those with limited proficiency in English, those from homes where the parents' reading levels and practices are low, and those with speech, language, and hearing handicaps are at increased risk of reading failure.

However, many children with robust oral language experience, average to above average intelligence, and frequent early interactions with literacy activities also have difficulties learning to read. Why? Programmatic longitudinal research, including research supported by NICHD, clearly indicates that deficits in the development of phoneme awareness skills not only predict difficulties learning to read, but they also have a negative effect on reading acquisition. Whereas phoneme awareness is necessary for adequate reading development, it is not sufficient. Children must also develop phonics concepts and apply these skills fluently in text. Although substantial research supports the importance of phoneme awareness, phonics, and the development of speed and automaticity in reading, we know less about how children develop reading comprehension strategies and semantic and syntactic knowledge. Given that some children with well developed decoding and word-recognition abilities have difficulties understanding what they read, more research in reading comprehension is crucial.

From Research to Practice

Scientific research can inform beginning reading instruction. We know from research that reading is a language-based activity. Reading does not develop naturally, and for many children, specific decoding, word-recognition, and reading comprehension skills must be taught directly and systematically. We have also learned that preschool children benefit significantly from being read to. The evidence suggests strongly that educators can foster reading development by providing kindergarten children with instruction that develops print concepts, familiarity with the purposes of reading and writing, age-appropriate vocabulary and language comprehension skills, and familiarity with the language structure.

Substantial evidence shows that many children in the first and second grades and beyond will require explicit instruction to develop the necessary phoneme awareness, phonics, spelling, and reading comprehension skills. But for these children, this will not be sufficient. For youngsters having difficulties learning to read, each of these foundational skills should be taught and integrated into textual reading formats to ensure sufficient levels of fluency, automaticity, and understanding.

Moving Beyond Assumptions

One hopes that scientific research informs beginning reading instruction, but it is not always so. Unfortunately, many teachers and administrators who could benefit from research to guide reading instructional practices do not yet trust the idea that research can inform their teaching. There are many reasons for this lack of faith. As Mary Kennedy

(1997) has pointed out, it is difficult for teachers to apply research information when it is of poor quality, lacks authority, is not easily accessible, is communicated in an incomprehensible manner, and is not practical. Moreover, the lack of agreement about reading development and instruction among education leaders does not bode favorably for increasing trust. The burden to produce compelling and practical information lies with reading researchers.

Most great scientific discoveries have come from a willingness and an ability to be wrong. Researchers and teachers could serve our children much better if they had the courage to set aside assumptions when they are not working. What if the assumption that reading is a natural activity, as appealing as it may be, were wrong and not working to help our children read? The fundamental purpose of science is to test our beliefs and intuitions and to tell us where the truth lies. Indeed, the education of our children is too important to be determined by anything but the strongest of objective scientific evidence. Our children deserve nothing less.

[1] See Fletcher and Lyon (in press) and Lyon and Moats (1997) for reviews of NICHD reading research findings. Contact the author for a complete set of references of published research from all NICHD reading research sites since 1963.

References

Adams, M. J. (1990). *Beginning to Read: Thinking and Learning about Print*. Cambridge, MA: MIT Press.

Edelsky, C., B. Altwerger, and B. Flores. (1991). *Whole Language: What's the Difference?* Portsmouth, NH: Heinemann.

Fletcher, J. M., and G. R. Lyon. (in press). *Reading: A Research-Based Approach*. Palo Alto, CA: Hoover Institute.

Foorman, B. R., D. J. Francis, J. M. Fletcher, C. Schatschneider, and P. Mehta. (1998). "The Role of Instruction in Learning to Read: Preventing Reading Failure in At-risk Children." *Journal of Educational Psychology* 90, 1–15.

Goodman, K. S. (1966). *Ken Goodman on Reading: A Common Sense Look at the Nature of Language and the Science of Reading*. Portsmouth, NH: Heinemann.

Gough, P. B., J. A. Alford, and P. Holley-Wilcox. (1981). "Words and Contexts." In *Perception of Print: Reading Research in Experimental Psychology*, edited by O. J. Tzeng and H. Singer. Hillsdale, NJ: Erlbaum.

Gough, P. B., C. Juel, and P. Griffith. (1992). "Reading, Spelling, and the Orthographic Cipher." In *Reading Acquisition*, edited by P. B. Gough, L. C. Ehri, and R. Trieman. Hillsdale, NJ: Erlbaum.

Just, C., and P. A. Carpenter. (1980). "A Theory of Reading: From Eye Fixations to Comprehension." *Psychological Review* 87, 329–354.

Kennedy, M. M. (1997). "The Connection Between Research and Practice." *Educational Researcher* 26, 4–12.

Liberman, A. M. (1992). "The Relation of Speech to Reading and Writing." In *Orthography, Phonology, Morphology, and Meaning*, edited by R. Frost and L. Katz. Amsterdam: Elsevier Science Publishers B.V.

Lyon, G. R., and L. C. Moats. (1997). "Critical Conceptual and Methodological Considerations in Reading Intervention Research." *Journal of Learning Disabilities* 30, 578–588.

Stanovich, K. E. (1994). "Romance and Reality." *The Reading Teacher* 47, 280–291.

Stanovich, K .E., R. F. West, and D. J. Freeman. (1981). "A Longitudinal Study of Sentence Context Effects in Second-grade Children: Tests of an Interactive-Compensatory Model." *Journal of Experimental Child Psychology* 32, 402–433.

Marcia D'Arcangelo   From *Educational Leadership,* October 1999, Vol. 57, No. 2, pp. 26–31

Learning About Learning to Read
A Conversation with Sally Shaywitz

Unlike speaking, reading is not an instinctive human ability. New imaging techniques now allow researchers to see how our neurocircuitry uses the brain's language system to both speak and read.

*N*euroscientist and professor of pediatrics at Yale University School of Medicine, Sally Shaywitz, along with her husband, Bennett Shaywitz, is codirector of the Yale Center for the Study of Learning and Attention. For 30 years, she has focused on understanding the brain mechanisms involved in reading. While developing "The Brain and Reading" video series, Marcia D'Arcangelo interviewed Dr. Shaywitz about her life's work.

We hear how advances in brain imaging technology let us see the brain at work. Because we wonder whether new discoveries can inform our instructional practice, learning about how the brain works is of great interest to educators today.

Educators have always been interested in the brain, but we scientists haven't had the ability to bring issues relating to the brain to education. But now, we can actually look at the working brain and examine what happens when a child tries to learn. These matters are very germane to what teachers need to know.

What do we really know about how the brain learns to read?

We know that whereas speaking is natural, reading is not. Children do not automatically read. They have to learn how to do it.

Through tens of thousands of years of evolution, men and women have developed the abilities to speak, to hear, and to listen. Every society has some form of spoken language. Put a baby in a speaking environment and that child will learn to speak. We don't have to teach children how to talk. As Stephen Pinker says, language is instinctive. But reading isn't. Reading is a recent development. Not every society reads. There isn't a little reading center in the brain. Humans haven't evolved that way. The neurocircuitry isn't set up to allow us to read.

But humans do have the capacity to read.

Over time, we have learned to use our neurocircuitry to read. The brain system that lends itself to reading is the language system. To read, a child has to use this wonderful, enriched, and robust language system to somehow get meaning from print. To do that, a child has to somehow transcode that print into language.

Are you saying that in order to read, we have to adapt, or train, our brain to perform in ways it wasn't naturally designed to work?

In essence, yes. We acquire the ability to do many things that we aren't born knowing how to do. Children have to develop the awareness that words are made up of sounds. And that print represents these sounds, or phonemes. For example, the word *bat* really has three phonemes, *b, a,* and *t,* so children have to develop this awareness. And then they have to develop the understanding that the letters on the page—the *b,* the *a,* and the *t*—represent these units of sound. When children reach this level of awareness, they're ready to learn to read. For some children, it's easy; for others, it's very difficult.

You and your group at Yale have used functional magnetic resonance imaging (fMRI) technology to analyze how the brain learns to read. Have you discovered why it is easy for some and difficult for others?

In one study, we examined very disabled readers and compared them with good readers. We found a difference in the brain activation patterns of the two groups when the task made increasing demands to break up words into their underlying phonologic structure or sound pattern.

This is very exciting and extraordinarily important.

One, it shows the functional organization of the brain for reading. Two, it shows what happens when people have trouble reading. And three, it shows when the problem occurs. Knowing all of this supports the view that reading is biologically based and lends substantial support to the phonologic hypothesis of how we read and why some people can't read.

Why is it important to understand that reading is biologically based?

We often blame children, particularly bright children who have trouble reading, for not being motivated enough or for not trying hard enough. As if somehow, it's their fault. But if we have evaluated the children, we know that they're trying hard, more than anyone can imagine. But they have nothing to show for it. Before, we could hypothesize that the child was very bright but had a real biologic difficulty making him or her unable to read. Now, we can look at an imaging pattern and say, "Aha, this is a real problem; this is as real as a broken arm that you might look at on X-ray."

Can we look at brain imaging patterns and tell which children will have trouble reading?

This technology has been an extraordinary advance, but I don't want to mislead people. We can't use it yet to diagnose an individual. Someone cannot get into the scanner and say, "Aha, I have an image, and I can have a diagnosis." But I have no doubt about the *potential* for this technology to diagnose people early and more precisely and then to actually examine the effects of interventions.

What difference, specifically, did you see in the brain patterns of good and poor readers?

Good readers had a pattern of activation in the back of the brain, the system that includes the occipital region, which is activated by the visual features of the letters; the angular gyrus where print is transcoded into language; and Wernicke's region, the area of the brain that accesses meaning. This posterior area is strongly activated in good readers, but we saw relative under-activation in poor readers.

As we asked good readers to do more and more phonologic processing—to look at single letters and tell whether they rhyme and then to look at and sound out words that they had never seen before—we could see an increase in activation in these areas. But when poor readers performed these same phonological tasks, they really didn't increase the activation in the back of the brain. There was a significant difference. What made it even more interesting was that there were differences in the front of the brain as well. When good readers read, an area in the front of the brain called the inferior frontal gyrus, or Broca's area, was activated. When poor readers read, that area was even more strongly activated.

What does this pattern of relative underactivation and overactivation in poor readers tell you?

We've interpreted this to mean that in going from print, from seeing letters, to language—which is the task of reading—poor readers have incredible difficulty. The relative increase in activation in the front of the brain reflects their effort. Sometimes when people can't read, they subvocalize. They say the word under their breath. This may represent additional effort to pronounce the word accurately.

It's incredible that we found this difference in the angular gyrus, the area that helps transcode one precept—say, the visual—to another, the linguistic. This makes sense given what we know about the cognitive process of reading, going from print to language. Clearly, we have a lot to learn, but now all investigators who have worked hard to understand reading and the brain have a place to focus future research. We can go to the next level of trying to understand the neural mechanisms that lie under reading and reading impairment.

In other words, the brain systems of poor readers process incoming print information differently from the way that the systems of good readers do.

Yes, there really is a difference in brain activation patterns between good and poor readers. We see the difference when people carry out phonologically based tasks. And that tells us that the area of difficulty—the functional disruption—in poor readers relates to phonologic analysis. This suggests that we focus on phonologic awareness when trying to prevent or remediate the difficulty in poor reading.

After poor readers master the reading process, do their brain activation patterns change, or are patterns of activation similar all their lives?

That's an important question that our research group at Yale is collaborating with investigators at Syracuse University (Anita Blachman) to address. Children who are poor readers are receiving a highly focused, phonologically based intervention, and they are imaged both before and after the intervention. We expect to have the results of this study within a few years.

Are the results you discovered with brain imaging consistent with what you find when you study readers cognitively?

They are. For example, a number of years ago we studied more than 300 children, most of whom were poor readers. When we examined these children on a range of tasks, the one that most significantly differentiated good readers from poor readers assessed phonemic awareness. For example, we asked children to say a word and remove a phoneme: "Can you say 'Germany' without 'ma'?" To do that, they have to segment that spoken word and pull out a part. Children who had difficulty with this phonologic processing task were also the poorest readers. One of the strongest predictors of who will be good readers is their phonemic awareness. The evidence we have that this is brain based converges nicely with behavioral information.

What are the implications of these studies for teaching reading?

Pretty strong evidence supports a phonologic model of reading. People have to be aware, clearly, that it's a complex issue. We want children to be able to read the word on the page. But we must also remember that we want them to read the word on the page to get to the meaning and the richness of the literature and the language. But if they don't know how to read the individual words, what can we do?

The most comprehensive reading program explicitly teaches about the sounds of language. It teaches children that words can be broken up into these smaller units of language, that the letters represent these units of language—phonics. But we also want to teach children about language and to build their vocabulary. We want them to have a knowledge base. We want them to practice reading and to read for meaning. So we want a balanced program. Although phonics is more important for some children than for others, all children can benefit from being taught directly how to break up spoken words into smaller units and how letters represent sounds.

You mentioned that children must practice reading. What is it about how the brain functions that makes practice important?

Think of brain pathways as circuits. The more we use them, the more they become reinforced. It's very important for children to read often. But if children can't read well, they're not going to want to read. But if we can give poor readers a sound foundation so that they know and can decode a group of words, they will have the phonologic skills to sound out words they've never seen before and will be encour-

aged to read. Once children know how to decode words, we want them to become fluent and automatic and be able to see words and read them without struggling. Only then will they have the resources left to enjoy what the word means and to think about the multiple meanings of what they're reading.

Can you give an example of how being taught directly about language can be more important for some children than for others?

We get very concerned about poor readers who are dyslexic, who have difficulties in phonology but have strong skills in reasoning, understanding, and comprehending. Their isolated skill in phonology is lacking, but all the other skills and understandings are there. These children often

have wonderful vocabularies. Imagine their frustration. They see a word in print but can't read it. Then someone says, "Oh, you don't know that?" But when they hear the word, they know it very well. It is important to identify these children as early as possible and to give them the help they need in the most intense, direct way possible.

Back in 1985, **Becoming a Nation of Readers** ***suggested that teaching phonics is not a useful practice after the early grades. Yet we have many children in the upper grades, including high school, who read poorly. Do children outgrow the need for direct phonics instruction?***

We know that brain systems are plastic, flexible, and responsive, but we have to give children the right substrate in terms of how we teach them. Children who have a biologically based difficulty can learn, but we have to present instruction in a more direct, more intense way over a longer duration. We should also clarify that today's research-based interventions are not our mother's phonics. Today's programs, for example, research-based interventions supported by the National Institute of Child Health and Human Development (NICHD), are balanced, comprehensive programs that include phonologic awareness, phonics, literature, vocabulary, fluency, and comprehension-strategy components.

Have your studies revealed any differences between boys' and girls' ability to learn to read?

We've examined this issue in several ways. We started the

Connecticut Longitudinal Study in 1983, when we identified a random group of more than 400 five-year-old boys and girls about to enter kindergarten. We didn't select these children because they had reading problems. The only criterion was that they attended public school in Connecticut.

We're still following over 90 percent of these children, who are now in their early 20s. We've tested them in reading and arithmetic every year. When we compare the boys' and the girls' reading scores, we don't see differences. That surprised us because the literature suggests that boys may have more problems. So, for all the children in our study, we asked their schools, "Has this child been identified as having a reading problem?" We found that four times as many boys as girls were identified as having a reading problem.

When we examined our data for an explanation, we found that teachers seemed to be using behavioral criteria. They saw that Johnny was a little more fidgety in class, a little more disruptive, so they selected little boys for further evaluation; little girls who were just sitting very nicely, very politely, but not reading, might not be identified.

Recently, haven't you found some brain-based gender differences in the ways that men and women read?

We found something rather remarkable. We examined brain activation patterns in men and women as they were sounding out nonsense words. We gave them two printed nonsense words and asked, "Do these two words rhyme?" Men activated an area on the left side of their brain, the inferior frontal gyrus, or Broca's area. When women did the same task, they indeed activated the left inferior frontal gyrus. But they activated the right as well. Equally interesting was that there was no difference in how quickly and accurately men and women could sound out nonsense words. This

tells us that men and women can get the same result by perhaps using different routes.

Are different mental challenges involved in learning to read and reading to learn?

The so-called simple view states that reading has two major components: identifying the single word—decoding—and comprehending—understanding what we read. We now are able to examine the process of decoding in terms of brain organization.

Comprehension is a lot more complicated. Obviously, to comprehend a printed word, we first have to decode it. But more is involved. We are studying that now.

What part of the brain is involved with processing meaning?

We speak of "this area of the brain" or "that area of the brain," but it's important to know that the brain is connected and that there are brain systems. These brain systems are forever communicating with one another. So even though for ease of communication we speak of specific areas, what we really have are networks that are communicating with one another constantly.

Having said that, I will note that an area of the brain that particularly has to do with meaning is Wernicke's area, in the temporal lobe of the brain. The temporal lobes are located on each side of the brain just behind the ears.

Teachers often find that some students can read and not understand a word whereas others can understand everything but have trouble decoding words. How are those problems different?

Some children, particularly as they get older, reach a high level of accuracy in identifying words, but still have diffi-

culty becoming fluent or automatic in their reading. They're very slow readers. And reading takes a great deal of energy. But those children or young adults can understand what they read. It just takes a lot out of them. It's very much an energy-consuming process.

Other children may read words rapidly but may not get the meaning. Children with a serious problem called hyperlexia can decode very well, but they can't comprehend. It's the inverse of dyslexia. Dyslexic children have the lower-level phonologic deficit, but intact higher-order skills that allow them to comprehend at high levels. Children with hyperlexia have terrific phonologic skills but can't comprehend. Hyperlexia is a relatively rare disorder, and affected children often experience other difficulties as well.

For all we know about the nature of reading, many misconceptions still exist about reading difficulties— dyslexia, for example.

One common misconception about dyslexia is that people see letters and words backward. That is unfortunate because I've seen many people for whom the diagnosis of dyslexia was delayed because they did not manifest reversal. People with dyslexia have no problem copying letters and words, and they don't copy words backward. They may make some reversals in writing but no more than other children do. They have difficulty naming things because dyslexia is a language difficulty, not a problem with visual perception.

These children can copy the word correctly. For example, they can copy *w-a-s* for *was* and say the letters correctly. But when we ask them what word they copied, they say, "saw." So it's not a question of having the visual, perceptual skills but of what they do with a word on the page. How do we bring the print to language? Again, the brain mechanism of going from print to language is phonologically based. We have to transcode the print. We have to appreciate that the print stands for words that can be broken into smaller phonologic units and that the grapheme, the letter or the letter groups, represents these bits of language. When we look at print, we activate areas in the back of the brain that have to do with vision, convert the print to language by using areas farther forward in the brain that have to do with transcoding, and then use areas of the brain that get to the meaning of language. The important thing to remember is that although for ease of communication the system is described as linear, in fact, information is transmitted bidirectionally and in parallel.

Educators are vitally interested in information that can help them

teach reading. Many middle school and high school teachers, in particular, haven't been taught how to teach reading.

I find it curious that teachers are often blamed for their students' poor reading. Of all the people to whom I lecture, the largest group, the most committed group, is teachers. They're the ones who want to know, "What do we know about reading? What can I take back to my classroom?" We haven't been able to provide teachers until recently with a knowledge base of what reading is all about. But fortunately, we—and when I say "we," I mean the whole scientific community that studies reading—now really understand the reading process from both cognitive and behavioral perspectives and, increasingly, from

neurobiological perspectives. This evidence supports the fact that reading is part of language. To read, we have to break up spoken words into smaller units, understand that letters represent sounds, have a knowledge base, have a vocabulary, and have the motivation and enjoyment.

Teachers now have a template, a scientifically based template, to guide them in how they teach reading. If they use this approach, they can actually make a difference. ■

Sally Shaywitz is Professor of Pediatrics at the Yale Child Study Center and at Yale University School of Medicine, 333 Cedar St., New Haven, CT 06510 (e-mail: sally.shaywitz@yale.edu). **Marcia D'Arcangelo** is a Producer on ASCD's Professional Development team (e-mail: mdarcang@ascd.org).

II

SECTION II

Word Structure

The History of the English Language

The History of the English Language

by Stephen Krensky

Language is something that most of us take for granted. Words seem to appear automatically in our heads; sentences pop out at our request. We hardly think about how and why we choose them. We read and write, speak and listen, as though we have done it always. This is not true, of course. We are not born with a language at the tip of our tongues, nor do we put on a language like a new winter coat. Learning a language is more like gathering leaves in October. We rake them up, either deliberately or at random, watching the pile grow larger as the leaves fall in ever increasing numbers.

Whether we remember it or not, there was a time for each of us before the leaves began to fall. A newborn baby does not speak a language; he simply gurgles. Gurgling is a sound he makes without thinking about it. But babies are smart. Soon they're imitating their parents, their brothers and sisters, and anybody else they meet. One thing all these people do is talk. They do not talk the same way everywhere, though. Different words are used in different places. In the United States a baby is a *baby*, but in France he is an *enfant* and in Germany a *Säugling*. A baby will naturally learn the language he hears. If it is French, he will come to speak French. If it is German, he will come to speak German. And if it is English, he will some day speak that.

The idea of language itself is a complicated one. When a baby cries for the first time, he is only reacting to discomfort. Babies cry when they're hungry or thirsty, frightened or hurt. Sometimes they cry because they're in a bad mood. Babies cry a lot. But when a baby realizes—as all babies do—that crying will bring help, he cries with a purpose. Crying has become an expression of his unhappiness. The deliberate use of this expression marks the beginning of the baby's language.

The notion of representing ideas with symbols can be traced back through recorded history, and undoubtedly it existed before the advent of writing. The existence of words, either written or spoken, is not as old as some other forms of language. Sign language, for example, probably preceded it. Even today we know the difference between an angry face and a smiling one without the need for words. And we still wave at people to greet them or to get their attention.

Sign language, though, is hampered by its need to be seen. A sign for help cannot be noticed at a distance, and it is useless at night. A cry for help would be heard in both instances. The development of speech might have followed when one particular cry for help was used by a group of people living together. At the same time, someone may have started mimicking the hiss of a snake or the crackle of burning wood. Before long a hiss might mean *snake,* and a crackling noise might stand for *fire.* And the creation of a few words would soon lead to others. We cannot prove that speech began in this fashion, but it's entirely possible.

Speech alone, though, is difficult to examine and even harder to preserve. Written languages do not have these drawbacks. These advantages undoubtedly led to their development, beginning with picture writing. The idea behind it was simple: a picture of an object identified that object. Rather than write *cow* to mean the four-legged animal that gives us milk, people drew a picture of a cow. We still draw pictures, though most of us don't think of them in terms of language. But the famous old saying "One picture is worth a thousand words" shows that words and pictures have been related for a long time. And if one picture could identify one object, a series of pictures could tell a story—the tale of a successful hunt or of building a home. A lengthy story, however, would take many pictures, an awkward practice. And some things are more complicated to draw than a cow. How would anybody draw a picture of right and wrong? Or how would we draw pictures to explain the history of the English language?

What was needed were written symbols to represent the sounds in spoken words. An alphabet is a collection of written symbols, each of which represents a different sound. When individual letters are grouped together, they form a word. A word can represent anything. *Love, hate, funny, sad, dog, run,* and *yellow* are all words, but they have different meanings. These words are formed with the Roman alphabet, which was passed along by the Romans during their European conquests. The Romans had not invented it, though. They had adapted it, as they adapted so many ideas, from the Greeks. The Greeks, however, had not invented it, either. Their alphabet had come from the Phoenicians and the Hebrews, who lived in the Middle East. The word *alphabet* itself comes from the first two letters of the Greek alphabet: *alpha* and *beta*. These names echo those of the first two letters of the Hebrew alphabet: *'aleph* and *bēth*.

The borrowing and adapting that have led to the modern Roman alphabet are similar to the evolution that has marked the English language as a whole. Neither has stood alone in its development. English is related to other languages, just as we are related to other people. We share features and habits of our parents and grandparents, our brothers and sisters, and even our cousins. Our inheritance may be the shape of a nose, the color of our eyes, or a particular sense of humor. For English the features and habits show up in its vocabulary, pronunciation, and sentence structure.

The influences that contributed to English are not without some confusing legacies. Words that sound alike, such as *waste* and *waist,* are not spelled alike; nor do they mean the same thing. And what about separate words with identical spellings but different meanings? We take a *bow* by bending at the waist, but a *bow* is also the front of a ship. Then, too, we shoot a *bow* and arrow. It's enough to make anybody dizzy. But beneath the confusion is a rich and varied pattern, the work of many tribes and nations over thousands of years. Yet English was hardly constructed with careful planning, as the Romans built their roads or the Egyptians raised their pyramids. It was not created by any one people, but created by many. Most of all, it was a by-product of invasion and conquest.

The common ancestor of English and many other languages is the Indo-European language. It was spoken in east-central Europe over five thousand years ago. Other languages were spoken then in other places, but they had no influence on the birth of English. Although the Indo-European language was not written down, we know which modern languages stem from it because they share certain similarities. One clue is in the vocabulary. Words like *father* and *winter,* for example, are similar even in languages that exist thousands of miles apart. So, while Persian and French, or English and Sanskrit, look and sound very different from one another, they are not as different as they seem.

The differences between them arose when the speakers of Indo-European broke up into smaller groups that migrated through Europe and Asia. The Indo-European people ended up spread out over two continents, and any language stretched that far was bound to snap into separate parts.

Some of the migrating people settled in and around what is now Germany. Their language, Germanic, divided into three main sections: East Germanic, North Germanic, and West Germanic. It is from West Germanic that English—as well as Dutch, Flemish, and Frisian—came.

Fifteen hundred years ago three tribes speaking a form of West Germanic lived among the lowlanders on the North Sea coast. Their languages were closely related, and the three tribes—known as the Angles, the Saxons, and the Jutes—understood one another. At about that time most of Europe was overrun by German tribes—Ostrogoths, Vandals, and Visigoths among them. It was continental Europe that attracted their attention, though, leaving Britain (as England was then known) to be invaded by the Angles, the Saxons, and the Jutes.

The natives of Britain were the Celts. They had been conquered over four hundred years earlier by the Romans, who had left some time before. The Celts were not at all united, apparently satisfied to fight among themselves. This proved their undoing. By the year 600 the Germanic invaders had driven the Celts into Wales, taken them into captivity, or killed them. And while the Romans had looked on Britain as merely an outpost, the Angles, the Saxons, and the Jutes had come to stay. In fact the Angles, being the biggest and most widely settled of the three tribes, eventually gave their name to the land, people, and language of their new home. *Engle* they were soon called, and *Engla land* their country. In time the name would shorten to *England.*

The Germanic invasion overlapped the Christian conversion of Britain. By 700 most of the Anglo-Saxons, as we call the descendants of the three tribes, had been adopted into the Roman Catholic Church.

The first manuscripts written in English appeared during this period. The Germanic invaders had originally brought their own alphabet with them, but English clerics, newly converted to Christianity, chose instead to record English speech with Latin, or Roman, letters. The next two centuries witnessed the development of Old English. (Old English is the name we give to the first phase of the English language.) It had four major dialects. Northumbrian and Mercian were spoken by the Angles, Kentish by the Jutes, and West Saxon by the Saxons. The most famous example of Old English literature, *Beowulf,* comes from Northumbrian. It is a long poem that tells of the Viking warrior-king Beowulf, who kills the monster, Grendel, and Grendel's mother, with a magic sword. He later sets out to defeat a ravaging dragon, and though he is successful, the victory costs him his life.

Many of the objects and ideas described in Old English in *Beowulf* and other works have remained with us. These words concern such integral parts of daily life that they have proven impossible to dislodge. *Day, night, father, mother, work, love, hate,* and *summer* would not be exactly recognizable in their Old English forms, but the similarities are clear. Old English parents were a *faeder* and a *mōdor.* The *grund* Beowulf walked on is the *ground* we walk on now. The seemingly mysterious *weorc,* which looks like something magical, is only the *work* we all know far too well. Not every word has changed, though. *Winter,* for example, is the same cold and snowy season today that it was a thousand years ago.

Beginning in about the eighth century the Vikings began to trouble the Anglo-Saxons. They were great explorers, the Vikings. Five hundred years before Columbus bumped into North America while searching for India, the Vikings had come and gone. But clearly not all Vikings enjoyed long sea voyages, and England was conveniently nearby.

The Viking attacks united the Anglo-Saxons

against their common enemy. Their combined strength was greatest under Alfred the Great (849-899), who succeeded to the West Saxon throne in 871. He defeated the northern invaders regularly until they were discouraged enough to give Anglo-Saxons some years of peace. Once he secured his domain, Alfred turned his attention to scholarship. The story is told that when he was a young boy, his mother promised a book of Anglo-Saxon poems to the first of her children who learned to read. Though Alfred had several older brothers, he won the book. His early affection for learning stayed with him his whole life. Because of Alfred and his successors the bulk of Old English writings are known to us in West Saxon. And Alfred was not satisfied with recording only English works. He began a translation of important Latin manuscripts (into what was then called *Englisc*), promoted an enlightened code of laws, and commanded all young freemen who had the means to learn to read. As a result England had a written standard of language and a richness of expression long before other European countries.

While King Alfred had confined the Vikings to one part of England during his reign, after his death they finally defeated the Anglo-Saxons. The fate of the conquered people, however, was not the one the Celts had suffered. There were bonds between the Vikings and the Anglo-Saxons that had not existed between the Anglo-Saxons and the Celts. The Viking language was also Germanic in origin, and their heritage had things in common with Anglo-Saxon customs. Also, the cultural and physical similarities made it easier for both the peoples and their languages to mingle. The legacy of this mingling is evident in the English vocabulary. The Vikings' other contributions reflect in sound and meaning their harsh life and cold homeland. *Rotten* eggs would only smell bad, monsters wouldn't be *ugly*, and we would not *gasp* or *gape* in surprise had not the Vikings come to England.

While some Vikings were invading England others were invading the rest of Europe. One such group secured for themselves the northwest part of France. Northmen they were called, having come from the north, but Normans they became. The Normans quickly took on French customs and attitudes, but they were not content for long with their French holdings. They invaded England under William the Conqueror in 1066, an invasion that was more than simply another Viking attack. The Normans were not interested in mingling with the Anglo-Saxons; they wished to rule them. After their victory at the Battle of Hastings the Normans soon achieved this aim. They replaced most of the English nobles with their own leaders and took control of the Church. Norman French became the language of everything important—literature, commerce, law, and religion. Latin remained the language of learning, but only because the Normans studied with it as well.

The barriers that had risen around Old English were as strong as the walls of any castle. No one in authority either spoke it or wrote it, no one was recording it, and anyone who cared about its past assuredly did so in secret. The peasants alone spoke English freely, which divided them even further from the Norman lords. While Robin Hood and his merry men, for example, spoke an Old English dialect when planning an ambush, the Sheriff of Nottingham was plotting against them in Norman French. But a language needs more than merry men to preserve it. Despite the wagging peasant tongues, had these barriers remained around English for five hundred years, it might have disappeared altogether.

That English survived was through some lucky circumstances. First, in 1204 the French captured the Norman holdings in France. This left the Normans to look on England not as a colonial possession but as their home. The situation worsened when some newly arrived French nobles tried to change the language of the English court from Norman French to Parisian French, the language of Paris. It didn't matter that the Normans had done the same thing to the Anglo-Saxons two hundred years earlier. They were certainly not going to tolerate any notions of French superiority. In protest, many of them turned to the unpretentious language of their subjects.

The Black Death also did its part. This plague swept through England killing thousands and thousands of people. Its worst effects were felt in the cities, where the Normans were concentrated. Once the plague passed, Anglo-Saxons began filling some professional posts because there were no longer enough Normans to fill the posts alone. Consequently English resurfaced above the lower classes. Meanwhile the ongoing Hundred Years' War (1337-1453) widened the breach between England and France, severing the political ties that remained.

The language that rose in the wake of the French retreat was not the Old English of King Alfred, however. There is a well-known parlor game that illustrates what had happened. In a roomful of people—perhaps twenty or more—one person thinks of a message and whispers it to whoever is next to him, who in turn passes it down the line. The first person writes down the message he whispered, and the last person speaks aloud the message he received. The two messages rarely match. In passing from person to person words have been added or dropped, heard wrong, or said badly. So, too, the English language had drifted. Three centuries of passing it down the line had wrought certain changes. Sentences were simpler and sentence construction more flexible. Complicated word endings had been nibbled at by repeated mumbling, and both long and short words had been disguised by changing pronunciation.

Middle English (the name we give to the second phase of the English language) was the language that emerged. The strong influence of Norman French was its most apparent feature.

Not surprisingly, this influence was strongest in areas of Norman concern and weakest in areas they ignored. For example, tending livestock was a chore mostly left to the Anglo-Saxon peasants. And so *cows* and *sheep* retained their native English names. The Normans, though, did take a great interest in their meals. *Beef* and *mutton* were Norman French words that Middle English adopted, as were the ways of preparing them—*roast, boil, stew,* and *fry.* A peasant might *eat* his meal in a *house,* but a Norman could *dine* in a *palace.* And after the meal, while the Anglo-Saxon was busy trying to keep *warm,* a Norman spent his time *painting, dancing,* and writing *poetry.*

As Middle English absorbed these words further events ensured its stature. In 1349 English was reinstated in the schools, and in 1362 it became the language of the courts. New literary works also supported the language's claim to respectability. Foremost among the writers of the time was Geoffrey Chaucer. Although he knew several languages, he chose to write in English. His most famous book, *The Canterbury Tales,* particularly captured the full flavor of Middle English while revealing it as a language of transition.

In Chaucer's writings and in other places Middle English words were not spelled uniformly. The development of printing, though, helped to end the resulting confusion. William Caxton printed the first book in English in 1475, beginning a tradition that greatly enlarged the permanent record of the language. Hand-written manuscripts, though beautiful, took a long time to complete. As a result their numbers were relatively few, and they were unavailable to the general population. Only the rich or scholarly had the means to afford them, and so these manuscripts basically reflected only their interests and their speech patterns. Printing made the written page accessible to many more people—people who enriched the language with new words and experiences. The printers' influence extended even to spelling, which achieved some printed uniformity that spread when other people began following their example.

This widening of background prepared the way for the beginning of Modern English (the name we give to our current speech). One major difference between Middle and Modern English is in how words are pronounced. In 1400 the final *e* in such words as *space* was pronounced. It sounded like the *e* in *father*. By 1600 the final *e* was silent. Similarly, the *ed* in words like *looked* and *cooked* was pronounced. *Lookedd* and *cookedd*, Chaucer would have said. Now, of course, we say *lookt* and *cookt*. A more sweeping change was the Great Vowel Shift, which is our name for what happened to the pronunciation of *a, e, i, o,* and *u.* For example, Chaucer said *about* like we say *aboot.* The shift finally stopped in the seventeenth century, and the basic sound of English hasn't altered much since. An enormous growth in vocabulary has also marked Modern English. In the eighth century English clerics seeking converts to Christianity used native words instead of Latin whenever possible. By doing so they hoped to make the conversion seem more familiar. Fourteenth- and fifteenth-century scholars, however, were trying to make their writings seem impressive, not familiar. Latin was still impressive, even if an increasing number of things were being written in English. It was not unusual to add a Latin or Latin-based word to an English text in the hope of improving its appearance. Whether or not any improvement took place, English gained a lot of words in the process. Before long people were adding Greek words to the language as well. At times the additions weren't necessary. Today a sad person can receive both *sympathy* and *compassion* from a considerate friend. He won't feel any better knowing that the first comes from the Greek and the second from Latin, but he probably won't feel any worse, either.

One thing that did not affect Modern English was another conquest. The defeat of the Spanish Armada in 1588 ended the last threat to English sovereignty that might have decidedly changed the language. And while England was establishing itself politically its literature was delivering the final blow to anybody who thought English inferior to other languages. The works of Sidney, Spenser, Jonson, Milton, and, most of all, Shakespeare displayed a solid literary foundation that the English people could point to with pride. In the late 1600's English even began competing with Latin as the language of scholarship. Sir Isaac Newton wrote about the laws of motion and gravity in his *Principia Mathematica,* a Latin work. Seventeen years later his study of light, *Optiks,* was published In English.

The stability that English had reached by the eighteenth century was unmatched in its earlier history. Some people were so pleased with it that they proposed freezing the language in place. They feared that importing more foreign words would corrupt the perfect state English had achieved. But how many foreign words are really too many? And how does one freeze a language? Their idea melted away in the realization that it was impossible to carry out.

It was true, though, that English had reached a juncture where rules setting forth its grammar and usage would prove useful. Looming large was the need for precise word definitions. An early English dictionary by Robert Cawdrey had appeared in 1604. It briefly defined about twenty-five hundred words, hardly enough for most purposes. Several other dictionaries were published in the next hundred and fifty years, with varying success, but none equaled the dictionary of Samuel Johnson, published in 1755. Dr. Johnson had spent eight years completing it. The dictionary contained forty thousand precise definitions, studded with a hundred and sixteen thousand quotations from literature to help illustrate meanings. It was a unique achievement. Mirroring the thoughts of his peers, Dr. Johnson had at first set out to secure the language permanently. By the time he had finished, he knew that language could not be caged, however noble the intent of the warden.

The establishment of dictionaries and other linguistic tools helped mold the general shape of the English language. In the last few hundred years most of the changes English has undergone have resulted from its geographic expansion. The isolation that fractured the ancient Indo-European language could not do the same thing to English. Such isolation no longer exists; the advances in transportation and communication have seen to that. Nonetheless some adjustments were inevitable.

American English is a notable example. Over two hundred million people speak it, far more than all the other English-speaking peoples put together. Their diverse cultural and ethnic backgrounds have decidedly influenced our language. The native Americans were the first to have an impact. They had names for things they made, like *moccasins* and *tomahawks,* and for animals unknown in Europe, like *moose, raccoons,* and *skunks.* The colonists had enough to do without thinking up new names, so they borrowed the existing ones. Later developments—after the American Revolution, when British influence had lessened—led to differences in spelling and vocabulary. We write *center* when the British write *centre;* we also write *color* for *colour, connection* for *connexion,* and *traveler* for *traveller.* The pattern of *-er* for *-re, -or* for *-our,* and one *l* for two is repeated in many words. The wrinkles in vocabulary are more complicated. While Americans find their way through the dark with a *flashlight,* the British use an electric *torch.* British babies ride around in *prams,* not *baby carriages,* and British *constables* keep law and order across the ocean from American *policemen.* These and other differences, however, affect the flavor more than the body of the language. Even a thick accent cannot prevent an Englishman from understanding his American counterpart.

The British Empire, of course, was not confined to North America, and English has grown in response to its far-flung contacts. From Arabic have come such words as *syrup* and *magazine;* the Chinese gave us *tea;* the native Australians threw us a *boomerang;* while from the West Indies hail the unlikely pair of *hurricane* and *barbecue.* Of all the world's languages only English remains important in so many countries. It is the predominant language of Canada, Australia, and New Zealand, as well as a major force in India, Pakistan, South Africa, and other former British territories.

Today the ages of conquest and exploration are over, but English continues to expand. Its growth is not the wild and unpredictable one of medieval times, yet it retains some surprises. New words have been formed with practical inventiveness. *Greenhouse* and *blackboard* were made by joining together existing words. *Laser* comes from another source; it is the sum of the first initials of *Light Amplification by Stimulated Emission of Radiation.* We can easily see why it was shortened. Other words, especially in the sciences, have been named for people. We *pasteurize* milk because Louis Pasteur invented the process. And the *watt,* a unit of electrical power, is named after James Watt, who invented the steam engine. Meanwhile words like *television* are created when the things they represent enter our experience.

English is now a language of over five hundred thousand words. In keeping with its history, about a third of these come from Old English and the Viking language, and two-thirds from the more recent French and Latin. We're not sure, in fact, whether some words came to English directly from Latin or passed through French along the way. The problem is like receiving a gift through the mail and deciding after it's been unwrapped whether it came first class or special delivery. But whatever their origin, English words currently make up the vast majority of the world's books and newspapers. Only Chinese is spoken by more people. Its influence, though, is essentially confined to mainland China.

We can never be certain about a language's future. Old English disappeared in England after the Norman invasion, but a cousin of it lives on in Modern Icelandic. Middle English gave way under the pressure of a growing vocabulary and changes in pronunciation, yet certain Scottish dialects retain much in common with it. About Modern English we can at least say that it will probably not undergo any radical transformations. Still, new words will be coined and old ones dusted off to be used again so long as people continue to write and speak. Definitions will shift, shrink, and expand depending on generations of interpretation. Following the course of the English language is like following a path through uncharted territory. It is easy to get lost along the way. A dictionary can't show us where the path ends, but like a good compass, it will always help us to keep our bearings.

III

SECTION III

Sound/Print Connection

Emergent Literacy: Research Bases

Barbara K. Gunn
Deborah C. Simmons
Edward J. Kameenui
University of Oregon

AREAS OF LITERACY KNOWLEDGE

Numerous frameworks have been set forth for categorizing areas of literacy knowledge (Mason & Allen, 1986; Morrow et al. 1990; Stahl & Miller, 1989; van Kleeck, 1990). Although these frameworks differ in structure, certain areas of literacy knowledge are common across the emergent literacy literature. The following structure, adapted from van Kleeck (1990) reflects those areas: awareness of print, knowledge of the relationship between speech and print, text structure, phonological awareness, and letter naming and writing. Each of these areas develops concurrently and interrelatedly, and continues to develop across the preschool and kindergarten period. Moreover, acquisition of these skills is an important part of early childhood literacy development, and substantially affects the ease with which children learn to read, write, and spell (Hiebert, 1988; van Kleeck, 1990; Weir, 1989).

Awareness of Print

Experiences with print (through reading and writing) give preschool children an understanding of the conventions, purpose, and function of print—understandings that have been shown to play an integral part in learning to read. Because certain terms are used differently across the emergent literacy research, the way we use a term may differ slightly from the way a particular author uses it; nonetheless the gist of the concept is retained. Generally, *awareness of print* refers to a child's knowledge of the forms and functions of print. For this review, we define *forms* as knowledge of the conventions of print, and *functions* as the purposes and uses of print. In this section, each of these types of print awareness is discussed in relation to the contribution it makes to a child's literacy knowledge.

From *What Reading Research Tells Us About Children With Diverse Learning Needs*, 1998, Lawrence Erlbaum Associates, Inc.

Conventions of Print. Children learn about print from a variety of sources, and in the process come to realize that although print differs from speech, it carries messages just like speech (Morrow et al., 1990). Eventually, children learn that print—not pictures—carries the story. As preschool children listen to stories they learn not only how stories are structured semantically in terms of ideas but also visually in terms of their appearance on the printed page. That is, text begins at the top of the page, moves from left to right, and carries over to the next page when it is turned (Ehri & Sweet, 1991).

Attention to conventions of print is also seen in the development of written language. Children begin writing even before they can form letters, and this early writing reveals children's early attention to the conventions of written language (van Kleeck, 1990). Hiebert (1988) characterized this as a developmental progression in which early attempts at messages may take the form of scribbles that take on characteristics of the writing system, such as linearity. Eventually, the scribbling is superseded by letter-like forms that, in turn, are replaced by letters, generally familiar ones such as those in the child's name.

Functional and varied experiences in reading and writing print help children develop specific print skills, which appear to play an integral part in the process of learning to read (Dickinson & Tabors, 1991; Mason & Allen, 1986; Scarborough & Dobrich,1994).Because of differences in parental support for literacy, however, children do not come to school with the same range of print-related experiences (Mason & Allen, 1986). The failure of some children to pick up on physical cues to the nature of reading (e.g., sounds are arranged temporally, whereas writing is arranged permanently in space) means that teachers may need to assess children's level of understanding about print concepts and, when necessary, plan instruction to develop such understanding (Jagger & Smith-Burke, cited in Mason & Allen 1986). This may be accomplished by extending opportunities for children to interact with oral and written language in meaningful contexts such as story reading sessions in which book-handling skills are discussed (Weir, 1989).

Purpose and Functions of Print. Children understand the purpose of print when they realize that words convey a message; they understand the function of print when they realize that messages can serve multiple purposes (van Kleeck, 1990). While knowledge about the conventions of print enables children to understand the physical structure of written language, the conceptual knowledge that printed words convey a message—that is, the printed words contain meaning independent of the immediate social context—also helps young children bridge the gap between oral and written language. Additionally, as a result of interacting with and observing adults in their environment using print, preschool children also understand the vocabulary of reading in instructional contexts such as read, write, draw, page, and story (Morgan, cited in Weir, 1989; van Kleeck, 1990). When formal instruction begins, the child who has this vocabulary about print-related phenomena is more likely to understand the basic vocabulary in the classroom.

Print serves a broad variety of functions. The scope of print functions ranges from very specific (e.g., making shopping lists, reading product labels, writing checks, reading street signs, looking up information) to very general (e.g., acquiring knowledge, conveying instructions, and maintaining relationships). Because all preschool children are not exposed to the same range of print-related experiences, their knowledge of these functions varies considerably. This variation in knowledge of the functions of print is related to daily routines in the child's home; it is developed more fully in a subsequent section on the role of family environment.

Developmental Patterns. Our review of research revealed that conclusions about factors promoting the development of awareness of print (i.e., knowledge of the purposes and processes of reading and the ability to recognize print embedded in environmental contexts) are limited. Lomax and McGee (cited in Hiebert, 1988; Weir, 1989) analyzed developmental patterns of children ages 3 to 6 on a hierarchy of reading-related skills and the ability to recognize print embedded in environmental contexts. According to their model of developmental patterns, awareness of print preceded graphic awareness, followed by phonemic awareness, grapheme–phoneme correspondence knowledge, and word reading.

Specifically, prekindergarten children demonstrated facility with only the early developing capabilities (e.g., awareness of print and graphic awareness), whereas gains by older children with succeeding capabilities (e.g., word reading) were reported to depend on proficiency with earlier skills. It appears that levels of preschool literacy competency do exist, and furthermore, these competencies may play a role in facilitating subsequent reading-related skills (Weir, 1989).

Relationship of Print to Speech

The ability to map oral language onto print is important for early reading and writing experiences. Through interaction with others who model language functions, children learn to attend to language and to apply this knowledge to literacy situations. In English, the relationship between oral language (speech) and written language (print) uses the equivalence between phonemes and graphemes. However, because talking and reading are different processes and produce different outcomes (Akinnaso, cited in Mason & Allen, 1986), we cannot assume that children learn this equivalence solely by mapping their knowledge of oral language onto written language (Mason & Allen, 1986). Typically, it has been viewed as a developmental process, rather than an accumulation of discrete skills. Letter knowledge and phonological awareness are constituent skills in children's ability to realize this relationship (Ehri & Sweet, 1991; van Kleeck, 1990), but even before progressing to that level of knowledge, children may participate in less conventional forms of reading and writing that reflect their initial ideas about the relationship between speech and print (Hiebert, 1988; van Kleeck, 1990). For example, children may initially adopt a strategy in which they use one grapheme to represent one sound in an entire syllable or word, such as "Sio" to represent Santiago (Ferreiro, cited in van Kleeck, 1990). This may be followed by invented spelling that although not yet conventional, does adhere to the correspondence in the English orthography (van Kleeck, 1990).

Although the communicative function of oral language might make the acquisition of written language a natural process (Goodman & Goodman, cited in Mason & Allen, 1986), research suggests that written language acquisition can be problematic—due in part to basic differences between the linguistic properties of oral and written language.

Citing Perera's framework, Mason and Allen (1986) summarized the physical, situational, functional, form, and structural differences between oral and written language, and considered the impact of those differences on language instruction in the classroom.

For example, certain *physical differences* exist between written and spoken language. Print is processed by eye whereas speech is processed by ear (Kavanagh & Matingly, cited in Mason & Allen, 1986). This means, for example, that it may take 6 minutes to write a paragraph from a speech, but only 1 minute to read it.

Because of differences in early literacy experiences, children may come to school with varying concepts about the distinctions between the physical cues of reading and the aural cues of spoken language. For example, Ferreiro and Teberosky (cited in Mason & Allen, 1986) found that children varied in their ability to distinguish between oral conversation and a fairy tale or a news item when a researcher "read" to them from a storybook or a newspaper. Such failure to pick up on physical cues that differentiate written from spoken language can be problematic for beginning readers. To help children succeed in relating oral language to print, teachers may need to assess children's knowledge about the differences between speech and print, then clarify and expand their understanding (Jagger & Smith-Burke, cited in Mason & Allen, 1986).

Situational differences between oral and written language are apparent. Oral language most often occurs in a face-to-face context where the listener has the opportunity to ask for clarification or information. In written language or text, however, readers and writers are usually separated. Consequently, the writer must assume that the reader has the knowledge to process and comprehend the text. The reader in turn, must move backward or forward in the print to clarify information (Mason & Allen, 1986).

The multiple *functions* of language children use depends on the context and the desired function of a given communication. Whereas oral language is generally used to express, explore, and communicate, written language is used as a means for expanding one's own thinking, by prompting comparisons and analysis (Mason & Allen, 1986). If children have not had extensive interaction with adults who model these language functions before coming to school, then the teacher must incorporate opportunities into the curriculum.

When English is seen in print *form*, each letter is a distinct visual form, and each word is distinct due to the spaces between the words (Mason & Allen, 1986). Other physical characteristics include indentation, punctuation, and capitalization. By contrast, in speech the boundaries between words and even phonemes may be obscured as Ehri (cited in Mason & Allen, 1986) illustrated in comparing the written "Give me a piece of candy" with the spoken "Gimme a pieca candy" (p. 6).

Finally, spoken and written language differ in *structure*. For example, speakers tend to be more redundant than writers, and speech is also more informal than writing, as evidenced by the greater frequency of incomplete sentences, slang expressions, and meaningless vocalizations that function as place holders for thought in spoken language (Perera, cited in Mason & Allen, 1986). For children who come to school with differing exposures to the written and spoken discourse structures, awareness of the structural differences between spoken and written language may not be evident and, therefore, may negatively affect the transfer from listening to reading comprehension.

Given the differences between oral and written language, what are the instructional implications for children who have difficulty making the link between their oral language experiences and formal instruction in reading and writing? Several studies have suggested that when text is designed to resemble speech, beginning readers can process it more readily. Allen (cited in Mason & Allen, 1986) found that primary-grade children performed better on inferential comprehension tasks when the texts were closely linked to the children's oral language. Seventy children of varied reading ability read dictated, peer-written, and textbook stories. Allen observed that even the least able readers inferred well when reading their own texts, and they inferred somewhat better on peer stories than textbook stories. Similarly, Amstersam (cited in Mason & Allen, 1986) reported that children who repeated and later recalled natural language versus primerese versions of fables gave more complete recalls and fewer unnecessary repetitions of the text than children who used the language of the text.

These general manipulations of beginning reading instruction designed to lessen the differences between speech and print may be helpful for at-risk children. However, further research is needed to determine the specific sources of difficulty that at-risk populations experience in transferring speech to print, and how those children might best be helped (Mason & Allen, 1986).

Comprehension of Text Structures

As the ability to map oral language onto print is important for early reading and writing experiences, awareness of story grammar or text structures is important in facilitating children's comprehension of spoken and written language (Just & Carpenter; Perfetti, cited in van Kleeck, 1990). Children come to school with differing exposures to grammatical and discourse structures (Mason & Allen, 1986). Those who have had exposure to oral or written texts through storybook reading dialogue in the home may be sensitive to the schematic structure of stories from a very young age (Applebee, cited in van Kleeck, 1990). In fact, children recognize such features as formal opening and closing phrases (e.g., "Once upon a time") as early as 2 years of age. They also abstract a structure for the organization of stories and use this structure in their own comprehension and writing.

In their analysis of the writing of 16 kindergarten children, Brown and Briggs (1991) found that age, prior knowledge, level of social interaction, and environmental experiences influenced the participants' awareness of story elements. Moreover, repeated reading activities as well as reading a wide variety of discourse structures can influence the content and organization of children's stories by facilitating comprehension and developing story knowledge (Brown & Briggs, 1990; Mason & Allen, 1986; van Kleeck, 1990).

Although comprehension of text structures facilitates children's comprehension, few empirical investigations have been conducted in this area with young children, thus limiting converging evidence.

Phonological Awareness

Phonological awareness is reviewed extensively in another chapter; however, in this chapter we review its role and integral relation to emergent literacy.

In an alphabetic writing system such as English, beginning readers must use the alphabetic code to understand the link between the sounds of speech and the signs of letters (Mason & Allen, 1986; Sulzby & Teale, 1991). Phonological awareness, or the ability to perceive spoken words as a sequence of sounds, is a specific auditory skill that is of crucial importance to reading ability in an alphabetic system. Because research has established a correlational, if not causal relation between phonological awareness and reading (Ehri & Sweet, 1991; Mason & Allen, 1986; Sulzby & Teale, 1991; van Kleeck, 1990), phonological awareness is often raised in discussions of early childhood literacy education (Sulzby & Teale, 1991). Indeed, of all the areas of literacy knowledge developed during the preschool years, none has been studied as extensively or related as directly to early reading as phonological awareness (van Kleeck, 1990).

However, Sulzby and Teale (1991) noted that although phonological awareness has long been tied to research and practice in the teaching of phonics and other decoding skills, it has been neglected in emergent literacy due to the tendency to view phonological awareness research as traditional and bottom–up in theory. Despite this perspective, some researchers have argued that the ability to deal with the codes of alphabetic language does not automatically arise out of environmental print awareness. Instead, they suggested that young children must be helped to notice that words encode sounds as well as meaning (Dickinson & Snow; Mason; Masonheimer, Drum, & Ehri, cited in Sulzby & Teale, 1991).

Precursory phonological awareness skills such as rhyming and alliteration can emerge in informal contexts before school, and are seen in young children who can neither read nor spell (Snow, 1991; van Kleeck, 1990). A general order for the emergence of other phonological awareness abilities typically begins when children divide sentences into semantically meaningful word groups. According to Fox and Routh (cited in van Kleeck, 1990), the ability to segment sentences into words emerges next, followed by the more phonologically based skill of segmenting words into syllables. The ability to segment words into phonemes comes last (in their study, one fourth of words were segmented into phonemes by age 3). This general order of emergence has been supported in other investigations; however, the children in those studies tended to be older (Ehri; Holden & MacGinitie; Huttenlocher; Liberman; Liberman, Shankweiler, Fisher, & Carter, cited in van Kleeck, 1990).

In contrast to the informal context in which they acquire other emergent literacy skills, most children require specific instruction to acquire the phonological awareness skill of segmentation, or the ability to segment words into their component phonemes, and often master it later than other foundations for print literacy (van Kleeck, 1990). It has also been suggested that general phonological awareness skills be taught in conjunction with letter-sound knowledge to facilitate reading acquisition. Based on their review of research on instruction in phonological awareness, Ehri and Wilce (cited in Sulzby & Teal, 1991) reported that young children can be taught phonological awareness prior to formal reading instruction if they have a certain amount of letter knowledge. Training studies reviewed by Mason and Allen (1986) also revealed the advantages of knowledge of letter-sound principles for reading and spelling. They reported that when children understand that words contain discrete phonemes and that letters symbolize these phonemes, they are able to use more efficient word recognition strategies than when they rely on nonphonetic strategies.

Mason and Allen (1986) summarized their review of phonological awareness research by noting that instructional studies have led to improved outcomes in reading, but questions remain about how to employ information about word-and-letter recognition strategies to improve instruction. The authors concluded that although it is important for children to learn about letter-sound relationships, it should not be at the expense of reading comprehension opportunities or independent reading activities. Similarly, Sulzby and Teale (1991) proposed that without fundamental understandings of the functions and uses of literacy (e.g., storybook reading, language play, written language use in everyday practices), children may not profit from phonological awareness instruction. They suggested future investigations of phonological awareness combine rigorous classroom-based research on phonological awareness training and its relation to overall early childhood curriculum.

Letter Knowledge

Both phonological awareness and letter recognition contribute to initial reading acquisition by helping children develop efficient word-recognition strategies such as detecting pronunciations and storing associations in memory. Letter knowledge, like phonological awareness, may be acquired either through formal instruction or incidentally. Through incidental learning, for example, many children gain at least some concepts and skills related to the formal aspects of print prior to school (Hiebert & Papierz, 1990). They learn about the functions of written language in storybooks and poems while they learn about the forms (e.g., letter naming and visual discrimination) of written language (Hiebert, 1988).

Letter knowledge, which provides the basis for forming connections between the letters in spellings and the sounds in pronunciations, has been identified as a strong predictor of reading success (Ehri & Sweet, 1991) and has traditionally been a very important component of reading readiness programs (van Kleeck, 1990). Knowing the alphabet and its related sounds is associated with beginning literacy. In fact, letter knowledge measured at the beginning of kindergarten was one of two best predictors of reading achievement at the end of kindergarten and first grade; the other predictor was phonemic segmentation skill (Share, Jorm, Maclean, & Matthews, cited in Ehri & Sweet 1991). Furthermore, an analysis of the relationship between literacy development and participation in literacy activities at home revealed that children's exposure to letter names and sounds during the preschool years was positively associated with linguistically precocious performance on selected literacy measures (Crain-Thoreson & Dale, 1992).

Within the scope of this review, several reasons were offered for the effect of letter knowledge in reading acquisition. Based on observations of

5-year-old children in New Zealand, Clay (cited in Mason & Allen, 1986) concluded that:

> before children learn to decode words in and out of context, they become able to use some letter-sound information to recognize, remember, and spell words. This is possible even if they are not taught the letter sounds, because the names of the alphabet letters provide clues to the phonemic representations in words. (p. 18)

Ehri and Wilce (cited in Ehri & Sweet, 1991) hypothesized that letter knowledge enables beginning readers to adapt to the task of pointing to words as they read them and figure out how printed words correspond to spoken words. It may also enable them to remember how to read the individual words they encounter in the text. "This knowledge of letters provides the basis for forming connections between the letters seen in spellings and the sounds detected in pronunciations, and for storing these associations in memory in order to remember how to read those words when they are seen again" (p. 446).

Although letter knowledge may be a strong component in preschool programs, children may also learn these skills at home. In a study of 59 parents of preschool children, Hildebrand and Bader (1992) found that children who performed high on three emergent literacy measures, including writing letters of the alphabet, were more likely to have parents who provided them with alphabet books, blocks, and shapes. The authors suggested that as children exhibit behaviors indicative of emergent literacy, parents and teachers can seize the teachable moments, and provide developmentally appropriate materials and interactions to further literacy development.

Whether letter knowledge is learned at home or at school, through word games or letters on the refrigerator, it appears to foster the development of subsequent reading strategies. However, further research is needed to provide more precise information about the kinds of instruction that are appropriate for children at varying stages of development and ability levels.

REFERENCES

Brown, D. L., & Briggs, L. D. (1991). Becoming literate: The acquisition of story discourse. *Reading Horizons, 32*(2), 139–153.

Bus, A. G., & van IJzendoorn, M. H. (1995). Mothers reading to their 3-year-olds: The role of mother–child attachment security in becoming literate. *Reading Research Quarterly, 30*, 998–1015.

Clay, M. (1979). *Stones—The concepts about print test.* Portsmouth, NH: Heinemann.

Copeland, K. A., & Edwards, P. A. (1990). Towards understanding the roles parents play in supporting young children's development in writing. *Early Child Development and Care, 56*, 11–17.

Crain-Thoreson, C., & Dale, P. S. (1992). Do early talkers become early readers? Linguistic precocity, preschool language, and emergent literacy. *Developmental Psychology, 28*(3), 421–429.

Dickinson, D. K., & Tabors, P. O. (1991). Early literacy: Linkages between home, school, and literacy achievement at age five. *Journal of Research in Childhood Education, 6*(1), 30–46.

Ehri, L. C., & Sweet, J. (1991). Fingerpoint-reading of memorized text: What enables beginners to process the print? *Reading Research Quarterly, 26*, 442–462.

Hiebert, E. H. (1988). The role of literacy experiences in early childhood programs. *The Elementary School Journal, 89*, 161–171.

Hiebert, E. H., & Papierz, J. M. (1990). The emergent literacy construct and kindergarten and readiness books of basal reading series. *Early Childhood Research Quarterly, 5*, 317–334.

Hildebrand, V. L., & Bader, L. A. (1992). An exploratory study of parents' involvement in their child's emerging literacy skills. *Reading Improvement, 29*(3), 163–170.

Katims, D. S. (1991). Emergent literacy in early childhood special education: Curriculum and instruction. *Topics in Early Childhood Special Education, 11*, 69–84.

Katims, D. S. (1994). Emergence of literacy in preschool children with disabilities. *Learning Disabilities Quarterly, 17*, 58–69.

Mason, J., & Allen, J. B. (1986). A review of emergent literacy with implications for research and practice in reading. *Review of Research in Education, 13*, 3–47.

McGee, L. M., & Lomax, R. G. (1990). On combining apples and oranges: A response to Stahl and Miller. *Review of Educational Research, 60*, 133–140.

Morrow, L. M. (1990). Preparing the classroom environment to promote literacy during play. *Early Childhood Research Quarterly, 5*, 537–554.

Morrow, L. M., O'Connor, E. M., & Smith, J. K. (1990). Effects of a story reading program on the literacy development of at-risk kindergarten children. *Journal of Reading Behavior, 22*, 255–275.

Pelligrini, A. D., & Galda, L. (1993). Ten years after: A reexamination of symbolic play and literacy research. *Reading Research Quarterly, 28*, 163–175.

Perera, K. (1984). *Children's writing and reading: Analyzing classroom language.* Oxford, England: Blackwell.

Roberts, B. (1992). The evolution of the young child's concept of word as a unit of spoken and written language. *Reading Research Quarterly, 27*, 125–138.

Scarborough, H. S., & Dobrich, W. (1994). On the efficacy of reading to preschoolers. *Developmental Review, 14*, 245–302.

Scarborough, H. S., Dobrich, W., & Hager, M. (1991). Preschool literacy experience and later reading achievement. *Journal of Learning Disabilities, 24*, 508–511.

Smith, C. B. (1989). Emergent literacy—an environmental concept. *The Reading Teacher, 42*(7), 528.

Snow, C. E. (1991). The theoretical basis for relationships between language and literacy in development. *Journal of Research in Childhood Education, 6*(1), 5–10.

Stahl, S. A., & Miller, P. D. (1989). Whole language and language experience approaches for beginning reading: A quantitative research synthesis. *Review of Educational Research, 59*(1), 87–116.

Stewart, J. (1992). Kindergarten students' awareness of reading at home and in school. *Journal of Educational Research, 86*, 95–104.

Sulzby, E., & Teale, W. (1991). Emergent literacy. In R. Barr, M. L. Kamil, P. B. Mosenthal, & P. D. Pearson (Eds.), *Handbook of reading research* (Vol. 2, pp. 727–757). New York: Longman.

Teale, W. H., & Sulzby, E. (1987). Literacy acquisition in early childhood: The roles of access and mediation in storybook reading. In D. A. Wagner (Ed.), *The future of literacy in a changing world* (pp. 111–130). New York: Pergamon Press.

van Kleeck, A. (1990). Emergent literacy: Learning about print before learning to read. *Topics in Language Disorders, 10*(2), 25–45.

Weir, B. (1989). A research base for pre kindergarten literacy programs. *The Reading Teacher, 42*, 456–460.

What Every Teacher Should Know About Phonological Awareness

by Joseph K. Torgesen and Patricia Mathes

Phonological awareness is rapidly becoming one of the most important educational "buzzwords" of this decade. Teachers are talking about it, parents are trying to understand it, and publishers of early reading materials are trying to include it. Yet, it is a concept that is easily misunderstood. Some confuse it with "phonics," and others consider it to be a part of general print awareness, and it is neither of these things. We must also be careful about how we teach it to children; unless we thoroughly understand the concept and its role in reading development, we may easily teach it in ways that produce no real benefit. This short essay is an attempt to share what is currently known about the nature of phonological awareness, why it is important in reading growth, why children differ from one another in their ability to acquire it, and how we may most effectively incorporate it into reading instruction. Although we currently know a great deal about this concept, there is still much that is not known, so we shall try to point out some of the questions along the way.

What is phonological awareness?

In order to understand the concept of phonological awareness, we must first know what a phoneme is. A phoneme is the smallest unit of sound in our language that makes a difference to its meaning. For example, the word *cat* has three phonemes, /k/-/a/-/t/. By changing the first phoneme, we can produce the word *bat*. Changing the second phoneme creates the word *cot*, and we can obtain the word *cab* by altering the final phoneme. Words in English (in fact, in all languages) are composed of strings of phonemes. This is fortunate, because it allows us to create all the words we will ever need by using various combinations of just 44 different speech sounds!

Speech scientists have discovered that the human brain is specifically adapted for processing many different kinds of linguistic information, and one part of our biological endowment allows us to process the complex phonological information in speech without actually being aware of the individual phonemes themselves. This is one of the human abilities that makes acquiring speech a natural process, so that almost everyone in the world learns to speak a language with very little direct instruction. As we will explain more fully later, learning to read requires that children become consciously aware of phonemes as individual segments in words. In fact, phonological awareness is most commonly defined as one's sensitivity to, or explicit awareness of, the phonological structure of words in one's language. In less formal language, it involves the ability to notice, think about, or manipulate the individual sounds in words.

One of the early signs of emerging sensitivity to the phonological structure of words is ability to play rhyming games and activities. In order to tell whether two words rhyme, the child must attend to the sounds in words rather than their meaning. In addition, the child must focus attention on only one *part* of a word rather than the way it sounds as a whole. As children grow in awareness of the phonemes in words, they become able to judge whether words have the same first or last sounds, and with further development, they become able to actually pronounce the first, last, or middle sounds in words. At its highest levels of development, awareness of individual phonemes in words is shown by the ability to separately pronounce the sounds in even multi-syllable words, or to tell exactly how two words like *task* and *tacks* are different (the order of the last two phonemes is reversed).

Acquiring phonological awareness actually involves learning two kinds of things about language. First, it involves learning that words can be divided into segments of sound smaller than a syllable. Second, it involves learning about individual phonemes themselves. As children acquire more and more conscious knowledge of the distinctive features of phonemes (how they sound when they occur in words, or how they feel when they are pronounced), they become more adept at noticing their identity and order when they occur in words. For example, while children in the first semester of first grade might be able to notice the first or last sound of a word like *man,* by the end of first grade, most children can easily, and relatively automatically, notice all the sounds in a more complex word like *clap.* At both beginning and more advanced levels, phonological awareness strongly supports learning about the ways that the words in our language are represented in print.

Why is phonological awareness important in learning to read?

When children learn to read, they must acquire two different kinds of skills. They must learn how to identify printed words, and they must learn how to comprehend written material. Their major challenge when they first enter school is to learn to accurately identify printed words, and

this brings them face to face with the alphabetic principle. English is an alphabetic language, meaning that words are represented in print roughly at the level of phonemes. For example, the word *cat* has three phonemes, and three letters are used to represent them; the word *which* has three phonemes, but five letters are used to represent them.

In our language, the alphabetic principle presents two important learning challenges to children. First, individual phonemes are not readily apparent as individual segments in normal speech. When we say the word *dog,* for example, the phonemes overlap with one another (they are coarticulated), so that we hear a single burst of sound rather than three individual segments. Coarticulating the phonemes in words (i.e., starting to pronounce the second phoneme (/r/) in the word *frost* while we are still saying the first phoneme (/f/) makes speech fluent, but it also makes it hard for many children to become aware of phonemes as individual segments of sound within words.

The second challenge presented by the alphabetic principle in our language is that there is not always a regular one-to-one correspondence between letters and phonemes. For example, some phonemes are represented by more than one letter (i.e., ch, sh, wh, ai, oi). In addition, sometimes the phoneme represented by a letter changes, depending on other letters in the word (*not* vs. *note, fit* vs. *fight, not* vs. *notion*), or pronunciation of parts of some words may not follow any regular letter-phoneme correspondence patterns, such as in *yacht* or *choir.* Variations in the way that phonemes are represented by letters present problems for some children in learning *phonics* skills in reading, while the coarticulation of phonemes in spoken language makes acquisition of *phonological awareness* a challenge for many children.

If understanding and utilizing the alphabetic principle in reading words presents such learning challenges for children, the obvious question, and one that has been repeatedly asked over the last century, is whether it is really necessary for children to understand the principle and master its use in order to become good readers. On the basis of research on reading, reading development, and reading instruction conducted over the past twenty years, we now know that the answer to this question is very strongly in the affirmative (Beck & Juel, 1995). Children who quickly come to understand the relationships between letters and phonemes, and who learn to utilize this information as an aid to identifying words in print, almost invariably become better readers than children who have difficulty acquiring these skills (Share & Stanovich, 1995).

There are at least three ways that phonological awareness is important in learning beginning word reading skills. These are:

1. *It helps children understand the alphabetic principle.* Without at least a beginning level of phonological awareness, children have no way of understanding how the words from their oral language are represented in print. Unless they understand that words have sound segments at the level of the phoneme, they cannot take advantage of an alphabetic script (Liberman, Shankweiler & Liberman, 1989). They will also not be able to understand the rationale for learning individual letter sounds, and the common request to "sound out" words in beginning reading will not make sense to them.

2. *It helps children notice the regular ways that letters represent sounds in words.* If children can notice all four phonemes in the word *flat,* it helps them to see the way the letters correspond to the sounds. This ability to notice the match between the letters and sounds in words has two potential benefits to children learning to read. First, it reinforces knowledge of individual letter-sound correspondences, and second, it helps in forming mental representations of words so

they can be accurately recognized when they are encountered in print again. Research has shown that the associations children form between the letters and sounds in words creates the kind of "sight word" representations that are the basis of fluent reading (Ehri, 1997).

3. *It makes it possible to generate possibilities for words in context that are only partially "sounded out."* For example, consider a first grade child who encounters a sentence such as "John's father put his bicycle in the car," and cannot recognize the fifth word. A relatively early level of phonological awareness supports the ability to search one's mental dictionary for words that begin with similar sounds. Thus, if the child knows the sound represented by the letter *b,* he/she can mentally search for words that begin with that sound and fit the context. As children acquire more knowledge of "phonics" and can "sound out" more letters in words, their search for words with similar phonemes in them can proceed much more accurately.

As should be clear from this analysis, phonemic awareness has its primary impact on reading growth through its effect on children's ability to phonetically decode words in text. Although phonetic decoding skills should never be considered the end goal of reading instruction (phonetic decoding is too slow and effortful to support fluent reading and good comprehension), research now shows that, for most children, these skills are a critical step along the way toward effective reading skills.

To illustrate concretely the impact that deficient phonological awareness can have on the growth of reading skills, Figure 1 (see following page) presents information on the growth of word reading ability in a group of children who began first grade with relatively low levels of phonological awareness (Torgesen, Wagner & Rashotte, 1994). At the beginning of first grade, these children's performance on measures of phonological awareness was in the bottom 20% of a large group of children who all had estimated general verbal ability in the normal range. The numbers at the right of the graphs represent average grade level score at the end of fifth grade of children above and below the 20th percentile. From the top panel, we can see that children with weak phonological awareness ended up about two grade levels below their peers in sight word reading ability, and the bottom panel shows that their phonetic reading skills were more than three grade levels below their peers. On a measure of reading comprehension, the children with weak phonological awareness obtained a grade score of 3.9, which was three years behind the score of 6.9 obtained by their peers.

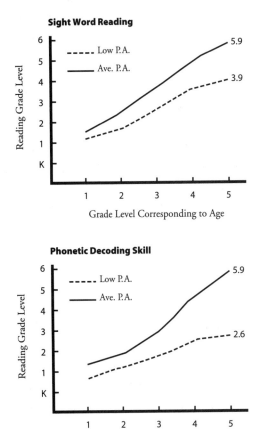

FIG. I: *Growth of sight word and phonetic decoding skill in children who begin first grade below the 20th percentile in phonological awareness*

Before we leave this section, it is important to remind ourselves that phonological awareness is not the only knowledge or skill required to learn to read. Longitudinal research has shown that phonological awareness is *necessary*, but not *sufficient* for becoming a good reader. Other phonological abilities may also affect children's ability to acquire phonetic decoding ability and sight word fluency, and a good vocabulary, general knowledge about the world, good thinking skills, and an interest in reading are clearly important in the development of reading comprehension.

What is the normal developmental course for phonological awareness?

Although reliable information about normal growth rates in phonological awareness is one of the questions remaining for further research, it is possible to outline some broad benchmarks of development for the early school years. There is even less information available for the preschool years, although a few studies have demonstrated beginning levels of phonological awareness in children as young as two-and-a-half to three years of age.

It is important to recognize that when we speak of phonological awareness in children as young as three years old, we are speaking of a very different level of this ability than is shown by most first grade children. The tasks used to assess phonological awareness in young children differ in at least two important ways from those used with older children. First, many of these tasks assess sensitivity to syllables and rhyme, which are more global aspects of the phonological structure of words than phonemes. These measures assess general *phonological sensitivity* rather than *phonemic awareness*. Second, some tasks, such as those that involve judging whether words have similar beginning sounds, require a less fully explicit knowledge of phonemes than tasks that ask children to pronounce or manipulate individual phonemes in words. Tasks that assess a more general level of phonological sensitivity (such as awareness of syllables or sensitivity to rhyme) are not as predictive of reading growth as measures that specifically assess awareness or sensitivity to phonemes in words.

Normally developing children enter kindergarten prepared to easily learn to play rhyming games and activities, and most of them can divide simple words into syllables by midyear (thus showing good general *phonological* awareness). By the end of kindergarten, a child who is developing normally in phonological awareness should be able to judge rhyming words and generate new words that rhyme with a given word. They should also be able to respond to measures of *phonemic* awareness that require them to compare words on the basis of their first sounds. Most children can also pronounce the first phoneme of simple words when asked a question like, "What is the first sound in the word *man*?"

By midway in the first semester of first grade, children who are developing normally in phonological awareness can reliably blend phonemes together to produce two-phoneme words such as *on, in, at,* or *bee.* Children at this stage of development can also say what word is left if a given sound is dropped from the beginning or end of a three-phoneme word (i.e., say *man* without saying the /m/ sound).

With the beginning of reading instruction, most children's ability to perform on measures of phonemic awareness increases rapidly. By the end of first grade, average children who have received at least a moderate degree of instruction in "phonics" can pronounce all the sounds in a three-phoneme word such as *dog, hat,* or *fan.* Their phoneme-blending skills are also much better by this time, and, without too much trouble, they can blend words containing three and four phonemes. From this point, further development in phonemic awareness occurs primarily in the form of increasing accuracy and fluency in the skills acquired during first grade.

What causes differences among children in phonological awareness?

When children enter school, there is substantial variability in their level of phonological awareness, and their response to instruction in kindergarten produces an even larger range of individual differences by the end of the school year. The factors that cause individual differences among children in phonological awareness when they enter school are genetic endowment and preschool linguistic experience.

Research conducted over the last 20 years has shown that children vary significantly "in the phonological component of their natural capacity for language" (Liberman, Shankweiler & Liberman, 1989). This phonological ability, or talent, is a trait that is strongly heritable. In other words, children can vary in their talent for processing the phonological features of language in the same way that they vary among one another in musical ability, height, or hair color. In fact, large-scale studies involving identical twins have shown that about half of all the variation in linguistically related phonological skills is inherited (Olsen, Forsberg & Wise, 1994).

Talent in the area of phonological processing can vary quite independently from other areas of intellectual ability, although many studies show that it is at least moderately correlated with general learning ability. It is clearly possible, for example, to be average or above average in general intelligence while being severely deficient in the ability to acquire phonological awareness. Sometimes a lack of talent for processing the phonological features of language produces noticeable effects on language and speech development prior to school entry, but frequently it does not. In other words, it is possible to have a genetically transmitted weakness in the area of phonological processing that does not affect speech, but does affect early reading development. The reason for this is that reading requires children to become consciously aware of the phonemic segments in words while speech does not. With this said, it is nevertheless true that subtle speech difficulties are a common correlate of early problems in acquiring phonetically based reading skills (Catts, 1993).

The child's preschool linguistic environment can also exert a strong influence on sensitivity to the phonological structure of words at the time of school entry. Early experience with nursery rhymes, for example, can help children begin to notice and think about the phonological structure of words. Several research studies have shown that children who know more about nursery rhymes at age three are those that tend to be more highly developed in general phonological awareness at age four, and in phonemic awareness at age six (Bryant, MacLean, Bradley & Crossland, 1990). There is also consistent evidence that children from different socioeconomic backgrounds enter school with significantly different levels of sensitivity to the phonological structure of words. Some very recent work has begun to verify that children who come from backgrounds in which they have been more frequently exposed to letters and their names and to various kinds of reading activities show more advanced phonological awareness upon school entry than those with less experience in these areas.

After children enter school, the growth of their phonological awareness depends not only on what they are taught, but on their response to that instruction. Reading programs that contain explicit instruction in "phonics" produce more rapid growth in phonological awareness than approaches that do not provide direct instruction in this area. In addition, children who respond well to early reading instruction grow much more rapidly in phonological awareness than those who experience difficulties learning early

reading skills. In this sense, phonological awareness is both a *cause* and a *consequence* of differences among children in the rate at which they learn to read. Those who begin reading instruction with sufficiently developed phonological awareness understand the instruction better, master the alphabetic principle faster, and learn to read quite easily. In contrast, those who enter first grade with weak phonological awareness do not respond well to early reading instruction and thus do not have the learning experiences or acquire the reading knowledge and skill that stimulates further growth and refinement of phonological awareness.

Can direct instruction in phonological awareness help children learn to read more easily?

There have now been many research studies showing that it is possible to stimulate growth in phonological awareness by direct training. Even when the phonological awareness training contains only oral language activities (does not include letters or instruction in letter-sound correspondences), it can have a positive effect on general growth of early reading skills (Lundberg, Frost & Peterson, 1988). However, we also know that the effectiveness of oral language training in phonological awareness is significantly improved if, at some point in the training, children are helped to apply their newly acquired phonological awareness directly to reading and spelling tasks (Bradley & Bryant, 1985). While most instructional programs in phonemic awareness begin with oral language activities, most also conclude by leading children to apply their newly acquired ability to think about the phonemic segments in words to reading and spelling activities. *This is a very important point.* Training in phonological awareness should never be considered an isolated instructional end in itself. It will be most useful as part of the reading curriculum if it is blended seamlessly with instruction and experiences using letter-sound correspondences to read and spell words.

We also know from recent research that training programs in this area must go beyond beginning levels of phonological awareness to activities that draw attention to the phonemes in words. Thus, programs that only teach rhyme or syllable awareness will not be as effective as those that require children to become aware of individual phonemes in words.

Unfortunately, it is in the area of instruction in phonological awareness that many of our most important unanswered questions still lie (Blachman, 1997). This, of course, does not mean that we should delay implementing what we know, but rather that we should be open to refinements in our knowledge in this area as research progresses. For example, we do not yet have specific information, beyond the simple distinction already made, about how much phonological awareness is optimal for beginning reading instruction. We might say, "the more the merrier," but if we concentrate too much time in developing more phonological awareness than is needed before we begin actual instruction in reading, this may be a waste of valuable instructional time. Further, it is not yet clear what the optimal combination of training tasks might be. We know that training using oral language activities can stimulate the growth of phonological awareness, but it is also clear that direct instruction in "phonics" and spelling can also produce development in this area.

Another important question is whether training in phonological awareness prior to the beginning of reading instruction can actually prevent serious reading disabilities. We know that classroom-level training or small group training in phonological awareness consistently produces improvements in reading growth for groups of children. However, in all studies conducted thus far, there has always been a large range of individual differences in response to the instruction, with the most phonologically impaired children showing the least growth in response to training.

It is very likely that classroom-level instruction in phonological awareness will not be sufficient to prevent reading disabilities in children who have serious deficiencies in phonological talent. These children will require more intensive, detailed, and explicit instruction in order to achieve the levels of phonemic awareness required to support good reading growth. Although we do not know precisely what such instruction might eventually look like, one program that has been used successfully to stimulate phonological awareness in severely impaired children and adults actually helps them to discover the mouth movements or articulatory gestures that are associated with each phoneme (Lindamood & Lindamood, 1984). One of the goals of this method of instruction is to provide a way for individuals to "feel" the sounds in words as well as hear them.

On the basis of very substantial and consistent research findings, it is clear at this point that instruction to enhance phonological awareness should be part of reading instruction for every child. This instruction will accelerate the reading growth of all children, and it appears to be vital in order for at least 20% of children to acquire useful reading skills. However, it is also clear that this instruction is only one small part of an effective overall reading curriculum. Good training in phonological awareness should be combined with systematic, direct, and explicit instruction in "phonics" as well as rich experiences with language and literature to make a strong early reading curriculum. This "balanced" reading curriculum should also include early and consistent experiences with writing, both as a means to help children learn more about the alphabetic principle and to enhance their awareness of reading and writing as meaningful activities. Of course, all this instruction should be provided within a supportive, rewarding context that provides instructional adjustments for children depending upon the different ways they respond to the basic reading curriculum.

References and Further Reading

Beck, I.L., & Juel, C. (1995). The role of decoding in learning to read. *American Educator, 19,* 8–42.

Blachman, B.A. (1997). Early intervention and phonological awareness: A cautionary tale. In B. Blackman (Ed.). *Foundations of Reading Acquisition and Dyslexia: Implications for Early Intervention.* Mahwah, NJ: Lawrence Erlbaum Associates.

Bradley, L., & Bryant, P. (1985). *Rhyme and Reason in Reading and Spelling.* Ann Arbor: University of Michigan Press.

Bryant, P., MacLean, M., Bradley, L., & Crossland, J. (1990). Rhyme and alliteration, phoneme detection and learning to read. *Developmental Psychology, 26,* 429–438.

Catts, H.W. (1993). The relationship between speech-language impairments and reading disabilities. *Journal of Speech and Hearing Research, 36,* 948–958.

Ehri, L.C. (1997). Grapheme-phoneme knowledge is essential for learning to read words in English. In J. Metsala & L. Ehri (Eds.). *Word recognition in beginning reading.* Hillsdale, NJ: Erlbaum.

Liberman, I.Y., Shankweiler, D., & Liberman, A.M. (1989). The alphabetic principle and learning to read. In Shankweiler, D. & Liberman, I.Y. (Eds.). *Phonology and reading disability: Solving the reading puzzle* (pp. 1–33). Ann Arbor, MI: University of Michigan Press.

Lindamood, C.H., & Lindamood, P.C. (1984). *Auditory Discrimination in Depth.* Blacklick, Ohio: SRA.

Lundberg, I., Frost, J., & Peterson, O. (1988). Effects of an extensive program for stimulating phonological awareness in pre-school children. *Reading Research Quarterly, 23,* 263–284.

Olsen, R., Forsberg, H., & Wise, B. (1994). Genes, environment, and the development of orthographic skills. In V.W. Beringer (Ed.). *The varieties of orthographic knowledge I: Theoretical and developmental issues* (pp. 27–71).

Share, D.L., & Stanovich, K.E. (1995). Cognitive processes in early reading development: A model of acquisition and individual differences. *Issues in Education: Contributions from Educational Psychology, 1,* 1–57.

Torgesen, J.K., Wagner, R.K., & Rashotte, C.A. (1994). Longitudinal studies of phonological processing and reading. *Journal of Learning Disabilities, 27,* 276–286.

From *Journal of Educational Psychology,* 1993, Vol. 85, pp. 453–465

Cross-Language Transfer of Phonological Awareness

Aydin Y. Durgunoğlu, William E. Nagy, and Barbara J. Hancin-Bhatt

The number of students from linguistically diverse backgrounds who are enrolled in U.S. schools is increasing rapidly (Hakuta & García, 1989). For these students, learning to read in English is one of the crucial components of academic success. Hence, how these students' first-language knowledge may affect their reading in a second language is of great pedagogical importance. In addition, the effects of first language on second-language reading (i.e., cross-language transfer) is also of theoretical interest, as evidenced by the increase in research devoted to this issue in the last few years. After two decades of little attention to cross-linguistic transfer, researchers in the area of second-language acquisition have returned to studying acquisition and production of second-language structures as a function of the characteristics of the first language (for reviews, see Gass & Selinker, 1983; Kellerman & Sharwood Smith, 1986; Odlin, 1989). However, despite a resurgence of interest in the effects of cross-language transfer on second-language reading, there has been very little systematic research on the role of first-language cognitive strategies and knowledge on beginning reading in a second language (for exceptions, see Faltis, 1986; Kendall, Lajeunesse, Chmilar, Shapson, & Shapson, 1987).

Cross-Language Transfer

Research with monolingual beginning readers has convincingly demonstrated the relationship between phonological awareness and reading acquisition. In this study, we have replicated this finding with Spanish-speaking children and have shown that phonological awareness in Spanish is closely related to Spanish word recognition. We have also replicated the finding that phonological awareness tests such as segmenting and blending are closely interrelated. However, the critical finding in our study is the cross-language transfer of phonological awareness. We have demonstrated the relationship between phonological awareness in Spanish and word recognition in English. Children who could perform well on Spanish phonological awareness tests were more likely to be able to read English words and English-like pseudowords than were children who performed poorly on phonological awareness tests. This effect was even more salient for those pseudowords that had different pronunciations in Spanish and in English. In short, phonological awareness was a significant predictor of performance on word recognition tests both within and across languages.

Phonological awareness, like other metalinguistic abilities, requires one to reflect on and manipulate the structural features of the spoken language (Tunmer et al., 1988). Unless a child can deliberately focus on the form rather than on the

Aydin Y. Durgunoğlu, William E. Nagy, and Barbara J. Hancin-Bhatt, Center for the Study of Reading, University of Illinois at Urbana-Champaign.

This work was supported in part by the Office of Educational Research and Improvement under Cooperative Agreement No. G0087-C1001-90 with the Reading Research and Education Center and in part by a grant from the Mellon Foundation. The publication does not necessarily reflect the views of the agencies supporting the research. We would like to thank Sofia Ariño-Martí, Kristen Knapp, Jim Kotowski, Montserrat Mir, and Kristen Saunders for their help in testing subjects and scoring the data and Georgia García for her comments. Most of all, we thank the children in our study and their principals and teachers for their cooperation. Portions of this research were presented at the April 1992 American Educational Research Association meetings in San Francisco.

Correspondence concerning this article should be addressed to Aydin Y. Durgunoğlu, who is now at the Department of Psychology and Mental Health, University of Minnesota, Bohannon Hall, Duluth, Minnesota 55812.

content of a word, the components in a word are not readily transparent. For example, a child saying *cat* is normally more interested in its meaning rather than in its structural components. However, once a child is able to reflect on the components of a language, it is likely that this metalinguistic awareness could be applied to an (alphabetic) second language as well.

Just as phonological awareness facilitates word recognition, schooling and learning to read can also facilitate phonological awareness. Because most of our subjects were already reading quite a few words in Spanish, we cannot address this question of directionality. However, regardless of the direction, both phonological awareness and word recognition in Spanish seem to transfer to word recognition in English. Although the two variables have some overlap, both contribute independently to performance on English word and pseudoword recognition.

The pattern of cross-language transfer summarized above indicates that it is possible to build on the strengths that a child already has in his or her first language. A child who already knows how to read in Spanish and who has a high level of phonological awareness in Spanish is more likely to perform well on English word and pseudoword recognition tests. In contrast, a child who has some Spanish word recognition skills but low phonological awareness tends to perform poorly on English transfer tests. Developing phonological awareness and word recognition skills in the first language is likely to help in second-language word recognition.

One could ask whether Spanish phonological awareness affects English word recognition directly or indirectly through its influence on English phonological awareness. We feel that this question incorrectly assumes that phonological awareness is developed specific to a particular language. We hold, on the contrary, that similar types of processing underlie both Spanish and English word recognition. For example, in both of these alphabetic languages, children need to identify the phonological subcomponents of the spoken words and understand how orthographic symbols are mapped onto those phonological subcomponents. Such metalinguistic awareness need not be language specific. When faced with a new language, children may need to acquire new phonemes (e.g., /th/ in English) or new orthographic patterns (e.g., *str-* in English) as well as new matches between phonological segments and orthographic patterns (e.g., pronunciation of *-un* is not like *put* as in Spanish but rather like *nut*).[5] More important, children need to understand which phonological units are salient in orthographic representation (e.g., syllables in Spanish but onset-rime units in English). Given this view of bilingual processing, it is not surprising that children who already have a wide knowledge base (i.e., recognize Spanish words well) and who have high metalinguistic awareness (i.e., exhibit phonological awareness) perform better on the English word and pseudoword reading tasks.

One could then question whether the relationship of phonological awareness measured in Spanish and learning to read English words can be legitimately characterized as cross-language transfer. We would operationalize cross-language transfer in terms of the following, educationally

very relevant, question: Would training students in phonological awareness in Spanish enhance their ability to read in English?

The results of the present study indicate that the answer to this question is yes, given two further points: (a) the results of studies of monolingual children in which training in phonological awareness has produced gains in learning to read, and (b) the assumption that the children in the present study gained their phonological awareness primarily through their first language, through their earlier experiences with spoken Spanish, and in particular, through the process of learning to read in Spanish. We feel that this latter assumption is warranted, given that the children had stronger proficiency in Spanish than in English, as indicated by their placement in the bilingual education program and corroborated by their pre-LAS scores. Moreover, the children had been learning English at school only for a short period of time, and this instruction was aimed (primarily) at developing initial oral proficiency, not at reading. As was pointed out, these children were able to read extremely few English words. In summary, we have supporting data that enable us to assume that these children gained their phonological awareness mainly through Spanish. Within the limits of a correlational study, then, we have found evidence for the cross-language transfer of phonological awareness.

Oral-Language Proficiency

One of the most common criteria used for entering and exiting students to and from bilingual education programs is English oral proficiency. In fact, a survey found that 92–94% of school districts used English oral proficiency (alone or in conjunction with other measures) to make entry/exit decisions (Fradd, 1987). Likewise, the schools in our study made placement decisions on the basis of both English oral proficiency and staff judgments. Our data support the caution expressed by several researchers (e.g., Moll & Diaz, 1985; Saville-Troike, 1984) that oral proficiency by itself is not a very reliable predictor of reading abilities. Performance on our oral proficiency tests did not have any significant correlations with word recognition or phonological awareness measures.

Of course, we were focusing on a very specific component of the reading process. Although word recognition is a crucial component of the reading process, it is not the only component. If we had focused on other components of the reading process or on other reading levels, oral proficiency may have played a more prominent role. For example, Verhoeven (1990) found that oral proficiency of Turkish children in Dutch (as measured by syntax and vocabulary knowledge) showed a higher correlation with Dutch reading comprehension than with word recognition measures. The apparent inconsistency between our results and those of Verhoeven underlines the importance of specifying which components of the reading process are involved, and under which condi-

---

[5] The issue of rimes that have varying pronunciations in English (e.g., *-ut*) that sometimes match the Spanish pronunciations is a topic that needs to be investigated.

tions, when one looks for cross-language transfer effects. We discuss this point further in the next section.

Studying Cross-Language Transfer

Cross-language transfer needs to be investigated under well-specified conditions with well-specified tasks. The question is not whether cross-language transfer occurs or whether oral language proficiency is a good predictor of reading performance. Rather, the question is one of condition-seeking (McLaughlin, 1987): Under what conditions do which components of the reading process reflect cross-language transfer? Under what conditions and for which components of reading is oral proficiency a good predictor? Our results indicate that cross-language transfer can occur in word recognition. Both phonological awareness and word recognition skills in Spanish are predictive of word recognition in English. In contrast, oral language proficiency in Spanish is not related to word recognition processes in English. Further research can elucidate which other skills and knowledge in a reader's first language affect certain components of the reading process in a second language.

Methodologically, another point needs to be highlighted. In our study we have not compared the performance of bilinguals with monolinguals but rather analyzed processing in the two languages of a bilingual (cf. Hakuta, Ferdman, & Diaz, 1987). What a child could do on specific tasks in the first language was used to predict what that child could do on specific tasks in the second language. However, to use this analytic, component-skills approach (cf. Haynes & Carr, 1990), a good model describing the interrelationship of the two sets of tasks is necessary. Monolingual reading research had provided us with a well-supported model that demonstrates the relationship between phonological awareness and word recognition in beginning reading, which we have used to investigate cross-language transfer. The exciting new developments in reading research are beginning to reveal more relationships between different components of the reading process that can be applied to research on bilingual reading.

References

Adams, M. J. (1990). *Beginning to read: Thinking and learning about print.* Cambridge, MA: MIT Press.

Ball, E. W., & Blachman, B. A. (1991). Does phonemic segmentation training in kindergarten make a difference in early word recognition and developmental spelling? *Reading Research Quarterly, 26,* 49–66.

Blachman, B. A. (1987). An alternative classroom reading program for learning disabled and other low-achieving children. In W. Ellis (Ed.), *Intimacy with language: A forgotten basic in teacher education* (pp. 49–55). Baltimore: Orton Dyslexia Society.

Bradley, L., & Bryant, P. (1985). *Rhyme and reason in reading and spelling.* Ann Arbor: University of Michigan Press.

Byrne, B., & Fielding-Barnsley, R. (1991). Evaluation of a program to teach phonemic awareness to young children. *Journal of Educational Psychology, 83,* 451–455.

Calfee, R. C., Lindamood, P., & Lindamood, C. (1973). Acoustic–phonetic skills and reading—Kindergarten through 12th grade. *Journal of Educational Psychology, 64,* 293–298.

Calfee, R. C., & Piontowski, D. C. (1981). The reading diary: Ac-

quisition of decoding. *Reading Research Quarterly, 16,* 346–373.

Carr, T. H., Brown, T. L., Vavrus, L. G., & Evans, M. A. (1990). Cognitive skill maps and cognitive skill profiles: Componential analysis of individual differences in children's reading efficiency. In T. H. Carr & B. A. Levy (Eds.), *Reading and its development* (pp. 1–56). San Diego, CA: Academic Press.

Carrell, P. L., & Eisterhold, J. C. (1983). Schema theory and ESL reading pedagogy. *TESOL Quarterly, 17,* 553–573.

Clay, M. M. (1979). *The early detection of reading difficulties* (3rd ed.). Portsmouth, NH: Heinemann.

Cummins, J. (1981). The role of primary language development in promoting educational success for language minority students. In California Office of Bilingual Bicultural Education (Ed.), *Schooling and language minority students: A theoretical framework* (pp. 3–49). Los Angeles: Evaluation, Dissemination and Assessment Center, California State University.

de Manrique, A. M. B., & Graminga, S. (1984). La segmantación fonológica y silábica en niños de preescolar y primer grado [The phonological and syllabic segmentation in preschool and first-grade children]. *Lectura y Vida, 5,* 4–14.

Devine, J. (1987). General language competence and adult second language reading. In J. Devine, P. L. Carrell, & D. E. Eskey (Eds.), *Research in reading in English as a second language* (pp. 73–85). Washington, DC: TESOL.

Dickinson, D. K., & Snow, C. E. (1987). Interrelationships among prereading and oral language skills in kindergartners from two social classes. *Early Childhood Research Quarterly, 2,* 1–25.

Duncan, S., & De Avila, E. A. (1986). *Pre-LAS.* Monterey, CA: CTB/McGraw-Hill.

Durgunoğlu, A. Y. (1988). Repetition, semantic priming and stimulus quality: Implications for the interactive-compensatory reading model. *Journal of Experimental Psychology: Learning, Memory, and Cognition, 14,* 590–603.

Durgunoğlu, A. Y., & Roediger, H. L. (1987). Test differences in accessing bilingual memory. *Journal of Memory and Language, 26,* 377–391.

Ehri, L. C. (1991). Development of the ability to read words. In R. Barr, M. L. Kamil, P. Mosenthal, & P. D. Pearson (Eds.), *Handbook of reading research* (Vol. 2, pp. 383–417). New York: Longman.

Ehri, L. C., & Wilce, L. S. (1980). The influence of orthography on readers' conceptualization of the phonemic structure of words. *Applied Psycholinguistics, 1,* 371–385.

Faltis, C. (1986). Initial cross-lingual reading transfer in bilingual second-grade classrooms. In E. E. García & B. Flores (Eds.), *Language and literacy research in bilingual education* (pp. 145–157). Tempe: Arizona University Press.

Foorman, B. R., Francis, D. J., Novy, D. M., & Liberman, D. (1991). How letter–sound instruction mediates progress in first-grade reading and spelling. *Journal of Educational Psychology, 83,* 456–469.

Fox, B., & Routh, D. K. (1984). Phonemic analysis and synthesis as word attack skills: Revisited. *Journal of Educational Psychology, 76,* 1059–1064.

Fradd, S. H. (1987). The changing focus of bilingual education. In S. H. Fradd & W. J. Tikunoff (Eds.), *Bilingual and bilingual special education: A guide for administrators* (pp. 1–44). Boston: Little Brown.

García, G. E. (1991). Factors influencing the English reading test performance of Spanish-speaking Hispanic children. *Reading Research Quarterly, 26,* 371–392.

Gass, S., & Selinker, L. (1983). *Language transfer in language learning.* Rowley, MA: Newbury House.

Goswami, U., & Bryant, P. (1990). *Phonological skills and learning to read.* Hillsdale, NJ: Erlbaum.

Gough, P. B., & Juel, C. (1991). The first stages of word recognition. In L. Rieben & C. A. Perfetti (Eds.), *Learning to read* (pp. 47–56). Hillsdale, NJ: Erlbaum.

Goyen, J. D. (1989). Reading methods in Spain: The effect of a regular orthography. *Reading Teacher, 42,* 370–373.

Hakuta, K., Ferdman, B. M., & Diaz, R. (1987). Bilingualism and cognitive development: Three perspectives. In S. Rosenberg (Ed.), *Advances in applied psycholinguistics* (Vol. 2, pp. 284–319). Cambridge, England: Cambridge University Press.

Hakuta, K., & García, E. E. (1989). Bilingualism and education. *American Psychologist, 44,* 374–379.

Haynes, M., & Carr, T. H. (1990). Writing system background and second language reading: A component skills analysis of English reading by native speaker-readers of Chinese. In T. H. Carr & B. A. Levy (Eds.), *Reading and its development: Component skills approaches* (pp. 375–421). San Diego, CA: Academic Press.

Heath, S. B. (1986). Separating "things of imagination" from life: Learning to read and write. In W. H. Teale & E. Sulzby (Eds.), *Emergent literacy: Writing and reading* (pp. 156–172). Norwood, NJ: Ablex.

Hudelson, S. (1984). Kan yu ret an rayt en ingles: Children become literate in English as a second language. *TESOL Quarterly, 18,* 221–238.

Juel, C. (1980). Comparison of word identification strategies with varying context, word type and reader skill. *Reading Research Quarterly, 15,* 358–376.

Juel, C., Griffith, P. L., & Gough, P. B. (1986). Acquisition of literacy: A longitudinal study of children in first and second grade. *Journal of Educational Psychology, 78,* 243–255.

Kellerman, E., & Sharwood Smith, M. (1986). *Crosslinguistic influence in second-language acquisition.* Elmsford, NY: Pergamon Press.

Kendall, J. R., Lajeunesse, G., Chmilar, P., Shapson, L. R., & Shapson, S. M. (1987). English reading skills of French immersion students in kindergarten and Grades 1 and 2. *Reading Research Quarterly, 22,* 135–159.

Liberman, I. Y. (1987). Language and literacy: The obligation of the schools of education. In W. Ellis (Ed.), *Intimacy with language: A forgotten basic in teacher education* (pp. 1–9). Baltimore: Orton Dyslexia Society.

Lomax, R. G., & McGee, L. M. (1987). Young children's concepts about print and reading: Toward a model of word reading acquisition. *Reading Research Quarterly, 22,* 237–256.

Lundberg, I., Frost, J., & Petersen, O. P. (1988). Effects of an extensive program for stimulating phonological awareness in preschool children. *Reading Research Quarterly, 23,* 265–284.

Maclean, M., Bryant, P., & Bradley, L. (1987). Rhymes, nursery rhymes, and reading in early childhood. *Merrill-Palmer Quarterly, 33,* 255–281.

Mann, V. A., Tobin, P., & Wilson, R. (1987). Measuring phonological awareness through the invented spellings of kindergartners. *Merrill-Palmer Quarterly, 33,* 365–391.

Mason, J., & Allen, J. (1986). A review of emergent literacy with implications for research and practice in reading. In E. Rothkopf (Ed.), *Review of research in education* (pp. 205–238). Washington, DC: American Educational Research Association.

McConkie, G. W., & Zola, D. (1981). Language constraints and the functional stimulus in reading. In A. M. Lesgold & C. A. Perfetti (Eds.), *Interactive processes in reading* (pp. 155–175). Hillsdale, NJ: Erlbaum.

McLaughlin, B. (1987). *Theories of second language learning.* London: Arnold.

Moll, L. C., & Diaz, S. (1985). Ethnographic pedagogy: Promoting effective bilingual instruction. In E. E. García & R. V. Padilla (Eds.), *Advances in bilingual education research* (pp. 127–149). Tucson: University of Arizona Press.

Morais, J., Cary, L., Alegria, J., & Bertelson, P. (1979). Does awareness of speech as a sequence of phones arise spontaneously? *Cognition, 7,* 323–331.

Odlin, T. (1989). *Language transfer.* Cambridge, England: Cambridge University Press.

Perfetti, C. A. (1985). *Reading ability.* New York: Oxford University Press.

Perfetti, C. A., Beck, I., Bell, L., & Hughes, C. (1987). Phonemic knowledge and learning to read are reciprocal: A longitudinal study of first grade children. *Merrill-Palmer Quarterly, 33,* 283–319.

Rayner, K., & Pollatsek, A. (1989). *The psychology of reading.* Englewood Cliffs, NJ: Prentice Hall.

Read, C., Yun-Fei, Z., Hong-Yin, N., & Bao-Qing, D. (1986). The ability to manipulate speech sounds depends on knowing alphabetic writing. *Cognition, 24,* 31–44.

Saville-Troike, M. (1984). What *really* matters in second language learning for academic achievement? *TESOL Quarterly, 18,* 199–219.

Seidenberg, M. S., & McClelland, J. L. (1989). A distributed, developmental model of word recognition and naming. *Psychological Review, 96,* 523–568.

Shanahan, T. (1984). Nature of reading–writing relation: An exploratory multivariate analysis. *Journal of Educational Psychology, 76,* 466–477.

Stanovich, K. E. (1982). Individual differences in the cognitive processes of reading: 1. Word decoding. *Journal of Learning Disabilities, 15,* 485–493.

Stanovich, K. E. (1986). Matthew effects in reading: Some consequences of individual differences in the acquisition of literacy. *Reading Research Quarterly, 21,* 360–406.

Stanovich, K. E. (1991). Word recognition: Changing perspectives. In R. Barr, M. L. Kamil, P. Mosenthal, & P. D. Pearson (Eds.), *Handbook of reading research* (Vol. 2, pp. 418–452). New York: Longman.

Stanovich, K. E., Cunningham, A. E., & Cramer, B. B. (1984). Assessing phonological awareness in kindergarten children: Issues of task comparability. *Journal of Experimental Child Psychology, 38,* 175–190.

Stanovich, K. E., & West, R. F. (1983). On priming by a sentence context. *Journal of Experimental Psychology: General, 112,* 1–36.

Stuart, M., & Coltheart, M. (1988). Does reading develop in a sequence of stages? *Cognition, 30,* 139–181.

Treiman, R. (1985). Phonemic analysis, spelling, and reading. In T. H. Carr (Ed.), *The development of reading skills* (pp. 5–18). San Francisco: Jossey-Bass.

Treiman, R. (1988). The internal structure of the syllable. In G. Carlson & M. Tanenhaus (Eds.), *Linguistic structure in language processing* (pp. 27–52). Dordrecht, Holland: D. Reidel.

Treiman, R., & Baron, J. (1983). Phonemic analysis training helps children benefit from spelling-sound rules. *Memory & Cognition, 11,* 382–389.

Tunmer, W. E., Herriman, M. L., & Nesdale, A. R. (1988). Metalinguistic abilities and beginning reading. *Reading Research Quarterly, 23,* 134–158.

Tunmer, W. E., & Nesdale, A. R. (1985). Phonemic segmentation skill and beginning reading. *Journal of Educational Psychology, 77,* 417–427.

Vellutino, F. R., & Scanlon, D. M. (1987). Phonological coding, phonological awareness, and reading ability: Evidence from a longitudinal and experimental study. *Merrill-Palmer Quarterly, 33,* 321–363.

Verhoeven, L. T. (1990). Acquisition of reading in a second language. *Reading Research Quarterly, 25*, 90–114.

Vygotsky, L. S. (1962). *Thought and language* (E. Hanfmann & G. Vakar, Eds. and Trans.). Cambridge, MA: MIT Press.

Wagner, R. K. (1988). Causal relations between the development of phonological processing abilities and the acquisition of reading skills: A meta-analysis. *Merrill-Palmer Quarterly, 34*, 261–279.

Wagner, R. K., & Torgeson, J. K. (1987). The nature of phonological processing and its causal role in the acquisition of reading skills. *Psychological Bulletin, 101*, 192–212.

Walley, A. C., Smith, L. B., & Jusczyk, P. (1986). The role of phonemes and syllables in the perceived similarity of speech sounds

for children. *Memory & Cognition, 14*, 220–229.

Wells, G. (1987). The learning of literacy. In B. Fillion, C. N. Hedley, & E. C. DiMartino (Eds.), *Home and school: Early language and reading* (pp. 27–46). Norwood, NJ: Ablex.

Williams, J. P. (1980). Teaching decoding with a special emphasis on phoneme analysis and phoneme blending. *Journal of Educational Psychology, 72*, 1–15.

Yopp, H. K. (1988). The validity and reliability of phonemic awareness tests. *Reading Research Quarterly, 23*, 159–177.

Zifcak, M. (1981). Phonological awareness and reading acquisition. *Contemporary Educational Psychology, 6*, 117–126.

Appendix

Words in the Matching Test

Target word	Alternatives		
Initial sounds the same, broken syllable			
*g*anas	luna	*g*ota	bota
*n*ene	base	*n*ota	cana
*c*oche	*c*arta	dedo	misa
*m*ono	lapiz	tiza	*m*adre
*t*oro	malo	arte	*t*ela
*p*era	*p*ino	risa	arbol
Initial two sounds the same, intact syllable			
*ca*pa	leche	*ca*ro	agua
*sa*po	*sa*la	yoyo	curso
*la*ta	pico	zero	*la*do
*bo*ca	casa	torre	*bo*ta
*ar*te	isla	once	*ar*pa
*ba*se	lobo	*ba*ja	pero
*mu*ral	*mu*jer	noche	poder
*va*so	loma	*va*ca	dulce
Initial two sounds the same, broken syllable			
*co*no	*co*rte	rampa	lindo
*la*va	gusto	mundo	*la*rgo
*bo*ta	curva	*bo*lsa	parte
*to*do	*to*rta	campo	busca
*pa*to	mares	color	*pa*rque
*fi*no	gana	*fi*nca	donde

Received November 12, 1991
Revision received December 2, 1992
Accepted January 6, 1993 ■

IV

SECTION IV

Decoding

THE ROLE OF DECODING IN LEARNING TO READ

BY ISABEL L. BECK AND CONNIE JUEL

A S ANYONE knows who has both read to young children and watched them begin learning to read, there is a great difference in the sophistication of their abilities in the two arenas. As an illustration, consider a typical activity in a first-grade classroom.

Twenty-six first graders are sitting on the floor around their teacher, Ms. Jackson. She opens a copy of McCloskey's (1941, 1969) *Make Way for Ducklings* and shows the children a double-page picture of two mallards flying over a pond. Jackson tells them that the birds are mallards, which are a kind of duck, and begins to read.

As the teacher reads, the children's attention, facial expressions, and giggles (for example, when a policeman stops traffic to let the mallards waddle across the road) suggest that they are enjoying the story. Their giggling also provides evidence that they understand the story. Even stronger evidence of their understanding is found in the discussion Jackson initiates. For example,

Isabel L. Beck is professor of education at the School of Education and senior scientist at the Learning, Research, and Development Center, both at the University of Pittsburgh. She has published widely in the area of reading comprehension as well as early reading acquisition. Connie Juel is the Thomas G. Jewell Professor of Education and director of studies in learning to read at the McGuffey Reading Center at the University of Virginia. She has published widely on literacy acquisition, including her recent book, Learning to Read and Write in One Elementary School *(Springer-Verlag: 1994). This article first appeared as a chapter in* What Research Has To Say About Reading Instruction *(1992), edited by S. J. Samuels and A. E. Farstrup, and is reprinted by permission of the International Reading Association.*

Reprinted with permission from the Summer 1995 issue of the *American Educator,* the quarterly journal of the American Federation of Teachers

The Role of Decoding

one of the questions she asks is why the mallards didn't want to live next to foxes and turtles. The only information given in the story is that "[Mrs. Mallard] was not going to raise a family where there might be foxes or turtles." The reason is not explained, yet the children are able to infer that Mrs. Mallard doesn't want to live next door to foxes and turtles because they might harm the ducklings.

The discussion also provides evidence that the children have control over some sophisticated language structures. Consider such complicated syntax as "But the people on the boat threw peanuts into the water, so the Mallards followed them all round the pond and got another breakfast, better than the first." When the teacher asks several of the children what that sentence means, none has difficulty capturing the notion that the mallards liked the peanuts more than what they had gotten to eat on their own.

Most children entering school have fairly sophisticated knowledge about language and stories. The children described here had enough knowledge of syntax, vocabulary, story elements, and aspects of the world around them to comprehend and enjoy *Make Way for Ducklings*. But no story in any first-grade preprimer can match the literary quality and level of language found in *Make Way for Ducklings*. Why? Because the children will be unable to read many words and therefore have no reliable way to translate the written text into their familiar spoken form of language. Until their word recognition skill catches up to their language skill, they are unable to independently read a story that matches the sophistication of their spoken vocabularies, concepts, and knowledge.

There has been much legitimate criticism of the reading materials used in early reading instruction. Although these materials need improvement, it is important to acknowledge that because children can recognize only a limited number of words, even the most creatively developed materials cannot compete with stories such as *Make Way for Ducklings*. Our goal as educators is to quickly provide children with the tools they need to read some of the marvelous stories gifted writers have created for them. The major tools we can give children are ones that allow them to decode printed words for themselves. To facilitate a discussion of the issues associated with helping children gain control of the code that links the printed word to the spoken word, let us first define some terms.

Defining Reading Terms

Various terms have been used to describe the way children come to recognize printed words. We begin with a discussion intended to sort out a set of easily confused terms: the code, decoding, word attack, word recognition, phonics, and sight words.

One dictionary definition of *code* is "a system of signals used to represent assigned meanings." Signals can be numbers (as in a military code), dots and dashes (Morse code), or letters (as in an alphabetic language like English). In themselves these signals are meaningless. They become meaning-bearing units only when an individual knows what meanings can be assigned to the signals. When an individual can apply meaning to signals, that person has learned to decode.

In written alphabetic languages such as English, the code involves a system of mappings, or correspondences, between letters and sounds. When an individual has learned those mappings, that person is said to have "broken the code." Now the individual can apply his or her knowledge of the mappings to figure out plausible pronunciations of printed words. Most of the time, competent adult readers do not need to apply their knowledge of the mapping system consciously to recognize the words they encounter. If they do encounter a word they have never seen before, however, they are able to bring their knowledge of the code to

bear in a deliberate and purposeful way.

A number of terms are used to describe the application of the code when reading. It may be useful to consider the terms in light of two extremes of attention a reader pays to the code. At one extreme readers apply their knowledge of the code immediately and without any apparent attention. The terms used to describe this immediate phenomenon are *word recognition, word identification,* and *sight word recognition.* At the other extreme, readers consciously and deliberately apply their knowledge of the mapping system to produce a plausible pronunciation of a word they do not instantly recognize, such as the name of a character an English-speaking reader might encounter in a Russian novel. The term associated with this self-aware "figuring out" is *word attack.*

Individuals involved in either extreme are decoding in that they are using symbols to interpret a unit that bears meaning. Hence, word recognition, word identification, word attack, and sight word recognition are all terms applied to decoding, albeit to decoding with different levels of conscious attention.

Two terms that can be confused are sight word *vocabulary* (sometimes called sight word recognition) and sight word *method.* The former is a critical goal of all reading instruction—that children come to respond to most words at a glance, without conscious attention. This goal should not be confused with the instructional strategy called the sight word method (also known as the whole word or look-say approach), in which words are introduced to children as whole units without analysis of their subword parts. By repeated exposure to words, especially in meaningful contexts, it is expected that children will learn to read the words without any conscious attention to subword units. Hence, sight word recognition, or the development of a sight word vocabulary, is a goal of sight word instruction.

The issue of instructional strategies brings us to the terms *phonics* and *word attack.* Phonics embraces a variety of instructional strategies for bringing attention to parts of words. The parts can be syllables, phonograms (such as *an*), other letter strings (such as *ple*), or single letters. The goal of phonics is to provide students with the mappings between letters and sounds but, unlike the goal of the sight word method, phonics is not an end point. Rather, phonics merely provides a tool that enables students to "attack" the pronunciation of words that are not recognizable at a glance; hence the term word attack.

The Importance of Early Decoding Skill

Early attainment of decoding skill is important because this early skill accurately predicts later skill in reading comprehension. There is strong and persuasive evidence that children who get off to a slow start rarely become strong readers (Stanovich, 1986). Early learning of the code leads to wider reading habits both in and out of school (Juel, 1988). Wide reading provides opportunities to grow in vocabulary, concepts, and knowledge of how text is written. Children who do not learn to decode do not have this avenue for growth. This phenomenon, in which the "rich get richer" (i.e., the chil-

dren who learn early to decode continue to improve in reading) and the "poor get poorer" (i.e., children who do not learn to decode early become increasingly distanced from the "rich" in reading ability), has been termed the Matthew effect (Stanovich).

The importance of early decoding skill can be illustrated through the findings of several studies. In a longitudinal study of fifty-four children from first through fourth grades, Juel (1988) found a .88 probability that a child in the bottom quartile on the Iowa Reading Comprehension subtest at the end of first grade will still be a poor reader at the end of fourth grade. Of twenty-four children who remained poor readers through four grades, only two had average decoding skills. By the end of fourth grade, the poor decoders still had not achieved the level of decoding that the average/good readers had reached by the beginning of second grade. The poor decoders also had read considerably less than the average/good readers, both in and out of school. They had gained little vocabulary compared with the good decoders and expressed a real dislike of both reading and the failure associated with reading in school.

Lesgold and Resnick (1982) found that a child's speed of word recognition in first grade was an excellent predictor of that child's reading comprehension in second grade. In a longitudinal study of children learn-

ing to read in Sweden, Lundberg (1984) found a .70 correlation between linguistic awareness of words and phonemes in first grade and reading achievement in sixth grade. Moreover, Lundberg found that of forty-six children with low reading achievement in first grade, forty were still poor readers in sixth grade.

Clay (1979) discusses results of a longitudinal study of children learning to read in New Zealand:

> There is an unbounded optimism among teachers that children who are late in starting will indeed catch up. Given time, something will happen! In particular, there is a belief that the intelligent child who fails to learn to read will catch up to his classmates once he has made a start. Do we have any evidence of accelerated progress in late starters? There may be isolated examples which support this hope, but correlations from a follow-up study of 100 children two and three years after school entry lead me to state rather dogmatically that where a child stood in relation to his age-mates at the end of his first year in school was roughly where one would expect to find him at 7:0 or 8:0 (p. 13).

What Helps Children Learn the Code

The studies reported above all point to the importance of arranging conditions so that children gain reading independence early. The task of learning to decode printed words is made easier when the child has certain prerequisite understandings about print. These include knowing that print is important because it carries a message, that printed words are composed of letters, and that letters correspond to the somewhat distinctive sounds heard in a spoken word. Often these prerequisites develop as a result of a child's having been read to (especially by an adult who has made occasional references to aspects of the print), having attended preschool and kindergarten programs, or having watched instructional television programs like *Sesame Street*. Let us look at these three prerequisites and why children sometimes have difficulty acquiring them.

Printed Words Carry Messages

First, young children need to know that some systematic relationship exists between printed symbols and spoken messages. They need to know that looking at the print itself is important to determine these messages. This idea is not as obvious as it may first appear. Storybooks contain colorful, enticing pictures designed to capture children's interest and attention. In comparison, the black marks at the bottom of the page are rather uninteresting. Likewise, print in the environment is often embedded in rich contexts that are more noticeable and "readable" than the print itself (e.g., for a child, the color and shape of a stop sign has more meaning than the letters forming the word *stop*).

Words Are Composed of Letters

Observations of children's first unguided attempts to use print show that they frequently find some distinctive feature of a word that acts as a cue to identify the word for them (Gates & Boeker, 1923; Gough & Hillinger, 1980). Often this distinctive feature will be tied to a picture or a page location (e.g., *police car* is the last string of letters on the page with a picture of a policeman). Or a child will remember distinctive fea-

tures of a particular word (e.g., *mallard* is a long string of letters with two straight lines in the middle). Initial letters are frequently used as recall cues (for instance, *duck* starts with a *d*). The problem with this approach is that for each additional word it is harder to find a single, distinctive cue (*d* for *duck* will no longer suffice when *deer* is encountered). At this point, reading can become an increasingly frustrating activity unless a better cue system is developed.

Children often try to combine distinctive features of words (for instance, first letters) with context cues to figure out an unknown word. This hybrid approach is not particularly reliable, however. For example, consider the difficulty a young child would encounter in figuring out an unknown word in the sentence "Mrs. Mallard_____ her eight ducklings." What word fits in the blank? It could be almost any verb. What if the child looked at the first letter (which in this case is *l*), or looked at the first and last letters (*l* and *s*) and approximate length (five letters)? Even with these three feature cues, the word might be *loves*, *likes*, *loses*, or *leads*, to list a few. Learning to look at *all* the letters is important.

Letters Correspond to the Sounds in Spoken Words

Once children know that words are composed of letters, they need to be able to map, or translate, the printed letters into sounds. In order to do that, children first need to be able to "hear" the sounds in spoken words—that is, to hear the /at/ sound in *cat* and *fat*, for example, and perceive that the difference between the two words lies in the first sound. (In this article slashes // indicate a speech sound.) If children cannot perceive these sound segments, they will encounter difficulty when trying to sound out words, in both reading and writing. This understanding has been termed phonemic awareness.

Phonemic awareness is not a single insight or ability. Rather, there are various phonemic insights, such as being able to rhyme words as in the cat/fat example above, or knowing that *fat* has three distinctive, yet overlapping and abstract, sounds. The last insight is particularly difficult because phonemes often overlap in speech (e.g., we begin saying the /a/ sound in fat while still uttering the /f/).

Although it is not clear how children gain phonemic awareness, certain activities do appear to foster it. Home factors such as time spent on word play, nursery or Dr. Seuss rhymes, and general exposure to storybooks appear to contribute to phonemic awareness. In a fifteen-month longitudinal study of British children from age three years, four months, Maclean, Bryant, and Bradley (1987) found a strong relationship between children's early knowledge of nursery rhymes and the later development of phonemic awareness. In addition, phonemic awareness predicted early reading ability. Both relationships were found after controlling for the effects of IQ and socioeconomic status.

There is growing evidence that phonemic awareness can be taught to young children and that such teaching can occur in a playful, interactive way. Lundberg, Frost, and Petersen (1988) showed that preschool children can be trained to manipulate the phonological elements in words. Their eight-month training program involved a variety of games, nursery rhymes, and rhymed stories. A typical game designed to foster syllable synthesis included a troll who told children what they would get as presents through the peculiar method of producing the words syllable by syllable. Each child had to synthesize the syllables in order to figure out what the troll was offering. Children who participated in the training showed considerable gains in some phonemic awareness skills—such as phoneme segmentation—compared with children who did not participate in the program. Positive effects of the preschool training were still evident in children's reading and spelling performance through second grade.

Clay (1979) found that many six-year-olds who were not making adequate progress learning to read could not "hear" the sound sequences in words. She adopted a phonemic awareness training program developed by the Russian psychologist Elkonin (1973) to train these children. Clay found that the children could learn and apply the strategy of analyzing the sound sequence of words. This strategy improved both their reading and their writing.

Unfortunately, many children come to school without phonemic awareness, and some fail to gain it from their school experiences. Juel, Griffith, and Gough (1985) found that well into first grade the spelling errors of many children were not even in the domain of what has come to be known as invented spellings (such as using the sounds captured in letter names to spell *light* as *lt* or *rain* as *ran*). These researchers found that many children entered first grade with little phonemic awareness and had difficulty learning spelling-sound relationships. For example, these children's misspellings of *rain* used in a sentence included such things as *yes, wetn, wnishire, rur,* and drawings of raindrops. The course of learning the code for these children will be different and more difficult than for children who are able to hear the sounds in spoken words and who know that these sounds can be mapped to letters.

Instructional Approaches

Given that letters and sounds have systematic relationships in an alphabetic language such as English, it stands to reason that those responsible for teaching initial reading would consider telling beginners directly what those relationships are. Indeed, until about 60 years ago this is what most teachers in the United States did. The techniques used, however, left much to be desired.

Phonics: The Past

It is important to recognize that phonics is not a single procedure. Under the label phonics can be found a variety of instructional strategies for teaching the relationship between letters and sounds. It appears that the kind of phonics practiced in the first decades of this century was an elaborated "drill and more drill" method. Diederich (1973) describes the scene:

Initial instruction in letter-sound relationships and pronunciation rules was done to death … children had

to learn so much abstract material by rote before doing any significant amount of reading (p. 7).

To illustrate more concretely what Diederich was describing, picture the following: It is October 1921, and forty first graders are seated at rows of desks. The teacher stands at the front of the class and points with a long wooden pointer to a wall chart that contains columns of letters and letter combinations. As she points to a column of short vowel and consonant *b* combinations, the class responds with the sound of each combination: /ab/, /eb/, /ib/, /ob/, /ub/. She goes to the next column and the class responds, /bab/, /beb/, /bib/, /bob/, /bub/. Then the teacher asks, "What's the rule?" The children respond in unison, "In a one-syllable word, in which there is a single vowel followed by a consonant.…" So it went day after day, with "letter-sound relationships and pronunciation rules … done to death."

It is no wonder that educators as prominent as William S. Gray described this kind of phonics as "heartless drudgery" and urged that it be replaced with what initially was termed the look-say approach and subsequently called the sight word or whole word method. The relief from extended drill with letter sounds, their synthesis into often meaningless syllables, and the recitation of rules of pronunciation is evident in Diederich's (1973) own response to the look-say method:

When [this] writer began his graduate study of education in 1928 ... no less an authority than Walter Dearborn had to send his students to observe several classes that were learning to read by the new "look-say" method before they would believe that it was possible. When prospective teachers like the students of Walter Dearborn discovered what a relatively painless process the teaching of reading could be, using the ... whole word approach, they were not disposed to demand evidence of superior results. It was enough to know that the new method worked about as well as the old and with far less agony (p. 7).

Look-Say

By the 1930s, the look-say method prevailed. The idea behind this approach was that children could learn to recognize words through repeated exposure without direct attention to subword parts. The existence of ideographic writing systems (like Chinese or Japanese Kanji, which is based on Chinese characters) shows that this type of visual learning can occur, but it is difficult. The characters are learned slowly. A child in Japan is expected to learn only seventy-six Kanji in first grade and 996 by the end of sixth grade. In contrast, many Japanese children enter school already reading Kana, which is based on phonetic segments. Most ideographic writing systems have been (or are in the process of being) replaced by alphabetic ones.

English is not an ideographic written language. To teach it as if it were ignores the systematic relationships between letters and the sounds that underlie them. Proponents of the look-say method have been quick to point out the imperfections of these relationships, which are most apparent in some high frequency words (e.g., *come, said*). It should not be overlooked, however, that the pronunciations of even these irregular words do not deviate widely from their spellings. We do not pronounce *come* as *umbrella,* or *said* as *frog.*

The look-say method continued virtually unchallenged until 1955, when Flesch, in his book *Why Johnny Can't Read,* vehemently attacked the approach and demanded a return to phonics. Although the general public and press reacted favorably to Flesch's book, it was rejected by reviewers in educational journals—chiefly because it took the form of a propagandistic argument that presented conclusions beyond what research evidence allowed. A decade later, Chall's (1967) *Learning to Read: The Great Debate* provided a reasoned presentation of the research with the conclusion that the evidence points to benefit from those programs that include early and systematic phonics. Subsequent researchers confirmed this advantage (e.g., Barr, 1972, 1974, 1975; DeLawter, 1970; Elder, 1971; Evans & Carr, 1983; Guthrie et al., 1976; Johnson & Baumann, 1984; Resnick, 1979; Williams, 1979).

Phonics: The Present

Several years ago, the National Commission on Reading, comprising a range of representatives from the research community (and sponsored in part by the National Institute of Education), developed a report that synthesized and interpreted the existing body of research on reading. The report, entitled *Becoming a Nation of Readers* (Anderson et al., 1985), observes in its discussion of early reading that "most educators" view phonics instruction as "one of the essential ingredi-

ents." It goes on to note: "Thus, the issue is no longer ... whether children should be taught phonics. The issues now are specific ones of just how it should be done" (pp. 36-37). Approaches to phonics instruction generally can be described by one of two terms—explicit phonics and implicit phonics, referring to the explicitness with which letter sounds (phonemes) are taught in a given approach.

In explicit phonics, children are directly told the sounds of individual letters (the letter *m* represents the /m/ in *man*). In implicit phonics, children are expected to induce the sounds that correspond to letters from accumulated auditory and visual exposure to words containing those letters (for instance, they would induce /m/ from hearing the teacher read *man, make,* and *mother* as she or he points to the words on the chalkboard). In terms of the effectiveness of one approach over the other, *Becoming a Nation of Readers* observes that "available research does not permit a decisive answer, although the trend of the data favors explicit phonics" (p. 42). Let us look more closely at both approaches, beginning with implicit phonics.

As noted above, in implicit phonics the sounds of individual letters are never pronounced in isolation. Instead, the child is expected to induce these sounds from reading words in stories and lists that contain similar spelling-sound patterns. Continuing with the *m* example, a child who encountered the new word *met* and who had seen and heard *man* and *make* would be instructed to think of other words that begin with the letter *m* in order to identify the sound at the beginning of the new word. In order to comply with the instructions, the child needs to be able to identify distinct sounds in spoken words to make a connection between the sound and the target letter. To be able to induce the sound of the letter *m* or the sound of the *et* phonogram, the child must be able to distinguish between the sound of the initial consonant and the rest of the word. This is a difficult task because in speech the sounds of individual letters actually overlap and blend as a word is pronounced. Thus, in actuality, the ability to extract the sound of a letter from a spoken word is more "in the mind" than "in the mouth."

A problem with implicit phonics is that many children fail to induce the sounds because they are unable to segment a word into distinctive sounds. It takes very sophisticated phonemic awareness to do so. Many children do not come to school with such awareness, yet implicit phonics requires this ability right from the start.

Explicit phonics requires less sophisticated phonemic awareness because the sounds associated with letters are directly provided. Explicit phonics, however, has its own potential problem; the sounds of some consonant letters cannot be said in isolation without adding a schwa, or /uh/ (e.g., the isolated sound of the letter *b* in *but* is distorted to /buh/). Do we harm children by telling them these distortions? Not if instruction in how to blend letter sounds is provided. In reviewing the research associated with this question, Johnson and Baumann (1984) noted that "there is no substance to the long-held belief that pronouncing sounds in isolation is detrimental" (p. 592). Similarly, the

THE ROLE OF DECODING

commission that developed *Becoming a Nation of Readers* concluded that "isolating the sounds ... and teaching children to blend the sounds of letters together to try to identify words are useful instructional strategies" (p. 42). Thus, the prevailing conclusion seems to be that isolating sounds offers an advantage when it is done in moderation and when it includes good blending instruction.

Explicit phonics is helpful because it provides children with the real relationships between letters and sounds, or at least approximations of them. But knowledge of letter-sound relationships is of little value unless the child can use that knowledge to figure out words. Whether children have learned the sounds of letters through implicit or explicit phonics, figuring out a new word still requires that the sounds of the letters be merged or blended.

We will return to the topic of blending in considering instructional issues. First we address another major issue associated with phonics—the relationship between what children learn in phonics and the stories they read.

Phonics and Reading Materials

We begin this section by recalling that among the serious problems Diederich (1973) pointed to about the way phonics was presented in the past was that "children had to learn so much abstract material [i.e., letter-sound relationships] by rote before doing any significant amount of reading" (p. 7). This "abstractness" problem can be eliminated by recognizing that adequate instruction gives students opportunities to apply what they are learning. Children need a lot of early experience reading meaningful material that includes many words that exemplify the sound-spelling patterns being introduced.

Current beginning reading programs tend to fall into two groups: (1) those in which there is a strong relationship between the sound-spelling patterns children are learning in their phonics lessons and the words in the stories they read, and (2) those in which this relationship is weak. To illustrate the differences, *Becoming a Nation of Readers* presented excerpts from two representative programs. Both excerpts came from material that would be read some time in or near November of first grade, when both programs would have introduced about thirty letter-sound relationships. A twenty-six-word passage from the weak-relationship program contained seventeen different words, out of which "only three (or 17 percent) could be decoded entirely on the basis of letter-sound relationships that [had] been introduced in the program's phonics lessons" (p. 45). In contrast, out of eighteen different words in the passage from the strong-relationship program, seventeen (or 94 percent) "could be decoded entirely on the basis of letter-sound relationships that students should know from the program's phonics lessons" (p. 46).

This gap in the percentage of decodable words results from the word selection process for the stories of each program. The first program selected high-frequency words that are likely to be in a young child's vocabulary. Word choice was not constrained by the letter-sound relationships or letter patterns introduced in the program's phonics lessons. In the second program, word choice was, to a large extent, constrained by the letter patterns introduced.

These two excerpts reflect the findings of Beck's (1981) analysis of eight beginning reading programs. The analysis included all the material students would read in the first third of each program. The percentage of decodable words in the four programs that based word selection on the letter-sound relationships introduced in their phonics lessons was 100 percent, 93 percent, 79 percent, and 69 percent, respectively. In contrast, the percentage of decodable words in the programs that selected their words from high-frequency lists was 0 percent for two programs, 3 percent for the third, and 13 percent for the fourth.

Problems arise when the relationship between what children learn in phonics and the stories they read is either too low or too high. When too few of the words are decodable it is questionable whether what is taught in phonics is of any use. On the other hand, when all but one or two of the words in a selection are constrained by the letter sounds introduced, it is virtually impossible to write interesting selections in natural sounding language. This is, in part, a result of exclusion of such high-frequency but irregular words as *said, come, have,* and *you.* At its extreme, excluding such words and overemphasizing the last few letter sounds introduced results in sentences of the "Dan had a tan can" variety.

Is there an optimal relationship between the letter sounds children are learning in phonics and the words in their readers? Clearly, the answer is no. *Becoming a Nation of Readers* makes the point that establishing a rigid guideline is a poor idea: "What the field of reading does not need is another index that gets applied rigidly. What the field does need is an understanding of the concepts at work" (p. 47). The concept at work is that a "high proportion of the words in the earliest selections children read should conform to the phonics that they have already been taught." However, "requiring that, say, 90 percent of the words ... conform to letter-sound relationships already introduced would destroy the flexibility needed to write interesting, meaningful stories" (p. 47).

The issues we have raised in the last two sections concern instructional strategies for teaching phonics and the relationship between what is learned in phonics and the selections children read. Having raised these issues in terms of existing instructional materials, let us turn to the teacher's role.

What Teachers Can Do

It is well established that basal reading programs are the most widely used resources for teaching reading in the elementary school. Although program implementation undoubtedly varies with individual teachers, there is strong evidence that the program teachers use heavily influences their classroom teaching (Diederich, 1973). Hence, we will frame our discussion of what

Learning
To Read

teachers can do in relationship to the kinds of programs in use.

Since the most widely used reading programs employ implicit phonics, this seems to be the most prevalent approach. In implicit phonics, individual sounds are not produced in isolation. However, we would encourage teachers to make the individual sounds available. As teachers told Durkin (1984), who observed them producing sounds in isolation even though their manuals did not recommend it, "Children need to hear the sounds" (p. 740).

Although we recommend making individual sounds explicitly available, we caution against using them in isolation. Specifically, we recommend that teachers start with a word the children already know from oral language, extract the sound from that word, and then place it back into the word. For example, in preparation for learning the sound of the letter *d*, the teacher can draw students' attention to a word like *duck* from a recent story or use a line from a nursery rhyme, such as "diddle, diddle, dumpling." Then the teacher should explain that the first letter of these words, called a *d*, represents the /d/ sound.

This strategy not only overcomes the problem in implicit phonics of requiring children to extract a sound from a spoken word, but it also reduces a potential problem in explicit phonics—the difficulty of saying the sounds of some of the consonant letters in isolation. By starting with strong words, extracting the sound from those words, and placing the sound right back into words, teachers can avoid the pitfalls of explicit phonics approaches in which a string of isolated letter sounds is accumulated.

As noted earlier, an important issue associated with phonics is blending. *Becoming a Nation of Readers* makes two important points that can be applied to this topic. The first is that blending "is a difficult step for many children. Until a child gets over this hurdle, learning the sound of individual letters … will have diminished value" (p. 39). The second point is that when children attempt to figure out a word by blending sounds, it is not necessary for them to produce a perfect pronunciation. Rather, they need to be able to "come up with approximate pronunciations—candidates that have to be checked to see whether they match words known from spoken language" (p. 38).

We have two suggestions for promoting children's blending ability. In one the teacher models decoding of unknown words by slowly blending their component letter sounds. A model of blending involves stretching out each component sound until it merges with the next sound and then collapsing the sounds together so the word can be heard more clearly. For example, the teacher could select a new word that will be encountered in an upcoming selection, let's say *met*, write it on the board, and demonstrate how one might go about sounding it out. She or he would note that the first letter, the *m*, represents the /m/ sound, like at the beginning of *mittens*. Next the teacher would produce /m/ and add the short *e*, first elongating the sounds, /mmee/, then collapsing them, /me/. Then the teacher would add the /t/, at first giving a slightly exaggerated, then a more natural, pronunciation of *met*.

It is not difficult to involve the children in practicing this strategy. For example, the teacher can write a word on the board and tell the children to think of the sound of the first letter and keep saying it until he or she points to the next letter, and keep saying the sound of the two letters until they add on the sound of the last letter.

Resnick and Beck (1976) note that an important feature of blending instruction is merging different sounds successively—that is, /m/, /me/, /met/. Teachers should avoid using sequences in which the merging does not occur until each sound has been produced, such as /m/, /e/, /t/, /met/. Among the reasons that successive blending is preferable is that it avoids the need to keep a string of isolated sounds in memory.

Blending instruction does not have to be tedious. Teachers can choose from a variety of active and fun possibilities. For example, the teacher might give large cardboard letters to some children and start a word by telling the child who has the card that says /m/ to stand up. Then the child whose card makes /m/ say /me/ can go up and stand next to the /m/ child, followed by the /t/ bearer, who can complete the word *met*. The teacher might then ask the child who can make *met* say *bet* to go up and change places with the /m/ child.

This last example brings us to the second instructional strategy that promotes blending. Here children are involved with many opportunities to make words and to experiment with and observe the results of a letter change. A traditional implementation of this strategy involves a variety of letter substitution techniques. For example, the teacher places a phonogram such as *an* on a flannel board and then puts various consonants in front of the pattern, having the children read the resulting words (e.g., *can, man*). Or the teacher places the letters *s, a, t* on a flannel board and after the children read *sat*, she or he changes the vowel so the word reads *sit*, then changes it again to read *set*. This technique can be extended so that children use their own letter cards (which they can make or get from the teacher) to create words by changing letters in all positions—for instance, *sat* to *sit* to *hit* to *hot* to *hop* to *mop* to *map*. By deleting, adding, or substituting letters, more complex sequences, such as *black* to *back* to *tack* to *tick* to *trick*, can be developed.

Building words in this fashion externalizes the blending process. It makes the process readily accessible to children by making it very concrete. Children physically handle the letter cards, attach sounds to them, and manipulate the cards to produce new words.

Now let us turn to instructional issues associated with the relationship between what children are learning in phonics and the words in the stories they read and consider what the teacher can do if the relationship is either too low or too high. First, if the selections do not use words that allow the children to practice what has been taught in phonics, the teacher will need to write or find materials that do.

One teacher developed a way to write stories that incorporated the sound spelling patterns introduced in the program she was using. Essentially, she made "little books" by revising some of the stories in the basal. She started with a selection and inserted new words whose letter-sound relationships had already been taught. She

found she was able to develop meaningful stories by adding and deleting various sentences, phrases, and words. Most often, her revised stories were longer than the original ones. Sometimes they were elaborated versions of the original stories, but frequently the deletion and addition of words allowed her to vary the plots of these stories.

The teacher reported that she enjoyed revising the selections, but found it very time consuming. Since all teachers cannot be expected to have the time or knack for making such little books, published materials are needed. Some published children's stories (such as Dr. Seuss's *The Cat in the Hat, Hop on Pop, Fox in Socks,* and *There's a Wocket in My Pocket*) can be used. If a book contains too many unknown words, the teacher could use it in a shared reading situation in which she reads some of the story to the children and the children read the parts (perhaps from a "Big Book") that contain the words with learned sound spelling patterns. Other sources of material that may be useful are nursery rhymes ("How now brown cow") and tongue twisters ("How many cans can a canner can…"). In addition, teachers can give children opportunities to write their own tongue twisters.

If the program being followed is too constrained in using only phonics-related words (the "Dan had a tan can" variety), the teacher needs to incorporate into the selections some high-frequency words that have lots of utility for future readings. The teacher also should include words of interest to the children and words that have appeared in the children's writings. So we might get "Dan had a big can full of tan monsters." Or the teacher can leave blanks in a story where the children can fill in words: "Dan had a ____ can full of ____. A ____ man took the can." Basically the teacher leaves blanks where adverbs, adjectives, and prepositional phrases could go. The children might copy and illustrate these stories, collecting them into storybooks that can be taken home and read to others. The teacher also can use these types of text in chart stories or Big Books.

Children's writing can be used to foster phonic skill. For this strategy to work, children must have the prerequisite understandings discussed earlier in the section on phonemic awareness. Bissex (1980) gives an example of how a child who could analyze words into spoken sounds gained knowledge of the code through writing. Bissex's five-year-old son, Paul, advanced by asking his mother questions concerning letter-sound relationships as he wrote. For example, Paul asked what made the "ch" sound in *teach,* to which his mother responded "c-h" (p. 12). Or this dialogue:

Paul: What makes the "uh" sound?
Mother: In what word?
Paul: Mumps.
Mother: u (p. 13).

To ask such questions, Paul had to have rather sophisticated phonemic awareness (for instance, he could segment the /uh/ sound in *mumps*). Likewise, teachers of young children may be able to foster such interaction as they respond to their young students' questions about how to write the sounds in certain words.

Just as teachers model blending to decode unknown words, they can model how to sound and blend sounds into written words. For example, "If I wanted to write the word *met* in a story, I'd first say the word to myself very slowly, /mmeett/. Then I'd think of the letter that makes the /m/ sound at the beginning of met and write it [writing the letter *m* on the board]. Then I'd think of what letter needs to be added to make it say /meee/ [adding the letter *e*]. Then I'd think of what letter needs to be added to make it say *met* [adding the letter *t*]." The teacher can encourage children to sound out and write the words in their stories in a similar manner.

As teachers can help children induce the code by repeatedly answering the question "What's this word?" they also can help them by answering "What letter stands for this sound in this word?" With either reading or writing, successful induction of the code will depend both on whether the child has the prerequisite understandings (i.e., phonemic awareness) and whether someone is around to answer these questions frequently. The fortunate child who has both of these conditions in place can learn the code even more quickly by being directly informed about the alphabetic code (e.g., through explicit phonics). The child who has little prerequisite knowledge about print and who lacks an informed partner in learning may need to *depend* on systematic and explicit phonics instruction. This child has fewer opportunities to induce the code through exposure to print and is thus more dependent on instruction to lay bare the alphabetic system.

The course of acquiring the code for a child like Paul, who at age five wrote above his workbench DO NAT DSTRB GNYS AT WRK (Bissex, 1980, p. 23), will be very different from that of the child who in the middle of first grade is spelling *rain* as *yes* or *wnishire*. Paul already had a good understanding of the alphabetic system and knew a fair amount about the code prior to first grade. He would have learned to read in first grade no matter what the instruction. Many children are not as fortunate as Paul. They depend almost exclusively on the instruction they receive in school to learn to read and write.

We have discussed the extreme importance of learning the code in first grade because early decoding reliably predicts reading comprehension in subsequent grades. Failure to teach the code in the most straightforward manner (e.g., through good, explicit phonics instruction coupled with reasonably constrained texts) would leave many children without the key to unlock the printed message. Children without this key cannot independently enter the world of quality literature; some may learn to dislike reading entirely. Each day that goes by without the child being able to read a book like *Make Way for Ducklings* is a day in which the knowledge and joy that can come from such reading are lost.

REFERENCES

Anderson, R.C., Hiebert, E.H., Scott, J.A., & Wilkinson, I.A.G. (1985). *Becoming a nation of readers: The report of the Commission on Reading*. Washington, DC: National Institute of Education.

Barr, R. (1972). The influence of instructional conditions on word recognition errors. *Reading Research Quarterly, 7,* 509-529.

Barr, R. (1974). Influence of instruction on early reading. *Interchange.* 5(4). 13-21.

Barr, R. (1975). The effect of instruction on pupil reading strategies. *Reading Research Quarterly, 4,* 555-582.

Beck, I.L. (1981). Reading problems and instructional practices. In G.E. MacKinnon & T.G. Waller (Eds.), *Reading research: Advances in theory and practice* (vol. 2, pp. 53-95). New York: Academic.

Bissex, G.L. (1980). *GNYS AT WRK: A child learns to read and write.* Cambridge, MA: Harvard University Press.

Chall, J.S. (1967). *Learning to read: The great debate.* New York: McGraw-Hill.

Clay, M.M. (1979). *Reading: The patterning of complex behavior.* Portsmouth, NH: Heinemann.

DeLawter, J. (1970). *Oral reading errors of second grade children exposed to two different reading approaches.* Unpublished doctoral dissertation. Teachers College, Columbia University, New York.

Diederich, P.B. (1973). *Research 1960-1970 on methods and materials in reading* (TM Report 22), Princeton, NJ: Educational Testing Service.

Durkin, D. (1984). Is there a match between what elementary teachers do and what basal reader manuals recommend? *The Reading Teacher, 37,* 734-744.

Elder, R.D. (1971). Oral reading achievement of Scottish and American children. *Elementary School Journal, 71,* 216-230.

Elkonin, D.B. (1973). U.S.S.R. In J. Downing (Ed.). *Comparative reading* (pp. 551-579). New York: Macmillan.

Evans, M.A., & Carr, T.H. (1983). *Curricular emphasis and reading development: Focus on language or focus on script.* Symposium conducted at the biennial meeting of the Society for Research on Child Development, Detroit, MI.

Flesch, R. (1955). *Why Johnny can't read.* New York: Harper & Row.

Gates, A.I. & Boeker, E. (1923). A study of initial stages in reading by preschool children. *Teachers College Record, 24,* 469-488.

Gough, P.B. & Hillinger, M.L. (1980). Learning to read: An unnatural act. *Bulletin of the Orton Society, 30,* 179-196.

Guthrie, J.T., Samuels, S.J., Martuza, V., Seifert, M., Tyler, S.J. & Edwall, G.A. (1976). *A study of the focus and nature of reading problems in the elementary school.* Washington, D.C.: National Institute of Education.

Johnson, D.D. & Baumann, J.F. (1984). Word identification. In P.D. Pearson (Ed). *Handbook of reading research* (pp. 583-608). White Plains, NY: Longman.

Juel, C. (1988). Learning to read and write: A longitudinal study of fifty-four children from first through fourth grade. *Journal of Educational Psychology, 80,* 437-447.

Juel, C., Griffith, P.L. & Gough, P.B. (1985). Reading and spelling strategies of first grade children. In J.A. Niles & R. Lalik (Eds.). *Issues in literacy: A research perspective* (pp. 306-309). Rochester, NY: National Reading Conference.

Lesgold, A.M., & Resnick, L.B. (1982). How reading disabilities develop: Perspectives from a longitudinal study. In J.P. Das, R. Mulcahy, & A.E. Wall (Eds.). *Theory and research in learning disability.* New York: Plenum.

Lundberg, I. (1984, August). Learning to read. *School Research Newsletter.* Sweden: National Board of Education.

Lundberg, I., Frost, J., & Petersen, O. (1988). Effects of an extensive program for stimulating phonological awareness in preschool children. *Reading Research Quarterly, 23,* 263-284.

Maclean, M., Bryant, P., & Bradley, L. (1987). Rhymes, nursery rhymes, and reading in early childhood. *Merrill-Palmer Quarterly, 33,* 255-281.

McCloskey, R. (1941/1969). *Make way for ducklings.* New York: Viking.

Resnick, L.B. (1979). Theories and prescriptions for early reading instruction. In L. B. Resnick & P.A. Weaver (Eds.), *Theory and practice of early reading* (vol. 2, pp. 321-338). Hillsdale, NJ: Erlbaum.

Resnick, L., & Beck, I.L. (1976). Designing instruction in reading: Interaction of theory and practice. In J.T. Guthrie (Ed.), *Aspects of reading acquisition.* Baltimore, MD: Johns Hopkins University Press.

Stanovich, K.E. (1986). Matthew effects in reading: Some consequences of individual differences in the acquisition of literacy. *Reading Research Quarterly, 21,* 360-406.

Williams, J.P. (1984). Reading instruction today. *American Psychologist, 34,* 917-922.

The Multisyllabic Word Dilemma

Helping Students Build Meaning, Spell, and Read "Big" Words

by Patricia M. Cunningham

Facility with multisyllabic words is essential for students as they read, write, and learn. Many big words occur infrequently, but when they do occur they carry much of the meaning and content of what is being read. English is a language in which many words are related through their morphology. This relationship is preserved through our spelling system. Students who learn to look for patterns in multisyllabic words will be better spellers and decoders. If they learn to look further and consider possible meaning relationships, they will increase the size of their meaning vocabulary stores. This article summarizes research and presents practical teaching strategies for developing facility with multisyllabic words.

Ten thousand new words—words never before encountered in print—is the number the average student encounters each year from fifth grade on (Nagy & Anderson, 1984). Most of these words are big words—words of seven or more letters and two or more syllables. To progress in reading, students must have strategies for decoding big words. In spite of this explosion of words during the intermediate school years and beyond, relatively little is known about how children learn to decode big words, and still less is known about how to teach children about them. Compounding the problem is the belief that phonics instruction is generally not undertaken after the early primary grades. The highly popular and influential report, *Becoming a Nation of Readers* (Anderson, Hiebert, Scott, & Wilkinson, 1985), added to this misconception when it recommended that "Except

From *Reading and Writing Quarterly: Overcoming Learning Difficulties*, 1998, Vol. 14, No. 2, pp. 189–218

in cases of diagnosed individual need, phonics instruction should have been completed by the end of the second grade" (p. 43). Another recommendation in this report was that, to be effective, phonics instruction must be related to the words children actually meet while reading. Because the percentage of multisyllabic words encountered in reading material before third grade is relatively small, instruction in decoding multisyllabic words before that time would have little effect.

The widely held belief that phonics instruction should be completed by the end of second grade is partly responsible for children getting so little help developing the decoding strategies necessary to unlock the pronunciation and meanings for those 10,000 new words they encounter each year. Another reason is the lack of agreement about what kind of instruction would be helpful. What can you do to help children decode 10,000 new words, most of which are going to be big words? In past decades, children were taught a set of syllabication rules and then were instructed to apply their phonics knowledge to the syllables once they were successfully divided. Syllabication rules are rarely taught these days, because teachers realized, and research demonstrates, that there is little relationship between knowing the rules and successful reading (Canney & Schreiner, 1977). Even when children can successfully divide words, they often cannot pronounce the word, because phonics rules that apply to one-syllable words often do not apply to bigger words.

Twenty years ago, instruction in what was termed *structural analysis* was a part of most upper-elementary reading curricula. This instruction usually included prefixes, suffixes, and Greek and Latin roots. These word parts were usually taught as clues for determining meanings of words rather than as clues for pronouncing unfamiliar-in-print words. Often the word parts emphasized were parts with low utility. *Intra,* for example, was taught as a prefix meaning "within," with the examples of *intramural* and *intrastate.* According to the *American Heritage Dictionary* (4th edition), there are 25 words that begin with the letters *intra.* In most of these, such as *intractable,* the *in,* not the *intra,* is the prefix. Six words, including *intramural* and *intrastate,* begin with the prefix *intra.* The only other words students would be helped to figure out the meaning of from the prefix *intra* were *intravenous, intrauterine, intracellular,* and *intracellularity!* In addition to the lack-of-utility problem, many of the prefixes taught had as many examples where the prefix did not add to the meaning of the word as those in which it did. *Mis* might help you figure out *misbehave* and *misdeal,* but it doesn't get you far with the meanings of *miscellaneous* and *mistletoe.*

Instruction about suffixes was often cluttered with grammatical jargon. The suffixes *ance* and *ence* were taught as ones that change the word from the verb form to the noun form and meaning "the condition or state of." It is doubtful that when students first encountered the word *difference* they thought of the word *differ* (which is actually lower in frequency than *difference*) and then used *differ* to figure out a meaning for *difference*—"the condition or state of differing!"

Finally, the usefulness of Greek and Latin roots is questionable. Shepard (1974) found that knowledge of Latin roots is not strongly related to knowledge of meanings of words but that knowledge of stems that are current English words is strongly related to the meaning of related words. Many students know meanings for words such as *collect* and *receive* who don't know anything about the Latin roots *lect* and *ceive.* But students who know the word *sane* have little trouble with the less frequent related word, *sanity.*

For a variety of reasons, this type of structural analysis is seldom found in upper-grade reading curricula today. Later in this article, when I recommend what kind of instruction might help children decode big words, the importance of morphological relationships will be highlighted, but it is important to note that the morphologically based instruction supported by research bears little resemblance to the rule-based, low-utility structural analysis done in the past.

In the remainder of this article I will look at what is known about multisyllabic words, which is not as much as we need to know but is a lot more than we knew when the previous generation of multisyllabic word instruction was created. The few studies that have carried out instructional approaches to increase students' ability to decode big words are reviewed, and a program of instruction, based on what is currently known, is outlined.

What the Research Tells Us About Big Words

The research base for the understanding of how big words work comes from the research into how students acquire word meanings, initiated by William Nagy and Richard Anderson as part of the research carried out by the Center for the Study of Reading, and from the spelling stage development research initiated by Ed Henderson and colleagues from the University of Virginia. Neither of these research lines investigated the decoding of multisyllabic words, but an understanding of how big words work from a meaning-and-spelling viewpoint will allow us to make inferences about the decoding processes involved.

Research Into the Development of Meaning Vocabulary

In 1984, William Nagy and Richard Anderson published a landmark study in which they analyzed a sample from Carroll, Davies, and Richman's (1971) *Word Frequency Book* to determine the number and relationships of words found in printed school English. On the basis of a sample of 7,260 words, Nagy and Anderson estimated that there are more than 400,000 distinct words (excluding proper nouns, numbers, and foreign words) in "printed school English" (Grades 3–9). Many of these words, however, are related semantically through their morphology. A child who knows the words *hunt, red, fog,* and *string* will have little difficulty with the meanings of *hunter, redness, foglights,* and *stringy.* Word relationships such as these are defined as *semantically transparent.* When you group the semantically transparent words together, instead of 400,000 plus words you have 88,500 word families. For each basic word known, most children know three or four other words.

Other word relationships exist but are not so readily apparent. Meaning relationships exist between *planet* and *planetarium, vicious* and *vice, apart* and *apartment*, but these will probably not be apparent to most children unless they are pointed out. Nagy and Anderson (1984) defined these types of meaning relationships as *semantically opaque*. If readers do, however, understand these more complex morphological relationships, then instead of 88,500 word families there would be 54,000 word families. If children knew or learned how to interpret these more morphologically complex relationships, they would know six or seven words for every basic word known.

When looking at all the words readers are apt to meet, affixed words (words with a prefix and one or more suffixes) outnumber basic (unanalyzable) words by a factor of four to one. These affixed words play an even greater role in reading than the 4:1 ratio would imply, because affixed words make up a larger percentage of low frequency words, and basic words are more apt to be high frequency words. When children are reading from the upper elementary grades onward, a large percentage of the new words they encounter will be affixed words. Nagy and Anderson (1984) estimated that approximately 60% of English words have meanings that can be predicted from the meanings of their parts and that, for another 10%, word parts give useful though incomplete information. The average fifth grader is apt to encounter 10,000 new words each year. Excluding proper nouns, numbers, abbreviations, and other "special" words, only 1,000 of these new words are probably truly new words, not related to other more familiar words.

Nagy and Anderson (1984) concluded that students learn most of their word meanings from wide reading and that facility with context and morphological relationships may determine how able they are to take advantage of the opportunities for new word learning presented by wide reading. They suggested that teaching words together as a family will call attention to the morphological relationships and will allow students to take better advantage of these relationships when reading on their own.

White, Power, and White (1989) confirmed the importance of morphology to the acquisition of word meanings by examining all words in the Carroll, Davies, and Richman (1971) corpus that began with the four most common prefixes. They found 782

words prefixed by *un,* 401 words prefixed by *re,* 313 words prefixed by *in/im/ir/il*(meaning "not"), and 216 words prefixed by *dis*. On the basis of a sample of these words, White et al. concluded that if students knew one of the three most common meanings for the base word, they would correctly infer the meaning of the prefixed word 81% of the time. Next, they estimated how many analyzable words containing these four prefixes students would be apt to meet in their reading from third to ninth grade. They estimated that the average third grader would encounter 230 words, the meaning of which would be obvious if the base word and the four prefixes were known. The average seventh grader would probably encounter 1,324 such words. White et al. further estimated that the number of analyzable words for each grade level would double if all prefixes, not just the most common four, were included. They concluded that:

> individual prefixed words are quite rare or infrequent—much too infrequent to learn on an individual basis. But because there are a great many of them, the need for morphological analysis arises often (p. 290).

To summarize what we know about big words from the investigations into the development of meaning vocabulary, we can conclude that readers encounter a large number of infrequently occurring words as they move through school. Most of these words are related morphologically to other words. Students learn word meanings from their reading, and both context and morphology are thought to account for a lot of their vocabulary development. Readers' morphological sophistication—the ability to gain information about the meaning, pronunciation, and part of speech of words from their prefixes, roots, and suffixes—is thought to play a large role in how effectively they deal with new, long words.

Research Into the Development of Spelling Abilities

In 1985, Henderson wrote:

> Those who set out to remember every letter of every word will never make it. Those who try to spell by sound alone will be defeated. Those who learn how to "walk through" words with sensible expectations, noting sound, pattern and meaning relationships

will know what to remember, and they will learn to spell English (p. 67).

The work of Henderson and his followers, most clearly laid out in *Words Their Way* (Bear, Invernizzi, Templeton, & Johnston, 1996), shows children progressing through a number of stages as they become fluent spellers (Zutell, 1998). The final stage, and the one of most interest for big words, is called *derivational constancy*. This is the stage at which children notice the sophisticated patterns represented by the spelling of multisyllabic words and also the stage in which morphology plays a dominant role. The rest of this discussion about spelling of big words will be based on research into words and children's spelling of words in the derivational constancy stage.

"Why does *bomb* have a *b* at the end and *sign* have a *g?*"
"Why is there a *c* in *muscle?*"
"Why is the second syllable of *composition* spelled with an *o* while a syllable that sounds the same in *competition* is spelled with an *e?*"

The answer to these questions is that spelling preserves the meaning linkages across words. The *b* at the end of *bomb* maintains the meaning relationship between *bomb* and other "relatives," such as *bombard* and *bombastic; signal, signature,* and other related words will explain the *g* in *sign;* and *muscular* will explain the *c* in *muscle.* The middle syllable of *composition* is spelled with an *o* because of its relationship to *compose.* Likewise, *competition* is related to *compete.*

Linguists believe that English spelling is more dependent on morphology than any other language. Most English morphemes have a single spelling even though their pronunciations vary. The past tense of the words *walked, crawled,* and *dated* are all spelled *e–d,* but the endings of these words have three different pronunciations. Vowels change pronunciations as word form changes, shown by the pronunciation of the *a* in *volcano* when it becomes *volcanic.* In many other languages, the spelling would reflect these changes in pronunciation. But in English, spelling maintains meaning links at the expense of sound (O'Grady, Dobrovolsky, & Aronoff, 1989). Templeton (1991) put it most succinctly when he said students need to learn that "Words that are related in meaning are often related in spelling as well, despite changes in sound"

(p. 194). In fact, when it comes to spelling big words, meaning, not sound, rules! To become a good speller from the middle grades on, you must abandon a "memorize the letters" strategy or a "write down the letters that stand for the sound" strategy and realize that even patterns that work in short words often don't work in longer words. You must develop a strategy in which you consider at some level what words might be related to this word.

Templeton (1992) reviewed the research that he and his colleagues have conducted on students' spelling development in the derivational constancy stage. In one set of studies, they set out to determine how aware middle-grade students are of the spelling–meaning connection. In interviews, students were asked if spelling made sense to them. They were also asked to decide if pairs of words, such as *please–pleasant, limb–limber,* and *logic–logician* were related. Some of these pairs were shown to the interviewees. Others did not see the pairs but heard the interviewer pronounce the words. They were also asked if the first *i* in words such as *define–definition* had the same sound in both words. If they replied that the sounds were different, they were asked why the spelling did not change to show that the sounds were different. Students gave a variety of responses, including:

"*Clinic* and *clinician* are related because of the spelling."
"I doubt that *sign/signal* come from one another. I don't think the origin sounds the same.
"*Origin* and *original* are not related because *original* means just something that is original and I don't know what the other one is and they don't sound alike." (Templeton, 1992, p. 259)

This interview study was followed by a study in which middle-grade students responded on a 5-point scale to items such as:

Spelling would make a lot more sense if words were spelled the way they sound.
In words like *please* and *pleasant,* it's good that the spelling of the underlined letters is the same because the meaning of the words is similar (p. 260).

On the basis of these studies, Templeton and his colleagues concluded that there was a wide range of understandings about spelling–meaning connections among these middle-grade students. Some students had developed some knowledge of derivational morphology, but most were uncertain about the nature and application of this knowledge.

In another set of studies that relate directly to the problems readers have reading polysyllabic words, Templeton and his colleagues (Templeton, 1992) investigated the ability of 6th–10th graders to spell and read derived forms of pseudowords. Subjects were given a made-up word such as *tefame* and a suffix such as *ation*. For some words, the words and suffixes were shown to them; for others they were only pronounced. Subjects were then asked to both pronounce and spell the pseudoword that would combine *tefame* with *ation* and fit in a sentence such as: "He was convinced by Jan's _____ of the book" (p. 256). Students at all grade levels were more successful at spelling the word (*tefamation*) than at pronouncing it. The explanation for this is probably that spelling it requires only that you know how to spell *ation* and that you must drop the *e* at the end of TEFAME. To read the word *tefamation*, however, requires changes in the pronunciation of the first *a* along with a change in accent (similar to the changes that occur as *profane* becomes *profanity*).

This "spelling easier than pronunciation" phenomenon is of particular interest because it is the opposite of what happens in the early years of learning to read and spell. In the early stages of literacy, children can read many more words than they can spell and must learn an arbitrary spelling system. (Why should *wait* be spelled w-a-i-t and *date* be spelled d-a-t-e?) Once big words become the literacy hurdle, however, the situation appears to reverse itself. Because the spelling system maintains the meaning links, spelling makes sense, and pronunciation becomes less predictable!

The meaning vocabulary researchers were seeking an explanation for the incredible vocabulary growth that occurs from the middle grades onward through school. The spelling researchers were looking for the particular patterns that older children must examine and notice if they are to become good spellers. Two groups of researchers, coming from different research traditions and asking different questions, separately

discovered morphology as a major player in the big-words game. Next I look at what the researchers whose interest was word recognition have contributed to our understanding of big words.

Research on Word Recognition

Within the last decade, advances in technology have allowed researchers, mainly in the areas of psychology and artificial intelligence, to investigate brain functions, eye movements, and other basic reading processes. The focus of this research was not on how to teach reading or on comparisons of various approaches but rather on what happens internally when we read and how this changes as readers move from beginning stages to more sophisticated reading. We know a great deal more today than we did two decades ago about basic reading processes.

For many years, it was generally believed that sophisticated readers sampled text. On the basis of predictions about what words and letters they would see, readers were thought to look at words and letters just enough to see if their predictions were confirmed. Eye-movement research carried out with computerized tracking has shown that, in reality, readers look at every word and almost every letter of each word (Rayner & Pollatsek, 1989). The amount of time spent processing each letter is incredibly small—only a few hundredths of a second. The astonishingly fast letter recognition within familiar words and patterns is explained by the fact that our brains expect certain letters to occur in sequence with other letters.

Although it is possible to read without any internal speech, we rarely do. Most of the time as we read, we think the words in our mind. We then check this phonological information with the information we have received visually by analyzing the word for familiar spelling patterns. Good readers use context to see if what they are reading makes sense. Context is also important for disambiguating the meaning of some words (I had a *ball* throwing the *ball* at the *ball*.). Occasionally, readers use context to figure out words. Most of the time, however, words are identified on the basis of their familiar spelling and the association of that spelling with a pronunciation. Context comes into play after, not before, the word is identified on the basis of the brain's processing of the letter-by-letter information it receives (Stanovich, 1991).

When presented with unfamiliar but phonetically regular words—*kirn, miracidium*—good readers immediately and seemingly effortlessly assign them a pronunciation. This happens so quickly that readers are often unaware that they have not seen the word before and that they had to "figure it out." Successful decoding occurs when the brain recognizes a familiar spelling pattern or, if the pattern itself is not familiar, searches through its store of words with similar patterns. This process of using other words with similar patterns to figure out the unfamiliar word is commonly called *decoding by analogy* (Adams, 1990; Goswami & Bryant, 1990).

When the word to be identified is a big word, readers "chunk" or divide the word into manageable units. They do this on the basis of the brain's incredible knowledge of which letters go together in words. A reader who did not immediately recognize the word *midnight* in print would divide between the *d* and the *n*. Seeing the word *Madrid* for the first time, the reader would divide after the *a*, leaving the *dr* together. Letters such as *dr*, which are often seen together in the syllables of words *(drop, dry, Dracula)*, "pull" together. Letters such as *dn*, which are almost never seen following each other in the same syllable, pull apart (Adams, 1990; Mewhort & Campbell, 1981).

To try to summarize what the brain does to identify words is to run the risk of oversimplification, but this seems necessary if we want our instructional practices to be compatible with what we know about brain processes. As we read, we look very quickly at almost all letters of each word. For most words, this visual information is recognized as familiar patterns with which spoken words are identified and pronounced (aloud or through internal speech). Words we have read before are instantly recognized as we see them. Words we have not read before are almost instantly pronounced on the basis of spelling patterns the brain has seen in other words. Big words are "chunked" on the basis of patterns that usually go together in other big words. Meanings are accessed through visual word recognition, but the sounds of words support the visual information and help to hold words in memory.

In addition to this basic research on how the brain functions to decode words, there is some information about word recognition and multisyllabic words. A number of studies have demonstrated that poor decoders have a difficult time reading polysyllabic words even when they can read single-syllable words (Just & Carpenter, 1987; Samuels, LaBerge, & Bremer, 1978). Perfetti (1986) concluded that the ability to decode polysyllabic words increases the qualitative differences between good and poor readers. Although the nature of the relationship is not completely clear, there is a strong relationship between reading level and morphological knowledge. Anderson and Davison (1988) concluded that because most longer words are morphologically complex, deficiencies in morphological knowledge may be a cause of poor readers' difficulties with long words. Freyd and Baron (1982) investigated the extent to which readers' use of structural analysis is related to their reading ability. They found a strong relationship and concluded that skilled readers use structural analysis in three ways: to recognize known words more efficiently, to remember the meanings and spellings of partially learned words, and to figure out the meanings and pronunciations of new words.

Nagy, Anderson, Schommer, Scott, and Stallman (1989) investigated the nature of the relationship between morphology and word recognition by measuring how quickly readers recognized words. Pairs of words were matched for frequency of occurrence but had widely differing frequencies when all the "relatives" of that word were included. *Slow* and *loud,* for example, occur equally frequently in text. When you add *slow*'s relatives—*slowed, slowing, slows, slower, slowest,* and *slowly*—you get a family frequency for *slow*. Adding *louder, loudest, loudly, loudness,* and *loudspeaker* to *loud* gives you a family frequency for *loud*. Nagy et al. argued that if *slow* and *loud* (and other similarly matched words) had equal recognition times, the effect of morphology on word recognition would be questionable. As it turned out, words such as *slow,* with high family frequencies, were recognized much more quickly and accurately than words such as *loud,* whose individual frequencies were the same but whose family frequencies were much lower. Nagy et al. concluded that morphology may help readers recognize words more efficiently and that speed of recognition is determined not just by frequency of the word but by frequency of parts.

We know from basic process research on reading that the major word recognition function in the brain is pattern detection. We also know that children have more difficulties reading longer words. We know from the meaning vocabulary research and the spelling research that the major patterns in multisyllabic words are morphological relationships. Although we don't know the exact nature of the relationship between morphology and the recognition of longer words, it is clear that there is a relationship. Becoming more morphologically sophisticated obviously helps readers access and construct meaning. But that knowledge of affixes and roots may be helpful in decoding and spelling words even where these units do not supply useful information about the meanings of words. There are three tasks involved in developing facility with big words: meaning, spelling, and reading. Recognizing the relationship among *compose, composer,* and *composition* will help with all three. Without sophisticated knowledge of Latin and Greek roots, it is unlikely that students will be helped to construct meaning for *perceive* or *deceive* on the basis of their knowledge of *receive*. If, however, they recognize that all three words share the same pattern of letters and are spelled and pronounced alike, comparing the words has helped them with two of the three tasks.

Given the accumulated research from meaning vocabulary, spelling development, and word recognition research, it seems obvious that work with big words should focus simultaneously on meaning, spelling, and reading. When confronted with a new word, students should first ask themselves: "Do I know any other words that look like this word?" Accessing these analogic words should help them pronounce the word. Once the word is pronounced and its pronunciation checked with the context of what is being read, readers should then ask the second question: "Are these look-alike words related to each other?"

What Research Tells Us About Teaching Readers to Decode Big Words

The ability to decode words is only one factor in reading comprehension. In addition to decoding, readers must access appropriate meanings, connect to prior knowledge, and use text strategies to construct appropriate meanings. But the ability to decode is a major factor in this complex process. Ehrlich, Kurtz-Costes, and Loridant (1993) investigated the cognitive and motivational determinants of reading comprehension in good- and poor-reading Parisian seventh graders. Subjects were given tests that measured reading comprehension, word recognition, metalinguistic knowledge, academic self-concept, and attributional beliefs. For good readers, academic self-concept was the only significant predictor of reading comprehension. In contrast, self-concept was not related to comprehension for poor readers. For poor readers, word recognition was the only significant predictor. Ehrlich et al. concluded that

> our poor readers were notably deficient in word recognition skill. Basic word decoding and perceptual skills are necessary in order to read; if a child lacks these cognitive skills, even the most adaptive attribution and self-efficacy beliefs will not magically reveal the meaning behind the text (p. 376).

John Shefelbine is one of the few researchers to investigate how children decode polysyllabic words. In a descriptive study, Shefelbine and Calhoun (1991) classified 36 sixth-graders as high, moderate, or low on the basis of their ability to decode polysyllabic nonsense words. These sixth-graders were then given a test of their ability to analyze real words, and their error patterns on the first 10 words missed were analyzed. The 12 high decoders showed equal facility with beginning and ending syllables and correctly pronounced 75% of the prefixes and suffixes. Moderate decoders were equally successful with the beginning syllables of words and with prefixes (which were often, but not always, the same unit) but were able to correctly pronounce ending syllables and suffixes only about half the time. Low decoders correctly pronounced only one third of beginning or ending syllables. They were able to correctly pronounce 75% of the prefixes but fewer than half of the suffixes. (Because the analysis was conducted on the first 10 words missed on a graded word list on which the words increased in difficulty, the words being missed by the high decoders were longer, less familiar, and probably more morphemically complex than the words being missed and analyzed by the low decoders. Had their attempts on the same words been compared, the discrepancies between the high and low groups would probably have been even greater.)

High decoders attended to almost all the letters in words and gave correct pronunciations to vowels 80% of the time. They rarely omitted any letters. This analysis was done only on the words they failed to correctly pronounce, so this is a very high level of accuracy. Moderate and low decoders, on the other hand, were two and four times more likely to omit syllables. On the basis of their analysis, Shefelbine and Calhoun (1991) concluded:

> Developing proficiency in identifying polysyllabic words entails a vicious circle in which students need to read many polysyllabic words successfully to learn likely letter patterns but knowing these same patterns is necessary for reading the words in the first place. Among poorer readers, this problem is compounded by a tendency to disregard or misinterpret relatively large proportions of letter information. Extensive reading at independent levels should help break this cycle, since students will be able to use context to identify at least some words. However, in both this instance and when words are pronounced by the teacher, students need to be encouraged to examine letter patterns once the word is identified (p. 176).

In an instructional intervention study (Shefelbine, 1990), 14 fourth graders and 15 sixth graders identified as having difficulty decoding polysyllabic words were given 5 hours of instruction (10 minutes for 30 days) in which they were shown how to use vowels and affixes to pronounce polysyllabic words and practiced decoding words after identifying these parts. When compared with a similar group of control students, the group that had received this short intervention demonstrated significantly greater ability to pronounce polysyllabic words that had never been included in the lessons. On the basis of this study, Shefelbine concluded that:

> Directly teaching students how to pronounce and identify syllable units and then showing them how such units work in polysyllabic words appears to be a worthwhile component of syllabication instruction and should help reduce or remediate this source of reading difficulty among intermediate students (p. 228).

In screening the students for this intervention, Shefelbine found that a large number of intermediate-grade children (15–20% of 8 fourth- and sixth-grade classes) had a great deal of difficulty identifying polysyllabic words. In one of his "low-level" sixth-grade classes, half of the students exhibited difficulty decoding big words.

In another instructional study, Lenz and Hughes (1990) taught 12 learning-disabled seventh-, eighth-, and ninth-graders a seven-step strategy for decoding polysyllabic words. The seven steps of DISSECT were: *d*iscover the context, *i*solate the prefix, *s*eparate the suffix, *s*ay the stem, *e*xamine the stem, *c*heck with someone, *t*ry the dictionary. Students were given six weeks of instruction (20–25 minutes daily) that included modeling, verbal rehearsal, practice, and feedback. Lenz and Hughes concluded that the training was effective in reducing oral reading errors and, for most students, resulted in increased comprehension of passages at their reading level.

In spite of the obvious (and empirically demonstrated) importance of multisyllabic-word decoding to reading comprehension, we know very little about what constitutes effective big word decoding instruction. In the following section, I outline a framework for such instruction. This framework builds on what we know about the morphological link among meaning, spelling, and reading and on the scant instructional research summarized in this section.

Research-Based Big Word Instruction

In 1992, Nagy, Osborn, Winsor, and O'Flahavan presented guidelines for instruction in structural analysis. These guidelines were based on their research with morphology and are intended to help students with the meaning part of developing fluency with big words. The five guidelines are summarized here.

1. Provide explicit explanations, including modeling, think-alouds, guided practice, and the gradual release of responsibility to the students.

When students encounter new words, say things like:

> "Here's a word I haven't seen before. The first thing I'll do is see whether I recognize any familiar parts —a prefix, stem, or suffix—or maybe it might be a compound. Okay, I see the stem. Now, I'll see if that meaning makes any sense in this sentence."

2. Rely on examples more than abstract rules, principles, or definitions. Begin with familiar words. Show nonexamples. Don't have them look for little words in big words (the *car* in *cargo*). Begin with word parts—leave derivational suffixes until later, and when you address them use example rather than definition such as "When you get frustrated you experience a lot of frustration," instead of "Frustration is the state or condition of being frustrated."

3. Recognize the diversity of English word structure and teach what is most useful. Avoid vague Latin roots—the *fer* in *transfer*, the *ceive* in *deceive* can help you spell, but they are not apt to be useful in meaning detection. Some suffixes and prefixes are found in hundreds of words; others occur infrequently.

4. Make the limitations of structural analysis clear, and always check meaning derived from structural analysis with context.

5. Use extended text in opportunities for application.

These guidelines, although intended for meaning, give us an excellent beginning point for building a multisyllabic word instructional framework that includes meaning, spelling, and decoding. If you were interested in spelling and decoding in addition to meaning, you would amend Guideline 3 to include noticing the spelling–decoding help presented by words such as *transfer* and *receive*. In pointing out nonexamples, as suggested in Guideline 2, you would help students notice that the *mis* in *mistletoe* does not help with meaning but is spelled and pronounced like other words that begin with *mis*.

If we are to teach the word parts that are most useful, we must know what these are. White, Sowell, and Yanagihara (1989) analyzed the words in the Carroll et al. (1971) corpus and found that 20 prefixes accounted for 97% of the prefixed words. Four prefixes—*un, re, in* (and *im, ir, il,* meaning "not"), and *dis*—accounted for 58% of all prefixed words. The prefixes accounting for the other 39% of the words were: *en/em, non, in/im* (meaning "in"), *over, mis, sub, pre, inter, fore, de, trans, super, semi, anti, mid,* and *under*. For suffixes, *s/es, ed,* and *ing* account for 65% of the suffixed words. Add *ly, er/or, ion/tion, ible/able, al, y, ness, ity,* and *ment,* and you account for 87% of the words. The remaining suffixes, each occurring in less than 1% of the words, were *er/est* (comparative), *ic, ous, en, ive, ful,* and *less*.

Because White, Sowell, and Yanagihara (1989) were looking at prefixes and suffixes only from the standpoint of helping with the meaning part of big words, they did not include in the count "unpeelable" prefixes and suffixes, such as the *con* in *conform* and the *ture* in *signature*. Arguing rightly that few children would be able to figure out the meaning of *conform* or *signature* by peeling away these parts, they deemed them not useful enough to be taught. When you consider not only meaning but also spelling and decoding, *con* and *ture* become very useful chunks.

In the remainder of this article I present a set of instructional guidelines and strategies that take into consideration meaning, spelling, and decoding. These guidelines and strategies can be used together or separately depending on the content subject being taught, the age and word fluency of the students, and the proclivities of the individual teacher.

Help Students Become Word Detectives On the Lookout For the Meaning, Spelling, and Decoding Relationships Shared By Words

There are two questions I would like to put into the mouths of every teacher of children from third grade through high school. These two questions are: "Do I know any other words that look and sound like this word?" and "Are any of these look-alike/sound-alike words related to each other?" The answer to the first question should help students with pronouncing and spelling the word. The answer to the second question should help students discover what, if any, meaning relationships exist between this new word and others in their meaning vocabulary stores. This guideline and these two simple questions could be used by any teacher of any subject area. Imagine that students in a mathematics class encounter the new word/phrase *improper fraction*. The teacher demonstrates and gives examples of these fractions and helps build meaning for the concept. Finally, the teacher asks the students to pronounce and look at both words and see if they know any other words that look and sound like these words. For *improper*, students think of:

impossible, important, impatient, imported
property, properly, proper
super, paper, kidnapper

For *fraction*, they think of:

fracture, motion, vacation, multiplication,
addition, subtraction

The teacher lists the words, underlining the parts that are the same, and asks students to pronounce the words emphasizing the part that is pronounced the same. The teacher then points out to the students that thinking of a word that looks and sounds the same as a new word will help you quickly remember how to pronounce the new word and will also help you spell the new word.

Next the teacher explains that words, like people, sometimes look and sound alike but are not related. If this is the first time this analogy is used, the teacher will want to spend some time talking with the students about people with red hair, green eyes, and so on who have some parts that look alike but are not related and others who are.

Not all people who look alike are related, but some are. This is how words work, too. Words are related if there is something about their meaning that is the same. After we find look-alike, sound-alike words that will help us spell and pronounce new words, we try to think of any ways these words might be in the same meaning family.

With help from the teacher, the children may discover that *impossible* is the opposite of *possible*, *impatient* is the opposite of *patient*, and *improper* is the opposite of *proper*. *Proper* and *improper* are clearly relatives! *Impossible, impatient,* and *improper* are probably "distant cousins" because they all have *im*, making them opposites. Depending on the students' word sophistication, someone might be able to point out that a *fracture* is a break into two or more parts and that *fraction* also involves parts.

Imagine that the students who were introduced to improper fractions on Monday by their math teacher and were asked to think of look-alike, sound-alike words and consider if any of these words might be "kinfolks" had a science teacher on Tuesday who was beginning a unit on weather and did some experiments with the students using *thermometers* and *barometers*. At the close of the lesson, the teacher pointed to these words and helped them notice that the *meters* chunk was pronounced and spelled the same and asked the students if they thought these words were just look-alikes or were related to one another. The students would probably conclude that they are both used to measure things and that the *meters* chunk must be related to measuring, like in *kilometers*. When asked to think of look-alike, sound-alike words for the first chunk, students thought of *baron* for *barometers* but decided these two words were probably not related. For *thermometer,* they thought of *thermal* and *thermostat* and decided that all these words had to do with heat or temperature.

Now imagine that this lucky class of students had a social studies teacher on Wednesday who pointed out the new word *international* and asked the two critical questions, an art teacher on Thursday who was having them do some *sculpture,* and an English teacher on Friday with whom they encountered the new word *foreshadowing*.

Throughout their school day, children from the intermediate grades up encounter many new words. Because English is such a morphologically related language, most new words can be connected to other words by their spelling and pronunciation, and many new words have meaning-related words already known to the student. Some clever, word-sensitive children become word detectives on their own. They notice the patterns and use these to learn and retrieve words. Others, however, try to learn to pronounce, spell, and associate meaning with each of these words as separate, distinct entities. This is a difficult task that becomes almost impossible as students move through grades and the number of new words increases each year. Readers do not need to be taught every possible pattern, because the brain is programmed to look for patterns. Some students, however, do not know what the important patterns in words are and that these patterns can help them with pronouncing, spelling, accessing, and remembering meanings for words. The simple procedure of asking the two critical questions for key vocabulary introduced in any content area would add only a few minutes to the introduction of key content vocabulary and would pay students back manyfold for that time.

Teach Students to Spell a Set of Big Words That Have the High Utility for Meaning, Spelling, and Decoding

To access words from our memory stores that have the same chunks as other words, we must not only be able to read the words, but we must also be able to spell them. Many students from the intermediate grades on can read more big words than they can spell. They may be able to read the word *confusion* but be unable to correctly spell it. Thus, when they see another word that begins with *con* or ends with *sion,* they cannot access *confusion* as the similar word. It would be helpful to older children who have difficulties decoding, spelling, or accessing meaning for big words to have a store of big words that they could read and spell and with which they associated meanings.

I created such a list by deciding which prefixes, suffixes, and spelling changes were most prevalent in the multisyllabic words students might encounter. I included all the prefixes and suffixes determined to be most common in White, Sowell, and Yanagihara's (1989) study. Because I wanted to create a list that would provide the maximum help with all three big-word tasks, I added prefixes and suffixes such as *con / com, per, ex, ture,* and *ian,* which were not included in White, Sowell, and Yanagihara's study because they were not considered helpful from a meaning standpoint. These prefixes are useful spelling–pronunciation chunks.

Having created the list of "transferable chunks," I then wanted to find the "most-apt-to-be-known" word containing each chunk. I consulted *The Living Word Vocabulary* (Dale & O'Rourke, 1981), which indicates for 44,000 words the grade level at which more than two thirds of the students tested knew the meaning of each. Because the test from which it was determined students knew the meanings also required them to read the word, one can also infer that at least two thirds of the students could decode/pronounce the word. My goal was to find words that two thirds of fourth graders could read and for which they would know at least one meaning. After much finagling, I created a list of 50 words that contain all the most useful prefixes, suffixes, and spelling changes. All but eight of these words were known by more than two thirds of fourth graders. Seven words—*antifreeze, classify, deodorize, impression, irresponsible, prehistoric,* and *semifinal*—were not known by two thirds of fourth graders but were known by two thirds of sixth graders. *International,* the most known word containing the prefix *inter,* was known by two thirds of eighth graders. Because this list of 50 words is apt to be known by so many intermediate-aged and older students, and because it so economically represents all the important big-word parts, I named it the *Nifty Thrifty Fifty;* it appears in Table 1.

There are endless possibilities for how the list might be used. First, however, students must learn to spell the words. Teachers might want to start a word wall (Cunningham, 1995) of big words and add five words each week to the wall. They might take a few minutes each day to "chant" the spelling of the words and talk about the parts of the word that could be applied to other words. This talking should be as "nonjargony" as possible. Rather than talking about the root word *freeze* and the prefix *anti,* the discussions should be about how antifreeze keeps your car's engine from freezing up and thus is protection against freezing. Students should be asked to think of other words that look and sound like *antifreeze* and then decide if the *anti* parts of those words could have anything to do with the notion of "against."

> What is an antibiotic against?
> What is an antiaircraft weapon?

For suffixes, the discussion should center around how the suffix changes how the word can be used in a sentence.

> A *musician* makes music. What do a *beautician, electrician, physician,* and *magician* do?
> When you need to *replace* something, you get a *replacement.* What do you get when someone *encourages* you?
> What do you call it when you *accomplish* something?

Spelling changes should be noticed and applied to similar words.

> *Communities* is the plural of *community.* How would you spell *parties? Candies? Personalities?*
> When we forget something, we say it was forgotten. How would you spell *bitten? Written?*

TABLE 1. THE NIFTY THRIFTY FIFTY

WORD	TRANSFERABLE CHUNKS		WORD	TRANSFERABLE CHUNKS	
Antifreeze[a]	Anti		International[b]	Inter	Al
Beautiful		Ful (y–i)	Invasion	In	Sion
Celebrate		Ate	Irresponsible[a]	Ir	Ible
Classify[a]		Ify	Midnight	Mid	
Communities	Com	Es (y–i)	Misunderstand	Mis	
Composer	Com	Er	Musician		Ian
Continuous	Con	Ous	Nonliving	Non	Ing (drop e)
Conversation	Con	Tion	Overpower	Over	
Deodorize[a]	De	Ize	Performance	Per	Ance
Different		Ent	Prehistoric[a]	Pre	Ic
Discovery	Dis	Y	Prettier		Er (y–i)
Dishonest	Dis		Rearrange	Re	
Electricity	E	Ity	Replacement	Re	Ment
Employee	Em	Ee	Richest		Est
Encouragement	En	Ment	Semifinal[a]	Semi	
Expensive	Ex	Ive	Signature		Ture
Forecast	Fore		Submarine	Sub	
Forgotten		En (double t)	Supermarkets	Super	S
Governor		Or	Swimming		Ing (double m)
Happiness		Ness (y–i)	Transportation	Trans	Tion
Hopeless		Less	Underweight	Under	
Illegal	Il		Unfinished	Un	Ed
Impossible	Im	Ible	Unfriendly	Un	Ly
Impression[a]	Im	Sion	Unpleasant	Un	Ant
Independence	In	Ence	Valuable		Able (drop e)

Note. All words are known by two thirds of fourth graders. [a] Known by more than two thirds of sixth graders. [b] Known by more than two thirds of eighth graders.

If this list is to become truly useful to students, they need to learn to spell the words gradually over time, and they need to be shown how the patterns found in these words can be useful in decoding, spelling, and spelled and pronounced by the students, there are hundreds of other words they can decode and spell and for which they can infer meanings. To prove this to myself, to you, and to your students, I used my computer to find all the words that contained certain parts. I then chose the words that could be gotten only from the prefixes, suffixes, and root words contained in the words on the Nifty Thrifty Fifty list. Next, I eliminated words of which very few students of any age would have heard. I was left with a list of more than 800 analyzable words—words whose meaning, spelling, and pronunciation could be determined by combining various parts of the Nifty Thrifty Fifty.

Facility with big words is essential for students as they read, write, and learn in all areas of school and life. Many big words occur infrequently, but when they do occur they carry a lot of the meaning and content of what is being read. English is a language in which many words are related through their morphology. This relationship is preserved through our spelling system. Students who learn to look for patterns in the big new words they meet will be better spellers and decoders. If they learn to look further and consider possible meaning relationships, they will increase the size of their meaning vocabulary stores. Patterns and morphological relationships are the keys to unlocking pronunciation, spelling, and meaning. All students should be issued these master keys.

References

Adams, M. J. (1990). *Beginning to read: Thinking and learning about print.* Cambridge, MA: MIT Press.

American heritage dictionary 1984. Boston: Houghton Mifflin.

Anderson, R. C., & Davison, A. (1988). Conceptual and empirical bases of readability formulas. In G. Green & A. Davison (Eds.), *Linguistic complexity and text comprehension* (pp. 23–54). Hillsdale, NJ: Erlbaum.

Anderson, R. C., Hiebert, E., Scott, J. A., & Wilkinson, I. A. G. (1985). *Becoming a nation of readers.* Washington, DC: National Institute of Education.

Bear, D., Invernizzi, M., Templeton, S., & Johnston, F. (1996). *Words their way: Word study for phonics, vocabulary, and spelling instruction.* Englewood Cliffs, NJ: Prentice-Hall.

Canney, G., & Schreiner, R. (1977). A study of the effectiveness of selected syllabication rules and phonogram patterns for word attack. *Reading Research Quarterly, 12,* 102–124.

Carroll, J. B., Davies, P., & Richman, B. (1971). *Word frequency book.* New York: American Heritage.

Cunningham, P. M. (1995). *Phonics they use: Words for reading and writing,* (2nd ed.). New York: HarperCollins.

Dale, E., & O'Rourke, J. (1981). *The living word vocabulary.* Chicago: World Book.

Ehrlich, M., Kurtz-Costes, B., & Loridant, C. (1993). Cognitive and motivational determinants of reading comprehension in good and poor readers. *Journal of Reading Behavior, 25,* 365–381.

Freyd, P., & Baron, J. (1982). Individual differences in acquisition of derivational morphology. *Journal of Verbal Learning and Verbal Behavior, 21,* 282–295.

Goswami, U., & Bryant, P. (1990). *Phonological skills and learning to read.* East Sussex, England: Erlbaum.

Henderson, E. H. (1985). *Teaching spelling.* Boston: Houghton Mifflin.

Just, M. A., & Carpenter, P. A. (1987). *The psychology of reading and language comprehension.* Boston: Allyn & Bacon.

Lenz, B. K., & Hughes, C. A. (1990). A word identification strategy for adolescents with learning disabilities. *Journal of Learning Disabilities, 23,* 149–163.

Mewhort, D. J. K., & Campbell, A. J. (1981). Toward a model of skilled reading: An analysis of performance in tachistoscoptic tasks. In G. E. MacKinnon & T. G. Walker (Eds.), *Reading research: Advances in theory and practice* (Vol. 3, pp. 39–118). New York: Academic Press.

Nagy, W., & Anderson, R. C. (1984). How many words are there in printed school English? *Reading Research Quarterly, 19,* 304–330.

Nagy, W., Osborn, J., Winsor, P., & O'Flahavan, J. (1992). *Guidelines for instruction in structural analysis* (Technical Report No. 554). Urbana–Champaign: University of Illinois, Center for the Study of Reading.

O'Grady, W., Dobrovolsky, M., & Aronoff, M. (1989). *Contemporary linguistics.* New York: St. Martin's Press.

Perfetti, C. A. (1986). Continuities in reading acquisition, reading skill and reading ability. *Remedial and Special Education, 7,* 11–21.

Rayner, K., & Pollatsek, A. (1989). *The psychology of reading.* Englewood Cliffs, NJ: Prentice-Hall.

Samuels, S. J, LaBerge, D., & Bremer, C. D. (1978). Units of word recognition: Evidence for developmental change. *Journal of Verbal Learning and Verbal Behavior, 17,* 715–720.

Shefelbine, J. (1990). A syllable-unit approach to teaching decoding of polysyllabic words to fourth- and sixth-grade disabled readers. In J. Zutell & S. McCormick (Eds.), *Literacy theory and research: Analysis from multiple paradigms* (pp. 223–230). Chicago: National Reading Conference.

Shefelbine, J., & Calhoun, J. (1991). Variability in approaches to identifying polysyllabic words: A descriptive study of sixth graders with highly, moderately, and poorly developed syllabication strategies. In J. Zutell & S. McCormick (Eds.), *Learner factor s/ teacher factors: Issues in literary research and instruction* (pp. 169–177). Chicago: National Reading Conference.

Shepard, J. F. (1974). Research on the relationship between meanings of morphemes and the meaning of derivatives. In P. L. Nacke (Ed.), *23rd National Reading Conference yearbook* (pp. 115–119). Clemson, SC: National Reading Conference.

Stanovich, K. E. (1991). Word recognition: Changing perspectives. In R. Barr, M. Kamil, P. Mosenthal, & P. D. Pearson (Eds.), *Handbook of reading research (Vol. 2,* pp. 418–452). New York: Longman.

Templeton, S. (1991). Teaching and learning the English spelling system: Reconceptualizing method and purpose. *Elementary School Journal, 92,* 185–201.

Templeton, S. (1992). Theory, nature and pedagogy of higher-order orthographic development in older children. In S. Templeton & D. Bear (Eds.), *Development of orthographic knowledge and the foundations of literacy: A memorial Festschrift for Edmund H. Henderson* (pp. 253–278). Hillsdale, NJ: Erlbaum.

White, T., Power, M., & White, S. (1989). Morphological analysis: Implications for teaching and understanding vocabulary growth. *Reading Research Quarterly, 24,* 283–304.

White, T., Sowell, J., & Yanagihara, A. (1989). Teaching elementary students to use word-part clues. *The Reading Teacher, 42,* 302–308.

Zutell, J. (1998). Word sorting: A developmental spelling approach to word study for delayed readers. *Reading & Writing Quarterly, 14,* 219–238.

Irene H. Blum
Patricia S. Koskinen

Repeated Reading: A Strategy for Enhancing Fluency and Fostering Expertise

Reflect on something you do well, something at which you are an expert. It may be cooking, playing tennis, teaching children to read, or a range of other activities. When asked to do this activity, you probably approach the task with confidence, knowing what you need to do and how you are going to do it. You can assess your own success and if you run into difficulty, you competently find a solution. In addition, you probably can tell others what they are doing right or wrong in relation to this task. It is likely you gained this expertise because, for some reason, you were motivated to practice repeatedly over a long period of time.

In our work with teachers and students, we have been focusing on developing an instructional setting that fosters expertise. In such an environment, students understand what they read, learn strategies to improve their reading, feel successful, and are motivated to practice. We have been especially interested in using repeated reading as an instructional strategy to develop fluency (i.e., smooth, accurate, natural, expressive reading) with beginning readers as well as with less proficient readers. This deceptively simple rehearsal strategy involves multiple readings and provides substantial practice in reading connected discourse. It enables novices to feel like experts as they acquire fluency.

From *Theory Into Practice,* Summer 1991, Vol. 30, No. 3

Fluency and Repeated Reading

While fluency has traditionally been a neglected goal in instruction, Allington (1983) stimulated an interest in examining the role of fluency in skilled reading. He reviewed a variety of sources that support the view that oral fluency should be regarded as a necessary feature of defining good reading, that readers can be helped to acquire fluency through training, and that fluency training improves overall reading ability.

In an effort to explore these ideas, researchers, using a variety of repeated reading strategies, have documented evidence of improved fluency as a result of training. Studies provide impressive evidence of improvement in both reading rate and accuracy (Chomsky, 1976; Dahl, 1974; Dowhower, 1987; Samuels, 1979). A growing body of work also adds support to the view that fluency training is linked to improving overall reading ability. There is considerable evidence that rereading improves reading comprehension (Dowhower, 1987; O'Shea, Sindelar, & O'Shea, 1985;), increases vocabulary (Elley, 1989; Koskinen & Blum, 1984), and helps students understand and remember more concepts (Bromage & Mayer, 1986; Taylor, Wade, & Yekovich, 1985). In addition, there are indications that repeated reading helps students feel more confident about their reading and is an activity in which they want to participate (Koskinen & Blum, 1984; Topping, 1987; Trachtenberg & Ferruggia, 1989).

Characteristics of Experts

While substantial support for the use of repeated reading can be found in the literature, a conceptual framework is needed in which to interpret some of its success and to support its wider use in instruction. The theory of automatic information processing as developed by LaBerge and Samuels (1974) emphasizes the importance of practice. According to this theory, practice enables beginning readers to achieve a level of automaticity in decoding so that they can focus attention on comprehension. Recent literature on expertise broadens our understanding of the nature of effective practice, noting the influence of task difficulty on comprehension monitoring behavior. In addition, this research clarifies the relationship between motivation and practice.

A review of the literature on expertise indicates common elements among experts: (a) They have extensive knowledge about their topic, (b) they have a variety of strategies for learning, and (c) they are highly motivated to practice (Meichenbaum & Biemiller, 1990). Not only is the knowledge of experts coherently organized and easily accessed (Bereiter & Scarmadalia, 1986), but these experts also employ a range of metacognitive skills. They efficiently select strategies to advance their learning and monitor their comprehension. When they encounter difficulties, they call upon fix-up strategies (Ericsson & Smith, 1989, cited in Meichenbaum & Biemiller, 1990). In addition, experts' high level of motivation leads to extensive practice over an extended period of time and in a range of settings (Ericsson, Tesch-Romer, & Krampe, 1989, cited in Meichenbaum & Biemiller, 1990). It appears that success begets success. Not only does practice enhance knowledge, but knowledge enhances interest, thereby stimulating continued motivation to practice.

Research by Meichenbaum and Biemiller (1990) with self-directed elementary students reveals that these child "experts" exhibit behavior that is similar to other experts in specific disciplines. Not only do these children have enhanced knowledge and motivation, they have a repertoire of effective learning strategies. These child "experts" engage in considerable metacognitive behavior, monitoring their own activities as well as those of others. In addition, they design new situations in which to develop their metacognitive abilities and extend their personal knowledge.

Of particular interest in this research with self-directed children is the relationship between task difficulty and behavior as an expert. The research results indicate that behavior as an expert is a function of setting. Children who were self-directed and "experts" in one setting did not necessarily behave in this self-directed "expert" way in another setting (e.g., going from the academic setting of the classroom to the creative setting of the art room). Meichenbaum and Biemiller (1990) suggest a need to view expertise "*not* as a characteristic of an individual . . . but rather as a reflection of the *fit* between the level of task demands (e.g. difficulty and interest levels) and the child's abilities (knowledge strategy and motivation)" (p. 33). They observed that self-directed children typically selected tasks at a moderate level of difficulty and were able to monitor their task behavior.

While some students develop expertise on their own, the research by Meichenbaum and Biemiller (1990) highlights the need to provide a classroom environment that allows less spontaneous learners to behave like experts. They propose that one way to create this environment is to provide activities that offer a wide range of difficulty levels so that each student can participate in activities where the cognitive demands of the task are not overwhelming, thus allowing the student to reflect on and monitor the task.

Repeated Reading and Expertise

In our efforts to design a learning environment that fosters literacy, helping students develop expertise has been an important component. We have been particularly interested in providing instructional opportunities where students are exposed to interesting and important content knowledge, where they acquire strategies for learning, and where they are motivated to extend and use their knowledge. Providing meaningful activities that students can complete successfully is a critical feature of this instruction.

Teachers have successfully used repeated reading in a variety of ways. Typically it has been used as an adjunct to regular instruction, providing repeated practice for fluency. More recently, however, teachers have begun to integrate it into the fabric of literacy instruction. Research on the use of successful methods includes repeated reading of passages (Dowhower, 1987; Herman, 1985; Samuels, 1979) and assisted repeated reading, where a live or audiotaped model of the passage is provided (Carbo, 1978; Chomsky, 1976). Another variation is paired repeated reading (Koskinen & Blum, 1984) where students work together reading short passages of text and evaluate both their own improvement and that of their partners.

Repeated reading appears to provide opportunities for learners to develop expertise by contributing to increases in knowledge of both content and strategy. In addition, increased knowledge and awareness of improvement provides considerable motivation for continued practice. Because it allows students at many different instructional levels to participate in the same activity and improve at their own pace, repeated reading responds to Meichenbaum and Biemiller's (1990) recommendation to provide activities at a wide range of difficulty levels.

The following is an example of one teacher's use of paired repeated reading as a fluency strategy that encourages the development of expertise (Blum & Koskinen, 1990):

> In a unit on monkeys, Mrs. B. read a group of second grade beginning readers the book *Curious George* (Rey, 1969) while the children read along with their own text. An audiotape of this story was then put in the listening center as part of the class audio library. During the students' independent practice time, students were asked to work in pairs, selecting a short 50 word or less segment from the book to read to a partner. This segment was to focus on something interesting they learned about George. Each student read the segment three times to their partner. After each reading, the reader rated his/her improvement on a five point Likert scale ranging from "fantastic" to "terrible," and then the listener commented on how their partner's reading improved.

This repeated reading activity fostered expertise in a variety of ways, described in the following sections.

Increasing Content Knowledge

Students reread specific story content at least four or five different times. They heard the whole text initially and interacted with it again when selecting the segment for repeated reading. This selection process often required students to reread larger portions of text to find an interesting segment upon which to focus.

Following the paired repeated reading activity, which involved reading and listening to a segment three times, the students became quite comfortable with this text. Not only were all students able to respond with at least one important idea they remembered about George, the repeated reading further expanded students' knowledge about George's actions and adventures. In addition, children demonstrated they had learned factual information about monkeys (e.g., that George came from Africa).

Increasing Strategy Knowledge

All the students were able to participate in the activity, both as readers and listeners. As readers, each was able to select a segment, reread the segment to a partner, and rate the reading. As partners, each was able to listen to the partner's reading and then identify a way the reading had improved. Through independent practice, students gained skill in rereading as a strategy for acquiring information.

In addition, the cooperative learning setting of repeated reading provided an opportunity for students to reflect on their reading improvement. By evaluating each of their successive readings, they practiced monitoring their success. The listener provided monitoring guidance by offering compliments on improvement (e.g., the reader knew more words, read more smoothly). This role of listener provided important support for the reader and developed the listener's metacognitive awareness of the critical features of fluent reading.

Increasing Motivation

By using literature as an introductory activity, Mrs. B. engaged students with inviting material. The expressive oral reading by the teacher not only stimulated interest, but also provided background knowledge and word identification support so students could confidently begin individual text reading. In Mrs. B.'s class, students' motivation to practice was provided initially by external teacher purposes and evaluation directions. However, internal motivation began to develop from students' observations of increased fluency, partners' compliments, and increased familiarity with content information.

Providing for Different Ability Levels

Although students in Mrs. B.'s group were functioning at very different levels (from pre-primer to first grade), her repeated reading activity was structured so that everyone was able to experience success. The initial reading of the text by the teacher provided a chance for students to hear smooth fluent reading. While most students could understand the story concepts, they could not decode many of the words. The teacher's oral reading greatly increased students' familiarity with the text, thereby decreasing the complexity of subsequent reading tasks.

Individual reading was conducted within a paired learning paradigm where students were encouraged to support each other. This meant students could ask their partners for information or help with difficult words. In other words, they were not facing this task alone.

By varying the length of the passage selected for rereading, students could also adjust the task's difficulty. Some readers selected 50-word passages while others were encouraged to select short passages. Some less proficient readers selected only one or two sentences for rereading after going to the listening center to get extra assistance in identifying an interesting part. Because of the inherent flexibility of repeated reading procedures, these students were able to work at a pace that was comfortable for their individual skill level.

Integrating Repeated Reading

As we found and as research shows, there are considerable benefits to using repeated reading as a strategy for fostering expertise while enhancing fluency and comprehension (Dowhower, 1987; Koskinen & Blum, 1984; Yaden, 1988). Repeated reading is a powerful strategy that is flexible and adaptable for classroom use. Thus, teachers and researchers have been exploring ways to integrate repeated reading practice more extensively into classroom instruction. Educators who have used shared book experiences and focused on whole language instruction have suggested procedures for using repeated reading as an integral part of instruction (Baskwill & Whitman, 1987; Butler, 1988; Butler & Turbill, 1985; Holdaway, 1979; Trachtenberg & Ferruggia, 1989).

An illustration of the integration of repeated reading into instruction is provided by the experience of a teacher working with second grade less proficient readers in a unit on monkeys (Blum & Koskinen, 1990). This teacher, Mrs. B., began by introducing literature selections to motivate interest in the theme. These included poems, such as "Five Little Monkeys" (Richards, 1972), and books, such as *The Monkey and the Crocodile* (Galdone, 1969).

These materials were repeatedly read as part of shared reading time, with an emphasis on appreciation of the various readings' language, content, and humor. Where applicable, character development was discussed. As the units proceeded, new materials were introduced and students participated in paired repeated readings, read-along activities, and research on related topics. In a writing component, the students worked individually and as a group to generate ideas and put together a child-authored text. The activities involved with creating this text—revising, editing, illustrating, etc.—created further opportunities for meaningful repeated reading.

This sequence of repeated reading activities within a theme based unit helped students feel like experts as they became fluent, comprehending readers. It provided a new depth of understanding that enhanced content and strategy knowledge as well as motivation. Concepts were expanded and reviewed in informational texts and child-authored materials. Children read and then restructured information both orally and in writing.

Presenting the same information in a variety of ways provides such a range of levels that all students can be assured some degree of success. The following section elaborates further on ways to vary the use of repeated reading so that it can be integrated more extensively into classroom instruction.

Variations

From our work with teachers over a period of years, we have found that they use repeated readings in a variety of creative ways. The example of theme based instruction in Mrs. B.'s classroom presents a number of these successful variations in both direct instruction and independent practice settings. Within each of these settings, motivation to practice was provided by adjusting the purposes for repeated reading and by using different types of materials and modalities.

Vary the Instructional Setting

Mrs. B. used repeated reading in both teacher-directed and independent-practice settings. During teacher-directed instruction, Mrs. B. guided students through repeated reading, modeling important features (e.g., fluent reading and active listening) during an activity where the group listened to an audiotape. She then helped students monitor their use of the strategy.

During independent practice, students had opportunities to use the information they gained about content (monkeys) and strategy (repeated reading and related monitoring behavior). By practicing repeatedly, students developed facility both in learning new information and refining the information they already possessed.

Vary Purposes for Rereading

During teacher-directed instruction, Mrs. B. used a variety of purposes to reinforce content knowledge and monitor comprehension. With narrative text, the purpose of the initial reading was enjoyment. Subsequent readings focused on such purposes as identifying motivations of characters and learning characteristics of monkeys. With informational text, the initial reading focused on finding out about monkeys. A second reading was done to identify one important idea. Purposes for reading child-authored text varied from checking to see if all important ideas were included to performing editing functions.

In addition, students practiced repeated reading as performance opportunities to share knowledge with others (e.g., a parent, visitors to the classroom, another group). By using different purposes, Mrs. B. was reinforcing and providing motivation to obtain both content and strategy knowledge. During independent practice time, she included rereading activities with a variety of purposes, such as planning an illustration or preparing to read to others.

Vary Materials

Mrs. B. provided many different materials for repeated reading. During directed instruction, she began with examples of narrative texts and then introduced a variety of expository materials. In addition, students used both group and individual child-authored materials. Independent practice included the use of all the variety of materials used in teacher directed instruction, including narrative and expository material on monkeys as well as group and individual writing that related to ideas about monkeys.

By using this variety of material, children had many opportunities to practice vocabulary and concepts, thereby increasing their knowledge base and decreasing the concept demands of the task. Interaction with each successive text enabled students to work with an expanded base of prior knowledge and to increase their familiarity with new words.

Vary Modalities

By varying modalities, Mrs. B. was able to add another dimension of richness to the repeated reading process. Children had the opportunity to read silently with a fluent model or a tape. In other activities, they read aloud with the model. Sometimes children reread a piece of text, either narrative or expository, that had been introduced earlier. Children participated in restructuring information both orally and in their writing. During independent practice, students reread orally and listened to others read aloud. Varying modalities not only enhances interest and motivation, but it also helps to moderate levels of difficulty by adjusting the cognitive demands of the task.

Conclusion

Repeated reading offers considerable benefits as a strategy for enhancing fluency and comprehension while fostering expertise. This approach seems to contribute to an increase in content and strategy knowledge as well as motivation. In addition, repeated reading procedures allow students to work at a level of difficulty where they can be successful. The unique features of this fluency strategy suggest a need for continued exploration of its use, particularly when it is integrated into instruction. Although considerable research supports repeated reading as an adjunct to instruction, there is limited controlled research on integrating repeated reading into literacy instruction. However, repeated reading is currently being used as an important part of whole language classrooms.

Certainly the conceptual base for integrating repeated reading into literacy instruction is sound. The need now is to look at it systematically. Research should investigate its effectiveness by varying purposes, materials, and modalities in both direct instruction and independent practice settings.

References

Allington, R. (1983). Fluency: The neglected goal. *The Reading Teacher, 36,* 556-561.

Baskwill, J., & Whitman, P. (1987). *Whole language sourcebook.* Richmond Hill, Canada: Scholastic-TAB Publications.

Bereiter, C., & Scarmadalia, C. (1986). Educational relevance of the study of expertise. *Interchange, 17,* 10-19.

Blum, I.H., & Koskinen, P.S. (1990). [Integrating writing and repeated reading.] Unpublished raw data.

Bromage, B.K., & Mayer, R.E. (1986). Quantitative and qualitative effects of repetition on learning from technical text. *Journal of Educational Psychology, 78,* 271-278.

Butler, A. (1988). Shared book experience. Crystal Lake, IL: Rigby.

Butler, A., & Turbill, J. (1985). *Towards a reading-writing classroom.* Portsmouth, NH: Heinemann.

Carbo, M. (1978). Teaching reading with talking books. *The Reading Teacher, 32,* 267-273.

Chomsky, C. (1976). After decoding: What? *Language Arts, 53,* 288-296.

Dahl, P.J. (1974). *An experimental program for teaching high speed word recognition and comprehension skills.* (Final Report of Project No. 3-1154). Washington, DC: National Institute of Education, Office of Research. (ERIC Document Reproduction Service No. ED 099 812).

Dowhower, S.L. (1987). Effects of repeated reading on second-grade transitional readers' fluency and comprehension. *Reading Research Quarterly, 22,* 389-406.

Elley, W.B. (1989). Vocabulary acquisition from listening to stories. *Reading Research Quarterly, 24,* 174-187.

Galdone, P. (1969). *The monkey and the crocodile.* New York: Houghton Mifflin/Clarion Books.

Herman, P.A. (1985). The effect of repeated readings on reading rate, speech pauses, and word recognition accuracy. *Reading Research Quarterly, 20,* 553-564.

Holdaway, R. (1979). Foundations of literacy. Portsmouth, NH: Heinemann.

Koskinen, P.S., & Blum, I.H. (1984). Repeated oral reading and the acquisition of fluency. In J. Niles & L. Harris (Eds.), *Changing perspectives on research in reading/language processing and instruction.* Thirty-third yearbook of the National Reading Conference (pp. 183-187). Rochester, NY: National Reading Conference.

LaBerge, D., & Samuels, S.J. (1974). Toward a theory of automatic information processing in reading. *Cognitive Psychology, 6,* 293-323.

Meichenbaum, D., & Biemiller, A. (1990, May). *In search of student expertise in the classroom: A metacognitive analysis.* Paper presented at the Conference on Cognitive Research for Instructional Innovation, University of Maryland, College Park, MD.

O'Shea, L.J., Sindelar, P.T., & O'Shea, D.J. (1985). The effects of repeated readings and attentional cues on reading fluency and comprehension. *Journal of Reading Behavior, 17,* 129-142.

Rey, H.A. (1969). *Curious George.* Boston: Houghton Mifflin.

Richards, L.E. (1972). Five little monkeys. In B. Martin & P. Brogan (Eds.), *Sounds around the clock* (pp. 108-109). New York: Holt, Rinehart & Winston.

Samuels, S.J. (1979). The method of repeated reading. *The Reading Teacher, 32,* 403-408.

Taylor, N.E., Wade, M.R., & Yekovich, F.R. (1985). The effects of text manipulation and multiple reading strategies on the reading performance of good and poor readers. *Reading Research Quarterly, 20,* 566-574.

Topping, K. (1987). Paired reading: A powerful technique for parent use. *The Reading Teacher, 40,* 608-614.

Trachtenberg, P., & Ferruggia, A. (1989). Big books from little voices: Reaching high risk beginning readers. *The Reading Teacher, 42,* 284-289.

Yaden, D. (1988). Understanding stories through repeated read-alouds: How many does it take? *The Reading Teacher, 41,* 556-560.

tip

From *The Reading Teacher*, 1989, Vol. 42, pp. 690–693

Fluency for Everyone: Incorporating Fluency Instruction in the Classroom

Timothy V. Rasinski

Although there is no universal agreement about what constitutes reading fluency, most authorities would agree that it refers to the smooth and natural oral production of written text.

Harris and Hodges (1981), for example, define fluency as expressing oneself "smoothly, easily, and readily," having "freedom from word identification problems," and dealing with "words, and larger language units" with quickness (p. 120). Thus, at a minimum one might expect the fluent reader to read orally with accuracy, quickness, and expression.

Achieving fluency is recognized as an important aspect of proficient reading, but it remains a neglected goal of reading instruction (Allington, 1983). Most basal reading programs give little recognition to fluency as an important goal, and few reading textbooks for prospective teachers provide an in-depth treatment of the topic.

Reading fluency often becomes a salient issue only when students demonstrate significant deficiencies. These students often are referred to corrective or remedial classes where they finally receive special instruction in the development of fluent reading.

How can classroom teachers teach fluency to their students? Several methods have been proven successful. These include repeated readings (Dowhower, 1987; Herman, 1985; Samuels, 1979), reading while listening or echo reading (Carbo, 1978; Chomsky, 1976; Gamby, 1983; Laffey & Kelly, 1981; Schneeberg, 1977; Van Der Leij, 1981), the neurological impress method (Heckelman, 1969), and reading in phrases (Allington, 1983; Amble & Kelly, 1970; Gregory, 1986).

One potential problem with these fluency training methods is that they were, in general, originally intended for use in corrective reading situations involving an instructor working with one, two, or a very small group of students. Despite many positive aspects of these methods, the focus of their application is overly narrow.

Teachers who wish to make fluency instruction an integral part of the regular reading curriculum may be at a loss in attempting to use corrective fluency methods in a way that is appropriate for the more normal reader.

Fortunately, the methods shown to be effective in helping less fluent readers suggest a set of principles that teachers may find helpful. In the remainder of this article those principles will be identified and discussed.

Proven Methods

Repetition

Achieving fluency requires practice with one text until a criterion level is achieved. Although the principle of repetition is often translated into repeated exposures to target words in isolation, research has shown that repetition is most effective when students meet the target words in a variety of texts or through repeated exposures to one text.

Although repetitions of texts may seem to be a dull activity, there are several ways to make it interesting and appealing. For example, young children love to hear their favorite stories read to them repeatedly (Beaver, 1982) and students enjoy working in pairs on repeated reading tasks (Koskinen & Blum, 1986).

Rasinski (1988) suggests several ways to use natural classroom events to encourage repeated readings. Activities such as putting on plays and having older students read short books to primary students require that students practice the text they will have to perform later on.

Modeling

Young students and other less fluent readers may not always know what fluent reading should be like. Poor readers, for example, usually are assigned to reading groups in which the predominant model of reading is other disfluent readers. It seems clear that students need frequent opportunities to see and hear fluent reading.

Because the most fluent reader in the classroom is the teacher, the teacher should be the primary model. The easiest and most stimulating way to do this is to read good children's literature to the class. Daily periods should be set aside for teachers (and other fluent readers) to read aloud.

Direct Instruction and Feedback

Research into metacognition in reading is demonstrating that it may be important for readers to be aware of what happens when they read and why they have reading problems. This awareness may be particularly helpful in the development of fluency.

Prior to reading aloud, the teacher could remind the class to listen to the expression in his or her voice during the reading, the speed at which the text is read, or when stops or pauses occur. A short discussion of these factors after the reading or before students' own oral reading could heighten students' sensitivity to their own reading.

Similarly, providing feedback to students after they read orally can facilitate growth in fluent reading. Koskinen and Blum (1986), for example, propose a model of instruction in which students are trained to provide feedback to each other. The reader benefits from a formative critique of his or her reading and the student critic benefits from a heightened metacognitive sense of what it means to be a fluent reader.

Support During Reading

The notion of scaffolding or support while performing is critical to the development of fluency, especially in the beginning stages or with students having difficulty. Support is achieved through the student hearing a fluent rendition of a passage while simultaneously reading the same text. Several types of support are available.

Choral reading is perhaps the most common form of support reading and is highly appropriate for the regular classroom. Here students read a selected passage in unison. The teacher needs to ensure that several fluent readers are part of the group or that his or her own voice leads the way in choral reading.

The neurological impress method (Heckelman, 1969) was designed as a remedial technique for use one on one. The teacher begins by reading slightly ahead of and louder than the student, and later, as the students gains in fluency, softly shadows the student's reading of the passage. Although labor intensive, the technique can be adapted for regular classroom use with aides, volunteers, or fluent classmates.

The use of tape-recorded passages is another way to provide support during reading. Carbo (1978) reported students making good progress in reading while simultaneously listening to passages on tape. This format is especially appealing as it allows students to work on their fluency independently. They may need to be reminded to concentrate on reading the passage, not simply listen passively to it.

Text Unit

Fluency involves reading texts in multi-word chunks or phrases. Word by word reading, even if it is accurate and fast, is not fluent reading. Timely reminders should drive the point home.

Research has shown (for example, Weiss, 1983) that marking phrase boundaries in student texts with a penciled slash or vertical line may aid fluency. Occasionally reading short texts such as poems, famous speeches, or popular songs marked in this way may help students develop and maintain a mature sense of phrasing.

Easy Materials

Fluency is best promoted when students are provided with materials that they find relatively easy in terms of word recognition, so that

they can move beyond decoding to issues of phrasing, expression, and comprehensibility of production. These materials help students develop a sense of power and confidence.

Teachers, then, need to stock their classroom libraries with books that represent a variety of difficulty levels and interests. For their independent reading, students can be directed to those materials that they will not find frustrating.

Combining Principles

These principles offer some building blocks and guidelines for developing reading instruction and activities that promote the development of fluency. Rather than think of them in isolation, teachers can design lessons and activities that combine two or more of these principles.

In her study of disfluent third graders, Carol Chomsky (1976) combined the principles of repetition and support. She had students listen to and read a tape-recorded text until they could read it with fluency. Then they received instruction in various components of the text.

In a similar vein Koskinen and Blum's (1986) instructional model for fluency combines repetition and direct instruction. Students read a text three times and receive formative feedback (direct instruction in fluency) from their peers. In both the Chomsky and Koskinen and Blum models, students made substantial improvements in fluency.

Hoffman (1987) and Aulls (1982) offer even more complex models of fluency instruction that combine elements of modeling, repetition, support, and direct instruction.

Teachers Empowered

The point is not that teachers should blindly endorse any of the models identified and described here. Rather, relying on the principles of fluency instruction, informed and creative teachers can design instructional activities that meet the unique needs of their classrooms. They can incorporate one or more principles into the stories that students encounter in their daily lessons or pleasure reading, and depending on students' progress can employ principles more or less strenuously.

Fluency is an issue that needs to be taken seriously in the reading classroom. The principles outlined here, while neither prescription nor panacea, offer teachers several tools for making their reading instruction reflect their own professional judgment.

Through the use of principles such as these, prepackaged and "teacher proof" reading programs that foster deskilling and promote a perception of teachers as incompetent can be turned back in favor of alternative and effective teacher-designed instruction.

REFERENCES

Allington, R.L. (1983). Fluency: The neglected reading goal. *The Reading Teacher, 36*, 556–561.

Amble, B.R., & Kelly, F.J. (1970). Phrase reading development training with fourth grade students: An experimental and comparative study. *Journal of Reading Behavior, 2*(1), 85–96.

Aulls, M.W. (1982). *Developing readers in today's elementary school*. Boston, MA: Allyn & Bacon.

Beaver, J.M. (1982). Say it! Over and over. *Language Arts, 59*, 143–148.

Carbo, M. (1978). Teaching reading with talking books. *The Reading Teacher, 32*, 267–273.

Chomsky, C. (1976). After decoding: What? *Language Arts, 53*, 288–296.

Dowhower, S.L. (1987). Effects of repeated reading on second-grade transitional readers' fluency and comprehension. *Reading Research Quarterly, 22*(4), 389–406,

Gamby, G. (1983). Talking books and taped books. *The Reading Teacher, 36*, 366–369.

Gregory, J.F. (1986). Phrasing in the speech and reading of the hearing impaired. *Journal of Communication Disorders, 19*(4), 289–297.

Harris, T.L., & Hodges, R.E. (Eds.). (1981). *A dictionary of reading*. Newark, DE: International Reading Association.

Heckelman, R.G. (1969). A neurological impress method of reading instruction. *Academic Therapy, 4*, 277–282.

Herman, P.A. (1985). The effect of repeated readings on reading rate, speech pauses, and word recognition accuracy. *Reading Research Quarterly, 20*, 553–564.

Hoffman, J.V. (1987). Rethinking the role of oral reading in basal instruction. *The Elementary School Journal, 87*(3), 367–373.

Koskinen, P., & Blum, I. (1986). Paired repeated reading: A classroom strategy for developing fluent reading. *The Reading Teacher, 40*, 70–75.

Laffey, J.L., & Kelly, D. (1981). Repeated reading of taped literature: Does it make a difference? In G. McNinch (Ed.), *Comprehension: Process and change*. (First Yearbook of the American Reading Forum). Hattiesburg, MS: University of Southern Mississippi Press.

Rasinski, T.V. (1988). Making repeated readings a functional part of classroom reading instruction. *Reading Horizons, 28*, 250–254.

Samuels, S.J. (1979). The method of repeated readings. *The Reading Teacher, 32*, 403–408.

Schneeberg, H. (1977). Listening while reading: A four year study. *The Reading Teacher, 30*, 629–635.

Van Der Leij, A. (1981). Remediation of reading-disabled children by presenting text simultaneously to eye and ear. *Bulletin of the Orton Society, 31*, 229–243.

Weiss, D.S. (1983). The effects of text segmentation on children's reading comprehension. *Discourse Processes, 6*(1), 77–89.

SECTION V

Spelling

Reading Research Quarterly
Vol. 34, No. 1
January/February/March 1999
©1999 International Reading Association
(pp. 102–112)

Shane Templeton

University of Nevada, Reno, USA

Darrell Morris

Appalachian State University, Boone, North Carolina, USA

Questions teachers ask about spelling

For a number of reasons, spelling is once again a significant concern among both the language arts community and the lay public. Much of the concern has to do with the perception that students are misspelling many more words in their writing than they used to—an observation that, apart from anecdotal reports, is difficult to document at a national level in the United States (Sabey, 1997). On the other hand, many school systems report that students' performance on standardized tests of spelling is poorer than in previous years. Parents are concerned about the misspellings they see coming home in their children's writing—a concern that exists in spite of "First Draft" being stamped at the top of the page.

Parents and many educators are concerned about invented or temporary spelling, fearful this will lead to a lifetime of poor spelling. They wish to see spelling books tucked under children's arms and brought home, a reflection of what they perceive to be the foundation of tried and true traditional educational values. Many teachers, however, share similar concerns. While they believe that some type of systematic spelling instruction is necessary, they are uncertain about the nature and degree of such explicit attention to spelling.

Of course, one might also observe that it has always been thus (Templeton, 1992). Spelling is so visible, so obvious, that it often assumes the role of a proxy for literacy and in that role is bound to generate controversy. Spelling has also been a flashpoint in the debate between more integrated, whole-language–oriented instruction and more structured, part-to-whole instruction. And inevitably, these concerns are often tied to political agendas.

Can research provide a reasoned if not confident response to these concerns? In both the laboratory and the classroom, researchers and teacher/researchers are suggesting that it can. Research in the following areas has yielded important implications for the learning and teaching of spelling: (a) investigations of the nature and development of word perception, (b) investigations of the development of spelling or orthographic knowledge, and (c) methodological investigations.

In spite of all the caveats one must offer when turning to methodological issues, it is nonetheless possible to derive some solid and perhaps reassuring implications for what we can do in the classroom. While we will not in this article explore the research into the nature and development of word perception, we do wish to note that this research complements in many ways the findings from research in the other areas.

Traditional and contemporary perspectives on spelling

In the past, because most people inside education and out believed that English spelling does not do a good job of representing the pronunciation of words, primary instructional emphasis was usually placed upon rote memory (Horn, 1969). Where rules seemed to work they were emphasized, but the rules were themselves many in number and often seemed to be honored in the breach as often as much as in the main. In recent years a more comprehensive understanding of the nature of English spelling has led to more promising instructional thrusts. More educators now understand that, while memory does play an important role in learning to spell, it does not play the *only* role (Henderson, 1990). Learning to spell should *also* be a process of coming to understand how words work—the conventions that govern their structure and how their structure signals sound *and* meaning (Berninger, 1994, 1995; Brown & Ellis, 1994; Read & Hodges, 1982; Templeton & Bear, 1992; Templeton & Morris, in press).

This reconceptualization of the role that spelling or orthographic knowledge can play in both writing and reading means that the learning and teaching of spelling cover a broader theoretical and practical terrain than in years past (Templeton, 1991). Instructional emphasis is placed on the exploration of *patterns* that can be detected in the sound, structure, and meaning features of words—as opposed to the single-minded focus on learning how to spell the 5,000-plus most frequently occurring words in writing or particular words that may be problematic for individual students.

In part, this understanding arises from a general consensus in the research community that the process of *writing* words and the process of *reading* words draw upon the same underlying base of word knowledge (Ehri, 1993; Gill, 1992; Perfetti, 1992; Templeton & Bear, 1992). The more students understand about the structure of words—their spelling or orthography—the more efficient and fluent their reading will be (Perfetti, 1992). Thus, orthographic or spelling knowledge is the engine that drives efficient reading as well as efficient writing.

Though gaining a foothold, this reconceptualization of spelling is still not widespread among educators. In fact, many teachers express concern that they do not have a strong foundation either in how to teach spelling or in the nature of the spelling system (Gill & Scharer, 1996; Henry, 1988; Moats, 1995; Morris, Blanton, Blanton, Nowacek, & Perney, 1995). This knowledge base may be as tenuous for the experienced teacher as it is for the novice. While many teachers may agree that spelling *patterns* should be the focus of instruction, teachers' knowledge of the nature and extent of these patterns often is limited, particularly as these patterns apply to *morphemic* or meaning-bearing elements in words (Moats & Smith, 1992).

There have been some efforts in recent years to address the need for a broader knowledge base with respect to spelling instruction; for example, in October 1992 *Language Arts* published a themed issue on spelling; *Primary Voices*, a publication of the National Council of Teachers of English (NCTE), had an issue dedicated to the teaching of spelling in November, 1996; and NCTE also sponsored a teleconference on the topic. But such efforts still do not reach most elementary and middle school teachers, and they often do not reflect the importance of the role that a more informed knowledge of the spelling system can play for teachers. Significantly,

these efforts often do not reflect the importance of pulling words out of the immediate contexts of reading and writing in order to examine and explore them for common patterns. This latter issue reflects the classic controversy in the field of literacy and language arts concerning the role of context in word learning—when does the context for word study cease to become meaningful and authentic? Is it when words are taken out of written context? Or is it when the examination of words outside of running text becomes dull, routinized, and lacking in active inquiry and exploration?

In an effort to broaden the current professional dialogue regarding spelling instruction, in the remainder of this article we will address teachers' most frequently asked questions about spelling. These questions have come from teachers in all contexts, preschool through university. We address them in a sequence that we hope provides a logical introduction to this important topic:

1. Why don't we just spell words the way they sound?
2. How *do* students learn to spell?
3. How should spelling words be selected and organized?
4. How do I determine my students' spelling levels?
5. Should I allow invented spelling? If so, for how long?
6. What types of instructional *activities* work best?
7. What type of spelling *strategies* should be taught?
8. How can I assess how my students are progressing?
9. How should instruction be adjusted for students with a learning problem in the area of spelling?

Teachers' most frequently asked questions about spelling

1. Why don't we just spell words the way they sound?

Because so many questions that teachers raise can be addressed by looking at the nature of the spelling system, we begin with a brief description of how the system represents sound and meaning. A timeless lament, the question "Why don't we just spell words the way they sound?" has arisen from generations of students and their teachers. T.S. Watt's poem "Brush Up Your English" (as cited in Taylor & Taylor, 1983) has become a classic of sorts, playing off of the different ways in which sounds can be spelled in English. It begins:

> I take it you already know
> Of tough and bough and cough and dough.
> Others may stumble but not you,
> On hiccough, thorough, tough and through... (p. 99)

As we'll see, however, what has been lost in a consistent letter-sound correspondence has been gained in the increasing tendency to spell meaningful word parts consistently. Cummings (1988) expressed it simply: In English, spelling must balance a *phonetic demand* that "sounds be spelled consistently from word to word" with a *semantic demand* that "units of semantic content be spelled consistently from word to word" (p. 461).

English spelling did start out as primarily an alphabetic or phonemic writing system, representing sounds in a fairly straightforward left-to-right matchup. It still has a strong alphabetic foundation, as illustrated by words such as *mat* and *stop*. However, as a succession of languages brought an influx of new vocabulary into English over the centuries—Germanic, Scandinavian, French, Latin, Greek, and Spanish—the way these words were spelled in the original language was usually brought in as well. This had the inevitable effect of moving spelling away from its straightforwardly alphabetic, letter-sound foundation.

There are *patterns*, however, in English spelling. These patterns provide a level of consistency that operates within and between syllables, and they complement the alphabetic level in providing consistent information about how sounds are spelled. These patterns explain, by the way, the occurrence of letters that do not themselves stand for a sound in a particular word: Such letters usually signal the pronunciation of *other* sounds within the word.

To illustrate how these patterns operate, let's begin with the alphabetically spelled word *scrap*. Each letter corresponds to a sound or phoneme in English. But consider the word *scrape*. Unless we use a different letter to represent the *long a* sound in the middle of the word, we need to signal how this pronunciation differs from *scrap*. The *e* in *scrape* does this for us: The common VC*e* spelling pattern allows us to distinguish what would otherwise be ambiguous spellings—such as using *scrap* to spell both *scrap* and *scrape*.

Patterns that signal pronunciation—or pronunciations that signal spelling patterns—occur in more structurally complex words as well. For example, we distinguish the word *scrapped* from the word *scraped* by doubling the final consonant before adding the inflectional ending -*ed*. This consonant doubling feature of English spelling is widespread: It most often indicates that the preceding vowel is *not* a long vowel. When a long vowel *is* present, it is usually followed by a single consonant, as in *scraped*.

It is important to note that the phenomenon of doubling consonants or dropping *e*'s goes well beyond the case of adding suffixes to base words, as in *scrapped/scraped*. It also applies within polysyllabic words to which no suffixes have been added. Consider the words *snazzy* and *lazy*. The short vowel in the first syllable of *snazzy* is kept short because it is followed by the double consonant that closes the syllable, while the long vowel in the first syllable of *lazy* is kept long because it is followed by a single consonant—the first syllable is left open, signaling a long vowel.

An awareness of these patterns helps students in both reading and spelling: When students encounter an unknown word in reading they can apply their knowledge of patterns to access the sound of the word. When students are writing and are unsure of a spelling, they can attend to the sounds they hear to generate the spelling. The traditional belief that there are so many ways to spell sounds that it is difficult to go from sound to spelling reveals a strictly alphabetic bias: As the groundbreaking research by Hanna, Hanna, Hodges, and Rudorf (1966) revealed many years ago, when the speller learns how patterns work the possibilities for correct spelling increase significantly because the speller has more information that can be brought to bear in order to generate the conventional spelling.

As have such luminaries as George Bernard Shaw and Theodore Roosevelt, one might argue that we should adopt a different spelling system altogether, one in which every sound has its own corresponding letter. Assume for a moment that we decided to do this: Whose pronunciation would we choose? For example, if we choose the standard British pronunciation the word that is presently spelled *park* might be spelled *pok* (/pahk/), or *pak* if we chose a variety of New England pronunciation. If we choose the midwestern pronunciation of *girl* we would spell it *girl* but perhaps *gull* if we chose a standard British pronunciation. Clearly, we can avoid some rather thorny territorial and linguistic battles by not trying *literally* to spell words the way they sound.

Perhaps the most important benefit from not literally spelling words the way they sound, however, is that we would lose the visual representation of meaning that is preserved among words that are members of a spelling-meaning family. The importance of meaning or morphological characteristics of English spelling was convincingly argued almost a century ago by a noted editor of the *Oxford English Dictionary* (Bradley, 1919) and re-emerged during the heyday of linguistic theory in the 1960s (C. Chomsky, 1970; N. Chomsky & Halle, 1968; Venezky, 1970). The morphological characteristics that are visually preserved in spelling reflect what Cummings (1988) has referred to as the *semantic demand* upon the spelling system: Units within words that represent meaning should be spelled consistently from one word to the next. Over the last two decades students' acquisition and understanding of this *spelling-meaning connection* (Templeton, 1979) have been investigated (e.g., Derwing, Smith, & Wiebe, 1995; Fowler & Liberman,

1995; Templeton & Scarborough-Franks, 1985). Note how the italicized spelling units in each of the word groups below remain the same across words, despite accompanying changes in sound:

con*demn*	*critic*	*please*	*similar*
con*demn*ing	*critic*ism	*pleas*ant	*similar*ity
con*demn*ation	*critic*ize	*pleas*ure	

These groupings illustrate the consistent spelling of meaning across base words and their derivatives. This consistency also occurs among Greek and Latin word elements, as in *judge/judi*cial/ad*judi*cate and *eco*nomics/*eco*logy. The consistent spelling of morphemic elements in English provides more than simply a helpful strategy for the writer; this consistency underlies the structural analysis skills that are applied when students encounter unfamiliar words during their reading as well (Aronoff, 1994; Derwing & Baker, 1986). This consistency, by the way, is an important reason why so many words are not spelled the way they sound.

Linguists describe these various characteristics of English spelling in different ways: alphabetic, orthographic, syllabic, morphemic. To capture these characteristics from an educational perspective, Henderson and Templeton (1986) referred to the different layers of information as *alphabetic*, *pattern*, and *meaning*:

- *Alphabetic* refers to the fact that there *are* a good number of words in English the spelling of which is primarily left to right, a fairly straightforward linear matching of letters and sounds.
- The *pattern* layer provides information about (a) sounds that a group or pattern of letters represents *within* a syllable—for example, the signaling of long vowels by silent letters; and (b) patterns *across* syllables, as in the closed VCCV pattern of *kitten* and *helmet* and the open VCV pattern of *pilot* and *hotel*.
- The *meaning* layer provides information through the consistent spelling of *meaning elements* within words, despite sound change, as in *solemn/solemn*ity and *critic/critic*ize.

2. How do students learn to spell?

The understanding of the alphabetic, pattern, and meaning layers in the spelling system develops over time and depends upon considerable experience with meaningful reading and writing. As with any other type of learning, learning about the spelling of words is *conceptual* learning and proceeds from a more concrete to a more abstract level of understanding and analysis. Online reading and writing are the conditions in which spelling knowledge is developed and exercised most fully. For most students, however, the explicit examination and exploration of words outside of actual reading and writing are necessary.

Several researchers have described this process in *developmental* terms in which learning to spell entails understanding increasingly abstract relationships that begin at the level of individual letters and sounds, and progressively advance through pattern and meaning (e.g., Ehri, 1993; Frith, 1985; Henderson, 1990; Templeton & Bear, 1992). Other researchers have emphasized that this progression is not simply the application of qualitatively different levels of analysis at each stage, but also involves complex processes in which a number of different strategies are called upon throughout the learning process (e.g., Read, 1994; Snowling, 1994; Treiman, 1993).

Spelling begins in the extended period of emergent literacy during which children learn much about the forms and functions of print. This understanding lays the groundwork for moving into the exploration of the *alphabetic* layer of spelling. With their knowledge of the names of the alphabet letters and an emerging awareness of sounds within spoken words, children create or invent their spelling as they write. In English, consonants emerge first in children's invented spellings, because they are more salient acoustically and in terms of articulation: for example, I LK TO P KBL (*I like to play kickball*). Vowels emerge somewhat later: I LIK TO PLA KEKBOL. This sequence reflects English-speaking children's analysis of the way words are represented in print. That is, once children know what a printed word unit is and how it corresponds to speech (Morris, 1993), their theory of how spelling works is driven by an *alphabetic* expectation: Sounds within words are matched up with letters in a linear left-to-right fashion.

In contrast to the alphabetic layer, the *pattern* layer is more conceptually advanced because learners come to understand that spelling does not always work in a strictly left-to-right fashion; groups or *patterns* of letters work together to represent sound. For example, in order to understand how the "silent e" works in words such as *make*, learners must be able to do the following: skip to the end of the word and think in a right-to-left fashion, grasping the notion that a letter can in fact not stand for a sound itself but provide information about the sound of another letter in the word. This understanding means that children grasp that the vowel/consonant/silent *e* functions as a single pattern or unit. The most salient indicator that students have begun to make this conceptual advance from a linear alphabetic conception of spelling is the appearance of silent letters in their invented spellings to represent long-vowel sounds: WE TIDE THE GAEM (*We tied the game*). These spellings reveal that students conceptually grasp the pattern principle.

When letter patterns within single syllables are understood, learners come to understand *syllable* patterns. The foundation for this understanding is laid when students grasp the consonant-doubling/e-drop principle as it applies to simple base words and suffixes: *bat + ing = batting*, but *rake + ing = raking*. Somewhat later developmentally, this principle comes around again when students learn that it also applies *within* polysyllabic words, in the case of closed and open syllables: CATLE (*cattle*; the first syllable contains a short vowel and is closed by the double consonant, just as in *batting*) and STOLLEN (*stolen*; the first syllable contains a long vowel and remains open, just as in *raking*). Notably, as students learn those conventions that govern the base word plus suffix spellings, they are underway in their developing understanding of simple principles of word combination: how compound words are created and come to mean what they do, and how base words and affixes combine. This understanding in turn provides the foundation for grasping the role of *meaning* in spelling: OPPISITION and COMPISITION are corrected by relating each word to its base, *oppose* and *compose*, in which the pronunciation and spelling of the vowel in the second syllable become clear.

To an engaging degree, learners recapitulate the historical development of English spelling (Cummings, 1988; Invernizzi, Abouzeid, & Gill, 1994; Templeton, 1976). Over the course of several years they move from learning how spelling represents *sound* to learning how spelling represents *meaning*, and this was the course English spelling followed as well. The majority of spellings in Old English (approximately A.D. 450–1066) were straightforwardly alphabetic—letters matched sounds in a left-to-right manner as in *mus* and *hus* (present-day *mouse* and *house*).

The *pattern* feature was introduced in a significant way with the influx of French into English after the invasion by William of Normandy (the coastal region of France across the channel from England) in 1066. Over the next two centuries, French spelling significantly influenced the writing of English—as for example the vowel patterns *ou* in *house* and *mouse* (OE *hus* and *mus*) and *ie* in French loanwords such as *brief* and *relief* (Scragg, 1974). Notably, Middle English developed from this mixture of French and English.

Later, during the Early Modern English period (the 16th and 17th centuries), Greek and Latin word elements were infused into English in greater numbers and were combined and recombined to create a large number of new words, a vocabulary that primarily reflected the scientific advances of the time.

There are good reasons for this parallel between development within the individual learner and development of the spelling system as a whole. The alphabetic strategy characteristic of Old English corresponds to the cognitive expectations of young, beginning readers and writers. As learners develop further their literacy skills through reading and writing, they assimilate words that include the spelling and meaning patterns that characterized words that came into English later, first with the influx of Norman French and later with the revival of interest in and use of Greek and Latin word elements. Eventually, the wide range of derivationally related words in the Greek and Latin component of the language becomes accessible through students' reading. Most of this segment of English vocabulary, comprising literally tens of thousands of words, also represents a more abstract conceptual domain.

From a developmental perspective, however, students by this time have the more advanced cognitive competence that allows them to explore these concepts and the multiple layers of information through which they are represented in spelling. Indeed, the common spelling of derivationally related words may be one of the most efficient and effective means of becoming aware of and organizing concepts that share a common underlying conceptual domain (Fowler & Liberman, 1995; Templeton, 1989). Consider, for example, how the common spelling reveals the common and perhaps surprising conceptual domain underlying the following words: *human*, *humanity*, *humane*, post*humous*, *humus*, ex*hume*.

3. How should spelling words be selected and organized?

As we have pointed out, most students do not discover the different layers of information and the corresponding sound and meaning patterns on their own. We assume, therefore, that it is necessary to take words out of running texts and organize them in ways that will facilitate awareness, understanding, and application of these patterns. How do we go about this selection and organization?

First, the words should be developmentally appropriate. They should reflect spelling features that students "use but confuse" when they write (Invernizzi et al., 1994, p. 160). Children who are alphabetic spellers will be using but confusing short-vowel spellings as well as several consonant blends and digraphs. Attempting to teach them long-vowel patterns, for example, would not be productive because the underlying word knowledge and conception of how the system works would not support memory for different long-vowel patterns. On the other hand, students who are using but confusing one-syllable long-vowel patterns *should* be examining such patterns. Attempting to teach these children polysyllabic words will not work because underlying word knowledge does not support memory for such words.

Second, the words should be organized according to spelling *patterns*. While younger students explore vowel patterns, for example, older students explore syllable patterns and spelling-meaning relationships. The latter include learning the simple combinatorial principles that govern the ways in which base words and affixes combine, as well as learning about the common meaning connection among words that share similar spellings.

Third, at the primary levels (Grades 1 through 3) the words should be known automatically as sight words in reading. At the intermediate levels (Grades 4 through 6) and beyond, while most words should be familiar to students through their reading, some *new* words may be included that are related in spelling and in meaning to the known words. This is the point at which teachers can direct students' attention to the morphemic aspects of words, because most students will not become explicitly aware of these spelling-meaning features unless they are pointed out. Indeed, most adults are not explicitly aware of these aspects (Fischer, Shankweiler, & Liberman, 1985; Fowler & Liberman, 1995).

Is there one place I can go to get the appropriate words for spelling, or do I have to find them myself? Because a number of contemporary published spelling programs purport to be developmentally based (Zutell, 1994), teachers should examine these programs, grade by grade, to see the extent to which they present features and patterns in a developmentally appropriate manner. If this is the case, then these published programs themselves can provide a ready source of words. In addition, a number of resources for teachers offer words organized according to pattern, and some have arranged these in a developmental progression (e.g., Bear, Invernizzi, & Templeton, 1996; Henry, 1996).

How many words should students be examining each week? Because primary emphasis should be placed on spelling patterns, there should be enough words to allow students the opportunity to discern one or more patterns. For learners in the late alphabetic stage—the latter half of first grade for most children—fewer than 10 words per week is appropriate. The words should be organized around common features or patterns, for example, consonant digraphs or the CVC short-vowel pattern. A few high-frequency words that are necessary for writing should be addressed beginning at this level as well. As learners move into the within-word pattern phase (roughly second and third grade), 10 to 12 words per week become the norm. From the syllable juncture stage on (fourth grade and beyond for most students), 20 words per week are standard. At these successive stages,

frequently misspelled words may continue to be added to the core list.

Students may also individualize their weekly lists by including particular words that they wish to spell. This can be highly motivating; these self-selected words can be words of particular interest to the students (dinosaur names, for example, are popular during a unit focusing on the earth's history) or words that continue to cause difficulty. Again, however, these words should not be the *only* spelling words the students have. Indeed, when spelling instruction is based exclusively on personalized lists that include only those words that each student is misspelling in his or her writing or on lists of frequently misspelled words, then students are inadvertently forced to focus on individual words rather than on spelling *patterns* that apply to large numbers of words. So, the best practice is to add a few self-selected words and frequently misspelled words to the core group of pattern words students will study each week.

4. How do I determine my students' spelling levels?

Just as reading instructional levels vary among students within a single classroom, so do spelling instructional levels (Horn, 1969; Manolakes, 1975; Morris, Nelson, & Perney, 1986). Determining the latter is important, because when students examine words that are at their appropriate developmental/instructional level they make more progress than if they attempt words and patterns that are at their frustration level (Morris, Blanton, Blanton, Nowacek, & Perney, 1995). It is true that for most students in a fourth-grade class the spelling instructional level will indeed be fourth grade; nonetheless, there will be some who are at a lower instructional level and some at a higher level.

Students' spelling levels may be determined by administering a qualitative spelling inventory, a series of graded lists with approximately 20 words per list (Schlagal, 1989) or a single list organized according to developmental levels (Bear et al., 1996). The inventory will reveal what spelling features students are using but confusing (Invernizzi et al., 1994) and also help teachers determine where their students fall along the developmental continuum of word knowledge. The results of these inventories may be expressed in two ways: in terms of grade level (Henderson, 1990; Schlagal, 1992) or in terms of developmental level (Bear & Barone, 1989; Bear et al., 1996). It is important to note, however, that regardless of criterion—grade level or developmental level—the results are equivalent. For example, a spelling instructional level of second grade corresponds to the *within-word pattern* stage; a spelling instructional level of fourth grade corresponds to the *syllable juncture* stage (Henderson, 1990; Henderson & Templeton, 1986).

5. Should I allow invented spelling? If so, for how long?

In a sense, invented spelling continues throughout our lives. We engage in it whenever we take a risk or have a go at a word about which we are uncertain (Cramer, 1998; Hughes & Searle, 1997; Wilde, 1992). We may forget whether *irrelevant* or *irrelevent* is correct, so rather than interrupting our writing to consult a dictionary we write down our best guess and know that we can check it out later.

The issue of invented spelling is of most concern, however, in the case of younger students. Among many parents and some state legislators, reaction against allowing invented spelling has been strong and often vehement. There are really two parts to the question of allowing invented spelling, however: (a) Should we allow young children to invent spellings as a means of developing phonemic awareness and getting them involved in meaningful writing from the start? and (b) How long should we allow invented spelling to go on before expecting children to learn conventional spelling?

First, the value of encouraging and allowing young children to invent their spelling has been strongly supported by well-conducted studies (Clarke, 1988; Ehri & Wilce, 1987; Huxford, Terrell, & Bradley, 1992; Read, 1986). When children attempt to represent their speech with letters, they are applying phonics in a truly authentic context. Along with other meaningful engagements with literacy—shared book experiences, rhyming games, categorization activities focusing on beginning sounds, and so forth—children become aware first of some individual sounds within syllables and then progress to full phonemic awareness, defined as the ability to attend consciously to both consonants and vowels within words.

How long do we let it go on before addressing conventional spelling? First of all, children become aware of the reality of conventional spelling quite early and will often ask teachers whether their invented spellings are right. So, while we do encourage them to "write down all the sounds you hear and feel when you say the word" (Bear et al., 1996, p. 40)—to continue to use words the spelling of which they're uncertain but which they wish to use in their writing—we also proceed with instruction in how the system works. We can begin this exploration of conventional spelling when children have attained full phonemic awareness (the middle of first grade for most children) and are representing consonants and vowels in their invented spelling. At this level, in fact, phonics and spelling instruction are very closely aligned. As children learn about the short-vowel sound, for example, they can examine the spelling of several simple CVC pattern words that include this short vowel (*bag, sat, big,* etc.)

and can be expected to spell these conventionally in their writing.

6. What types of instructional activities work best?

Of the few methodological studies that have been conducted, none answers to everyone's satisfaction the question of whether spelling is learned primarily through reading and writing or primarily through the systematic examination of words. This is probably the wrong question to pose, however. Rather, researchers and practitioners should be interested in the relative contributions of these different types of engagements with words. While this situation is not different than any other question in language arts (e.g., vocabulary development, grammatical usage), it is particularly controversial in spelling because to many educators the mere mention of instructional activities in the same company with spelling means an endorsement of the mind-numbing skill-and-drill paradigm of the past. We must keep in mind, however, that this reflects our own instructional histories; it does not necessarily foretell the instructional future.

What does emerge from the research is the suggestion that *some* examination of words is necessary for most students. Accurate, automatized knowledge of basic spelling patterns is at the heart of skilled reading and writing (Adams, 1990; Perfetti, 1992). Although such word knowledge is best developed through contextual reading and writing, many students require careful teacher guidance and much practice if they are to internalize foundational spelling patterns. Even those who appear to be good spellers can benefit from instruction. Again, one reason for this is that students are usually not explicitly aware of the nature and function of different types of orthographic information and features—the wide-ranging applicability of the consonant doubling/ e-drop principle, for example, and the relationship between spelling and meaning patterns (Chomsky, 1970; Templeton, 1989). Becoming explicitly aware of these features enables students to extend their word knowledge in consequential ways (Derwing et al., 1995; Fischer et al., 1985; Fowler & Liberman, 1995; Goulandris, 1994). In fact, Fischer et al. (1985) observed that "spelling is not a skill that is fully acquired as a part of an elementary education" (pp. 438–439).

Bussis, Chittenden, Amarel, and Klausner (1985) described the brain as an "exquisitely designed pattern detector," but they also pointed out that it "depends on adequate information to word efficiently" (p. 66). This is where explicit spelling instruction comes in. Explicit instruction involves teacher-directed as well as student-directed examination of words. Teacher directed does not mean teaching spelling rules—in fact, trying to teach spelling through rules is one of the least effective approaches one can take (Hanna et al., 1966; Horn, 1969). What teacher-directed learning *does* involve is organizing the examination of words in such a way as to guide students to an understanding of how particular spelling features and patterns operate. This type of exploration is effective because it requires an active search for *pattern* (Derwing et al., 1995; Goulandris, 1994; Henry, 1988). For example, when young students examine the different spelling patterns for the *long a* sound in single-syllable words they may come to the realization that the spelling does not occur randomly: if the *long a* sound occurs at the end of the word it will most often be spelled *ay* and only occasionally *ey*; if it occurs in the middle of the word it will most often be spelled *a-consonant-e* or *ai*.

Another example of explicit spelling instruction involves the teachers organizing the exploration of derivational patterns. For example, most fifth graders know the meaning of the word *solemn* but are likely to misspell it in their writing as SOLEM. By pairing the known word, *solemn*, with the unfamiliar word *solemnity*, therefore, we accomplish two objectives. First, the spelling of the known word is explained: Students can hear the pronunciation of the *n* in *solemnity*, and this is the clue to the spelling of the silent *n* in solemn. Second, students' vocabularies are expanded: Because they understand the meaning of *solemn* well enough to understand it in their reading and use it in their writing, they can learn the related word *solemnity*. In other words, if students know one word in a spelling-meaning family there is the potential to learn many other words in that same family.

Given the importance of spelling patterns, what types of instructional *activities* best facilitate detection and abstraction of patterns and, at the same time, reinforce memory for the spelling of specific words? Actually, a number of promising activities have recently been reported in the literature. *Word sorts* engage students in categorizing words according to sound, spelling pattern, and meaning (Barnes, 1989; Bear et al., 1996; Morris, 1982; Weber & Henderson, 1989). They can be teacher directed (closed) or student directed (open) (Bear et al., 1996; Cramer, 1998). For example, students in the within-word pattern phase of word knowledge could sort words according to vowel pattern; in such sorts there is always a miscellaneous category (represented below by a *?*) for words that do not follow the target categories:

cat	*make*	*car*	*?*
mad	race	star	fall
flat	game	hard	ball
cap	place	mark	
grab	plate	park	
	rake		

Word sort activities involve students in *comparing, contrasting*, and *classifying* words—considering words from a variety of perspectives. Bear et al. (1996) emphasized the importance of comparing those words that do fit into a particular category with those that don't. This type of engagement with words will for most students lead to the abstraction of spelling patterns and the sounds to which they correspond.

Game-like formats such as board games and card games can also be effective if they focus on words that reflect spelling patterns. Word-building activities also facilitate abstraction of pattern: word wheels, flip charts, making words (Cunningham, 1995). Spelling or word study notebooks may be used to record, collect, and organize information about words and spelling patterns.

7. What type of spelling strategies should be taught?

The strategies that we can help students learn to support their spelling are derived from the type of thinking that occurs during word study activities. One of the most powerful strategies for determining the spelling of a word about which a student is unfamiliar is to try to think of a word that is similar in terms of sound or meaning. Psychologists have referred to this strategy as reasoning *by analogy*. We know that younger students as well as older ones are capable of this type of reasoning about words (Gaskins, 1992; Goswami, 1988; Treiman, 1993). This strategy should be modeled for students, however, because many will not discover it on their own.

For example, consider the student who has spelled *nature* as NATCHER. The teacher shows her the word *picture*, which she already knows how to spell. By directing the child's attention to the similar sound and spelling pattern in the known word *picture*, the teacher helps the child become aware of and remember the spelling of *nature*. At the same time, she is modeling a way of thinking about words: *If you're not sure about the spelling of a word, try to think of another word you know that may provide a clue.* Similarly, the common error among older students of misspelling an unaccented vowel, as in OPPISITION, is addressed by showing a word that is related in terms of spelling and meaning, *oppose*. Showing students that *opposition* is derived from the base word *oppose* reinforces the structural-meaning relationships that are preserved in the spelling system—as well as modeling a strategy for thinking about words.

A tried and true strategy for learning individual words is the *look, say*, and *write* strategy (Horn, 1969). Given our understanding of the role of analogy in learning to spell, however, to this sequence we would add *think*: Look, say, *think*, and write. As the student looks at and pronounces a particular word, he or she should think about other words that may have the same spelling and/or meaning pattern.

Students also need to think strategically about what they already know about the spelling of a word and realize that this will help them focus more specifically on a particular error. They should be shown how to look at their misspellings in the context of the whole word. In the past, many teachers have inadvertently sent the message that, when a spelling error occurs, "the whole word is wrong." This is bad pedagogy because word knowledge is not an all-or-none affair. When a student misspells a word (RECK for *wreck*), we should first show her how much she *already knows* about the word—which is, most likely, most of the word. She has erred on just one or at most a couple of letters. By first reinforcing what is correct and then moving to what needs to be fixed up, we show students *how* to look at their misspellings. They need to realize that they have not missed the *whole* word but rather just a part of it—in effect, they already *know* most of the word.

While acknowledging the importance of learning spelling patterns, many educators suggest that teaching about them should occur incidentally, in the context of authentic reading and writing activities. While this practice should be encouraged, there are problems when it is endorsed as the *sole* means of promoting spelling development. First, the classroom teacher needs to have knowledge about both the spelling system and spelling development to do this, and we have already noted that many, perhaps most, teachers would admit that they do not feel confident of their expertise in this area. Second, most learners need adequate *time* spent examining words and patterns in order to lock in the spelling pattern, leading to the automaticity that serves both writing *and* reading. Though important, incidental teaching and learning are usually not sufficient for this level of processing.

8. How can I assess how my students are progressing?

Teachers can assess students' *application* of their spelling knowledge by examining the students' writing. This also provides information about what students are using but confusing and therefore need to study. The most straightforward assessment of students' spelling *knowledge* involves the administration of a good spelling inventory (see Bear et al., 1996; Morris, Blanton, Blanton, Nowacek, & Perney, 1995; Schlagal, 1992). Administering these inventories at the beginning and again at the end of the school year can give teachers a clear picture of the spelling gains made by their students. These periodic assessments can be included in students' portfolios, thereby providing dramatic evidence to students and parents of the progress over the course of the school year. Where standardized assessments often will not yield dramatic evidence of growth, these assessments will, because they can document growth within developmental levels. Morris, Blanton, Blanton, and Perney (1995) also found that student performance on 6-week review tests (administered cold, before study) provides an accurate, ongoing measure of spelling achievement.

Weekly spelling pretests and posttests also yield information, although ironically the Monday pretest is probably the more important measure. This is because the pretest tells the teacher how much prior knowledge individual students bring to the task of learning a list of 15–20 spelling words. The child who can spell 50% of the words *before* study will have a better chance of internalizing the weekly spelling patterns than a child who can spell only 10% of the pretest words.

Friday posttests also are important, providing a purpose for weekly study and review. However, as all teachers know, some students do well on the Friday posttest and then misspell the same words one week later in a composition. This often happens when students are placed at a frustration level (as opposed to instructional level) in the spelling curriculum. Through hard effort and brute memory, these students can score 90% correct on a weekly posttest; however, they are unable to internalize the underlying pattern knowledge—represented in the weekly word list—that leads to long-term spelling effectiveness.

9. How should instruction be adjusted for students with a learning problem in the area of spelling?

Research has shown that students who experience significant difficulty with spelling follow the same developmental course as other students, but do so at a slower pace (Worthy & Invernizzi, 1990). In such cases, it is critical to provide spelling instruction at the appropriate developmental level, regardless of the students' age and grade. Once the appropriate spelling instructional level is established—be it alphabetic, within-word pattern, or syllable juncture—instruction can be adapted by focusing on fewer words at a time, teaching spelling patterns in an explicit manner, and providing for copious amounts of practice and review.

Conclusion

Cummings observed, "It seems probable that a better understanding of the American English orthographic system would lead us toward a better teaching of literacy" (1988, p. 463). While educators have learned much over the past three decades about how the learner develops orthographic knowledge, our knowledge base with respect to the overall spelling system has lagged behind. This has been costly for instruction because development must always be interpreted in terms of some end process or knowledge domain to be learned. To plan effective instruction, the teacher must know not only where the student presently is, but where he or she needs to go next; this calls for knowledge of the spelling system. The challenge ahead is to blend our understanding of the developing learner with a better understanding of the system to be learned. This can be done, and such an accomplishment could potentially improve not only the teaching of spelling but also the teaching of other literacy processes, including writing and reading fluency and vocabulary development. The spelling of words objectifies language and words in direct ways. An understanding of the system is beneficial for *all* learners, students and teachers alike.

REFERENCES

ADAMS, M.J. (1990). *Beginning to read: Thinking and learning about print*. Cambridge, MA: MIT Press.

ARONOFF, M. (1994). Morphology. In C.A. Purves, L. Papa & S. Jordan (Eds.), *Encyclopedia of English studies and language arts: Vol. 2* (pp. 820–821). New York: Scholastic.

BARNES, G.W. (1989). Word sorting: The cultivation of rules for spelling in English. *Reading Psychology, 10*, 293–307.

BEAR, D.R., & BARONE, D. (1989). Using children's spellings to group for word study and directed reading in the primary classroom. *Reading Psychology, 10*, 275–292.

BEAR, D.R., INVERNIZZI, M., & TEMPLETON, S. (1996). *Words their way: Word study for phonics, vocabulary, and spelling instruction*. Englewood Cliffs, NJ: Prentice-Hall.

BERNINGER, V.W. (Ed.). (1994). *The varieties of orthographic knowledge: Theoretical and developmental issues* (Vol. 1). Dordrecht, The Netherlands: Kluwer.

BERNINGER, V.W. (Ed.). (1995). *The varieties of orthographic knowledge: Relationships to phonology, reading, and writing* (Vol. 2). Dordrecht, The Netherlands: Kluwer.

BRADLEY, H. (1919). *On the relations between spoken and written language*. Oxford, England: Clarendon Press.

BROWN, G.D.A., & ELLIS, N.C. (Eds.). (1994). *Handbook of spelling: Theory, process, and intervention*. Chichester, England: John Wiley.

BUSSIS, A., CHITTENDEN, E., AMAREL, M., & KLAUSNER, E. (1985). *Inquiry into meaning: An investigation of learning to read*. Hillsdale, NJ: Erlbaum.

CHOMSKY, C. (1970). Reading, writing, and phonology. *Harvard Educational Review, 40*, 287–309.

CHOMSKY, N., & HALLE, M. (1968). *The sound pattern of English*. New York: Harper & Row.

CLARKE, L. (1988). Invented versus traditional spelling in first graders' writings: Effects on learning to spell and read. *Research in the Teaching of English, 22*, 281–309.

CRAMER, R. (1998). *The spelling connection: Integrating reading, writing and spelling instruction*. New York: Guilford Press.

CUMMINGS, D.W. (1988). *American English spelling*. Baltimore: Johns Hopkins University Press.

CUNNINGHAM, P. (1995). *Phonics they use* (2nd ed.). New York: HarperCollins.

DERWING, B.L., & BAKER, W.J. (1986). Assessing morphological development. In P. Fletcher & M. Garman (Eds.), *Language acquisition: Studies in first language development* (2nd ed., pp. 326–338).

Cambridge, England: Cambridge University Press.

DERWING, B.L., SMITH, M.L., & WIEBE, G.E. (1995). On the role of spelling in morpheme recognition: Experimental studies with children and adults. In L.B. Feldman (Ed.), *Morphological aspects of language processing* (pp. 3–27). Hillsdale, NJ: Erlbaum.

EHRI, L.C. (1993). How English orthography influences phonological knowledge as children learn to read and spell. In R.J. Scales (Ed.), *Literacy and language analysis* (pp. 21–43). Hillsdale, NJ: Erlbaum.

EHRI, L., & WILCE, L. (1987). Does learning to spell help beginners learn to read words? *Reading Research Quarterly, 22*, 47–65.

FISCHER, F., SHANKWEILER, D., & LIBERMAN, I.Y. (1985). Spelling proficiency and sensitivity to word structure. *Journal of Memory and Language, 24*, 423–441.

FOWLER, A.E., & LIBERMAN, I.Y. (1995). The role of phonology and orthography in morphological awareness. In L.B. Feldman (Ed.), *Morphological aspects of language processing* (pp. 157–188). Hillsdale, NJ: Erlbaum.

FRITH, U. (1985). Beneath the surface of developmental dyslexia. In K.E. Patterson, J.C. Marshall, & M. Coltheart (Eds.), *Surface dyslexia* (pp. 301–330). London: Routledge & Kegan Paul.

GASKINS, R.W. (1992). Using what you know to figure out what you don't know: An analogy approach to decoding. *Reading and Writing Quarterly, 8*, 197–221.

GILL, C.H., & SCHARER, P.L. (1996). "Why do they get it on Friday and misspell it on Monday?" Teachers inquiring about their students as spellers. *Language Arts, 73*, 89–96.

GILL, J.T. (1992). The relationship between word recognition and spelling. In S. Templeton & D.R. Bear (Eds.), *Development of orthographic knowledge and the foundations of literacy: A memorial Festschrift for Edmund H. Henderson* (pp. 79–104). Hillsdale, NJ: Erlbaum.

GOSWAMI, U. (1988). Orthographic analogies and reading development. *Quarterly Journal of Experimental Psychology, 40A*, 239–268.

GOULANDRIS, N. (1994). Teaching spelling: Bridging theory and practice. In G.D.A. Brown & N.C. Ellis (Eds.), *Handbook of spelling: Theory, process, and intervention* (pp. 407–423). Chichester, England: John Wiley.

HANNA, P.R., HANNA, J.S., HODGES, R.E., & RUDORF, H. (1966). *Phoneme-grapheme correspondences as cues to spelling improvement*. Washington, DC: United States Office of Education Cooperative Research.

HENDERSON, E.H. (1990). *Teaching spelling* (2nd ed.). Boston: Houghton Mifflin.

HENDERSON, E.H., & TEMPLETON, S. (1986). A developmental perspective of formal spelling instruction through alphabet, pattern, and meaning. *Elementary School Journal, 86*, 305–316.

HENRY, M.K. (1988). Beyond phonics: Integrated decoding and spelling instruction based on word origin and structure. *Annals of Dyslexia, 38*, 258–275.

HENRY, M.K. (1996). *Words: Integrated decoding and spelling instruction based on word origin and word structure*. Austin, TX: Pro-Ed.

HORN, T. (1969). Spelling. In R.L. Ebel (Ed.), *Encyclopedia of educational research* (4th ed., pp. 1282–1299). New York: Macmillan.

HUGHES, M., & SEARLE, D. (1997). *The violent E and other tricky sounds: Learning to spell from kindergarten through grade 6*. York, ME: Stenhouse.

HUXFORD, L., TERRELL, C., & BRADLEY, L. (1992). "Invented" spelling and learning to read. In C. Sterling & C. Robson (Eds.), *Psychology, spelling, and education* (pp. 159–167). Clevedon, England: Multilingual Matters.

INVERNIZZI, M., ABOUZEID, M., & GILL, J.T. (1994). Using students' invented spellings as a guide for spelling instruction that emphasizes word study. *Elementary School Journal, 95*, 155–167.

MANOLAKES, G. (1975). The teaching of spelling: A pilot study. *Elementary English*. 52, 243–247.

MOATS, L. (1995). *Spelling: Development, disabilities, and instruction*. Baltimore: York Press.

MOATS, L., & SMITH, C. (1992). Derivational morphology: Why it should be included in assessment and instruction. *Language, Speech, and Hearing in the Schools, 23*, 312–319.

MORRIS, D. (1982). "Word sort": A categorization strategy for improving word recognition ability. *Reading Psychology, 3*, 247–259.

MORRIS, D. (1993). The relationship between children's concept of word in text and phoneme awareness in learning to read: A longitudinal study. *Research in the Teaching of English, 27*, 133–154.

MORRIS, D., BLANTON, L., BLANTON, W.E., NOWACEK, J., & PERNEY, J. (1995). Teaching low-achieving spellers at their "instructional level." *Elementary School Journal, 96*, 163–178.

MORRIS, D., BLANTON, L., BLANTON, W., & PERNEY, J. (1995). Spelling instruction and achievement in six classrooms. *Elementary School Journal, 96*, 145–162.

MORRIS, D., NELSON, L., & PERNEY, J. (1986). Exploring the concept of "spelling instructional level" through the analysis of error-types. *Elementary School Journal, 87*, 181–200.

PERFETTI, C. (1992). The representation problem in reading acquisition. In P. Gough, L. Ehri, & R. Treiman (Eds.), *Reading acquisition* (pp. 145–174). Hillsdale, NJ: Erlbaum.

READ, C. (1986). *Children's creative spelling*. London: Routledge & Kegan Paul.

READ, C. (1994). Review of Shane Templeton and Donald R. Bear (Eds.), Development of orthographic knowledge and the foundations of literacy: A memorial Festschrift for Edmund H. Henderson. *The American Journal of Psychology, 107*, 471–476.

READ, C., & HODGES, R. (1982). Spelling. In H. Mitzel (Ed.), *Encyclopedia of educational research* (5th ed., pp. 1758–1767). New York: Macmillan.

SABEY, B. (1997). *Metacognitive responses of syllable juncture spellers while performing three literacy tasks*. Unpublished doctoral dissertation, University of Nevada, Reno.

SCHLAGAL, R. (1989). Constancy and change in spelling development. *Reading Psychology, 10*, 207–232.

SCHLAGAL, R. (1992). Patterns of orthographic development into the intermediate grades. In S. Templeton & D.R. Bear (Eds.), *Development of orthographic knowledge and the foundations of literacy: A memorial Festschrift for Edmund H. Henderson* (pp. 31–52). Hillsdale, NJ: Erlbaum.

SCRAGG, D.G. (1974). *A history of English spelling*. New York: Barnes & Noble.

SNOWLING, M. (1994). Towards a model of spelling acquisition: The development of some component skills. In G.D.A. Brown & N.C. Ellis (Eds.), *Handbook of spelling: Theory, process, and intervention* (pp. 111–128). Chichester, England: John Wiley.

TAYLOR, I., & TAYLOR, M.M. (Eds.). (1983). *The psychology of reading*. New York: Academic Press.

TEMPLETON, S. (1976, December). *The spelling of young children in relation to the logic of alphabetic orthography*. Paper presented at the 26th annual meeting of the National Reading Conference, Atlanta, GA.

TEMPLETON, S. (1979). Spelling first, sound later: The relationship between orthography and higher order phonological knowledge in older students. *Research in the Teaching of English, 13*, 255–264.

TEMPLETON, S. (1989). Tacit and explicit knowledge of derivational morphology: Foundations for a unified approach to spelling and vocabulary development in the intermediate grades and beyond. *Reading Psychology, 10*, 233–253.

TEMPLETON, S. (1991). Teaching and learning the English spelling system: Reconceptualizing method and purpose. *Elementary School Journal, 92*, 183–199.

TEMPLETON, S. (1992). New trends in an historical perspective: Old story, new resolution—Sound and meaning in spelling. *Language Arts, 69*, 454–463.

TEMPLETON, S., & BEAR, D.R. (Eds.). (1992). *Development of orthographic knowledge and the foundations of literacy: A memorial Festschrift for Edmund H. Henderson*. Hillsdale, NJ: Erlbaum.

TEMPLETON, S., & MORRIS, D. (in press). Spelling. In P.D. Pearson, M. Kamil, R. Barr, & P. Johnston (Eds.), *Handbook of reading research* (Vol. 3). White Plains, NY: Longman.

TEMPLETON, S., & SCARBOROUGH-FRANKS, L. (1985). The spelling's the thing: Older students' knowledge of derivational morphology in phonology and orthography. *Applied Psycholinguistics, 6*, 371–389.

TREIMAN, R. (1993). *Beginning to spell*. New York: Oxford University Press.

VENEZKY, R. (1970). *The structure of English orthography*. The Hague, The Netherlands: Mouton.

WEBER, W., & HENDERSON, E.H. (1989). A computer-based program of word study: Effects on reading and spelling. *Reading Psychology, 10*, 157–171.

WILDE, S. (1992). *You kan red this!: Spelling and punctuation for whole language classrooms, K–6*. Portsmouth, NH: Heinemann.

WORTHY, M.J., & INVERNIZZI, M. (1990). Spelling errors of normal and disabled students on achievement levels one through four: Instructional implications. *Annals of Dyslexia, 40*, 138–151.

ZUTELL, J. (1994). Spelling instruction. In A.C. Purves, L. Papa, & S. Jordan (Eds.), *Encyclopedia of English studies and language arts* (Vol. 2, pp. 1098–1100). New York: Scholastic.

Received December 16, 1997
Final revision received February 13, 1998
Accepted March 6, 1998

Spelling: The Difference Instruction Makes

by Louisa Cook Moats

Born to Spell?

Many teachers believe that "good spellers are born and not made." There is truth to the saying: current research on the genetics of reading and spelling disability (dyslexia) does affirm that these skills are genetically predispositioned, with spelling achievement being even more highly heritable than reading (Pennington, 1995). Both spelling and reading skills are distributed on a normal continuum in the general population, but spelling is a more difficult skill to acquire, and it remains the weakest skill in adults whose reading problems are remediated. Like other characteristics that are influenced by genetics, spelling achievement can be modified and improved with direct teaching, and there are many reasons why spelling should be taught.

Relationship of Spelling and Reading

Spelling is closely linked to word recognition in grades K–2. It is a very good predictor of basic reading skill during the early stages of reading development (Tangel and Blachman, 1995). The linguistic skills that underlie both word recognition and spelling are phonological awareness and sound-symbol linkage—both of which are quite unrelated to visual-spatial memory. Our so-called "visual" memory for words relies on a specific

From *The California Reader,* Summer 1997

orthographic memory system that is intimately linked with the language centers of the brain. Orthographic memory for words, in turn, is quite dependent on the quality of completeness of the learner's understanding of language structure at the phoneme, syllable, and morpheme levels. Learning to spell improves phoneme awareness and word recognition.

Stages of Development

Understanding of word structure and its relationship to print proceeds in predictable stages that are marked by new insights into language structure as well as the learning of specific words (Moats, 1995; Read, 1986; Templeton and Bear, 1992; Treiman, 1993). Children's inventive spellings, which have been the focus of considerable research in the last 20 years, reflect their growing knowledge of English phonology and orthography. However, most children do not teach themselves all that they need to know about spelling simply through exposure to print. Better spelling achievement is gained when instruction is direct, systematic, and focused on active exploration of language structure at the child's instructional level (see Moats, 1995, Tangel and Blachman, 1995, and Templeton and Bear, 1994, for discussion of the evidence). Effective teaching informs children directly about the sounds in words; the consistent spellings for vowels, consonants, syllables, and morphemes; the origin of words; and the meaning of words. Effective spelling instruction is linked as well to word identification and writing.

Phonetic or inventive spelling is a necessary but insufficient step to learning conventional spelling.

Children who spell phonetically are using the alphabetic principle (print represents the sounds of speech) and are signaling readiness for formal instruction, which should begin for most children in mid-first grade. Direct instruction should emphasize what is logical, frequent, and predictable in the spelling system of English. Grouping words for spelling instruction only on the basis of meaningful thematic links is not a supportable practice for most children, who need assistance deciphering how the orthographic code works at several levels of language organization.

What to Teach in Spelling

Orthographic Concepts and Specific Word Knowledge

Because written English is not a phonetic system of representation, the immature learner's strategy of phonetic (sound by sound) transcription must be replaced eventually by specific knowledge of English orthography. High frequency "sight" words must also be practiced and remembered lest they be learned incorrectly (*when/whenn; thay/they*). Children are to learn that there is not one symbol for each speech sound, but that most phonemes are represented by letter combinations conforming to patterns and generalizations (e.g., /k/ is spelled *ck* after stressed short vowels). Those correspondences vary, with more than one spelling possible for many speech sounds (/f/ = *f, ff, ph, gh*). The possibilities for spelling are often constrained by the position of the sound in a word (/f/ spelled *ff* at the ends of words only).

Children also need to learn that subtle features in the pronunciation of words are not represented in spelling, such as the /ch/ sound in *nature* and the /j/ sound that begins *dress*. Finally, they must realize that letter strings represent other aspects of word structure—sometimes the word's meaning (*straight vs. strait*) language of origin (*antique and ballet*), part of speech (*accept vs. except*) or relationship to other words (*mnemonic, amnesty, amnesia*).

Sound/Symbol Correspondence

Children need to learn the predictable consonant and vowel correspondences that form the common syllable types in English. During beginning spelling instruction, phoneme awareness is enhanced when children segment words by sound before spelling them. Words that follow a spelling pattern can be grouped and sorted, compared to others, discussed, and written to dictation until learned. Activities can be thought-provoking and focused on discovery of a pattern in many examples.

When children understand the patterns of sound-symbol and syllable correspondences within words, specific words are easier for children to remember. In general, we remember what makes sense to us, and spelling is no exception.

Common and unpredictable words (*they, do, said, were,* etc.) should be practiced, a few at a time, from the middle of first grade, using the multisensory routine of saying and writing simultaneously. Techniques such as tracing on a rough surface while the word is slowly pronounced can increase memory for the letters. These "non-family" words must be practiced many times by some children. Poor spellers who continue to demonstrate phonological weaknesses usually struggle with specific linguistic entities, such as inflections (*–ed, –s*) and the /r/ sound after vowels (as in *girl*), and benefit from slow, sequential lessons that focus on one concept or pattern at a time.

Word Structure and Word Origin

The morpheme structure of words needs to be emphasized from fourth grade on (Chomsky,

1970). Academic language includes many words of Anglo-Saxon, Latin, and Greek origin in which morphology determines both spelling and meaning but has a complex relationship to phonology. Word relationships are key at this level, as in *vary, variety, variable,* and *various.* Many words with common roots are pronounced differently, although the spelling of a meaningful root may stay constant, as in *sign/signal/resignation.*

Without planful instruction involving preselected lists, children cannot learn these constructions explicitly; examples encountered in reading and writing are too infrequent to support pattern recognition. Words such as *define, definition, indefinite,* and *definitive* do not often occur together in text, but must be grouped together for instruction if their relationship will be apparent.

A basic 10 to 15 minutes per day of directed word study fosters the word knowledge so important for vocabulary acquisition, reading, and writing. Even the poorest spellers benefit from such teaching. Intelligent spelling does have a place in every classroom.

References

Chomsky, C. (1970). Reading, spelling, and phonology. *Harvard Educational Review*, 40, pp. 287-309.

Moats, L.C. (1995). *Spelling: Development, disability, and instruction.* Baltimore, MD: York Press.

Pennington, B. (1995). Genetics of learning disabilities. *Journal of Child Neurology*, 10, pp. 569-577.

Read, C. (1986). *Children's creative spelling.* Boston: Routledge and Kegan Paul.

Tangel, D.M., and B.A. Blachman (1995). Effect of phoneme awareness instruction on the invented spelling of first grade children: A one year follow-up. *Journal of Reading Behavior*, 27, pp. 153-85.

Templeton, S., and Bear, D.B. (1992). *Development of Orthographic Knowledge and the Foundations of Literacy: A Memorial Festschrift for Edmund Henderson.* Hillsdale, NJ: Lawrence Erlbaum.

Treiman, R.T. (1993). *Beginning to spell.* New York: Oxford University Press.

Louisa Moats, Ed.D., was a Visiting Scholar for the '95–'97 school year with the Sacramento County Office of Education and the CSUS Center for the Improvement of Reading Instruction. She developed the Blueprint for Professional Development and the Reading Leadership Training Grant (AB 3482) materials to educate the public about the California Reading Initiative. She is currently Project Director of the NICHD Early Intervention Project in Washington DC. She has been interested in spelling errors since her doctoral work at Harvard University and has published many articles, chapters, and a book on the subject. She is co-author of a major new spelling basal program.

From *American Educational Research Journal*, Winter 1996, Vol. 33, No. 4

A Cognitive Theory of Orthographic Transitioning: Predictable Errors in How Spanish-Speaking Children Spell English Words

Olatokunbo S. Fashola, Priscilla A. Drum, Richard E. Mayer, and Sang-Jin Kang

University of California, Santa Barbara

Schools in the United States serve a large and increasing number of Spanish-speaking students who are making the transition to English language literacy. This study examines one aspect of the transition to English literacy, namely, how Spanish-speaking students spell English words. Samples of 38 students who speak Spanish at home (Spanish-speaking group) and 34 students who speak English at home (English-speaking group) listened to a list of 40 common English words dictated to them by the teacher and wrote down each word one at a time. Spanish-speaking students produced more errors that were consistent with the correct application of Spanish phonological and orthographical rules (i.e., predicted errors) than did English-speaking students, and the groups generally did not differ in their production of other kinds of spelling errors (i.e., nonpredicted errors). Theoretical and practical implications for bilingual education are discussed.

OLATOKUNBO S. FASHOLA is an Associate Research Scientist at the Center for Research on Education of Students Placed at Risk, Johns Hopkins University, 3505 North Charles Street, Baltimore, MD 21218. Her specializations are reading, language development, emergent literacy, problem solving, and bilingual education.

PRISCILLA A. DRUM is a Professor Emeritus of Education, University of California, Santa Barbara. She can be contacted at RR2 Box 3940, Pahoa, HI 96778. Her specializations are reading and language development.

RICHARD E. MAYER is a Professor in the Department of Psychology, University of California, Santa Barbara, CA 93106. His specialization is educational psychology.

SANG-JIN KANG is an Assistant Professor in the Department of Education, Yonsei University, Seoul, 120-749, Korea. His specializations are statistics and measurement and multilevel modeling.

A pressing issue facing American education today is how to address the instructional needs of language-minority students. The demographics of the American public school population are changing such that more students are now coming from homes in which languages other than English are the primary languages spoken (National Center for Education Statistics, 1995; National Commission on Migrant Education, 1992). In the United States, there are more than 3.5 million non-English-speaking students in kindergarten through Grade 12. In California alone, there are 1.2 million K–12 non-English-speaking students, and that number has more than doubled over the past decade (California State Department of Education, 1992). The largest component of this group is students who speak Spanish at home.

As the demographics of the American public school population change, educators must develop methods of instruction that are sensitive to student needs. This study focuses on one segment of the changing school population, namely students who speak Spanish as their first language. The topic of interest is their orthographic transitioning as they change from learning to spell in Spanish to learning to spell in English. In particular, this research study examines differences in how Spanish-speaking students who are making the transition to English and English-speaking students learn to spell in English.

In this study, we hypothesized that transitioning children whose first language is Spanish may initially operate in English spelling according to a systematic and predictable set of rules. In short, we hypothesized that, when they make errors, transitioning children are likely to use the rules of spelling in Spanish to spell words in English. With experience and proper instruction, their spelling will eventually change from transitional orthography to fully acquired bilingual orthography in both languages.

Examples of Phonetic and Orthographic Sources of Error in Spelling

Given the central role of basic language skills in the development of literacy, we focused on the process of spelling by elementary school students who are transitioning from Spanish to English language use in school. When a transitioning student makes a spelling error, the source may be a lack of knowledge of spelling rules. In this case, the child will make random spelling errors, which we call nonpredicted errors. Alternatively, a student may be correctly applying spelling rules from Spanish that are inappropriate for English. In this case, the child will produce errors that can be predicted on the basis of Spanish phonology and orthography, which we call predicted errors.

For example, consider a writing assignment in which an elementary school student who is transitioning from Spanish to English writes "I tok a lok on cavul." From the point of view of English spelling rules, this student produced three misspelled words, namely, "tok," "lok," and "cavul." However, from the point of view of Spanish spelling rules, the three words represent the closest approximation to sounds in Spanish for the words *took, look*, and *cable*, respectively. Because the "oo" and middle "b" sounds in English do not have identically corresponding sounds in Spanish, Spanish-speaking students may hear them as the closest Spanish sounds ("o" and "v," respectively). In this case, the student is producing the correct spelling of words as they would be pronounced using Spanish phonemes. In short, some spelling errors may result from adjusting English phonology to fit within the Spanish phonological system.

Consider another writing assignment in which a student produces the following sentence: "I was driming of a triqui jero." From the point of view of English spelling rules, there are three spelling errors: "driming," "triqui," and "jero." From the point of view of Spanish spelling rules, however, these three words represent correct applications of Spanish phonological and orthographic rules to the sounds for "dreaming," "tricky," and "hero," respectively, as they are pronounced in English. In short, some spelling errors may result from correct application of Spanish orthographic rules to the sounds of English words, such as using "i" for the /ee/ sound, "qu" for the /k/ sound, and "j" for the /h/ sound.

A Componential Analysis of a Word Dictation Task

In a word dictation task, a word is presented orally and the student writes the word. According to a componential analysis of the cognitive processes involved in the word dictation task, when an English word is presented orally, the following cognitive processes occur:

(a) *construction of a sensory representation*—the student receives the sensory information aurally and holds the input in sensory memory,

(b) *construction of a phonetic representation*—the student converts the sensory information into a phonetic representation in working memory (i.e., a series of phonemes) by matching it with known sounds from long-term memory, and

(c) *construction of an orthographic representation*—the student converts the phonetic representation into an orthographic representation (i.e., a series of letters) in working memory by matching each phoneme with a known letter or letter string from long-term memory.

The student then translates the orthographic representation into a written response.

What are the sources of spelling errors? According to this cognitive model of the word dictation task, errors in the written response can be attributed to errors in the construction of a sensory representation, a phonetic representation, or an orthographic representation. A sensory error occurs when the student has a hearing disorder that prevents the sounds from being heard properly. In this case, the student is unable to produce a sensible written response. Our focus is not on physically based hearing disorders, so we do not explore the role of sensory errors in this study.

A phonetic error occurs when the sensory representation (i.e., the received sound) does not correspond to a known phoneme in long-term memory, so the student is most likely to represent the sound as a known phoneme that is similar to the received sound. For example, for a word containing "sh," a Spanish-speaking student who does not possess the "sh" sound in long-term memory may perceive the sound as "ch." A spelling error will occur if the student then converts the "ch" phoneme into the "ch" digraph orthographically. We refer to this process as a phonetic processing bug.

An orthographic error occurs when the phonetic representation corresponds to a letter or letter string in long-term memory that is different from the English letter or letter string. For example, for a word containing the /h/ phoneme, a Spanish-speaking student may correctly map the "h" sound as a phonetic representation but convert that sound into the *j* grapheme as an orthographic representation. This results in a spelling error if the English spelling is based on the "h" sound being represented orthographically as *h*. We refer to this process as an orthographic processing bug.

Predicted Errors Based on a Cognitive Theory of Transitional Spelling

In this study, we examined phonetic and orthographic sources of spelling errors for Spanish-speaking children who were transitioning to literacy in English. In particular, we examined spelling errors for eight English allophones that could be predicted on the basis of the application of correct Spanish phonological and orthographical rules to English words.

Table 1 lists the actual and predicted spellings for each of five words in each of eight categories. The following subsections present phonological and orthographic descriptions of the eight categories, including explanations for the predicted spelling errors.

Category 1: /k/ Allophone

Velar voiceless stops are represented by the same sound, namely the /k/ phoneme, in both languages. In English, the medial orthographic spelling forms are written as *ck* or *cc*, whereas, in Spanish, the corresponding orthographic forms are *c, k,* and *qu*. The model predicts that Spanish transitional spellers will tend to use the *c* or *k* consonant or the *qu* digraph to spell the /k/ sound.

Category 2: /h/ Allophone

The English voiceless glottal fricative /h/ exists in both languages. The orthographic representation of the sound in English is *h*, whereas, in Spanish, the orthographic representation is *j*. The model predicts that Spanish transitional spellers will tend to substitute the *j* grapheme for the *h* grapheme.

Table 1
Actual and Predicted Spelling for Words in 8 Categories

Actual spelling	Predicted spelling
Category 1 (cc and ck become c, k, qu)	
soccer	socer, soker, soquer
locker	locer, loker, loquer
packet	pacet, paket, paquet
ticket	ticet, tiket, tiquet
tricky	tricy, triky, triqui
Category 2 (h becomes j)	
handball	jandball
happy	japi
hero	jero (giro)
handbag	janbag
handle	jandul
Category 3 (sk becomes sc, squ)	
basket	bascet, basquet
risky	risci, risqui
asking	ascing, asquing
masking	mascing, masquing
frisky	frisci, frisqui
Category 4 (b becomes v)	
cable	cavul
habit	havit
treble	trevul
rebel	revul
fabric	favric
Category 5 (all becomes oll, ol, o, al)	
football	futboll, futbol, futbo, futbal
wall	woll, wol, wo, wal
tall	toll, tol, to, tal
stall	stoll, stol, sto, stal
tall	foll, fol, fo, fal
Category 6 (a becomes ei, ell, ey)	
baby	beibi, bellbi, beybi
case	ceis, cells, ceys
baseball	beisbol, bellsbol, beysbol
flame	fleim, flellm, fleym
vase	veis, vells, veys
Category 7 (oo becomes o, u)	
took	tok, toke
book	bok, boke
looking	loking
soot	sot, sote
rooster	ruster
Category 8 (ea and ee become i)	
dreaming	driming
beanbag	binbag
meaning	mining
beetle	bitul
seam	sim

Category 3: "sk" Blend

The word-internal consonant cluster written as *sk* in English does not exist in Spanish orthography. The closest orthographic sequence in Spanish for the sound of this consonant cluster is *sc* or *squ*, whereas it is represented in English orthography using *sk*. Therefore, the predicted error of the Spanish-speaking students is to replace *sk* with *sc* or *squ*, whereas a person using Spanish orthography would not be expected to represent the "sk" blend using *k*.

Category 4: /b/ Allophone

The English-voiced bilabial stop /b/ exists in both languages and is orthographically represented as *b* in English. In Spanish, when this sound exists in an intervocalic position, it is pronounced as a voiced bilabial fricative and is represented orthographically as *b* or *v*. The Spanish-speaking students are thus expected to process the medial preconsonantal voiced bilabial stop phonetically as a voiced bilabial fricative and to represent it orthographically as *v*.

Category 5: "all" Cluster

First, the /a/ vowel is pronounced as an /a/ sound in English and an /o/ sound in Spanish; the corresponding orthography is *a* in English and *o* in Spanish. Second, the alveolar lateral /l/ is a phoneme in both languages; in English, however, it is orthographically represented as *l* or *ll*, while in Spanish it is orthographically represented only as *l*. When the alveolar lateral /l/ appears at the end of a word as part of the /al/ phoneme, Spanish-speaking students tend to either write it as one letter or eliminate the letters altogether. The predicted errors—*al, o, ol,* and *oll*—can be attributed to both phonetic and orthographic differences between English and Spanish.

Category 6: /e/ Vowel

Some English words containing "a" involve the tense midfrontal vowel represented by /e/. Because the Spanish vowel system involves only central vowels, the /e/ vowel may be perceived by Spanish-speaking students as a diphthong. The closest phonetic representation of this sound in Spanish is [ey], which is represented in Spanish orthography by the digraph *ey, ei,* or *ell*. The *ll* digraph could be used because it represents a voiced palatal fricative /y/, which is part of the [ey] diphthong. Therefore, Spanish-speaking children are expected to spell the words in this category using *ey, ei,* or *ell*.

Category 7: /u/ and /U/ Phonemes

Some English words containing *oo* involve the high back tense vowel /U/, which exists only in the English language. The closest Spanish sound is the midback vowel /u/, represented orthographically in both languages as *o*. Therefore, the predicted error of the Spanish-speaking children is to replace *oo* with *o*, whereas a person using Spanish orthographic rules would not be expected to represent the "o" phoneme using the geminated vowel digraph *oo*. Sometimes Spanish-speaking children may perceive the sound as the high back vowel /u/, represented in Spanish orthography as *u*. When this happens, Spanish-speaking children are also expected to spell this phoneme using the letter *u*.

Category 8: /i/ Phoneme

English words containing *ee* or *ea* involve the same phoneme in English and Spanish, namely the high frontal vowel /i/. In Spanish, this vowel phoneme is written orthographically as *i*. The Spanish-speaking children are expected to spell words in this category using the letter *i* instead of the vowel digraph *ee* or *ea*.

Literature Review

Phonetic Factors Affecting Communicative Competence

Knowledge of phonics constitutes an important component underlying communicative competence. To be communicatively competent in English, a student needs to hear and produce sounds in the same way as the native speakers of the language. Even acknowledging that there are different dialects, accents, and idiolects, native speakers of the language still sound more alike than different. In the process of learning to read, write, and spell, the phonetic qualities of a language represent one of the qualities that contribute to a child's ability to spell words correctly (Adams, 1990; Ehri, 1989).

Although an analysis of the phonological similarities and differences between Mexican Spanish and American English is beyond the scope of this article, there are important differences in the two languages. In particular, some sounds exist in English but not in Spanish (like "sh" in "shoe"), some sounds exist in Spanish but not in English (like "rr" in "correo"), and some sounds exist in both languages (such as "a" in "baby"). For example, if a Spanish-speaking child is attempting to spell an English word such as *shoe*, the child has to first learn to hear the "sh" phoneme, which exists only in English, and then later write it using the correct grapheme.

Another factor that influences transitioning is the relationship between the two orthographic systems that the children are using to spell. In this case, both the English and the Spanish orthographic systems use an alphabetic system. Sometimes the systems have the same letters; as is the case with the phonemes, however, there are symbols that exist in one language but not the other (e.g., *ñ* in Spanish). As a further complication, there are symbols that exist in both languages (such as *v*) but that represent two different sounds, or two sounds that exist in both languages but are represented using two different symbols (like /h/, represented by *h* in English and *j* in Spanish).

Orthographic Factors Affecting Communicative Competence

Knowledge of orthography constitutes a second major component of communicative competence. The English orthography system is written in an alphabetic form that identifies its smallest units phonetically. This orthographic system consists of 26 alphabetic letters (21 consonants and 5 vowels) that can be used to orthographically represent at least 44 phonemes (Stockwell, Bowen, & Martin, 1965). The English orthographic system does not have a strong letter-to-phoneme relationship, and this lack of consistency can be a troubling aspect of English orthography for novices (Bradley, 1969). According to Bradley (1969), when the spoken form of the language changed from Old English, the spelling did not; as a result, many inconsistencies arose between the written and spoken forms of English.

The Spanish alphabet has 30 graphemes, 5 of which are vowels, 22 of which are single letters, and 3 of which are digraphs (Cressey, 1978). In learning the Spanish alphabet, one learns the digraphs as part of the regular alphabet. In the Spanish orthographic system, the 30 graphemes generally represent the 30 sounds that exist in the Spanish phonology system. This relatively lawful correspondence between letters and sounds is not generally true in English. The expectation of a one-to-one sound-to-grapheme correspondence is a major issue when discussing transitional orthography issues because Spanish has a much more phonetically consistent orthographic system than English. Spanish-speaking spellers are at a disadvantage because they have not had much experience dealing with the exceptions to the rules of spelling.

The English system has three vowel systems, one that consists of tense vowels, one that consists of lax vowels, and one that consists of diphthongs. On the other hand, Spanish-speaking spellers are taught to write and read using only one vowel system (i.e., the full vowel system), and, when they encounter other types of vowels, they are at a disadvantage because they do not know how to represent them. An example of this is that the Spanish-speaking spellers would be apt to substitute the two Spanish vowel graphemes for a perceived English diphthong. Rather than write the word *b(a)seball*, the student would be more apt to write the word *b(ei)sball, b(ai)sball, b(eis)b(ol)*, or *b(ais)b(ol)*. Also, if any two or more vowels appear side by side in the Spanish system, they are usually pronounced in their original forms (as full vowels) and not altered depending on letters preceding or following them.

Understanding Students' Spelling Errors

A Spanish-speaking child who has fully transitioned to English language literacy understands, consciously or unconsciously, the orthographic and phonemic systems in both languages. A thesis of this study is that the "errors" made as a result of the interaction between these two languages should be further examined not just according to the standards of the rules of one language (English) but according to the standards of the rules of both languages. The end result is that transition should be evaluated as a developmental process. Children who make these errors are capable of "getting their message across," and eventually, when full transition is acquired, the frequency of these "errors" will diminish.

Several studies have examined the systematic nature of spelling errors among second-language spellers and have concluded that differences between the two languages are the sources of the spelling errors (Luelsdorff, 1986; Temple, 1979; Zutell & Allen, 1988). Luelsdorff's (1986) project was similar to this one in that he made specific predictions for the spelling errors, but there were two major differences. The first difference was that he used the Slavic languages instead of Spanish, and the second difference was that he did not have a control group to serve as a contrast for his predictions. Temple (1979) examined the English spelling errors of Spanish-speaking students, but his study lacked some of the methodological and theoretical features of our study. He did not have a control group of English speakers with which to compare the spelling results of his population and to affirm that the findings were indeed a result of the spelling systems. Also, he did not administer a controlled spelling test but instead described the errors that the children made, and he did not provide a theoretical analysis of phonetic aspects or the properties of the two languages.

The closest study to the one described in this report was conducted by Zutell and Allen (1988), who investigated the effect of Spanish pronunciation and spelling rules on children's English spelling strategies. Specifically, Zutell and Allen proposed that the students in their study would "generate unique patterns of errors based on their own pronunciation of English words and on the possible interference from their knowledge of Spanish letter-name-sound relationships" (p. 334). One hundred eight bilingual students in Grades 2, 3, and 4 were given a list of 20 words, with five categories of errors and four words per category. The five categories of errors included long "e" vowel (as in *seat*) and long "a" (as in *case*), the initial consonants "y" and "h," and finally the consonant blend "sp." Three of the categories in the Zutell and Allen study were used in this study (long "a," long "e," and "h"). Because there was no English-speaking control group, there was no way to ascertain that the errors were indeed Spanish-influenced errors. Another difference between the two studies is that Zutell and Allen (1988) predicted only one misspelling for each word, whereas in this study there were sometimes two or three predicted spellings based on a cognitive analysis of transitional spelling. Furthermore, in the study reported here, the predictions were based on phonological and orthographic rules for differences in spelling between the two languages, but Zutell and Allen (1988) discussed orthographic differences only from a letter name perspective.

Conclusion

This study has both theoretical and practical implications. On the theoretical side, the results show that students who are transitioning from Spanish to English may misspell English words by systematically applying the phonological and orthographical rules of Spanish. In our study, differences in the pattern of spelling errors of Spanish-speaking and English-speaking students can be understood by recognizing that Spanish-speaking students sometimes apply correct Spanish phonologic and orthographic rules to the spelling of English words. Aside from these kinds of errors (which we call predicted errors), Spanish-speaking and English-speaking students do not generally differ in how they misspell English words (which we call nonpredicted errors). Overall, the pattern of results provides support for a cognitive model of transitional spelling based on phonological and orthographic processes.

On the practical side, these results provide implications for fostering English language literacy in Spanish-speaking students. Our study of spelling errors provides evidence for the idea that acquiring literacy in a second language is tied to and builds upon literacy in one's first language. Teachers of language-minority students would benefit from recognizing when students' errors in English occur as a result of their applying rules that are correct in their native language. For example, teachers of limited-English-proficient Latino students would benefit from knowing the phonological and orthographic rules of Spanish so that they could better recognize predictable spelling errors. Rather than simply marking a predicted error as incorrect, the teacher could explicitly point out that the phonological or orthographic rule in English is different from the one in Spanish. In conclusion, both teachers and test designers who are working with bilingual and transitioning populations need knowledge of orthographic and phonological transitioning errors so that they can differentiate transitioning errors from random errors.

Overall, as would be expected, children from lower grade levels made more spelling errors than did children from higher grade levels. For some categories of sounds, there was an interaction pattern in which native English-speaking children improved more than Spanish-speaking children or in which English-speaking students produced low error rates at both grade levels. It may take more time for Spanish-speaking children to improve their English spelling than it does for English-speaking children, presumably because Spanish-speaking students must learn how to spell in two languages, whereas English-speaking students can concentrate on learning just one language.

A limitation of this study is that it is based on a relatively small sample taken from a single region in the United States. However, it should also be noted that approximately one third of the Spanish-speaking students in the United States live in California, and, of these, almost half live in Los Angeles County, the site of our sample.

Students who are transitioning from Spanish to English language have a somewhat more difficult task than monolingual English-speaking students. The Spanish-speaking students in this study had at least partial exposure to phonology and orthography in both languages and were transferring these skills to English. The goal for the monolingual spellers is to eventually master the phonological and orthographic rules for just one language. Bilingual spellers, however, have much more to accomplish. They have to understand the functional values of orthographic images in English and Spanish, which means that the spellers should be able to apply these values to the words when encountered in both languages.

Students who are engaged in transitional orthography have had partial exposure to a second language and sometimes are using skills used in their primary language to spell words in their second language. This is the point at which the "errors" are being made. The errors, however, are a part of problem solving and also a part of learning, because the process that leads to these errors is a result of communicative competence in several areas. What the Spanish-to-English transitioning students have not acquired, however, is strategic knowledge that prepares them with a plan about where and/or when to apply these rules correctly. This kind of strategic knowledge results from properly mediated learning. Moreover, Barnitz (1982) stated that, in addition to understanding phonemic differences between the two languages, it is also important to understand more complex structures such as morphemes and the roles that they play in orthography later on.

Many authors have discussed the issue of bilingualism and that of bilingual orthography, but few have addressed how to teach transitional orthography so that bilingual students will maintain their orthographic skills in both languages. For example, Hailer (1976) argued that children should initially be taught in their own languages and then gradually acquire English language skills. The goal of such a program should be to convert gradually from the native language of instruction to the English language medium of instruction, but emphasis is put on the fact that it must be gradual and strategic.

For the most part, the immigrants discussed in this study plan to and usually do retain their own individual cultures through language, literacy, food, and so forth. They are usually in constant contact with their homeland, because it is connected to the United States. Thus, these immigrants cannot be expected to discard their original language for English; both languages are still of use to them, and they are expected to function in both environments. A good transitional orthography program should help to ease the process, because the rules of pronunciation and orthography in both languages are recognized. Assistance at home for literacy is an important issue, especially when parents may be literate in Spanish but not in English

(Ylenalto, 1980). Finally, Hornberger (1989) argued that transitional orthography programs should be voluntary rather than forced, because the eventual results of a program stem from how it is seen by the learner.

In conclusion, if transitional spellers do not learn correctly, they may remain in the transitional stage, and the "orthographic pidgin" will then become a permanent structure, similar to an orthographic Creole. Research such as ours suggests that teachers who are familiar with Spanish phonology and orthography will be able to help Spanish-to-English transitional spellers achieve competence in both languages.

Notes

This study was made possible by a Graduate Research Mentorship Program Fellowship awarded by the Graduate Division of the University of California, Santa Barbara. We wish to thank Almedia Jacqueline Toribio, Guillermo Solano-Flores, and Maria Araceli Ruiz-Primo for their consultations concerning Spanish phonology and orthography. We also are grateful to the principal, teachers, and students of the cooperating elementary school, who must remain anonymous in order to protect student confidentiality.

[1]There were 11 boys and 8 girls in the younger Spanish group, 7 boys and 7 girls in the younger English group, 12 girls and 7 boys in the older Spanish group, and 11 boys and 9 girls in the older English group. A chi-square test revealed that the proportion of boys and girls in the Spanish and English groups did not differ significantly, $\chi^2(1) = 0.421$, *ns*. Students classified as limited English proficient lacked basic communication skills in English, but their level of Spanish proficiency was not assessed. All Spanish-speaking students were Latino; most English-speaking students were Caucasian, some were Asian American, and none were African American.

[2]Welch tests (Howell, 1992) conducted on the data in Table 2 produced results generally consistent with the results of the analyses of variance reported in the text.

References

Adams, M. J. (1990). *Beginning to read: Thinking and learning about print*. Cambridge, MA: MIT Press.

Barnitz, J. (1982). Orthographies, bilingualisms, and learning to read English as a second language. *Reading Teacher, 35*, 560–567.

Bradley, H. (1969). *On the relations between spoken and written language, with a special reference to English*. Folcroft, PA: Folcroft Press.

California State Department of Education. (1992). *Language census report for California public schools*. Sacramento: Author.

Cressey, W. (1978). *The sound patterns of English*. New York: Harper & Row.

Ehri, L. C. (1989). The development of spelling knowledge and its role in reading acquisition and reading disability. *Journal of Learning Disabilities, 22*, 356–365.

Hailer, R. M. (1976). *Meeting the needs of the bilingual child. A historical perspective of the nation's first transitional bilingual education law: Chapter 71A of the Acts of 1971, Commonwealth of Massachusetts*. Boston: Massachusetts State Department of Education.

Hornberger, N. H. (1989). Continua of biliteracy. *Review of Educational Research, 59*, 271–296.

Howell, D. C. (1992). *Statistical methods for psychology* (3rd ed.). Belmont, CA: Duxbury Press.

Luelsdorff, P. (1986). *Constraints of error variables in grammar: Bilingual misspelling orthographies*. Amsterdam: Benjamins.

National Center for Education Statistics. (1995). *A first look: Findings from the*

National Assessment of Educational Progress. Washington, DC: Office of Educational Research and Improvement.

National Commission on Migrant Education. (1992). *Invisible children: A portrait of migrant education in the United States*. Washington, DC: Author.

Stockwell, R. P., Bowen, J. D., & Martin, J. W. (1965). *The sounds of English and Spanish*. Chicago: University of Chicago Press.

Temple, C. (1979, November). *Learning to spell in Spanish*. Paper presented at the National Reading Conference, San Antonio, TX.

Ylenalto, O. (1980). Reading ability and differences in the middle and upper primary school. In J. Kavanagh & R. Venezky (Eds.), *Orthography, reading, and dyslexia*. Baltimore: University Park Press.

Zutell, J., & Allen, J. (1988). The English spelling strategies of Spanish-speaking bilingual children. *TESOL Quarterly, 22,* 333–340.

Manuscript received March 16, 1996
Revision received June 16, 1996
Accepted June 24, 1996

SECTION VI

Vocabulary Development

Language Development During Elementary School: The Gap Widens

by Andrew Biemiller

A wide range of differences in children's language exists when they begin kindergarten. The fact that some of these differences can be related to experiences before kindergarten suggests that schooling can provide an opportunity to *compensate* to some degree for differences in early language experiences in home and child care. Unfortunately, the limited available evidence also suggests that current practices in kindergarten and early primary grades do little to foster vocabulary and language development. In later grades, somewhat more is done to encourage language development. However, evidence suggests that the gap between advantaged and disadvantaged children continues to widen during the elementary years, although this effect is less severe when teachers give more attention to vocabulary and language.

In Chapter One, we saw that the growth of language from grades 1 to 6 involves going from roughly 2000 root words and idioms to over 8000. Growth in vocabulary from grades 1 to 3 *may* be slower than grades 4 to 6 (Anglin, 1993). If the rate is faster in grades 4 to 6, this accelerated rate of vocabulary acquisition is probably due to *reading*, and probably applies only to children whose vocabulary and reading skills are at or above the median.

This chapter is about normal school practices with respect to promoting language development. Chapters Four, Five, and Six will examine experimental and proposed school approaches for improving language development.

We have seen how variations in home experience greatly affect the growth of children's language and vocabulary. This indicates that we *can* initiate policies which promote better language development. For a long time, educators, politicians, and the public at large have believed that schooling provided the best opportunity to "compensate" for variations in home experience. In many school systems, children now begin school or its equivalent at age four (e.g., Head Start, four-year-old kindergarten). In others, the school day for kinder-

From *Language and Reading Success,* 1999, Brookline Books

gartners has been lengthened to provide more learning opportunities (e.g., full-day kindergarten programs).

However, it may come as a surprise to readers of this book that I will be arguing that *school experience often does little to foster language growth in the early elementary years* (kindergarten to grade 2). In the later elementary years, when greater attention is often given to vocabulary and related skills, cumulative deficits in vocabulary may be too great to be readily overcome.

Vocabulary and Reading Success

Why do I suggest that there is limited opportunity for language growth in the primary years? Let us begin with a story by Wesley Becker. Having implemented a very successful reading program (DISTAR) which resulted in bringing groups of severely disadvantaged children to average or "grade level" performance in first and second grade, Becker found that children from his program "lost ground" in *reading comprehension* to more advanced children in grade 3 (Becker, 1977). "Losing ground" didn't mean becoming less competent, but merely that the children didn't gain competence as fast as "average" children. Becker stressed that as a group these same children did continue to achieve as well as more advantaged children in math. He took this as evidence that the children were capable of learning when taught. He argued that the children's slow progress in reading comprehension reflected a solvable problem of lack of vocabulary, rather than an issue of underlying ability.[18]

When he examined the reading comprehension test used (the Metropolitan Achievement Test), Becker realized that it and other standardized reading comprehension tests showed a marked increase in vocabulary demands starting around third grade. He realized that traditional school basal readers restricted vocabulary to a few hundred words in grade 1 and an additional thousand or less in grade 2. This was done to keep the print word identification load manageable, and to avoid confronting children with new vocabulary while they were acquiring and consolidating print skills (sight-word identification, phonics, use of printed punctuation). However, when a great deal of the language children encounter in school activities was restricted to items normally found in the oral vocabulary of most six-year-old children (e.g., the Dolch list and the

---

[18] It is important to note that the children who participated in the DISTAR program continued to outperform control children from similar backgrounds. As noted in Adams (1990), they had lower dropout rates, higher percentages of high school graduations, and higher percentages of acceptances to college (Gersten & Keating, 1987).

most common 1000 words), there was little opportunity to expand vocabulary and language skills. *This meant that the main source of language growth continued to be the home (and peers) until well into middle elementary school.* Unfortunately, this also meant that "disadvantaged" children *continued* to have restricted language learning opportunities as their education proceeded.

Becker concluded that disadvantaged children probably needed more direct attention to their language and vocabulary if they were to have a chance at keeping up with their more advantaged peers. I should add that the same is true for children whose first language is not English.

Is there other research to support Becker's contention that disadvantaged children who *can read* show achievement deficits after grade 2? Unfortunately, yes. Jeanne Chall and her colleagues, Vicki Jacobs and Luke Baldwin, similarly found that working class children with strong word identification skills progressively lost ground from second to seventh grade; their vocabulary and reading comprehension scores — above grade level in grades 2 and 3 — were well behind grade level by grade 7. Vocabulary gaps appeared first (in fourth grade), then word recognition (in grade 6), and finally, reading comprehension (noticeably, in grade 7) (Chall, Jacobs, & Baldwin, 1991).

Why were the children in Chall's study "above grade level" (as a group) in grade 2, but below grade level by grade 7? As Becker noted, in grade 2, the vocabulary demands of *reading* comprehension tests are relatively low, largely because most children's skills for identifying words in print are not strong in grade 2. Chall's children had had a good reading program and were somewhat above average in reading skills at the end of grade 2. However, by grade 7 a much larger proportion of children have mastered word identification skills. Variation in the vocabulary and comprehension tests at this grade level reflect differences in the range of words *understood* rather than the range of words that can be *read*. Note, however, that words that can't be read still won't be understood in print.

The Limited Effects of Schooling on Vocabulary Development

Maria Cantalini (1987) found direct evidence that schooling in kindergarten and grades 1 and 2 has no impact on vocabulary growth. Her study of school "readiness" contrasted January- or February-born children (the oldest children in Ontario classrooms) with November- and December-born children (the youngest). In this research design, "young" first-grade children were about the same age as "old" kindergarten children but had an additional year of schooling. The same contrast was made for "young" second-grade children and "old" first-graders.

Cantalini assessed their vocabulary (Peabody Picture Vocabulary Test), and reading and mathematics achievement (WRAT). She found that there was *no* difference between the old kindergarten and young first-graders in vocabulary, nor between the old first-graders and young second-graders. Observed vocabulary differences between the "young" and "old" groups were entirely due to *age*, not school experience. She also found that "young" first-grade children made, on average, *half* the progress in reading as "old" first-grade children. The same was true in grade 2.

This study took place in a mixed rural-urban school district with traditional kindergarten and primary programs. This meant a combination of free or center-based play and a relatively small amount (30–40 minutes) of teacher-directed whole class activities in kindergarten. The primary programs involved traditional basal reading instruction. Like most North American kindergarten and primary programs, the programs Cantalini studied had *no* small-group activities that were primarily concerned with building listening vocabulary and comprehension rather than building reading (word identification) skills.

Frederick Morrison and his colleagues, Megan Williams and Greta Massetti, have reported virtually identical findings for vocabulary in studies conducted in North Carolina (1998). Again, the average vocabularies of "young" first-graders were about the same size as those of "old" kindergarten children at the end of the school year.

Cantalini's and Morrison's findings are not evidence that kindergarten and early elementary programs *can't* help children expand their language. The point is simply that many programs *don't* promote language growth — as both Becker and Chall found. We will look at programs that *do* promote language development in kindergarten and later grades in the next two chapters.

Levels of Language Challenge in the Upper Elementary Grades

Jeanne Chall and Sue Conard (1991) examined levels of vocabulary demand ("readability") in "reading" and "content area" (social studies, science) texts in elementary and high schools. They found vocabulary demands *lower* in "reading texts" than in the content area books. *They also found that well under half of "average" fourth- and sixth-grade students (as determined by a standardized achieve-*

ment test) were able to comprehend "grade level" science and social studies texts. The few "below average" students in their sample were at an even greater disadvantage. In short, the vocabulary "challenge" was above what many students could handle. At the same time, *reading* texts were found to be well below student abilities. Chall and Conard recommended reversing this pattern — challenging and extending students' language in their reading or language arts instruction, while making an effort to ensure that students can understand texts from which they are expected to learn subject content. Although not stated explicitly, it is also clear that students at markedly different levels of reading comprehension will require different texts unless the less advanced students receive substantial vocabulary assistance while reading.

Acquiring Vocabulary "From Context"

Many reading theorists acknowledge that children bring large vocabulary differences to school, and that primary programs do little to redress such differences (e.g., Anderson, 1996; Nagy & Herman, 1987) These theorists argue that with adequate reading skills (word identification), children will be able to acquire larger vocabularies through reading widely. This assumes that children will expand their vocabularies as a result of reading many books — in other words, that children will learn new words "from context."

Is there evidence to support the assumptions that children with limited vocabularies can improve this situation by reading widely, and that they can learn new words "from context" without having definitions supplied? As is often the case in education, the answer is "yes and no." The strongest evidence *for* acquiring large English vocabularies is the successful performance of some children who enter school speaking no English but proceed to do well academically. This is especially true for children who enter an English-speaking school by the beginning of first grade (Wright, Kane, & Deosaran, 1976), and for children whose parents place a high value on educational achievement. However, the available data suggests that many children who enter school from non-English-speaking families continue to lag behind English-speaking children in vocabulary (Biemiller, 1998; Valdes, 1998).

Evidence about adding new vocabulary items. Only a few studies have examined the learning of new lexical items "from context," that is, without formal instruction. One of the earliest was Werner and Kaplan's famous monograph (1952). They would provide a sentence including a pseudoword that represented an unfamiliar concept. For example, "A corplum may be used for support.") They would ask what a child thought *corplum* meant. Then they would supply another sentence ("Corplums may be used to close off an open space,") and so on through five sentences.

Werner and Kaplan carried out this procedure with children in grades 3 to 7. Even after having heard all five sentences, only 7% of third-grade children could arrive at the meaning Werner and Kaplan had intended. By grade 7, less than half did so. (For Werner and Kaplan, "corplum" was a stick or piece of wood.) Clearly, even younger children would have great difficulty acquiring truly *new* words (with new referents) by this means. Elshout-Mohr and van Daalen-Kapteijns (1987) report similar results with college students. Results were especially poor for "less verbally able" college students. New "words" were rarely understood completely, and "low verbal ability" college students were entirely unable to infer correct meanings for them.

Carol Fraser (in press) studied English word acquisition by eight French-speaking college students who were studying English. She had them read a complex passage in economics. They reported using several strategies to cope with unknown words — seeking assistance, consciously trying to infer word meanings, and simply skipping a word. Overall, about a quarter of "new words" (as identified by the students) were retained. Fraser's findings suggest that a combination of inference and checking inferences with an English speaker was most effective (leading to 50% retention), while checking with others or inferring alone were less effective, and of course "ignoring" was ineffective. Bear in mind that these findings refer to college students who were specifically trained to infer words.

William Nagy, Patricia Herman, and Richard Anderson (1985) did find some slight evidence of word learning from context. They had eighth-grade children ("average and above-average readers") read one of two 1000-word passages. Fourteen difficult words were identified for each passage (e.g., *envision, levee*). Students knew about half of these words without reading the passages. After reading a passage, they showed an average gain of about *one* word! They were more likely to acquire words which occurred several times in a passage than those which occurred only once. *Below average* readers, who most need to acquire larger vocabularies, were not included in the study.

Other studies (which will be described in Chapter Four) have indicated somewhat higher rates of vocabulary acquisition from *unassisted* inference. For example, Warwick Elley (1989) reports that an average of three words might be acquired from listening to a story three times during a week. (The Nagy, Herman, and Anderson study provided a single 20-minute period to read a thousand-word passage — allowing for it to be read two or three times, but not requiring that this be done.) Perhaps students can only infer meaning for one unfamiliar word while reading a story or other text. Elley's finding involved three readings. We do not know if more contextual experiences (e.g., reading or listening to thousands of words in a week or several stories) could lead to acquiring more new words.

It should be noted that in the Nagy and Anderson study, there were relatively few difficult words in proportion to the total text. In general, it seems probable that when there are more unfamiliar words in a passage, it becomes harder to learn new words. I assume that "learning from context" implies an understanding of that context. As the proportion of unfamiliar words increases, understanding declines (Freebody & Anderson, 1983; Marks, Doctorow, & Wittrock, 1974). As we have seen, some studies indicate that less "verbally able" students do very poorly at inferring meanings of unknown words (e.g., Elshout-Mohr & van Daalen-Kapteijns, 1987; Robbins & Ehri, 1994; Werner and Kaplan, 1952). This may reflect the consequences of starting with a smaller vocabulary — so that whatever passage is used for "context" contains *more* unfamiliar words for "less able" or lower vocabulary students than for others. Such students may also have some constitutional difficulty which makes word-learning more difficult. It is likely that the two conditions exacerbate each other.

Contextual Vocabulary Acquisition: Evidence from Miscue Studies. Additional evidence on the effect of passage difficulty on student ability to comprehend and to acquire new vocabulary comes from studies of reading "miscues" or oral reading errors. The study of oral reading errors or "miscues" has been a useful way to examine the role of context and meaning in the reading process (Allington, 1984; Biemiller, 1994; Goodman, 1973). A number of studies have consistently shown that children make proportionately fewer "contextual" miscues[19] — errors that reflect attention to the *meaning* of the passage — when their overall error rate is over 4–5% (A. Adams, 1991; Biemiller, 1979, 1994; Blaxall & Willows, 1984) This suggests that when error rates exceed 4–5% of running words, the "understanding" of the text is sufficiently disrupted so that readers are no longer able to use context to facilitate word identification. It seems probable that lack of knowledge of more than 4–5% of running words would

---

[19] "Contextual errors" are errors that are syntactically and semantically consistent with the prior context of the passage being read.

similarly make inferring word meanings unlikely.

Cumulative Vocabulary Deficits. Children who enter third or fourth grade with restricted vocabularies relative to the texts being used will have greater difficulty in comprehending these reading materials and greater difficulty in adding to their vocabulary through reading. This leads to what I call a *cumulative vocabulary deficit* — restricted vocabulary makes it harder to add new vocabulary and probably leads to reduced amounts of reading. Reduced reading in turn continues to restrict vocabulary development. This is what Keith Stanovich (1986) called a "Matthew Effect" in reading — better readers read more and continue to improve both their vocabulary and print skills, while poor readers read less and make little progress.

Summary. I agree with the overall conclusion of Beck & McKeown (1991) that "learning from context does not come easily or in large quantities" (p. 801). They provide a useful summary:

> From the research that has been done, what can be concluded about the role of printed context in accounting for vocabulary growth during the school years? The ubiquitous finding that learning word meanings from context does not seem to occur with particular ease suggests three possible explanations to account for vocabulary growth: One is that learners encounter such a huge number of contextual word-learning opportunities that impressive growth is possible even when the effect of each opportunity is minute. A second explanation is that oral contexts continue to play a major role in vocabulary learning throughout the school years. A third explanation is that vocabulary size and growth have been substantially overestimated. Because available data do not allow selecting with confidence among these three explanations, there seems to be a clear need for research that will clarify the issues. Research is needed that will give some insight into the contribution of oral context to vocabulary growth. Also needed are large-scale studies of vocabulary size that correct for the problems of earlier research in that area. (p. 803)

I will add to their conclusion the general hypothesis that we learn most of our *root* words when we encounter them in context (spoken or print) and *ask* for word meanings — usually asking a teacher or a friend, sometimes "asking" a dictionary. In addition, a number of words are taught by teachers without students asking for them, or are explicitly defined in books. Less frequently, we intentionally infer the meaning of unfamiliar words. I suspect that only rarely do we acquire root word meanings "incidentally" — without conscious effort. (The acquisition of derived word meanings may well occur through context, if there is a learning process required.[20] At present, there seems to be no research examining children's and adolescent's actual word acquisition practices.[21]

Other Sources of Vocabulary Acquisition

"Structural" or Morphological Analysis. Jeremy Anglin's (1993) study of vocabulary development suggests that for about 40–50% of words known by children, there was direct evidence that they worked out meanings by overtly combining prefixes and suffixes (e.g., *un-, -able*) with known root words or by analyzing compound words into their components. In the upper elementary grades, instruction in vocabulary strategies of this type is often referred to as "structural analysis." Children are made aware of the role of prefixes, suffixes, etc. in constructing and determining word meaning. They are typically also taught basic dictionary skills (alphabetizing, using dictionary definitions, using pronunciation guides), though not often given much opportunity to consolidate such skills through extended practice (Durkin, 1979). White, Power, and White (1989) provide an excellent analysis of the power of structural analysis (or "morphological" analysis, as they and Anglin call it). White et al. also provide much information on widely used prefixes and suffixes. Unfortunately, there is no major study directly examining the consequences of extended instruction in using word-learning strategies (Graves, in press). However, in view of Anglin's evidence that children commonly use such word-learning strategies, it seems reasonable to include instruction of these in an effective language program. In Chapter Five, I will describe one successful experimental effort to teach children to use prefixes to identify words. I recommend readers to Graves, Juel, and Graves's (1998) chapter on vocabulary development, and especially the sections on "using word parts" and "using the dictionary."

The Role of Controlled-Vocabulary Readers or "Basals." In some states and provinces, most primary and some upper elementary children read "basal" readers. By definition, a basal reader series adds vocabulary at a planned rate and

---

[20] I suspect that with many derived words (e.g., *unhappy* as opposed to *happy*), there may be no intentional word learning — the word is understood just as a plural or past tense is understood without an elaborate semantic process.

[21] My colleagues and I are presently engaged in research on how children and adolescents learn new words.

level, and ensures frequent use of a word once introduced. In the primary years, this keeps the print word identification load manageable. For older children (grades 3 to 6), this ensures coverage of a specifiable vocabulary. Unfortunately, vocabulary loads are often kept fairly low in basal readers (Chall, 1983; Chall & Conard, 1991; Bond & Dykstra, 1967/1997). Thus while the basal model provides a potential curriculum approach to building vocabulary, in practice the basal method has led to overly low levels of vocabulary being introduced (Chall & Conard, 1991). Worse, the same books are often used with all children, ensuring vocabulary overload for some and lack of challenge for others. No effort is made to assess vocabulary or comprehension levels of children relative to the textbooks being used.

In many other states and provinces, an emphasis on "whole language," "novel study," etc. has led to a de-emphasis or abolition of basal readers, replacing them with "trade books" — books written for children and for parents to read to children, or children's literature. Such books are generally written with less concern for using or introducing a specific vocabulary, and usually do not involve deliberate sequences of increasing vocabulary load. For children with above-average vocabularies and above-average reading (word identification) skills, challenging trade books and novels may well be superior to vocabulary-controlled basal readers because they offer a wide vocabulary and sometimes a higher level of narrative or expository complexity. However, for children with below average vocabulary *or* reading skills, the use of trade books may *reduce* the opportunity to build vocabulary and language skills.

For example, a study of the effects of "whole language" instruction on third-graders in a Canadian school district found an overrepresentation of children performing *below* the 25th percentile on standardized tests (Glasspool & Hutton, 1993). The same study also showed an overrepresentation of children *above* the 75th percentile, suggesting that for those whose reading (word identification skills) and vocabulary levels were *high*, the shift to trade books was advantageous.

An important issue centers around the relative effectiveness of using basals which deliberately introduce and repeat new vocabulary, versus the currently-popular approach of having children repeatedly reading the same story as a means of building vocabulary and comprehension. We will revisit this issue in the next chapter.

Conclusion

Schools now provide little or no alternative language support in the primary years to compensate for differences in experience before age five. In the upper elementary years, some direct language and vocabulary instruction is provided, but the rapidly increasing language demands of texts are greater than many students can handle successfully.

When we allow children to arrive at third or fourth grade unprepared for the vocabulary and other language demands of post-primary schooling, we reduce their chances for further educational progress even if they have become effective "readers" at the level of identifying words in print. For children who arrive at fourth grade with significantly below-average vocabularies and language skills, understanding "fourth grade texts" is rather like trying to climb a cliff at the base of a hill. If one has the requisite language, one is already at the top of the cliff and can continue to go up the educational hill. But those missing the necessary language (mostly vocabulary) are at the bottom of the cliff. They try to scramble up while others continue to extend their knowledge.

Schooling cannot "compensate" for *all* constitutional and experiential differences. But surely we can do better than the zero school effect on vocabulary growth observed in two studies described here. There is evidence that language can be substantially affected by experiences in which children are exposed to a wider range of meaningful vocabulary and the meanings of unfamiliar words are explained.

References

Adams, A. (1991). The oral reading errors of readers with learning disabilities: Variations produced within the instructional and frustrational ranges. *Remedial and Special Education, 12*(1), 48–55.

Allington, R. (1984). Oral reading. In P. D. Pearson (Ed.), *Handbook of Reading Research* (Vol. 1, pp. 829–864). New York: Longman.

Anderson, R. C. (1996). Research foundations to support wide reading. In V. Greanery (Ed.), *Promoting reading in developing countries*. Wilmington, DE: International Reading Association.

Anglin, J. M. (1993). Vocabulary development: A morphological analysis. *Monographs of the Society for Research in Child Development*, Serial No. 238, *58*.

Beck, I., & McKeown, M. (1990). Conditions of vocabulary acquisition. In R. Barr, M. I. Kamil, P. B. Mosenthal, & P. D. Pearson, (Eds.), *Handbook of Reading Research,* Vol. 2 (pp. 789–814). New York: Longman.

Becker, W. C. (1977). Teaching reading and language to the disadvantaged: What we have learned from field research. *Harvard Educational Review, 47*, 518–543.

Biemiller, A. (1979). Changes in the use of graphic and contextual information as functions of passage difficulty and reading achievement level. *Journal of Reading Behavior, 11*, 307–318.

Biemiller, A. (1994) Some observations on beginning reading instruction. *Educational Psychologist, 29*(4), 203–209.

Biemiller, A. (1998, April). *Oral vocabulary, word identification, and reading comprehension in English second language and English first language elementary school children.* Paper presented at the annual meeting of the Society for the Scientific Study of Reading, San Diego, CA.

Blaxall, J., & Willows, D. M. (1984). Reading ability and text difficulty as influences on second graders' oral reading errors. *Journal of Educational Psychology, 76,* 330–341.

Bond, G. L., & Dkystra, R. (1967/1997). The cooperative research program in first-grade reading instruction. *Reading Research Quarterly, 32,* 345–427. (Reprint of the original article which appeared in 1967)

Cantalini, M. (1987). *The effects of age and gender on school readiness and school success.* Unpublished doctoral dissertation. Toronto, Canada: Ontario Institute for Studies in Education.

Chall, J. S. (1967/1983). *Learning to read: The great debate.* New York: McGraw-Hill.

Chall, J. S., & Conard, S. S., (1991). *Should textbooks challenge students?* New York; Teachers College Press.

Chall, J. S., Jacobs, V. A., & Baldwin, L. E. (1990). *The reading crisis: Why poor children fall behind.* Cambridge, MA: Harvard University Press.

Durkin, D. (1979). What classroom observations reveal about reading comprehension. *Reading Research Quarterly, 14,* 518–544

Elley, W. B. (1989). Vocabulary acquisition from listening to stories. *Reading Research Quarterly, 24,* 174–186.

Elshout-Mohr, M., & van Daalen-Kapteijns, M. M. (1987). Cognitive processes in learning word meanings. In M. G. McKeown & M. E. Curtis (Eds.), *The nature of vocabulary acquisition* (pp. 53–72). Hillsdale, NJ: Erlbaum.

Fraser, C. (in press). Lexical processing strategy use and vocabulary learning through reading. *Studies in Second Language Acquisition.* (to appear in the June, 1999 issue)

Freebody, P., & Anderson, R. C. (1983). Effects of vocabulary difficulty, text cohesion, and schema availability on reading comprehension. *Reading Research Quarterly, 18,* 277–294.

Glasspool, J., & Hutton, G. (1993, August). *Enhancing reading instruction for young boys.* Paper presented at a symposium on Whole Language Instruction at the annual convention of the American Psychological Association, Toronto, Canada.

Goodman, K. S. (1973). Miscues: Windows on the reading process. In K. S., Goodman (Ed.), *Miscue analysis: Application to reading instruction.* Champaign-Urbana, IL: ERIC Clearinghouse of Reading and Communication, N.C.T.E.

Graves, M. F., Juel, C., & Graves, B. B. (1998). *Teaching reading in the 21st century.* Boston, MA: Allyn & Bacon.

Graves, M. F. (in press). A vocabulary program to complement and bolster a middle-grade comprehension program. In B. M. Taylor, P. van den Broek, & M. F. Graves (Eds.), *Reading for meaning: Fostering comprehension in the middle grades.* New York: Teachers College Press.

Marks, C. B., Doctorow, M. J., & Wittrock, M. C. (1974). Word frequency and reading comprehension. *Journal of Educational Research, 67,* 259–262.

Morrison, F. J., Williams, M. A., & Massetti, G. M. (1998, April). *The contributions of IQ and schooling to academic achievement.* Paper presented at the Annual Meeting of the Society for the Scientific Study of Reading, San Diego, CA.

Nagy, W. E., Herman, P. A., & Anderson, R. C. (1985). Learning words from context. *Reading Research Quarterly, 20,* 233–253.

Nagy, W. E., & Herman, P. A. (1987). Breadth and depth of vocabulary knowledge: Implications for acquisition and instruction. In M. G. McKeown & M. E. Curtis (Eds.), *The nature of vocabulary acquisition* (pp. 19–36). Hillsdale, NJ: Erlbaum.

Robbins, C., & Ehri, L. C. (1994). Reading storybooks to kindergartners helps them learn new vocabulary words. *Journal of Educational Psychology, 86,* 54–64.

Stanovich, K. E. (1986). Matthew effects in reading: Some implications of individual differences in the acquisition of literacy. *Reading Research Quarterly, 21,* 360–406.

Valdes, G. (1998). The world outside and inside schools: Language and immigrant children. *Educational Researcher, 27,* 4–18.

Werner, H., & Kaplan, B. (1952). The acquisition of word meanings: A developmental study. *Monographs of the Society for Research in Child Development, 15,* (Serial No. 51, No. 1).

White, T. G., Power, M. A., & White, S. (1989). Morphological analysis: Implications for teaching and understanding vocabulary growth. *Reading Research Quarterly, 24,* 283–304.

Wright, E. N., Kane, T., & Deosaran (1976). *Every student survey: Students' background and its relation to program placement.* Toronto, ON: Toronto Board of Education, Report # 36.

Teaching Vocabulary to Improve Reading Comprehension

by William E. Nagy

Introduction

Vocabulary knowledge is fundamental to reading comprehension; one cannot understand text without knowing what most of the words mean. A wealth of research has documented the strength of the relationship between vocabulary and comprehension. The proportion of difficult words in a text is the single most powerful predictor of text difficulty, and a reader's general vocabulary knowledge is the single best predictor of how well that reader can understand text (Anderson and Freebody 1981).

Increasing vocabulary knowledge is a basic part of the process of education, both as a means and as an end. Lack of adequate vocabulary knowledge is already an obvious and serious obstacle for many students, and their numbers can be expected to rise as an increasing proportion of them fall into categories considered educationally at risk. At the same time, advances in knowledge will create an ever-larger pool of concepts and words that a person must master to be literate and employable.

Reasons for Failure of Vocabulary Instruction

Why does much vocabulary instruction often fail to increase comprehension measurably? There are two basic ways to account for this failure.

From *Teaching Vocabulary to Improve Reading Comprehension*, 1988, International Reading Association

The first is that most vocabulary instruction fails to produce in-depth word knowledge. A number of studies indicate that reading comprehension requires a high level of word knowledge—higher than the level achieved by many types of vocabulary instruction. Only those methods that go beyond providing partial knowledge, producing in-depth knowledge of the words taught, will reliably increase readers' comprehension of texts containing those words. The implication is that teachers should augment traditional methods of instruction such as memorizing definitions with more intensive instruction aimed at producing richer, deeper word knowledge.

A second reason for the failure of vocabulary instruction to improve reading comprehension measurably relates to the comprehensibility of texts containing some unfamiliar words. One does not need to know every word in a text to understand it. In one study, the researchers found that one content word in six could be replaced by a more difficult synonym without significantly decreasing comprehension (Freebody and Anderson 1983).

Hence, *redundancy of text* explains the failure of vocabulary instruction to improve comprehension. If a certain proportion of unfamiliar words in the text does not measurably hinder comprehension, then instruction on these words would not measurably improve it. In fact, inferring the meanings of unfamiliar words in text is itself a major avenue of vocabulary growth (Nagy, Anderson, and Herman 1987; Nagy, Herman, and Anderson 1985). By implication, what is needed to produce vocabulary growth is not more vocabulary instruction, but more reading.

These two accounts of the failure of some vocabulary instruction to improve comprehension appear to have almost contradictory implications for instruction. Yet the two are not mutually exclusive; they give complementary perspectives on the complex relationship between vocabulary knowledge and reading comprehension.

Partial Word Knowledge

The first reason given that vocabulary instruction often fails to produce measurable gains in reading comprehension is that much instruction does not produce a sufficient depth of word knowledge. There are degrees of word knowledge, ranging from "I think I've seen that word before" to "That's what I did my dissertation on." But what depth of word knowledge should teachers try to impart to their students? How well do readers have to know words to benefit from them in their reading?

This question can be answered in part by looking at studies that have tried to increase reading comprehension through vocabulary instruction. The level of word knowledge required for comprehension is shown by the types of vocabulary instruction that succeed or fail to produce gains in comprehension.

From the published research on vocabulary instruction, we can piece together a fairly consistent picture of the effectiveness of different types of instruction in increasing reading comprehension. In synthesizing this research, I will draw most heavily on McKeown et al. (1985), Mezynski (1983), Pearson and Gallagher (1983), and Stahl and Fairbanks (1986). Several valuable articles on this topic can also be found in the April 1986 *Journal of Reading*, a special issue devoted to vocabulary instruction.

Problems of Traditional Methods of Vocabulary Instruction

Much vocabulary instruction involves the use of definitions—some combination of looking them up, writing them down, and memorizing them. Another commonly used method involves inferring the meaning of a new word from the context. Neither method taken by itself, however, is an especially effective way to improve reading comprehension.

Definitional Approaches

Traditionally, much vocabulary instruction has involved some variety of a definitional approach: students learn definitions or synonyms for instructed words. There are obviously better and worse versions of this approach, and one should not conclude that definitions are not useful in vocabulary instruction. But definitions alone can lead to only a relatively superficial level of word knowledge. By itself, looking up words in a dictionary or memorizing definitions does not reliably improve reading comprehension.

The first problem with definitional methods of instruction is that many definitions simply are not very good. Here is a definition from a well-written school dictionary (*American Heritage School Dictionary* 1977):

> **mirror:** any surface that is capable of reflecting enough light without scattering it so that it shows an image of any object placed in front of it

This definition may be accurate, but it is hard to imagine that anyone who does not already know the meaning of the word could be helped by the definition. Most of the content words in the definition are less likely to be familiar to the student then the word *mirror* itself.

Here are some other definitions taken from the glossary of a basal reader:

> **siphon:** to pull water from one place to another
>
> **migration:** moving from one place to another
>
> **image:** likeness
>
> **baleen:** substance like horn that grows in plates in a whale's mouth and that is used to filter food from the water

These definitions are simply not accurate, at least not for the readers who need to use them. Note, for example, that *likeness* is relatively rare, occurring less than twice in a million words of text, whereas *image*, the word it is used to define, is far more frequent, occurring twenty-three times per million words of text (Carroll, Davies, and Richman 1971). *Likeness* is also one of the few English words ending in *–ness* that is semantically irregular. As for the definition of *baleen*, the words *horn* and *plates* may be frequent enough, but they are being used with meanings that are probably not at all familiar to students.

Definitions given in glossaries are also not always appropriate to the selection being read. In one basal reader, for example, *tragic* is defined in the glossary as very sad. The word *tragic* occurs in one selection in the following context (spoken by a blind boy walking through Pompeii): "Too bad! The tragic poet is ill again. It must be a bad fever this time, for they're trying smoke fumes instead of medicine. I'm glad I'm not a tragic poet."

Even when definitions are accurate, they do not always contain enough information to allow a person to use the word correctly. This is especially true of definitions for words for concepts with which the learner is unfamiliar. Shefelbine (1984) and others have used the following activity to communicate this point to teachers. Take some definitions of words that represent truly unfamiliar concepts—such as those in the list below—and try to do what students are often asked to do: "For each word, write a sentence in which it is used correctly." I suggest that readers actually take the time to try this activity, to experience the full force of the point: Definitions do not teach you how to *use* a new word. The definitions that follow appear in *Webster's Third New International Dictionary* (1961):

epiphenomenal: having the character of or relating to an epiphenomenon

epiphenomenon: a phenomenon that occurs with and seems to result from another

etaoin shrdlu: a combination of letters set by running a finger down the first and then the second left–hand vertical banks of six keys of a linotype machine to produce a temporary marking slug not intended to appear in the final printing

kern: to form or set (as a crop of fruit)

khalal: of, relating to, or constituting the second of four recognized stages in the ripening of a date in which it reaches its full size and changes from green to red or yellow or a combination of the two colors

squinch: a support (as an arch, lintel, or corbeling) carried across the corner of a room under a superimposed mass (as an octagonal spire or drum resting upon a square tower)

stative: expressing a bodily or mental state

stirp: the sum of the determinants of whatever nature in a fertilized egg

There are two reasons why it is difficult to write meaningful sentences, given only a definition. One is that definitions alone tell little about how a word is actually used. This problem is especially acute for children, who are less able than adults to use information that is available in definitions (Miller and Gildea 1987).

Another reason that it is difficult to write a sentence for a truly unfamiliar word, given only the definition, is that definitions do not effectively convey new concepts. One can think of it this way: Why isn't a glossary of biological terms an adequate substitute for a biology textbook? The answer in part is that important information about biological concepts and their interrelations simply does not fit into definitions.

This brings us to perhaps the most basic reason that knowledge of definitions is not adequate to guarantee comprehension of text containing the words defined: reading comprehension depends on a wealth of encyclopedic knowledge and not merely on definitional knowledge of the words in the text.

Take, for example, a narrative in which a bat is seen flying around. Definitional features of *bat*—the fact that bats are mammals rather than birds—may well be totally irrelevant in comprehending the text. Understanding the text may depend more on a knowledge of bats, or a knowledge of folklore about bats, that would not necessarily be included in a definition.

The point is not that definitions are never to be used in vocabulary instruction; on the contrary, they will play an essential role in most vocabulary instruction. But definitions as an instructional device have substancial weaknesses and limitations that must be recognized and corrected. How this can be done will become clearer from the discussion of intensive approaches to vocabulary instruction.

Contextual Approaches

Another common approach to teaching vocabulary is the use of context. A teacher might write a sentence or two containing the word to be learned on the board and ask students to figure out what the word means. There is no question that learning from context is an important avenue of vocabulary growth and that it deserves attention and practice in the classroom. But context, used as an instructional method by itself, is ineffective as a means of teaching new meanings, at least when compared with other forms of vocabulary instruction.

The problem is that, for the most part, a context may look quite helpful if one already knows what the word means, but it seldom supplies adequate information for the person who has no other knowledge about the meaning of a word. Consider the following sentence used to illustrate context clues involving contrast: "Although Mary was very thin, her sister was obese." Contrast is clearly involved, but the exact nature of the contrast is clear only to someone who already knows the meaning of *obese*. The problem becomes

obvious when one attempts to substitute other words for the word whose meaning is supposed to be inferred. There is no reason, for example, for a word in this position to refer to an extreme value on the scale; an author could easily have used the word *normal* in this contest. Given only this sentence context, one can think of other words that relate to other possible implicit contrasts— for example, *charitable* (in her description of Mary), or *unconcerned* (about her health). Nor is there any reason to restrict guesses about the meaning of a new word to synonyms; meanings can be expressed by phrases, such as "not jealous," that would fit in this context.

Note that this example involves the use of contrast, a relatively informative type of context clue. In most cases, what appears to be a fairly informative context would allow an even wider range of possible substitutions.

Natural and Instructional Contexts

One motivation for having students try to figure out word meanings from context is to help them develop word-learning strategies to use on their own. Practice in these strategies should definitely be part of an approach to vocabulary building. However, the teacher must face up to the dilemma posed by any attempt to teach such strategies: most contexts in normal text are relatively uninformative. The context around any unfamiliar word tells us something about its meaning, but seldom does any single context give complete information (Deighton 1959; Shatz and Baldwin 1986). More informative contexts can be constructed (see Gipe 1979), but to the extent that they are informative, they are likely to be unnatural and hence defeat the purpose of training students in strategies for inferring word meanings from real texts.

A good context might help a student figure out the meaning of a less familiar synonym for a known word, but a single context is in general not adequate for teaching a new concept. If the goal is to teach students strategies, both teachers and students must accept partial word knowledge, some degree of uncertainty, and occasionally misleading contexts (Beck, McKeown, and McCaslin 1983). If the goal is to get a good grasp on the meaning of a new word, one will have to use highly artificial contexts, multiple contexts, or some other sort of supplemental information.

Combining Definitional and Contextual Approaches

A combination of definitional and contextual approaches is more effective than either approach in isolation; such mixed methods do, in general, increase reading comprehension (Stahl and Fairbanks 1986). Indeed, it would be hard to justify a contextual approach in which the teacher did not finally provide an adequate definition of the word or help the class arrive at one. Likewise, a good definitional approach includes sentences that illustrate the meaning and use of the words defined.

An example can often convey a meaning more vividly than a definition and help students relate what may be a very abstract and general definition to their own experience. For example, according to one school dictionary, the word *expand* in one sense means "to increase in one or more physical dimensions, as length or volume." A simple sentence such as "The balloon expanded as she blew air into it" might be helpful, perhaps even necessary, for the reader to make sense of such a general definition. It should be noted, of course, that it is the combination of definition and context that communicates the meaning effectively. The context alone, for example, "The balloon—as she blew it up," allows many interpretations: grew larger, burst, stretched, became taut, became more transparent, and so on.

Providing a natural context is often essential in teaching students how a word is used. Consider the definition of *cater*, meaning "to act with special consideration." Even if a student somehow grasped the connotations of this sense of the word (which the definition does not adequately convey), the student might produce a sentence such as "The mayor catered when the corporate executives visited the city."

Qualities of Effective Vocabulary Instruction

To be effective, then, vocabulary instruction must provide both adequate definitions and illustrations of how words are used in natural sounding contexts. But does supplying both definitions and contexts guarantee gains in reading comprehension? Not necessarily. It is safe to say that good definitions and contexts are minimal requirements for good instruction, but by no means do they exhaust what can be put into a good vocabulary lesson.

Based on surveys of available research (see Stahl 1986; Graves and Prenn 1986; Carr and Wixson 1986), three properties of vocabulary instruction that are effective in increasing reading comprehension can be identified: integration, repetition, and meaningful use.

Integration

The first property of powerful vocabulary instruction is that it integrates instructed words with other knowledge. This emphasis in instruction is an outgrowth of schema theory. For our purposes here, the essence of schema theory lies in two points: (1) that knowledge is structured—it consists not of lists of independent facts, but of sets of relationships, and (2) that we understand new infor- mation by relating it to what we already know.

Repetition

Repetition in word knowledge is related to what has been called the "verbal efficiency hypothesis" (Perfetti and Lesgold 1979), or the "bottleneck hypothesis." According to this hypothesis, a reader has only limited processing capacity available for tasks that require conscious attention. If the reader can decode well and knows all of the words in the text well, then identifying the words of the text can proceed more or less automatically so that most of the reader's attention can be given to comprehension.

Reading with understanding depends, then, on low-level processes such as decoding and word recognition proceeding smoothly without much conscious attention. Any interruption of the processes that are automatic for skilled readers can diminish comprehension. To take an extreme case, if a reader must struggle to decode the word *hippopotamus*, by the time that word has been recognized the reader may have forgotten what the rest of the sentence is about. Conversely, if this same reader is skillful in decoding, he or she can give more attention to the meaning of the sentence.

According to the verbal efficiency hypothesis, limited knowledge of word meanings can have the same sort of detrimental effect on comprehension that poor decoding skills may have. Being able to identify or produce a correct definition for a word does not guarantee that one will remember its meaning quickly and effortlessly during reading. Vocabulary instruction must therefore ensure not only that readers know what the word means, but also that they have had sufficient practice to make its meaning quickly and easily accessible during reading.

It should be stressed that repetition is necessary and worthwhile, at least for some words. According to available research, many encounters with a new word are necessary if vocabulary instruction is to have a measurable effect on reading comprehension (Stahl and Fairbanks 1986; McKeown et al. 1985).

How does a teacher provide multiple encounters with new words without having instruction become boring? The answer lies in the third property of effective vocabulary instruction, which I have labeled "meaningful use."

Meaningful Use

Effective vocabulary instruction helps the learner to use the instructed words meaningfully. One motivation for this property is simply that students learn more when they are actively involved. Another is what has been called "depth of processing." Simply stated, the more deeply some information is processed, the more likely it is to be remembered. In other words, vocabulary instruction that makes students think about the meaning of a word and demands that they do some meaningful processing of the word will be more effective than instruction that does not. A third motivation for instruction that requires learners to use the word meaningfully is, to put it simply, that you get what you train for. There is a big difference between being able to say what a word means and being able to use it. Knowing the definition of a word is often not enough to use the word properly. Conversely, we use and understand many words quite well without being able to define them. (How many educated adults can formulate a good, noncircular definition of *if*?)

If one's goal is to enable students to parrot definitions, drill on definitions is probably the most appropriate instructional technique. But if students are expected to deal with instructed words in context, the words must be encountered in context during instruction (McKeown et al. 1985). And if students are expected to learn to use words meaningfully in reading or writing, then instruction must include meaningful use of the words. Effective vocabulary instruction requires students to process words meaningfully—that is, make inferences based on their meanings—and includes tasks that are in some ways parallel to normal speaking, reading, and writing.

References

The American Heritage School Dictionary, 1977. Boston: Houghton Mifflin.

Anderson, R. C., and P. Freebody. 1981. Vocabulary knowledge. In *Comprehension and Teaching: Research Reviews*, ed. J. Guthrie, 77–117. Newark, DE: International Reading Association.

Beck, I., M. McKeown, and E. McCaslin. 1983. All contexts are not created equal. *Elementary School Journal* 83:177–81.

Carr, E., and K. Wixson. 1986. Guidelines for evaluating vocabulary instruction. *Journal of Reading* 29: 588–95.

Carroll, J. B., P. Davies, and B. Richman. 1971. *Word Frequency Book*. New York: American Heritage.

Deighton, D. 1959. *Vocabulary development in the classroom*. New York: Bureau of Publications, Teachers College, Columbia University.

Freebody, P., and R. C. Anderson. 1983. Effects on text comprehension of different proportions and locations of difficult vocabulary. *Journal of Reading Behavior* 15: 19–39.

Gipe, J. 1979. Investigating techniques for teaching word meanings. *Reading Research Quarterly* 22: 263–84.

Graves, M., and M. Prenn. 1986. Costs and benefits of various methods of teaching vocabulary. *Journal of Reading* 29: 596–602.

McKeown, M., I. Beck, R. Omanson, and M. Pople. 1985. Some effects of the nature and frequency of vocabulary instruction on the knowledge and use of words. *Reading Research Quarterly* 20: 222–35.

Mezynski, K. 1983. Issues concerning the acquisition of knowledge: Effects of vocabulary training on reading comprehension. *Review of Educational Research* 53: 253–79.

Miller, G., and P. Gildea. 1987. How children learn words. *Scientific American* 257(3): 94–99.

Nagy, W., R. C. Anderson, and P. Herman. 1987. Learning word meanings from context during normal reading. *American Educational Research Journal* 24: 237–70.

Nagy, W., P. Herman, and R. C. Anderson. 1985. Learning words from context. *Reading Research Quarterly* 20: 233–53.

Pearson, P. D., and M. Gallagher. 1983. The instruction of reading comprehension. *Contemporary Educational Psychology* 8: 317–44.

Perfetti, C., and A. Lesgold. 1979. Coding and comprehension in skilled reading and implications for reading instruction. In *Theory and Practice of Early Reading* (Vol. 1), ed. L. B. Resnick and P. Weaver. Hillsdale, N.J.: Erlbaum.

Schatz, E. K., and R. S. Baldwin. 1986. Context clues are unreliable predictors of word meanings. *Reading Research Quarterly* 21: 429–53.

Shefelbine, J. L. 1984. *Teachers' decisions about the utility of dictionary tasks and the role of prior knowledge*. Paper presented at the annual meeting of the National Reading Conference, St. Petersburg, FL.

Stahl, S. 1986. Three principles of effective vocabulary instruction. *Journal of Reading* 29: 662–68.

Stahl, S., and M. Fairbanks. 1986. The effects of vocabulary instruction: A model-based meta-analysis. *Review of Educational Research* 56: 72–110.

Webster's Third New International Dictionary of the English Language, Unabridged. 1961. Springfield, MA: G. & C. Merriam.

Reading Storybooks to Kindergartners Helps Them Learn New Vocabulary Words

by Claudia Robbins and Linnea C. Ehri

In sessions conducted individually, kindergartners who were nonreaders listened to an adult read the same storybook twice, 2–4 days apart, and then completed a posttest measuring their knowledge of the meanings of 22 unfamiliar words, half of which had appeared in the story. Some target words occurred twice in the story and some only once, so children heard some words four times and some words twice. Children recognized the meanings of significantly more words from the story than words not in the story, thus indicating that storybook reading was effective for building vocabulary. Gains were greater among children with larger entering vocabularies. Four exposures to words appeared to be necessary but not sufficient for higher rates of word learning. Findings confirm that story listening contributes modestly to young children's vocabulary growth.

The vocabulary growth occurring in elementary school children is substantial and significant and has received attention from a number of researchers (Anderson & Freebody, 1981; Beck, Perfetti, & McKeown, 1982; Becker, 1977; Calfee & Drum, 1986; Chall, 1987; Graves, 1986; McKeown & Curtis, 1987). Estimates of both average vocabulary size and yearly growth vary considerably (Dale, 1965; Joss, 1964; Lorge & Chall, 1963; Nagy & Anderson, 1984; Rinsland, 1945; M. E. Smith, 1926; M. K. Smith, 1941;

From *Journal of Educational Psychology*, 1994, Vol. 86, pp. 54–64

Templin, 1957). However, all studies show that children continue to acquire new words beyond the initial language acquisition years and that children's vocabularies grow by thousands of words each year during the elementary school years. Moreover, vocabulary size is strongly correlated with children's overall school achievement (Wells, 1986). Because vocabulary plays an important role in both communication effectiveness and academic success, it is important to understand how young children achieve their vocabulary growth.

According to Werner and Kaplan (1950a, 1950b), children learn the meanings of words under two conditions: (a) through direct and explicit reference by adults when they name objects or define words and (b) through incidental encounters with words in verbal contexts. Incidental encounters include hearing words in conversations, on television, and in stories. In these situations, word meanings may not be expressed or accessible. Therefore, children who encounter new words incidentally must use indirect contextual and implicit information to discern meanings.

Sternberg (1987) and Sternberg and Powell (1983) delineated factors that affect the learning of new words from incidental encounters in verbal contexts. Learning from context is influenced by the number of occurrences of the unknown word, the concreteness of the word, the helpfulness of the surrounding context, and the importance of the unknown word for understanding the surrounding context. It is also influenced by individual differences in the abilities to separate relevant information from irrelevant information; to combine selected information to form a cohesive, plausible whole; and to relate new information to previous knowledge. Thus, both the specific contexts of words and individual abilities are thought to contribute to the incidental learning of new words.

Before the age of 2 years, children seem to learn new words more easily from social interaction and direct references than from indirect sources. Vocabulary growth before age 2 years is positively correlated with social interactions but not with television viewing (Nelson, 1973). In contrast, children aged 3–5 years can acquire new words from television (Rice & Woodsmall, 1988; Sachs & Johnson, 1976). Thus, by the time children enter elementary school, they can effectively use both direct and indirect references to learn new words.

There are various ways that school children increase their vocabularies. One is from direct instruction in the classroom. However, studies indicate that direct instruction does not account for much of the vocabulary growth displayed by school children (Jenkins & Dixon, 1983). For example, Durkin (1979) found that in Grades 3–6 a very small percentage of classroom time (0.4% to 1.0%) was spent on direct vocabulary instruction. In one study of intensive vocabulary training, 27 fourth graders realized an average gain of only 85 targeted words in 19 weeks (Beck et al., 1982). This gain is far short of the estimated 1,000–3,000 words that children are known to acquire in that length of time (Joss, 1964; Nagy & Anderson, 1984).

Because classroom instruction does not account for vocabulary growth, school-age children must learn much of their vocabulary incidentally from verbal contexts. Studies by Jenkins, Stein, and Wysocki (1984); Nagy, Anderson, and Herman (1987); and Nagy, Herman, and Anderson (1985) have indicated that children do learn vocabulary incidentally from texts during Grades 3–8. Nagy et al. (1987) have concluded that an average amount of reading probably accounts for

one third of a child's annual vocabulary growth and that regular, wide reading can result in substantial and permanent vocabulary growth.

Before third grade, however, it is unlikely that children increase their vocabularies substantially through reading because they encounter few if any unfamiliar words in the books they are required to read at school. Their oral language is more advanced than the vocabularies found in these books because only the most frequent words are used to construct primary-grade reading materials (Clifford, 1978; Strickland, 1971).

On the other hand, children do learn new vocabulary while listening to stories. Wells (1986) found that the frequency with which children heard stories was positively associated with their teachers' assessments of their vocabulary size at age 10 years. Elley (1989) reported that 7- and 8-year-olds who heard the same stories three times in their classrooms demonstrated some gain in identifying the correct meanings of target words on a multiple-choice test. This gain increased significantly when the teacher discussed the target words during the reading. Similarly, studies by Feitelson, Kita, and Goldstein (1986) and Eller, Pappas, and Brown (1988) showed that kindergartners' and first-graders' vocabularies could be augmented by listening to stories. In the Elley, Feitelson et al., and Eller et al. studies, children demonstrated some ability to use newly acquired words in other tasks.

Although supportive of the influence of story listening on vocabulary growth, the conclusions that can be drawn from these studies are limited. In the Feitelson et al. (1986) study, inspection of their observational records revealed that teachers mediated story readings by reviewing the meanings of words that they thought first graders might not know. Thus, children may have learned new words not from listening to stories but rather from attending to discussions of the unfamiliar words.

In the Eller et al. (1988) study, after subjects listened to the same stories several times, each child was asked to read the stories aloud. Because the children were nonreaders, they "pretend read" the stories by turning pages and recalling the stories from memory. In their tellings, the children were observed to use the language of the stories including words considered unusual in kindergartners' discourse. This was taken as evidence by Eller et al. that the children had acquired new vocabulary from listening to the stories. However, it may be that these children memorized and repeated the text that they heard without knowing what the novel words meant. Children who use unfamiliar words appropriately in their pretend reading of a familiar story are not necessarily exhibiting productive vocabulary knowledge. Eller et al. did not demonstrate that kindergartners could use the novel words in other situations. Moreover, neither Feitelson et al. (1986) nor Eller et al. showed that young children could identify the meanings of the novel words they heard in stories. Thus, conclusions about story reading as a direct cause of vocabulary growth remain tentative in these studies.

Leung and Pikulski (1990) studied whether kindergartners and first graders could identify the meanings of novel words that they heard in stories. They replicated the Eller et al. (1988) study by using the same two picture storybooks, but they used a pretest-posttest design that included controls who did not hear the storybooks. After hearing each story, subjects from the experimental group were asked to pretend read the books. In addition, both experimental and control subjects were asked to tell the meanings of 20 target words from the stories before and after the experimental treatment. Results support Eller et al.'s finding that repeated exposure to stories increased children's use of target words in their pretend readings. However, there was no significant difference between the experimental and control groups in vocabulary gain as evidenced by subjects' ability to verbally define the target words. Leung and Pikulski suggested

that vocabulary gains might have been demonstrated if the design had used a multiple-choice test of word meanings.

The purpose of our study was to extend this line of research regarding the effects of listening to stories on children's vocabulary growth. Kindergartners listened to a story twice and then completed a multiple-choice vocabulary test assessing their knowledge of 11 unfamiliar target words occurring in the story. Comparable words not appearing in the story were included as controls in the test. Some target words appeared twice in the story and some only once. Children's entering vocabulary knowledge was assessed with the Peabody Picture Vocabulary Test–Revised (PPVT–R; Dunn & Dunn, 1981). Of interest was whether exposure to the target words in stories would improve children's knowledge of the words over that of control words, whether the number of exposures to words would influence learning, and whether children's entering vocabulary knowledge would influence gains. Our aim was to verify results of the study by Elley (1989) in which children with weak vocabularies exhibited greater gains. Our concern with Elley's results was that a ceiling effect may have suppressed gains in children with larger vocabularies.

Discussion

Results of this experiment support the hypothesis that kindergartners expand their recognition vocabularies when they listen to stories at least twice and hear unfamiliar words repeated in the stories. This finding supports and extends the findings of other research on vocabulary acquisition from stories (Elley, 1989; Jenkins et al., 1984; Leung & Pikulski, 1990; Nagy et al., 1985; 1987). Nagy et al. (1987) found that children aged 8 years and older learn vocabulary from their own silent reading, and they suggested that younger children should learn vocabulary from listening to stories. Elley (1989) found that 7- and 8-year-old children learn vocabulary from listening to stories. The present study showed that 5- and 6-year-old nonreading kindergartners can acquire new vocabulary from listening to stories. Vocabulary effects were detected with a multiple-choice test, thus supporting the recommendation of Leung and Pikulski that this type of test is more sensitive than the type they used requiring subjects to tell the meanings of target words.

One feature of our study that might be perceived as a weakness is the absence of a delayed posttest. However, Elley (1989) found only a 2–3% decline in performance from the immediate to the delayed posttest. It is likely that our findings would persist over time as well.

In the present study, prior vocabulary knowledge was the only subject-related variable to significantly affect vocabulary growth from listening to stories. Children with larger vocabularies learned more words than children with smaller vocabularies. This finding is discrepant with Elley's (1989) results. He divided subjects into four ability groups that were based on vocabulary pretest scores and calculated the percentage gain from pretest to posttest for each group. Subjects in his lowest group exhibited the highest percentage gain, whereas subjects in the other three ability groups exhibited about the same gain. However, differences between groups were not tested statistically, and a ceiling effect may have suppressed scores in the higher ability groups.

Our finding provides one more example of the Matthew effect, that is, the idea that the rich get richer while the poor get poorer (Stanovich, 1986). Applied to vocabulary growth, this means that as children get older, the gap between those with sizeable vocabularies and those with small vocabularies grows larger and larger.

Why should vocabulary size influence how easily children learn the meanings of new words from context? Sternberg and Powell (1983) suggest that the causal relationship is bidirectional. Students who are more skilled at using context cues are those who comprehend text well and have a rich knowledge base so that they are better able to infer the meanings of unfamiliar words. Likewise, students who have more elaborate knowledge of words and their definitions can construct richer semantic representations of text. Present findings support this relationship. Children with larger existing vocabularies were better able to use contextual clues to learn more new vocabulary words.

Not only vocabulary size but also other factors may partially explain why children with smaller vocabularies learned fewer new words. Perhaps these children were less experienced in listening to stories and therefore attended to the overall plot rather than to new words. Or perhaps they were less interested in or motivated to learn new words. Perhaps some aspect of intelligence other than vocabulary may have been responsible, such as short- or long-term memory deficits.

Although vocabulary growth was statistically significant, the effect size was modest. The heard-not heard main effect accounted for 19% of the within-subjects variance, and the mean gain from hearing words in stories was 1.24 words or 16% of the maximum gain possible. Listening to stories might have promoted greater vocabulary growth if more of the words had been heard at least four times and if target words had been better gauged to prior vocabulary level. The fact that subjects scored close to chance level on the words not heard in stories suggests that most of the words were difficult.

Nevertheless, our modest gains are consistent with those in other studies (Elley, 1989; Nagy et al., 1985; 1987). Nagy et al. (1987) found that children who read difficult words in a text knew 3.3% more of these words than those who had not read the texts. Elley (1989) reported gains of 15% for 7- and 8-year-old children who heard words in stories. In our study, subjects who heard words knew 11.3% more of the words than those who had not. It should be noted that some researchers consider percentage estimates highly dubious because they depend so much on the criteria for knowing a word and on the nature of the cues in the relevant texts, thus limiting conclusions about the extent of general vocabulary growth that can be expected from listening to stories.

One possible reason why contexts facilitated vocabulary growth to the extent that they did in the present study is that we were careful to ensure that contexts clarified the meanings of our target words. This was done by verifying that pseudo-words substituted for the target words could be defined correctly by adults who were administered this task. Because authors of children's text probably do not give special attention to the more difficult words they use in their writing, our results may overestimate the likelihood that readers will learn the meanings of unfamiliar words they encounter in their reading. Our results, however, suggest that authors of children's texts should take special steps such as those we took to ensure that more difficult words are embedded in meaning-clarifying contexts because this would certainly be beneficial to children's vocabulary acquisition.

There are several procedures that, if used, might have increased the vocabulary gains observed in the present study: including target words additional times in stories, discussing the new words, and embedding new words in interesting, meaningful stories. Elley (1989) suggests that stories having attractive characters with whom children readily identify, stories having humor, and stories with a high action plot all help children attend to the text. Neither story used in this study was humorous or had a high-action plot, and children may have had difficulty identifying with the main characters, a shepherd in *The Boy Who Cried Wolf,* a resident of the tropics in *The Crocodile's Tale.*

Greater vocabulary growth might also have occurred if more of the target words had been nouns. In the present study, many more verbs than adjectives or nouns were taught. Elley (1989) reported that children improved 24% on nouns but only 6% on adjectives and verbs from a vocabulary list with an even distribution of nouns, adjectives, and verbs.

Although the steps suggested above might have produced modest improvements in vocabulary learning in the present study, none of these steps addresses the major weakness of contexts for boosting word learning. As Pressley, Levin, and McDaniel (1987) point out, contexts may be effective for clarifying the meanings of unfamiliar words, but this clarification may do little to help subjects remember the meanings of the words. Comprehension of meanings is very different from and does not guarantee memory for meanings, particularly when several new words are encountered at the same time. Many studies have shown that word learning is much more effective when subjects are helped to form mnemonic connections between unfamiliar words and their meanings than when they are helped to simply understand the meanings of the words (Levin, Levin, Glasman & Nordwall, 1992; Pressley et al., 1987). In the present study, this may explain why subjects with higher PPVT–R scores exhibited superior vocabulary growth. It was not that they were better able to figure out the meanings of target words but rather that they possessed superior ability to retain associative connections between words and their meanings in memory.

Contrary to our expectations, several factors were not found to affect learning in the present study. Sternberg, Powell, and Kaye (1983) suggest that the helpfulness of surrounding context influences learning. Both Elley (1989) and Nagy et al. (1987) reported significant correlations between vocabulary gain scores and the helpfulness of the surrounding context. Also, the number of pictorial occurrences (Elley, 1989) and the syllable length of words (Nagy et al., 1987) have been associated with vocabulary gain from exposure to a text. However, in the present study, none of these variables was correlated significantly with the probability of learning a word. Perhaps the variability of values on our measures was insufficient. For example, most of our words were embedded in clear contexts as indicated by adults' high rate of success in defining pseudowords substituted for the target words. Perhaps our word sample was too small. Perhaps the context clarity measure was weak because it was obtained from adults rather than children. Perhaps our illustrations did not portray criterial details of target words. The fact that our words were heard whereas words in the other studies were read may have mitigated the effect of syllable length. Because the underlying causes are unclear and may have to do with inadequate stimuli or measures, no conclusions about these variables' lack of importance should be drawn from the present findings. We mention these findings to prompt further study of their importance.

One factor that appeared to influence word learning probabilities was the number of times that children heard the word. Only words that were heard four times were associated with higher rates of acquisition whereas words heard only two times exhibited low rates. However, there were several words exposed four times that did not have high learning probabilities. This reduced the correlation between frequency of exposure and learning $(r = .14, p > .05)$. This indicates that hearing a word four times is no guarantee that it will be learned. Four exposures may be necessary but not sufficient for learning words from context. These findings are similar to Jenkins et al.'s (1984) results where learning did not occur with two exposures but was significant with six exposures. Also, Beck et al. (1982) found that greater exposure to vocabulary words yielded superior learning.

Findings of our research carry implications for practice. They indicate that reading stories aloud to young school children will contribute to their vocabulary growth and that children with larger vocabularies are more apt to learn new words from listening to stories than are children with meager vocabularies. Because vocabulary size is associated with school achievement (Wells, 1986) and affects language comprehension, it is implicated in reading success. Our findings support the recommendation of the Commission on Reading (Anderson, Hiebert, Scott, & Wilkinson, 1985) that teachers and parents should read aloud to young primary school children daily as a means of fostering language and literacy acquisition. Of course, to be effective, the books that are read to children must contain some words whose meanings are unfamiliar but not so many unfamiliar words as to limit their comprehension of the stories.

While reading to children benefits vocabulary acquisition, we must recognize that the contribution is not as substantial as researchers and educators commonly believe, as, for example, in Anderson et al.'s (1985) assertion, "The single most important activity for building the knowledge required for eventual success in reading is reading aloud to children" (p. 23). Effects of exposure to stories were significant but small in the present study. In a recent review of studies reporting effects of reading to children on their growth in language and literacy, Scarborough and Dobrich (in press) conclude that effects are present in these studies but unexpectedly modest.

Because children with weaker vocabularies are less likely to learn new words from listening to stories than children with larger vocabularies are, teachers may need to provide more explicit vocabulary instruction for children with smaller vocabularies. One possible method is to discuss the meanings of words used in stories that are read aloud. This suggestion is supported by Elley's (1989) finding that 7- and 8-year-old children learned more new words from listening to stories when the teacher explained words during the reading sessions than when there was no explanation. Teachers may also need to provide experiences that assist children with weaker vocabularies to become involved in the story. It may be that some children do not concentrate during story time because their vocabularies are poor. If more words are explained during story time, children with weaker vocabularies may learn more new words and may enjoy the stories more. Perhaps the most effective step that teachers can take to assist vocabulary learning is to help students create effective ways to remember the meanings of new words, either through the use of keywords or root words (Pressley et al., 1987).

References

Anderson, R. C., & Freebody. P. (1981). Vocabulary knowledge. In J. T. Guthrie (Ed.), *Comprehension and teaching: Research reviews* (pp. 77–117). Newark, DE: International Reading Association.

Anderson, R. C., Hiebert, E. H., Scott, J. A., & Wilkinson, I. A. G. (1985). *Becoming a nation of readers.* Washington, DC: National Institute of Education.

Beck, I. L., Perfetti, C. A., & McKeown, M. G. (1982). Effects of long-term vocabulary instruction on lexical access and reading comprehension. *Journal of Educational Psychology, 74,* 506–521.

Becker, W. C. (1977). Teaching reading and language to the disadvantaged—What we have learned from field research. *Harvard Educational Review, 47,* 518–543.

Calfee, R. C., & Drum, P. A. (1986). Research on teaching reading. In M. C. Wittrock (Ed.), *Handbook of research on teaching* (3rd ed., pp. 804–849). New York: Macmillan.

Chall, J. S. (1987). Two vocabularies for reading. In M. G. McKeown & M. E. Curtis (Eds.), *The nature of vocabulary acquisition* (pp. 7–17). Hillsdale, NJ: Erlbaum.

Clifford, G. J. (1978). Words for schools: The applications in education of the vocabulary researches of Edward L. Thorndike. In P. Suppes (Ed.), *Impact of research on education: Some case studies* (pp. 107–198). Washington, DC: National Academy of Education.

Dale, E. (1965). Vocabulary measurement: Techniques and major findings. *Elementary English, 42,* 895–901, 948.

Durkin, D. (1979). What classroom observations reveal about reading comprehension instruction. *Reading Research Quarterly, 14,* 481–533.

Eller, R. G., Pappas, C. C., & Brown, E. (1988). The lexical development of kindergartners: Learning from written context. *Journal of Reading Behavior, 20,* 5–24.

Elley, W. B. (1989). Vocabulary acquisition from listening to stories. *Reading Research Quarterly, 24,* 174–187.

Feitelson, D., Kita, B., & Goldstein, Z. (1986). Effects of listening to series stories on first graders' comprehension and use of language. *Research in the Teaching of English, 20,* 339–356.

Graves, M. F. (1986). Vocabulary learning and instruction. In E. Z. Rothkopf (Ed.), *Review of research in education* (pp. 49–89). Washington, DC: American Educational Research Association.

Jenkins, J. R., & Dixon, R. (1983). Vocabulary learning. *Contemporary Educational Psychology 8,* 237–260.

Jenkins, J. R., Stein, M. L., & Wysocki, K. (1984). Learning vocabulary through reading. *American Educational Research Journal, 21,* 767–787.

Joss, M. (1964). Language and the school child. *Harvard Educational Review, 34,* 203–210.

Leung, C. B., & Pikulski, J. J. (1990). Incidental learning of word meanings by kindergarten and first-grade children through repeated read aloud events. In J. Zutell, S. McCormick, M. Connolly, & P. O'Keefe (Eds.), *Literacy theory and research: Analyses from multiple perspectives.* (39th yearbook of the National Reading Conference). Chicago: National Reading Conference.

Levin, J., Levin, M., Glasman, L., & Nordwall, M. (1992). Mnemonic vocabulary instruction: Additional effectiveness evidence. *Contemporary Educational Psychology, 17,* 156–174.

Lorge, I., & Chall, J. (1963). Estimating the size of vocabularies of children and adults: An analysis of methodological issues. *Journal of Experimental Education, 32,* 147–157.

McKeown, M. G., & Curtis, M. E. (1987). *The nature of vocabulary acquisition.* Hillsdale, NJ: Erlbaum.

Nagy, W. E., & Anderson, R. C. (1984). How many words are there in printed school English? *Reading Research Quarterly, 19,* 304–330.

Nagy, W. E., Anderson, R. C., & Herman, P. A. (1987). Learning words from context during normal reading. *American Educational Research Journal, 24,* 237–270.

Nagy, W. E., Herman, P. A., & Anderson, R. C. (1985). Learning words from context. *Reading Research Quarterly 20,* 233–253.

Nelson, K. (1973). Structure and strategy in learning to talk. *Monographs of the Society for Research in Child Development, 38*(1–2, Serial No. 149).

Pressley, M., Levin, J., & McDaniel, M. (1987). Remembering versus inferring what a word means: Mnemonic and contextual approaches. In M. McKeown & M. Curtis (Eds.),

The Nature of Vocabulary Acquisition (pp. 107–127). Hillsdale, NJ: Erlbaum.

Rice, M. L., & Woodsmall, L. (1988). Lessons from television: Children's word learning when viewing. *Child Development, 59,* 420–429.

Rinsland, H. D. (1945). A basic vocabulary of elementary school children. New York: Macmillan.

Sachs, J. S., & Johnson, M. (1976). Language development in a hearing child of deaf parents. In W. von Raffler-Engel & Y. LeBrun (Eds.), *Baby talk and infant speech: Proceedings* (pp. 246–252). Amsterdam: Swets & Zeitlinger.

Scarborough, H., & Dobrich, W. (in press). On the efficacy of reading to preschoolers. *Developmental Review.*

Smith, M. E. (1926). An investigation of the development of the sentence and the extent of vocabulary in young children. *University of Iowa Studies in Child Welfare, 3,* No. 5.

Smith, M. K. (1941). Measurement of the size of general English vocabulary through the elementary grades and high school. *Genetic Psychology Monographs, 24,* 311–345.

Stanovich, K. E. (1986). Matthew effects in reading: Some consequences of individual differences in the acquisition of literacy. *Reading Research Quarterly, 16,* 32–71.

Sternberg, R. J. (1987). Most vocabulary is learned from context. In M. G. McKeown & M. E. Curtis (Eds.), *The nature of vocabulary acquisition* (pp. 89–l05). Hillsdale, NJ: Erlbaum.

Sternberg, R. J., & Powell, J. S. (1983). Comprehending verbal comprehension. *American Psychologist, 38,* 878–893.

Sternberg, R. J., Powell, J. S., & Kaye, D. B. (1983). Vocabulary building. In A. C. Wilkison (Ed.), *Classroom computers and cognitive science* (pp. 122–143). San Diego, CA: Academic Press.

Strickland, R. G. (1971). Language in the schools. In C. E. Reed (Ed.), *The learning of language* (pp. 389–403). New York: Appleton-Century-Crofts.

Templin, M. (1957). *Certain language skills in children.* Minneapolis: University of Minnesota Press.

Wells, G. (1986). *The meaning makers: Children learning language and using language to learn.* Portsmouth, NH: Heinemann.

Werner, H., & Kaplan, E. (1950a). Development of word meaning through verbal context: An experimental study. *Journal of Psychology, 29,* 251–257.

Werner, H., & Kaplan, E. (1950b). The acquisition of word meanings: A developmental study. *Monographs of the Society for Research in Child Development. 15*(1, Serial No. 51).

SECTION VII

Comprehension

Sarah L. Dowhower

Supporting a strategic stance in the classroom: A comprehension framework for helping teachers help students to be strategic

Many teachers find it challenging to take a strategic approach to comprehension. This article presents one approach that encourages strategic and student-centered processing of text.

From *The Reading Teacher,* 1999, Vol. 52, pp. 672–683

A second grader, Colin (pseudonym), proudly announced that he has been using many of the ideas from the comprehension bulletin board to increase his understanding of books. "I've been guessing ahead, making pictures in my head, and deciding what I'm going to read for, before I start a book," he said. "These really helped me to think harder about the book and figure out what the author was trying to say when I'm reading by myself." The teacher, Mrs. E, complimented Colin for being so "strategic." The class had had strategy lessons and discussions on prediction, visual imagery, and purpose setting throughout the quarter and the children found many books that worked with these strategies. Mrs. E decided that since these three strategies were becoming independent, it was time to expand the children's repertoire. Using a flexible framework of comprehension teaching (presented in this article), she began planning how to build on what the students knew about strategies to teach two new techniques for using prior experiences and visually organizing content. These were natural extensions of the three strategies the children were already using spontaneously.

Both the most devout whole language champion and the most adamant direct instruction advocate would concede that Colin is making good progress in learning to be strategic. Both theoretical camps would say that strategies allow readers to be autonomous and in control of the comprehension process and that good readers use them effectively. Not all, however, would agree as to how best to accomplish this strategic stance (e.g., Carnine, Silbert, & Kameenui, 1997; Clay, 1991; Weaver, 1994). Is it programmed by the teacher, naturally left to the child to do alone, or achieved by a middle ground of instruction in a natural, supportive way?

Some research suggests that there is "little teaching of cognitive strategies in contemporary classrooms" (Pressley, Symons, Snyder, & Cariglia-Bull, 1989, p. 17). Data collected over 10 years indicate that only 1 out of 10 cooperating teachers working with early field preservice elementary education students taught reading strategies (Dowhower, 1998). In a seminal study on comprehension, Durkin (1978–1979) concluded that while many teachers believe they were teaching comprehension, most often they were assessing instead of directly explaining *how* to comprehend. Although Durkin's work came under some criticism because of the criteria she used to define instruction (Heap, 1982; Hodges, 1980), there is supporting evidence that her hypothesis—teachers are more interrogators than instructors—is valid (Kurth & Greenlaw, 1980; Mason, 1983; Wendler, Samuels, & Moore, 1989).

There are valid reasons why many novice and experienced teachers find it challenging to take a strategic approach to comprehension. Preservice and inservice teachers in classes and workshops report that they "seldom saw real strategy teaching either in their K–12 schooling or college reading methods classrooms." Some confused the term *strategy teaching* with instructional techniques teachers might use rather than strategies children might learn. "Reading instruction textbooks," they said, "gave minimal assistance in learning to teach children to use strategies." Like Durkin (1981), they found little help with strategies in the basal manuals. Furthermore, research by Wendler et al. (1989) suggests that even with good teacher preparation, confusion between assessment and direct teaching of comprehension is still evident.

In an attempt to encourage teachers and their students to adopt a strategic stance like the classroom described in the scenario above, this article presents an approach to comprehension instruction that teachers and I have dubbed the comprehension strategy framework. This framework has evolved out of work with preservice and inservice elementary teachers in our search for ways to support and encourage both strategic and student-centered processing of text. The first section gives a description of and rationale for elements of the framework, including an example of a lesson taught in Colin's second-grade class. The second section is a brief overview of how the framework fits into current literacy trends in strategy teaching. The final sections describe how to use the framework and teacher comments as to its efficacy.

Comprehension strategy framework

Still new to the whole idea of teaching to develop strategic readers, Colin's teacher turned to the comprehension strategy framework to organize how she would present new strategies and connect them with those the children were already using. "I see the framework helping me achieve two goals," said Mrs. E, "students internalizing and self-regulating the strategies; and me, as a teacher, building a schema for good planning and strategy instruction."

The format of the framework is an adaptation of Ringler and Weber's (1984, pp. 70–72) three phases of the interactive stage of teaching (prereading, active reading, and postreading), as well as a blending of Baumann and Schmitt's (1986) "what, why, how and when" of comprehension instruction and literature teacher-student discussion techniques. The framework has three parts or phases:

The *Prereading* phase includes three activities: (a) eliciting prior knowledge, (b) building background and relating that to prior knowledge, and (c) focusing on the specific strategy to be taught—specifically *what* the strategy is and *why* it is being taught. This gives the students a simple description or definition of the strategy (declarative knowledge), how its acquisition will help them become better readers (conceptual knowledge), and a brief model of how the strategy works (procedural knowledge) (see Appendix A, Part I).

The *Active Reading* phase (see Appendix A, Part II) involves a cycle or repetition of three activities: (a) students setting a purpose for reading the specific section of text, (b) silent reading and self-monitoring, and (c) "working the story." *Working the story* means discussion that helps children become a part of what they have read as well as the process of reading. It does not include interrogation from the teacher. This conversation includes the naming and continuous personal demonstration of the strategies ("I found myself doing _____ to understand this part better"). It is where students "hear what they (the authors) have to say, but examine it, weigh it and judge for themselves" (quote by author Tyrone Edwards, source unknown). It is where the awareness of theme(s) gradually develops as the story unfolds.

The Active Reading phase is repeated with several sections of text until the end of the passage, concluding with a final discussion of the strategies learned and the text theme(s) generated. Discussion should involve *when* the strategy would be used (and not used), the kinds of text *where* the strategy works (and does not), and *how* to evaluate its use. Special care should be taken to situate the strategy in the bigger picture of the reading process and support the students' coordination of the network of strategies they are beginning to bring under control (Clay, 1991). Important to this final discussion is the constructing of themes (abstractions linking the text to other texts) that requires the students to actively process what they read at higher levels. "By providing just the right degree of scaffolding, through the use of questions and comments, the teacher can support students as they attempt to construct a theme and at the same time, shift responsibility for the task to students" (Au, 1992, p. 107)

The final *Postreading* phase (see Appendix A, Part III) entails independent activities by students either individually or in groups: (a) recall of content, (b) reader response, (c) extensions of text, (d) strategy use and transfer, and (e) informal or self-assessment. Students or teachers may choose one or more of the activities according to the text, student need, or appropriateness. For instance, to address both efferent and aesthetic responses (Rosenblatt, 1994), students might sequence the events correctly (recall of content) or write in their journals about what they got out of the text or how they would react or feel about the character or situation (reader response). The students might practice the strategies "in flight"; for example, they might talk about how they use the strategies with a partner as they reread the story (strategy use and transfer). They could retell the story into a tape recorder for the teacher to informally assess comprehension or complete a self-assessment checksheet to indicate which strategies they used independently with new books during silent sustained reading (SSR) time (assessment). Encouraging students to recommend to peers books that fit one or more of the strategies in their repertoire is a way of weaving together strategy use and transfer and self-assessment.

To help the reader visualize the parts of the framework and how they work together to facilitate comprehension, Figure 1 gives a structural overview of the various components. The framework, as presented, is constructed as if the strategy is new for the students and this is the first time it is targeted. The components should be adapted as the students learn to use the strategy independently and integrate it with others.

Example of how the framework works

Because linking prior knowledge and constructing pictures of story content are connected with prediction and visualization (strategies that the children were already using independently), Colin's teacher decided to introduce the new strategies of Experience-Text-Relationship (ETR) and Visual Structures. ETR is a technique linking prior experiences with what is read in the text and forming some relationship between the two. Visual Structures are diagrams or pictures of the content of the text. Using the framework helped Colin's teacher plan how to present the strategies and adapt her instruction as the children became more strategic (i.e., using the strategy spontaneously during reading).

Figure 2 is the scenario of the lesson growing out of the teacher's plan represented in Appendix B. The text used, a second-grade story entitled "New Girl at School" (Delton, 1986), is about a little girl's experiences the first week in a new school. The girl's change of feelings over a week's time is not explicitly told. Because most children could relate to being in a new situation and the story lends itself well to a diagram using the 5 days of the week, Experience-Text-Relationship and Visual Structure strategies were taught together.

Rationale for framework elements

The section below discusses the rationale for elements of the framework including text division, cycles of instruction (purpose setting,

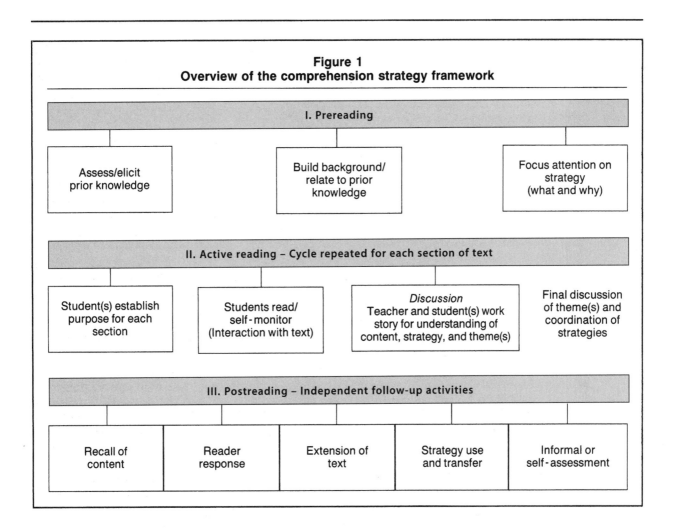

Figure 1
Overview of the comprehension strategy framework

I. Prereading

| Assess/elicit prior knowledge | Build background/ relate to prior knowledge | Focus attention on strategy (what and why) |

II. Active reading – Cycle repeated for each section of text

| Student(s) establish purpose for each section | Students read/ self-monitor (Interaction with text) | *Discussion* Teacher and student(s) work story for understanding of content, strategy, and theme(s) | Final discussion of theme(s) and coordination of strategies |

III. Postreading – Independent follow-up activities

| Recall of content | Reader response | Extension of text | Strategy use and transfer | Informal or self-assessment |

silent reading, and discussion of the strategy and content), and construction of general theme(s) or central meaning of the text.

Text chunked in cycles of instruction. The framework is set up differently from the typical lesson in which teachers ask the students to read the whole text at once. Instead, the teacher divides the text into sections before the lesson. These sections can be as small as a sentence or as large as several chapters. The cycles (purpose setting, silent reading, and discussion) allow for more opportunities to stop and think publicly about what was read and the construction of understanding. Importantly, the cycles allow students to explore both the theme and the strategy throughout the story—for building big ideas (possible themes) in the story and reinforcing practice of comprehension strategies along the way.

Purpose setting emphasis. Armbruster (1991), Ogle (1986), and others (see Blanton, Wood, & Moorman, 1990, for a review of the research) suggest it is important for learners to have a clear purpose for reading because it facilitates comprehension. "Before even beginning the first sentence of a text, knowledgeable readers know how to approach and frame a reading experience with a sense of purpose, need, and direction" (*Standards for the English Language Arts*, 1996, p. 31). Thus, each cycle begins with setting a purpose for reading the specific chunk of text. Because teacher-directed purpose setting has many problems, Blanton et al. (1990) suggest that the goal be to gradually replace teacher-set purposes with jointly established ones and then ultimately to individually and independently set student purposes. By setting a rea-

Figure 2
Scenario of actual lesson plan

Lesson continued (major components of the framework in bold)

Later, in a literature circle group, Mrs. E said, "Yesterday we chose a new story to read together called 'New Girl at School.' It is a good story to learn other strategies similar to ones you have been practicing. Good readers use strategies all the time as they read. That is why we are building a list of the strategies on the bulletin board. The story is about a girl moving to a new home and school. Did that ever happen to you? How did you feel?" **(Prereading: Building background/assessing and relating to prior knowledge)**

"This story will help you to learn two new strategies to understand what you read. The first is called Experience-Text-Relationship, or ETR for short. It gets us thinking about what has happened in our lives and how that fits with the character's experiences. We are also going to draw a picture or diagram of the story's events to better see the things that happen and how they fit together (visual structures). You may have used these strategies but never realized it." **(Prereading: Focusing attention on what the strategies are and why they are good to use)**

"Look at the picture on the first page of the story. How might Marcia be feeling on her first day at the new school? Let's read pp. 13–14 silently to see if this is so." **(Active reading: Purpose setting)** After reading silently—"If we were to draw a face on our chart as to how Marcia feels, what would it be? Why? Let's list the reasons (events) below the face that caused her to feel this way. What might you be saying if you were Marcia?" **(Discussion of visual structures and ETR)** The lesson continued like this over several cycles with purpose setting and the use of the children's predictions, silent reading, discussion, and "working of the story." Students added to the chart after each section of text and also discussed how these events related to their lives and any themes they saw.

At the end of the story the teacher asked, "How is this story like an experience you had? Look at the picture we built on the chart paper and tell us what the author might be trying to say in this story. What can we learn from Marcia's experience that will help us?" **(Final discussion of theme)**

Finally, the teacher asked, "*What* did we do to understand the story better?" One student said, "We talked about how our experiences were like the girl's and drew a picture to show the parts of the story and how her feelings changed over the week at school." "Let's add ETR and visuals to our comprehension strategy bulletin board," suggested Mrs. E. "*When* could we use these strategies again?" The students suggested they could draw a picture of the parts when they were having problems remembering and making sense of a story. When the story is like something that happened to them, they could use what has happened to them to figure it out. **(Final discussion of new strategies)**

During the discussion, Colin noticed that before they were reading, the group was setting a purpose for reading by guessing (predicting) what would happen. Other students commented how they could picture various incidents with Marcia and her schoolmates as they read (visualization). These were strategies already on their strategy bulletin board and taught previously. The teacher commented that she was delighted to see the students naming as well as incorporating learned strategies with new ones as ways of building their understanding of what they read. **(Coordination of other known strategies)**

After the final culminating discussion, the children independently reread the text to find examples of events that would support the different feelings Marcia had during the story. **(Postreading: Recall using the visual)** They wrote events beside the facial expression to support Marcia's feelings (see Appendix B). They also wrote in their journals about their feelings as if they had been a new student in Marcia's classroom. **(Postreading: Reader response)**

son to read themselves, students have a stake in finding the answer or testing a hypothesis. They learn a behavior critical to expert reading. Other guidelines suggested by Blanton et al. (1990) include (a) setting a single purpose rather than multiple purposes, (b) sustaining the purpose throughout the selection, and (c) discussing the purpose as the first activity after the reading is completed.

Silent reading emphasis. After the purpose setting, the format requires the students to silently read a text segment. There are several reasons for asking students to read the text silently. First, much of the reading instruction in our local elementary schools occurs within the context of oral round-robin reading or some variation. There is little support for either of these oral reading practices in the literature.

Compared to independent silent reading, round-robin reading actually decreased comprehension in several studies (Lynch, 1988; Santa, Isaacson, & Manning, 1987). In addition, results of several studies suggest that silent reading is more effective for learning than oral reading (Armbruster, 1991). Oral reading draws attention to errors and increases off-task behavior. A final argument is that silent reading is more authentic to real life than oral reading. Seldom do adults read aloud, except for possibly the litany in church or a story to a young child. The bulk of our adult reading is done silently.

• *Strategy instruction embedded in literature discussions.* As suggested by Fielding and Pearson (1994), we need to teach strategies that students can use every day within whole texts and give students time to talk about them. In other words, give "many occasions for students to talk to a teacher and one another about their responses" (p. 62). This situated cognition within good literature allows "students to internalize effective comprehension strategies through repeated situations in which they read and discuss whole text with a teacher and peers" (p. 67). These types of text discussions of content and strategies have been rare in classrooms (Durkin, 1978–1979, 1984; Mason, 1983). Furthermore, we have recent evidence that students are more highly involved and engaged in the literacy act when given opportunities to discuss by responding, challenging, questioning, and sharing opinions about the meaning of text (Almasi, McKeown, & Beck, 1996).

Theme(s) and focused discussion. A theme is the central idea of the text or the "big idea." It might be literal (e.g., girl moves to a new school); psychological, involving forces such as emotions and needs influencing the character's actions (e.g., a new girl's need for acceptance); or philosophical, encompassing universal truths (e.g., acceptance comes with time). Reading scholars suggest that themes should be at the heart of text discussions because (a) the process helps students query and develop insights beyond the literal (Lehr, 1988), and (b) "through constructing their own themes, students come to understand and appreciate literature on their own terms, not just the teacher's terms" (Au, 1992, p. 110). Teachers should scaffold the discussion with questions and comments through-

out the lesson to help students construct their own themes. While the teacher initially has several possible themes in mind that give the big picture, it is important that the final theme come from the students or be jointly constructed by the students and teacher. Likewise, different groups of students may construct multiple themes for the same text.

Using the strategy framework

As opposed to teaching just a single strategy, the framework can be a flexible, generic vehicle for teaching a repertoire of comprehension strategies. There are a number of strategic processes good readers use that can be taught. These include activating background knowledge, predicting, generating visual images, summarizing, self-questioning, analyzing text for story grammar elements, inferencing, distinguishing important information, synthesizing, monitoring, and learning to repair faulty comprehension (Goodman, Watson, & Burke, 1996; Pearson, Roehler, Dole, & Duffy, 1992; Pressley et al., 1992; Weaver, 1994).

Although there are many research-based techniques or methods in the literature that address these strategic processes, teachers new to strategy teaching find it more comfortable to concentrate on a few at first. This is consistent with what Pearson et al. (1992) suggest—initially learning a few strategies that can be applied to a wide variety of texts. Once teachers have a schema for teaching strategies, transfer to multiple strategies suggested in the literature is easier (e.g., reciprocal teaching or read aloud).

Less complex comprehension techniques include Directed Reading-Thinking Activities, Experience-Text-Relationship, Visual Structures, Story Grammars, or K-W-L (What I *K*now, What I *W*ant to Learn, What I *L*earned). These five have a classroom research base, address a range of strategic processes, can be used with varied types of text and genres, and can be adapted to various reading levels, content areas, and student needs. Importantly, there is evidence that they can transfer to independent reading. For those readers unfamiliar with these techniques the following is a brief overview with resources for further reference and exploration:

• Directed Reading-Thinking Activity (DR-TA) is a technique that encourages prediction and validation. First identified by Stauffer (1969, 1975) and applicable to both expository and narrative text, DR-TA uses a cycle in which the reader first predicts from the title or initial picture, then reads a segment of the text to validate those predictions, and predicts again from the new information. Reading, validating predictions, and then predicting again are a series of steps repeated until the end of the text. The same strategic prediction and validation cycle can be adapted to emergent readers who cannot read independently using Directed Listening-Thinking Activity (DL-TA) or Directed Seeing-Thinking Activity (DS-TA) (Dalton & Dowhower, 1985). (For other DR-TA references see Haggard, 1988; Tierney, Readence, & Dishner, 1995, pp. 213–222; Walker, 1996a, pp. 194-196.)

• Experience-Text-Relationship (ETR) is a strategy technique for linking background experiences and schemata (E) to narrative story text (T), before, during, and after reading. The result is the development of an insight or relationship (R) between the children's experiences and the text. ETR was developed from research at Kamehameha Schools with Hawaiian children (Au, 1979). (For other ETR references see Au, 1993; Mason & Au, 1990; Walker, 1996a, pp. 198–201.)

• Visual Structures is a general name given to spatial learning techniques such as graphic organizers, maps, chains, charts, continuums, webs, trees, grids, matrices, or diagrams that provide a visual representation of the content of narrative or expository text. Their purpose is to help students better understand important text ideas and how they are related. The information from a visual structure also aids summarization and allows for use of multiple modalities. (For references see Alvermann, 1991; Griffin, Malone, & Kameenui, 1995; Jones, Pierce, & Hunter, 1989; McGee & Richgels, 1985; Piccolo, 1987; Tierney et al., 1995, pp. 328–333, 346–352.)

• Story Grammar or Story Structure is perhaps the most researched comprehension technique. The terms are applicable to and include narrative story parts such as character or events, as well as the ways that content area texts (expository) are organized. Often story structure elements are written out as in frames (Cudd & Roberts, 1987; Fowler, 1982) or organized with visual structures such as maps and webs. Story structure elements are used for assessing (i.e., retelling) as well as teaching comprehension (Marshall, 1983). (For other references see Armbruster, Anderson, & Ostertag, 1989; Davis & McPherson, 1989; McGee & Richgels, 1985; Tierney et al., 1995, pp. 353–365.)

• K-W-L is a widely used self-questioning technique to help tap prior *knowledge* (K), set purposes for reading by determining what the students *want* to know (W), and identify new concepts *learned* (L). First researched by Ogle (1986), the technique is often (but not exclusively) used in the content area subjects. In its more developed form, K-W-L is called K-W-L Plus with a writing component consisting of mapping and summarization (Carr & Ogle, 1987). (For other K-W-L references see Tierney et al., 1995, pp. 379–384; Walker, 1996a, pp. 225-228.)

The changing nature of comprehension instruction

The framework described here attempts to encourage a more current perspective of strategy teaching. The last 4 decades have seen several waves of comprehension research and instruction, each very different in their emphasis. The 1960s and 1970s had a strong task-analysis flavor with both decoding and comprehension seen as sets of hierarchical skills that, taught in sequence, defined good reading instruction. The logic was that practice in completing comprehension questions and various skill activities would develop reading ability (Pearson et al., 1992). During this time there was a strong movement to teach the numerous subskills in a direct instruction mode because comprehension could best be achieved by teaching skills to some level of mastery (Rosenshine, 1980). Vestiges of this skill-based approach are still seen today in various direct instruction models (e.g., Carnine et al., 1997).

The 1980s brought a cognitive-based view of comprehension, ushering in terms such as *direct explanation* and *explicit comprehension instruction* to differentiate the approach from the *direct instruction* of the 1970s. Reading was seen by researchers as a more complex, interactive process, and teaching strategies became more credible than skills because they implied megacognitive control, higher levels of thinking, active choice, and active processing (Dole, Duffy, Roehler, & Pearson, 1991). During the 1980s and into the early 1990s, a strong cognitively focused research base suggested comprehension strategies (ways a reader monitors and makes sense of text) are important components of expert reading and can be taught (Dole et al., 1991; Fielding & Pearson, 1994; Pearson, 1985).

As productive as it was, the 1980s approach to strategy learning could be characterized as a transmission model, mostly teacher directed with large doses of direct explanation and modeling of comprehension strategies, emphasis on a few skills in isolated context, and short-term, quick-fix implementation (see Pressley et al., 1992, for a summary). Although rooted in the direct explanation tradition, there is a new look in the late 1990s to the 1980s perspective. This new look may provide potential solutions to the debate on how to facilitate strategic reading as we move into the next century. Several major shifts in thinking have occurred, in part, because of the current holistic movements in literacy.

Student's use of comprehension strategies is situated within a broader context of what a competent reader does. Researchers are seeing cognitive strategies as one facet of the overall concept of a competent reader. For example, studies in the last 5 years at the National Reading Research Center suggest that expert readers are also engaged readers who are motivated, knowledgeable, socially interactive, and strategic (Alvermann & Guthrie, 1993; Gambrell, 1996; Guthrie, 1996; Guthrie & McCann, 1997; Morrow, 1997). In addition, Almasi et al. (1996) found that use of comprehension strategies was both a sign of active engagement and a stimulus for that engagement.

Strategy development is seen in a more constructivist and collaborative light. Several theories are influencing how we currently conceptualize strategy teaching. These include (a) Reader Response Theory/Transactional Theory (Pressley et al., 1992; Rosenblatt, 1978, 1994), (b) Motivation and Engagement Theory (Cambourne, 1988), and (c) Self-Extending/Inner Control Theory (Clay, 1991). Literature Circles (Daniels, 1994), The Book Club (McMahon & Raphael, 1997), Questioning the Author (Beck, McKeown, Hamilton, & Kucan, 1997), and Instructional Conversations

(Goldenberg, 1992–1993) are recent approaches for facilitating collaborative discussions. The general thrust of these theories and approaches is that awareness and joint social construction of strategies and meaning are best learned through

---

The framework described here attempts to encourage a more current perspective of strategy teaching.

---

teacher-student and peer-led discussions and explanatory responses during reading. When strategy use is a joint effort (by students and teacher), the teacher engages in both responsive teaching in instructional conversations (Tharp & Gallimore, 1988) and instructional scaffolding (Beck et al., 1997; Pearson & Fielding, 1991).

As opposed to strict teacher control, strategy learning is more cognitively situated in student needs and demands of the reading task. Strategies are taught in context, as part of the topic or text being explored, not in isolation. Guthrie (1996) suggests that "when students' need to know determines the type and amount of strategy instruction, strategies are likely to be adapted and used widely" (p. 438).

Because of this cognitively situated viewpoint, strategy development and use is best supported "in flight" or what Fountas and Pinnell (1996) call "on the run." This means that demonstrations of new strategies and comments that reinforce existing strategies are woven into the ebb and flow of discussion of literature, by both teachers and students (Beck et al., 1997; Clay, 1991; Fountas & Pinnell, 1996; Goodman et al., 1996; Pressley et al., 1992; Smith & Elley, 1994; Walker, 1996b; Weaver, 1994). In other words, students and teachers learn to make public or explicit their overt thinking process and ways they have found to make sense of what they read as they read.

Isolated strategy teaching is being replaced by an emphasis on learning a repertoire of strategies as well as the coordination and flexible orchestration of those strategies. Duffy (1993), in rethinking the research on strategy instruction, suggests the goal is to build a repertoire of diverse comprehension strategies—not isolated strategies learned for their own sake—an "integrated set...within an overall global plan for being strategic" (p. 243). Most recently, the International Reading Association/National Council of Teachers of English Standards for the English Language Arts support this global plan for a strategic stance. The document specifically addresses the need for students to be able to apply a wide range of strategies for comprehension, interpretation, evaluation, and appreciation to a wide range of text (*Standards for the English Language Arts*, 1996).

Also, the Standards (1996) endorse the concept that teacher explanation and modeling of reading strategies and independent practice contribute to students' proficiency in comprehension. However, direct teacher explanation, modeling, and practice are currently thought of in more fluid, informal, and less structured ways than the explicit comprehension model of the 1980s. For instance, Goodman et al. (1996) suggest more spontaneous short minilessons (individual or group) to help move readers "back in low gear" so they can focus on specific process for meaning (p. 50). Walker (1996b) suggests "phasing in to demonstrate and name strategies and phasing out to let students use new strategies independently" (p. 289). This is done with "I" statements about how one personally gains meaning—all within conversations that focus on cultivating and orchestrating a repertoire of strategies while reading.

In addition to a repertoire perspective, there is an increased emphasis on self-assessment of multiple comprehension strategies. Experts suggest the use of self-report rubrics, checklists, and portfolio entries (DeFina, 1992; Lipson & Wixson, 1991; Rhodes, 1993; Walker, 1996a, 1996b) to help students document and monitor personal strategies "in flight." The rationale is that asking students to evaluate their increasing use of strategies draws their attention to the strategies and their positive effects (Walker, 1996a) as well as empowers them to read more difficult text (Clay, 1991) and be more self-efficacious (Schunk & Zimmerman, 1997).

Developing a strategic stance

Both beginning and experienced teachers have found the comprehension strategy framework to be helpful in promoting a strategic stance in their classrooms. Many veterans had never viewed reading instruction this way. "I thought teaching reading was just asking comprehension questions and having some discussion on what the author meant," a first-grade teacher admitted. One fourth-grade teacher conceded that "Deep down, I didn't believe my students could be strategic and use these strategies independently—I was wrong, and I'm so proud of them." " It was not easy at first to learn to teach this way, but the terms what, why, how and when, more than anything else, gave me the actual words to explain the process of being strategic to students. The framework helped me build my own stance of teaching for strategy development," said a second-grade teacher. "This concept has changed how I teach in every subject," several others commented. Finally, teachers reported that their students approached national and the state proficiency tests more strategically and they were more confident and efficacious in reading harder material. One student teacher found that as she encouraged responsibility for strategies, the passive low achievers flourished. "I know what I can do to figure out what I'm reading!" said a remedial student.

Several weeks after Mrs. E's lesson: After practicing ETR and Visuals with different stories, Mrs. E knew that the strategies had been internalized and had empowered her students when they clamored at the beginning of a new story, "Don't tell us, we know! We'll use ETR and tell all we know about this topic (referring to the title) before we start reading the story. During the story we will keep thinking about how the story is like our lives and we could also make a picture of the story parts. Right? Those are ways we can understand the story better."

Conclusion

Perhaps the fiercest theoretical debate around the issue of strategic processes today is not the concept of strategies that help readers become competent. "It is about who should control formation of that strategic system" (Clay, 1991, p. 344). Does the student do it alone, or does the teacher provide programmed help or monitoring? The various theories and models in today's literature indicate the answer lies between both positions. As opposed to the 1970s and 1980s instruction, educators view strategy use as only one facet of competency, embedding strategy learning in the ebb and flow of literature discussions, encouraging the coordination and use of a repertoire of strategies, and emphasizing student control and self-assessment "in flight" or "on the run." Fountas and Pinnell (1996) make the subtle distinction that reading instruction is teaching for strategies.

Direct instruction, in its purest sense, is often thought of as the antithesis of student-centered whole language (teacher-as-deliverer as opposed to teacher-as-facilitator). Heller (1995) suggests that a wise combination of direct instruction and student-centered activity is the goal for which classroom teachers should strive. Instructional scaffolding (challenging and assisting students to work at the edge of their competence) is one way to bridge the two contradictory models (Pearson & Fielding, 1991).

Duffy (1993) posits the most important thing is that strategic reading requires strategic teachers, which in turn requires strategic staff development (both preservice and inservice).

That is, if low achievers are to be strategic (i.e., if they are to be flexible adapters of strategies as needed to construct meanings), their teachers must themselves be strategic (i.e., flexible adapters of professional knowledge in response to students' developing concepts), and the teachers of teachers must also be strategic (i.e., adapting innovations and research findings to teachers' situations and involving them as co-constructors of knowledge rather than telling them what to do). (p. 245)

Toward these goals, I encourage both novice and experienced reading teachers, who want to establish a strategic stance, to experiment with and adapt the framework in their classrooms. However, a caveat is necessary. The framework is not a prescription or script to be followed verbatim, but a broad schema or flexible guide to be built anew, adapted, and co-constructed as the competence level of students change. By facilitating the first foray into strategy teaching, the framework can act as an instructional scaffold model for teachers and, in turn, their students.

Dowhower teaches at Miami University in Oxford, Ohio, USA. She may be contacted at Miami University Dolbois European Center, Château de Differdange, Impasse du Chateau #1, L-4524, Grand Duchy of Luxemburg.

References

Almasi, J.F., McKeown, M.G., & Beck, I.L. (1996). The nature of engaged reading in classroom discussion of literature. *Journal of Literacy Research, 28,* 107–146.

Alvermann, D.E. (1991). The discussion web: A graphic aid for learning across the curriculum. *The Reading Teacher, 45,* 92–99.

Alvermann, D.E., &. Guthrie, J.T. (1993). Themes and directions of the National Reading Research Center. *Perspectives in reading research, No. 1.* Athens, GA and College Park, MD: National Reading Research Center.

Armbruster, B.B. (1991). Silent reading, oral reading, and learning from text. *The Reading Teacher, 45,* 154–155.

Armbruster, B.B., Anderson, T.H., & Ostertag, J. (1989). Teaching text structure to improve reading and writing. *The Reading Teacher, 43,* 130–137.

Au, K.H. (1979). Using the experience-text-relationship method with minority children. *The Reading Teacher, 32,* 678–679.

Au, K.H. (1992). Constructing the theme of a story. *Language Arts, 69,* 106–111.

Au, K. H. (1993). *Literacy instruction in multicultural settings.* New York: Harcourt Brace Jovanovich.

Baumann, J.F., & Schmitt, M.C. (1986). The what, why, how, and when of comprehension instruction. *The Reading Teacher, 39*, 640 – 646.

Beck, I.L., McKeown, M.G., Hamilton, R.L., & Kucan, L. (1997). *Questioning the author: An approach for enhancing student engagement with text*. Newark, DE: International Reading Association.

Blanton, W.E., Wood, K.D., & Moorman, G.B. (1990). The role of purpose in reading instruction. *The Reading Teacher, 43*, 486 – 493.

Cambourne, B. (1988). *The whole story: Natural learning and the acquisition of literacy in the classroom*. Auckland, New Zealand: Scholastic.

Carnine, D.W., Silbert, J., & Kameenui, E.J. (1997). *Direct instruction reading* (3rd ed.). Columbus, OH: Merrill.

Carr, E., & Ogle, D. (1987). K-W-L plus: A strategy for comprehension and summarization. *Journal of Reading, 30*, 626 – 631.

Clay, M. (1991). *Becoming literate: Construction of inner control*. Portsmouth, NH: Heinemann.

Cudd, E., & Roberts, L.L. (1987). Using story frames to develop reading comprehension in a 1st grade classroom. *The Reading Teacher, 41*, 74 – 79.

Dalton, S., & Dowhower, S. (1985). *The directed seeing thinking activity and the directed listening thinking activity* (Early Education Bulletin No. 10). Honolulu, HI: Center for Development of Early Education, Kamehameha Schools—Bishop Estate.

Daniels, H. (1994). *Literature circles: Voice and choice in the student-centered classroom*. York, ME: Stenhouse.

Davis, Z.T., & McPherson, M.D. (1989). Story map instruction: A road map for reading comprehension. *The Reading Teacher, 43*, 232 – 240.

DeFina, A. (1992). *Portfolio assessment*. New York: Scholastic.

Delton, J. (1986). The new girl at school. In W. Durr (Ed.), *Adventures* (pp. 12 – 20). Boston: Houghton Mifflin.

Dole, J.A., Duffy, G.G., Roehler, L.E., & Pearson, P.D. (1991). Moving from the old to the new: Research on reading comprehension instruction. *Review of Educational Research, 61*, 239 – 264.

Dowhower, S. (1998). *A ten-year survey of reading strategy teaching in elementary schools*. Unpublished raw data.

Duffy, G.G. (1993). Rethinking strategy instruction: Four teachers' development and their low achievers' understanding. *The Elementary School Journal, 93*, 231 – 247.

Duffy, G.G., Roehler, L.R., Sivan, E., Rackliffe, G., Book, C., Meloth, M.S., Vavrus, L.G., Wesselman, R., Putnam, J., & Bassiri, D. (1987). Effects of explaining the reasoning associated with using reading strategies. *Reading Research Quarterly, 22*, 347 – 368.

Durkin, D. (1978 – 1979). What classroom observations reveal about reading comprehension instruction. *Reading Research Quarterly, 14*, 481 – 533.

Durkin, D. (1981). Reading comprehension instruction in five basal reading series. *Reading Research Quarterly, 16*, 515 – 544.

Durkin, D. (1984). Is there a match between what elementary teachers do and what basal reader manuals recommend? *The Reading Teacher, 37*, 734 – 744.

Fielding, L.G., & Pearson, P.D. (1994). Reading comprehension: What works. *Educational Leadership, 51*(5), 62 – 68.

Fountas, I.C., & Pinnell, G.S. (1996). *Guided reading*. Portsmouth, NH: Heinemann.

Fowler, G.L. (1982). Developing comprehension skills in primary students through the use of story frames. *The Reading Teacher, 37*, 176 – 179.

Gambrell, L.B. (1996). Creating classroom cultures that foster reading motivation. *The Reading Teacher, 50*, 14 – 25.

Garner, R. (1992). Metacognition and self-monitoring strategies. In S.J. Samuels & A.E. Farstrup (Eds.), *What research has to say about reading instruction* (2nd ed., pp. 236 – 252). Newark, DE: International Reading Association.

Goldenberg, C. (1992 – 1993). Instructional conversations: Promoting comprehension through discussion. *The Reading Teacher, 46*, 316 – 326.

Goodman, Y.M., Watson, D.J., & Burke, C.L. (1996). *Reading strategies: Focus on comprehension* (2nd ed.). Katonah, NY: Richard C. Owen.

Griffin, C.C., Malone, L.D., & Kameenui, E.J. (1995). Effects of graphic organizer instruction on fifth-grade students. *The Journal of Educational Research, 89*(2), 98 – 107.

Guthrie, J.T. (1996). Educational contexts for engagement in literacy. *The Reading Teacher, 49*, 432 – 445.

Guthrie, J.T., & McCann, A.D. (1997). Characteristics of classrooms that promote and motivations and strategies for learning. In J.T. Guthrie & A. Wigfield (Eds.), *Reading engagement: Motivating readers through integrated instruction* (pp. 128 – 148). Newark, DE: International Reading Association.

Haggard, M.R. (1988). Developing critical thinking with the directed reading-thinking activity. *The Reading Teacher, 41*, 526 – 533.

Hansen, J., & Pearson, P.D. (1983). An instructional study: Improving the inferential comprehension of good and poor fourth-grade readers. *Journal of Educational Psychology, 75*, 821 – 829.

Heap, J.L. (1982). Understanding classroom events: A critique of Durkin, with an alternative. *Journal of Reading Behavior, 14*, 391 – 411.

Heller, M. (1995). *Reading-writing connections: From theory to practice* (2nd ed.). New York: Longman.

Hodges, C.A. (1980). Commentary: Toward a broader definition of comprehension instruction. *Reading Research Quarterly, 15*, 299 – 306.

Jones, B.F., Pierce, J., & Hunter, B. (1989). Teaching students to construct graphic representations. *Educational Leadership, 46*(4), 20 – 25.

Kern, R.G. (1989). Second language reading strategy instruction: Its effects on comprehension and word inference ability. *The Modern Language Journal, 73*, 135 – 149.

Kletzien, S.B. (1991). Strategy use by good and poor comprehenders reading expository text at differing levels. *Reading Research Quarterly, 24*, 67 – 85.

Kurth, R.J., & Greenlaw, M.J. (1980, December). *Research and practices in comprehension instruction in elementary classrooms*. Paper presented at the annual meeting of the American Reading Conference, Sarasota, FL. (ERIC Document Reproduction Service No. ED 195 931)

Lehr, S. (1988). The child's developing sense of theme as a response to literature. *Reading Research Quarterly, 23*, 337 – 357.

Lipson M.Y., & Wixson, K.K. (1991). *Assessment and instruction of reading disability: An interactive approach*. New York: HarperCollins.

Lynch, D. (1988). Reading comprehension under listening, silent and round robin reading conditions as a function of text difficulty. *Reading Improvement, 25*(2), 98 – 104.

Marshall, N. (1983). Using story grammar to assess reading comprehension. *The Reading Teacher, 36*, 616 – 620.

Mason, J. (1983). An examination of reading instruction in third and fourth grades. *The Reading Teacher, 36,* 906–913.

Mason, J., & Au, K.H. (1990). *Reading instruction for today* (2nd ed.). Glenview, IL: Scott Foresman.

McGee, L.M., & Richgels, D.J. (1985). Teaching expository text structure to elementary students. *The Reading Teacher, 38,* 739–748.

McMahon, S.I. & Raphael, T.E. (1997). *The book club connection.* New York: Teachers College Press.

Morrow, L.M. (1997). *Literacy development in the early years.* Boston: Allyn & Bacon.

Ogle, D.M. (1986). K-W-L: A teaching model that develops active reading of expository text. *The Reading Teacher, 39,* 564–570.

Pearson, P.D. (1985). Changing the face of reading comprehension instruction. *The Reading Teacher, 38,* 724–737.

Pearson, P.D., & Fielding, L. (1991). Comprehension instruction. In R. Barr, M. Kamil, P. Mosenthal, & P.D. Pearson (Eds.), *Handbook of reading research, Vol. II* (pp. 815–860). New York: Longman.

Pearson, P.D., Roehler, L.R., Dole, J.A., & Duffy, G.G. (1992). Developing expertise in reading comprehension. In S.J. Samuels & A.E. Farstrup (Eds.), *What research has to say about reading instruction* (2nd ed., pp. 145–199). Newark, DE: International Reading Association.

Piccolo, J. (1987). Expository text structure: Teaching and learning strategies. *The Reading Teacher, 40,* 838–847.

Pressley, M., El-Dinary, P.B., Gaskins, I., Bergman, J.L., Almasi, J., & Brown, R. (1992). Beyond direct explanation: Transactional instruction of reading comprehension strategies. *The Elementary School Journal, 92,* 513–555.

Pressley, M., Symons, S., Snyder, B., & Cariglia-Bull, T. (1989). Strategy instruction research comes of age. *Learning Disability Quarterly, 12*(1), 16–31.

Rhodes, L.K. (1993). *Literacy assessments.* Portsmouth, NH: Heinemann.

Ringler, L.H., & Weber, C. (1984). *A language-thinking approach to reading.* New York: Harcourt Brace Jovanovich.

Rosenblatt, L.M. (1978). *The reader, the text, the poem: The transactional theory of literacy work.* Carbondale, IL: Southern Illinois University Press.

Rosenblatt, L.M. (1994). The transactional theory of reading and writing. In R.B. Ruddell, M.R. Ruddell, & H. Singer (Eds.), *Theoretical models and processes of reading* (4th ed., pp. 1057–1092). Newark, DE: International Reading Association.

Rosenshine, B. (1980). Skill hierarchies in reading comprehension. In R.J. Spiro, B.C. Bruce, & W.F. Brewer (Eds.), *Theoretical issues in reading comprehension* (pp. 535–554). Hillsdale, NJ: Erlbaum.

Santa, C.M., Isaacson, L., & Manning, G. (1987). Changing content instruction through action research. *The Reading Teacher, 40,* 434–438.

Schunk, D.H., & Zimmerman, B.J. (1997). Developing self-efficacious readers and writers: The role of social and self-regulatory processes. In J.T. Guthrie & A. Wigfield (Eds.), *Reading engagement: Motivating readers through integrated instruction* (pp. 34–50). Newark, DE: International Reading Association.

Smith, M.W. (1991). Constructing meaning from text: An analysis of ninth-grade reader responses. *Journal of Educational Research, 84,* 263–271.

Smith, J.W.A., & Elley, W.B. (1994). *Learning to read in New Zealand.* Katonah, NY: Richard C. Owen.

Standards for the English Language Arts. (1996). Newark, DE: International Reading Association and Urbana, IL: National Council of Teachers of English.

Stauffer, R.G. (1969). *Directing reading maturity as a cognitive process.* New York: Harper & Row.

Stauffer, R.G. (1975). *Directing the direct reading-thinking process.* New York: Harper & Row.

Swanson, B.B. (1988). Strategic preferences of good and poor beginning readers. *Reading Horizons, 28,* 255–261.

Tharp, R., & Gallimore, R. (1988). *Rousing minds to life: Teaching, learning and schooling in a social context.* Cambridge, England: Cambridge University Press.

Tierney, R.J., Readence, J.E., & Dishner, E.K. (1995). *Reading strategies and practices: A compendium* (4th ed.). Boston: Allyn & Bacon.

Walker, B.J. (1996a). *Diagnostic teaching of reading* (3rd ed.). Englewood Cliffs, NJ: Merrill.

Walker, B.J. (1996b). Discussions that focus on strategies and self-assessment. In L.B. Gambrell & J.F. Almasi (Eds.), *Lively discussions!* (pp. 256–296). Newark, DE: International Reading Association.

Weaver, C. (1994). *Reading process and practice: From socio-psycholinguistics to whole language* (2nd ed.). Portsmouth, NH: Heinemann.

Wendler, D., Samuels, S.J., & Moore, V.K. (1989). Comprehension instruction of award-winning teachers, teachers with master's degrees, and other teachers. *Reading Research Quarterly, 24,* 382–400.

AUTOMATICITY AND INFERENCE GENERATION DURING READING COMPREHENSION

Richard Thurlow
Widener University, Chester, Pennsylvania, USA

Paul van den Broek
University of Minnesota, Minneapolis, Minnesota, USA

A reader must simultaneously carry out many cognitive processes while moving through a text. Each process could demand all the reader's attention and prevent any other process from occurring. However, as a reader's skill develops, some of these processes begin to demand less and less attention, thus freeing attentional resources for other, simultaneous processes. The development of automaticity is a hallmark of skilled reading, yet there are questions regarding which processes truly become automatic with practice. We intuitively know that we make a wide variety of inferences as we read that both clarify and enrich a text. However, research provides evidence that only a minimum of these inferences occur automatically. Because educators should make use of this research, recommendations are given here for fostering automaticity in inference generation.

Try to *not* think about an elephant. Not very easy, is it? The very mention of the word makes you think about it. You can't stop yourself; it's automatic. Now read the following passage:

> *Toby wanted to get Chris a present for his birthday.*
> *He went to his piggy bank.*
> *He shook it. There was no sound.*

It is quite apparent that the lack of sound means Toby has no money to buy a present. Yet at no point does the passage mention the words "money" or "buy." We don't struggle to understand why Toby would shake the bank or even to know that the "it" that he shook was indeed the bank. In fact, it would be difficult for most skilled readers to stop themselves from filling in the missing pieces. As with the "elephant" example, there is an automatic nature to the process, a sense that comprehension occurs outside of our control.

The fact that there are cognitive processes beyond our control

From *Reading and Writing Quarterly: Overcoming Learning Difficulties*, 1997, Vol. 13, No. 2, pp. 165–181 seems, at first blush, to be a weakness. If ideas come to our mind unbidden, won't our mind become cluttered with unneeded information? Perhaps, but if some cognitive processes did not function without conscious effort, we would barely be able to function at all.

When learning a task, our cognitive system is inundated with new information to which we must attend. This is a problem because our attentional resources have a limited capacity. In addition, any processing of the information that we must undertake further strains that capacity. For example, if a friend were to recite to you a list of seven or eight random numbers, you would probably have no trouble reciting the list back. However, you *would* have difficulty reciting the list in reverse order. The attention it requires to change the order of the list diminishes the amount of attention available to remember the numbers.

With repeated practice, even complex tasks can eventually require less attention; that is, they can become more automatic. For instance, it takes a great deal of attention to coordinate using the clutch and accelerator when learning to drive a standard transmission. With practice, these actions eventually occur without any cognitive effort. An important result of an increase in the automaticity of a skill is an increase in attentional resources available for other skills (e.g., talking to a passenger, something novice drivers can find distracting). In addition, automatic processes usually occur very quickly, which is probably related to why they use fewer resources. Earlier, when you read the word *elephant,* the concept "elephant" very likely was active in your mind before you even finished reading the word.

There are, then, benefits of processes that operate outside our direct control. First, they place little demand on our attentional resources. Second, they work very quickly and without effort. A cognitive process that is automatic improves our capacity to handle information because we can devote attention to other tasks while that process proceeds.

In this article, we focus on inferential processes in reading and the question of whether those processes are automatic. First, we discuss an area of debate regarding the nature of an automatic process. Then we examine the importance of inference generation during reading comprehension and some constraints on comprehension that inferences help us overcome. Next, we describe research that investigates which inferences appear to be automatic. Finally, we discuss characteristics of skilled reading that are related to the automaticity of inference generation and some educational implications.

THE NATURE OF AUTOMATIC PROCESSES

There is considerable disagreement among researchers on what exactly defines a process as being automatic (cf. Kahneman & Treisman,

1984; Posner & Snyder, 1975; Schneider, Dumais, & Shiffrin, 1984). To understand this debate, note that in the discussion above, various characteristics of "automaticity" are implied: Automatic processes (a) are initiated and run their course outside of conscious control, (b) demand few attentional resources, (c) are effortless, (d) produce little interference with other tasks, and (e) are fast.

The first two characteristics—initiation/execution without conscious control and low demands on attention—describe the mechanism of automatic processes. They are, in essence, the defining characteristics of automaticity and thus are agreed upon by most researchers. However, they are theoretical constructs that cannot be observed directly, but only through their effects on overt behaviors. This is where the other three characteristics—effortless, fast, and producing little interference—enter the scene. They describe possible behavioral consequences of a process being automatic. A particular task will be performed *more* quickly, with *less* effort, and with *less* interference, when it occurs in an automatic fashion than when it occurs via a conscious process. Because of this, automaticity should be viewed as a *relative* concept.

Trouble starts when one proposes that automatic processes are fast (or effortless or create little interference) in an *absolute* sense. Such proposals lead to the adoption of absolute criteria for automaticity, such as: for a process to be automatic it needs to be completed within a certain amount of time (usually within hundredths or tenths of a second), to take no effort whatsoever, or to show no interference with other cognitive tasks. Tempting though these criteria may be, they are inaccurate. Take, for example, the contraction reflex of the iris when a bright light is shone into the eye. This reflex is a stereotypical example of an automatic process, yet it would be disqualified by at least two of the above criteria: the muscle contraction may take several seconds, and it will consume measurable amounts of energy. The interference criterion is also limited: although "automatic" processes such as driving may not interfere with performance on relatively simple secondary tasks, they frequently do interfere with performance on more complex tasks such as navigating an unfamiliar city.

The use of absolute criteria for automaticity leads to disagreements, because for any criterion one can find exceptions. Thus, a particular process may be relatively automatic by virtue of being much faster than its conscious counterpart, and may still be slow by an absolute standard. The same applies to the other properties of automaticity mentioned. Although many automatic processes *are* very fast, require little effort, and show little interference with the execution of other tasks in an absolute sense, it is possible for a process to be automatic even though it lacks one or more of these properties. Thus, automaticity is a *relative* rather than an *absolute* concept (cf. Schneider, Dumais, & Shiffrin, 1984).

INFERENCE GENERATION IN READING COMPREHENSION

Reading involves a complex combination of cognitive processes that particularly can be hampered by our limited attention and greatly helped by the development of automaticity in those processes. As a reader moves through a text, the first task is to identify letters and words. Novice readers expend virtually all of their resources in this effort. This is one reason that their oral reading is jerky and lacks inflection; they have no attentional resources available to think about what the words mean as a unit. Skilled readers identify words automatically and therefore are able to simultaneously determine what the combinations of words—the phrases or sentences (e.g., *There was no sound*)—mean as a unit. Readers must go further and integrate each new sentence into the context provided by the rest of the text. In the "Toby" text, even the seemingly simple step of integrating the final sentence with the preceding sentences involves multiple inferences: deciding that the lack of sound is related to the shaking (previous sentence) of the piggy bank (two sentences earlier), and its implication that the bank is empty. Our concern is with automaticity in this integration process and with the role that inferences play in connecting the many ideas present in a text.

The ultimate goal of the reading process is an integration of the text material into a complete, or *coherent,* representation in the reader's memory. The memory representation is constructed from the reader's comprehension of the ideas in the text and the relations that tie those ideas together. At its simplest level, a coherent memory representation of a text such as the story about Toby would consist of the characters and events described and the various relations among them (Graesser & Clark, 1985; Kintsch & van Dijk, 1978; Trabasso, Secco, & van den Broek, 1984). Toby, Chris, and the piggy bank would be included in such a representation, as would the relations among them: Toby's goal of buying a present for Chris, and the actions he takes to meet that goal (see Figure 1). In contrast, a representation that reflects a lack of understanding of some of the relations in the story would be less coherent (see Figure 2). The degree of coherence in a reader's representation corresponds to the degree of completeness in the reader's memory for text ideas and the relations among them. The more complete, or coherent, the representation, the more complete the reader's comprehension (Trabasso et al., 1984; van den Broek, 1989).

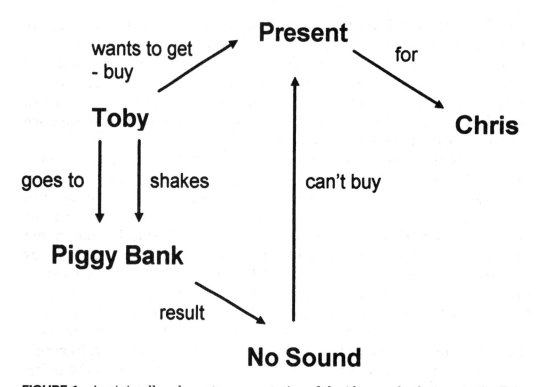

FIGURE 1 A minimally coherent representation of the ideas and relations in the Toby story.

However, as in the Toby passage, texts usually are incomplete in that they do not present every piece of information relevant to making sense of the message. Readers are required to fill in, or *infer,* the missing information from background knowledge about the topic. Thus, texts are potentially incoherent for any reader lacking in background knowledge. By filling in missing information (such as the fact that piggy banks, when shaken, usually make noise if they contain money—see Figure 3), the skilled reader creates cohesive ties that overcome these potential breaks in coherence (Halliday & Hassan, 1976).

In addition to leaving out information, texts also will often leave implicit the *relation* between adjacent sentences. For instance, our sample story offers no explanation for why Toby went to his piggy bank. We easily infer that his goal of wanting to get a present caused him to check his bank, yet it is an inference that must be made to maintain coherence (Figure 3). Again, the reader draws on background knowledge to fill gaps in the memory representation of the text.

The identification of relations becomes even more difficult when related pieces of information are distant from each other in the text. This will be done intentionally by writers of mystery stories. Information is given early in the story that is crucial to understanding or explaining events that occur much later. It also occurs unintentionally in instructional texts that are "unfriendly" to readers. If the relevance of distant information is not seen and a connection is not inferred between it and the related new information, the reader's representation will be less coherent. Inferences are required to bridge disjointed, partial, or distant information, and to make sense of each new sentence in the context of the rest of the text.

It can be seen, then, that there are several constraints imposed on a reader that can influence one's ability to maintain coherence while reading, and that inference processes are essential for dealing with these constraints. One constraint is the information provided (or rather, not provided) by the text. Any relevant information not stated in the text, including implied relations between adjacent as well as distant sentences, must be inferred by the reader. The difficulty of doing so will vary with the amount of information that is missing. A second constraint is the reader's level of background knowledge relevant to the text material. In order to fill in missing text information, the reader must have that information available in memory. Furthermore, any inferred information needs to be compatible with the information in the text. A third constraint on a reader is the limited cognitive resources available. We cannot hold the entire text in our

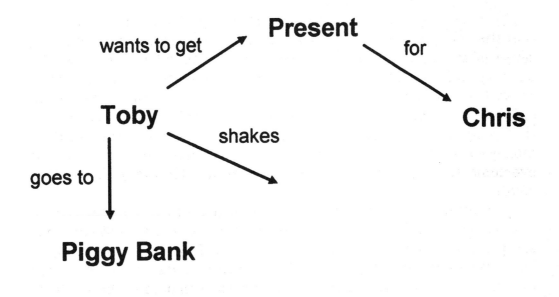

FIGURE 2 A less coherent representation, which is missing some of the relations between ideas.

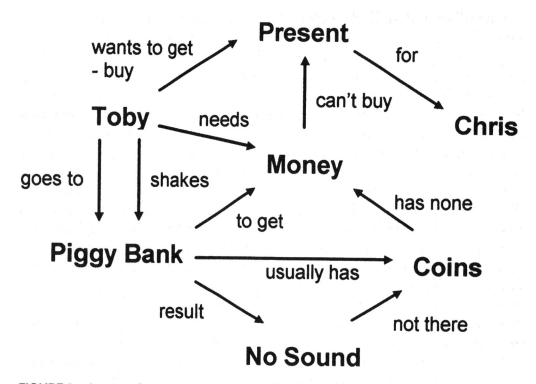

FIGURE 3 A very coherent representation of both explicit and implicit text information.

attention at one time to examine how each sentence relates to all the others. Instead, we must integrate each new sentence only with adjacent information, unless we retrieve earlier, distant information from memory.

A fourth constraint on a reader's ability to maintain coherence is the reader's own standard for coherence (van den Broek, Risden, & Husebye-Hartmann, 1995). Readers differ in the degree of coherence that they pursue. Some readers may be satisfied when they understand each individual fact or event. Others may aim for grasping the relations among various pieces of information. Still others may not be satisfied until they know the theme or moral of the text. These differences are reflected in the amount of effort that readers invest in handling difficult inferences, missing information, ambiguity, or simply a lack of clarity. The differences may have their origin in a variety of sources. For instance, some readers will not worry about complete comprehension and will ignore breaks in coherence, while other readers may simply be unaware that a coherence break has occurred, or may not have the ability to remedy it. Even within a reader the standards for coherence vary, depending on the situation and the reader's goals. For example, we typically are more relaxed about the amount of coherence in a text when we read it for entertainment than when we read it to study for an examination.

Unskilled and skilled readers differ in their ability to negotiate the constraints detailed above, such as a lack of background information. In general, skilled readers are more likely to make coherence-building inferences than are unskilled readers. Consider the following sentences: *Oxygen-depleted blood flows through the pulmonary arteries to the lungs. Then the oxygenated blood returns to the heart.* There is a causal relation between these sentences that is left implicit and requires background knowledge (*passage through the lungs oxygenates the blood*). Better readers will slow down and spend more time reading and re-reading passages when such implicit relations are unfamiliar (Bransford, Stein, Vye, Franks, Auble, Mezynski, & Perfetto, 1982). In contrast, poor readers are often unaware that there are implicit connections among sentences, and so they fail to make even simple inferences of relations that are required to create a coherent representation. Thus, skilled readers are better able to monitor their comprehension as they read a text and are more likely to take time to resolve problems. Poor readers can read quickly through a difficult passage and believe that they understand it quite well, even when they do not.

Interestingly, the fact that skilled readers are quick to make inferences can cause them problems from which less skilled readers are spared. This can be the case, for example, when a text violates the reader's initial expectations. Consider the following example: *The pickpocket stood before the black-robed judge entered the courtroom to convene the jury* (Just & Carpenter, 1987). By the time skilled readers reach the middle of this sentence, they tend to have inferred that the pickpocket is standing in front of the judge, whereas poor readers are less likely to draw that inference. For the good readers this causes a problem when they read on and must change their image of what has occurred. Readers who do not draw the early inference experience no such difficulty (Just & Carpenter, 1987).

Consequently, if a reader is motivated to extract a coherent message from a text, and has the relevant background knowledge and skills to make the necessary inferences, comprehension can be achieved. Skill in inference generation seems to entail two aspects: (a) rapid and reliable recognition of when to *initiate* inference making, and (b) efficient and effective *generation* of the actual inference. If these processes occur automatically, it should improve the likelihood that a coherent representation is created, because it will expand the reader's capacity for both monitoring comprehension and making inferences.

AUTOMATICITY IN INFERENCE MAKING

Are inferences made automatically as readers progress through the text? The topic of automaticity in inference generation is clouded by the large number of potential inferences that may be generated during reading. Consider the following short section of a story: *Janet's dog Brutus slammed into the table in his enthusiasm. Later she surveyed the broken shards of her rare vase.* There are many inferences that *could* be made when reading this passage. First, inferences connect anaphors to their referents. *Anaphors* are those terms that refer to a character or object in a new way. For example, in the first sentence, readers infer that Brutus is the enthusiastic male referred to by the pronoun "his." In the next sentence, readers infer first that Janet is the topical "she" of the sentence, and then that Janet is the owner of the former vase who is attached to the pronoun "her." It would also be anaphoric to add *The* animal *looked at her with sad eyes.* These are implicit references, no matter how obvious they seem. Readers must infer the connections.

A second category of inferences that are important to make while reading are those that are logically required for maintaining *causal* coherence; that is, establishing the causal relations among events. In this short passage, readers must infer that the vase was on the table that was bumped, and that the vase was caused to fall and subsequently break when the table moved. Again, as in the inferences about Toby, these seem obvious to most readers. Yet, it is clear that the reader must supply information about how things occur in the world and why people do what they do in order for causal connections to be made between the sentences.

Third, there are a number of likely inferences whose generation would be subject to individual differences. For instance, many readers would infer that the shards were located on the floor, but they could just as easily be thought of as being on the table. Or, some might infer that Brutus' tail was involved in the accident. Such inferences may be part of a complete and coherent representation of the text, but we wish to distinguish between likely, or logically *consistent* inferences, and necessary, or logically *required* inferences. This distinction is central to the debate regarding automaticity in inference generation.

Finally, there are many inferences that could add to the richness of a reader's understanding of the passage, which would not be related to maintaining coherence. For example, a reader could infer that Janet was upset or that Brutus would now be spending more time outdoors. Again, readers will differ considerably in which of these inferences might be made.

These four classes of potential inferences can be broken into two distinct categories (Long, Seely, Oppy, & Golding, 1996; McKoon & Ratcliff, 1992; Vonk & Noordman, 1990). The first two, anaphoric and causal, are inferences that are *required* for maintaining coherence. The others, likely and enriching, are inferences that *elaborate* on the meaning of the text. Even though there is agreement that readers are capable of making all of these inferences, a debate exists regarding whether or not the inferences are made automatically during the reading process. The debate exists in part because of a "catch" in studying inferences. If we have subjects read a passage and then ask them questions about inferred material (how did the vase get broken?), we can assume that those who give an answer are able to make the inference. However, we can't be sure that the answer to the question was inferred as the text was read. The inference could have been made at the time the question was asked. Any research that relies on asking people about what they have read is subject to this catch. However, there are methodologies (e.g., reading time, word recognition, etc.) that do examine the reading process as it occurs and that lead to greater consensus in the field.

For instance, anaphoric resolution, the first inference mentioned above, has long been accepted as essential for maintaining coherence (Kintsch & van Dijk, 1978; McKoon & Ratcliff, 1992) and has been shown to occur routinely and automatically during reading. First, subjects slow down their reading when explicit references are replaced with anaphors (Haviland & Clark, 1974) or when anaphors are distant from their referents (Lesgold, Roth, & Curtis, 1979). Additionally, readers slow down more for distant anaphors than for close ones. They slow down even more when coherence is broken by an anaphor without any referent (Cirilo, 1981). Even more compelling are findings that readers are quicker than usual to recognize a word from a text immediately after it has been referred to anaphorically. This suggests that the word indeed is the focus of their attention when that word is required for anaphoric coherence (Dell, McKoon, & Ratcliff, 1983). By testing subjects as they read, researchers have shown that readers infer very quickly, and with little effort, the connections between anaphors and their referents *as they are reading*.

Causal inferences are also viewed as essential for maintaining coherence (Warren, Nicholas, & Trabasso, 1979; Graesser & Clark, 1985; Trabasso et al., 1984), and similar methodologies indicate that they are also generated *during the reading process*. For example, reading times increase when the number of required causal inferences increases (Bloom, Fletcher, van den Broek, Reitz, & Shapiro, 1990), and when causally related items are more distant from each other, or when important causal information is missing (van den Broek & Thurlow, 1990). Additionally, as was true for anaphors, concepts that are required to maintain causal coherence are active in attention when they are needed for making an inference (Long & Golding, 1993; Long,

Golding, & Graesser, 1992; Thurlow, 1991). So, causal relations are also inferred quickly as readers move through a text. However, some studies that have examined individual differences show a weaker pattern of results for less skilled readers, implying that they may not make these inferences automatically (Long, Oppy, & Seely, 1994; Thurlow, 1991).

Thus, the inferences described earlier as required for coherence are made automatically during the reading process, at least by more skilled readers. Research into the inferences we described as elaborative shows weaker and sometimes contradictory evidence as to whether they occur during reading.

One such elaborative inference is called an *instrument inference*. For example, if a text describes one person stabbing another, a likely inference would be for a reader to think that a knife was the instrument used in the act of stabbing. Or if a text were describing a person writing a letter, it would be consistent to infer that the writer was holding a pen. Research has not strongly supported the idea that this type of inference occurs routinely during reading (Singer, 1988). However, note that the inferences suggested here—a knife to stab and a pen to write—are not the only inferences that might be made in those settings. Any sharp object, like a pair of scissors, can be used to stab, and many objects, even a computer, can be used to write a letter. There are fewer constraints on those inferences that are merely consistent with the text (a pen, pencil, etc., was used) than on those that are needed to make sense out of the text (the vase was knocked over by the dog).

Another type of elaborative inference is sometimes called a *forward inference*. Most readers have experienced a situation in which they *just know* what is going to happen next in a story. If our story about Brutus had started with a sentence explaining that Janet had just placed her delicate, rare vase on the table, readers might infer that the vase would be broken as they read about Brutus slamming into the table and before the text mentioned broken shards. There are studies demonstrating that such inferences can be made during reading, but, as was found for instrument inferences, only if the text constrains the reader's expectations sufficiently (Duffy, 1986; Husebye-Hartmann, 1992). It seems that readers need to be "set up" for such inferences to be generated reliably.

In light of such studies, researchers are coming closer to agreeing on a "minimalist" view regarding which inferences are made automatically during reading (McKoon & Ratcliff, 1992). In this view, only those inferences that are *required* to maintain coherence are seen as being automatic. The distinction between required and elaborative inferences is important for educators because readers must make the required inferences to create a coherent representation. Developing automaticity for making those inferences therefore promotes the likelihood of complete comprehension. However, because research supports only a minimalist view of automatic inference generation, the implication might be taken that readers do not or cannot generate elaborative inferences automatically. There are a number of reasons why we should consider that some elaborative inferences may be made automatically.

Consider first the limits of the research described above. Most of the research is looking at performance on tasks across a large number of subjects who vary considerably in skill and motivation. Few studies have investigated individual differences in inference generation. If only a subset of the subjects are making inferences as they read, that information can be lost in group data. Some of the research mentioned earlier suggests that better readers are more likely to generate causal inferences automatically (Long, Oppy, & Seely, 1994; Thurlow, 1991). The same could be true for elaborative inferences. Additionally, research cited here has shown that some inferences can be demonstrated only by using text material that strongly constrains which inferences the reader might make (Duffy, 1986; Husebye-Hartmann, 1992). Almost by definition, elaborative inferences are highly subject to individual differences in motivation, background knowledge, and attentional resources. We can't assume that because a group of individuals do not all make the *same* inference that none of them are making *any* inference.

Now, consider the intuitive sense we have that some elaborative inferences occur quickly and outside of our control. Try this for yourself. When reading the following sentences (from Collins, Brown, & Larkin, 1978), pause after each and consider what meaning is conveyed and how each sentence integrates with the others.

He plunked down five dollars at the window.
She tried giving him $2.50 but he refused to take it.
So when they got inside, she bought him a bag of popcorn

When asked about this text, most readers report that they infer, after reading the first sentence, that a transaction is occurring. They make this inference, without any conscious effort, even though it should not be required. After the second sentence they report that they still believe a transaction is occurring, but now they are making up elaborations that allow the text to make sense. When reading the last sentence, most readers experience a sudden shift in their interpretation of the second sentence. The new information provided in that sentence compels the reader to make new inferences that are much more coherent. The "AHA!" feeling is so automatic that it is just as difficult to suppress as thinking about that elephant.

We have now discussed several influences on whether or not an inference will be made automatically: (a) whether the inference is required to maintain coherence, (b) whether the text compels the reader strongly toward an inference, (c) whether the reader has the relevant background knowledge readily available, and (d) whether the reader is motivated and has an appropriate standard of coherence. We also know that as a reader develops automaticity in one reading skill, his or her capacity increases for either handling more information, or employing simultaneous processes—both of which will improve the likelihood of complete comprehension. From an educational perspective, then, we would like to know how we might improve a reader's ability to generate inferences automatically.

EDUCATIONAL IMPLICATIONS

Recall our statement that skill in inference generation entails both recognition of when to initiate inference making, and generation of the actual inference. Certain characteristics of skilled readers have implications for both of these aspects.

First, it is apparent that skilled readers do have a goal of constructing a coherent memory representation. They make, at least, a minimum number of automatic inferences that help integrate new material with the previous text. If integration is difficult, they will take time to work out the difficulty with elaborations. A recommendation for reading instruction is to make sure developing readers are aware that the pieces of a text are meant to go together and that they, the readers, have a task to find out how the pieces fit. One instructional technique would be to inform students that the author *also* has a task. The author's task is to make the pieces easy to put together. Class discussions can examine the students' beliefs about the author's overall message and how well different sections of the text contribute to that message. By evaluating how well authors have succeeded at their task, the students will explore the difficulties in their own task.

Second, skilled readers have strategies and criteria for repairing coherence breaks. They re-read difficult passages; they look back in the text for more information; they even make up their own explanations that make sense. These are all teachable skills, and instruction in such strategies is important (Irwin; 1986). However, readers should also be taught to be conservative in using these strategies. For one thing, not *all* relevant information is required for coherence. Often, all a reader needs is a sufficient way to integrate new text information (van den Broek, Risden, & Husebye-Hartmann, 1995). In addition, difficult passages often will become clearer simply by reading further. Part of the instruction in these strategies should focus on recognizing when the application of such strategies is called for (i.e., likely to be successful) and when it is not efficient.

Finally, skilled readers can make inferences automatically only if they are careful in the use of their attentional resources. That is, they must attend to the most important material for making inferences. Research suggests some ways that skilled readers focus their attention. One way is to keep track of the most important topic information and to direct attention to any new material referring to the same topic either directly or anaphorically. To use one of our earlier examples, readers might keep their attention focused on Janet and Brutus, as their story goes on, because they are referred to again and again. This is called a *leading edge* strategy, and it fits well with research regarding the automatic nature of anaphoric inferences (Kintsch & van Dijk, 1978; Miller & Kintsch, 1980). Another way to focus attention would be to keep track of text information that is likely to play an important causal role. This might include the goals and motives of characters, or actions that have occurred but have not yet had a consequence. Again, as Janet's story unfolds, readers might focus their attention on the fact that the vase was broken, because up to this point, nothing has happened as a consequence of the accident. This is called a *current state* strategy, and it is supported by research into the automatic nature of causal inferences (Fletcher & Bloom, 1988; Fletcher, van den Broek, & Arthur, 1996). A recommendation for instruction would be to assist readers in attending to these aspects of a text—for instance, asking questions about common referents (What did Toby shake?), causal relations (Why did Toby shake the bank?), and also likely causal consequences (What do you think Toby will do now?). However, for better readers, these questions can be too simple to interest them. They may already be making those inferences automatically. Questions of an elaborative nature would challenge them to think beyond the obvious (How did Toby feel?; Does he like Chris enough to keep trying?).

In summary, skilled readers can, and do, make inferences *automatically* as they read through a text. They must, however, be motivated to maintain a coherent representation, and they must have sufficient background knowledge for those inferences to be made. As beginning readers develop automaticity in more basic skills (e.g., decoding), they expand their capacity to make the numerous inferences required for comprehension. Similarly, when readers can make those required inferences automatically, they will have resources available for making elaborative inferences that will add to the richness of the reading experience.

REFERENCES

Bloom, C. P., Fletcher, C. R., van den Broek, P. W., Reitz, L., & Shapiro, B. P. (1990). An on-line assessment of causal reasoning during text comprehension. *Memory & Cognition, 18,* 65–71.

Bransford, J. D., Stein, B. S., Vye, N. J., Franks, J. J., Auble, P. M., Mezynski, K. J., & Perfetto, B. A. (1982). Differences in approaches to learning: An overview. *Journal of Experimental Psychology: General, 111,* 390–398.

Cirilo, R. K. (1981). Referential coherence and text structure in story comprehension. *Journal of Verbal Learning and Verbal Behavior, 20,* 358–367.

Collins, A. M., Brown, J. S., & Larkin, K. (1978). Inference in text understanding. In R. J. Spiro, B. C. Bruce, & W. F. Brewer (Eds.), *Theoretical issues in reading comprehension* (pp. 385–407). Hillsdale, NJ: Lawrence Erlbaum Associates.

Dell, G. S., McKoon, G., & Ratcliff, R. (1983). The activation of antecedent information during the processing of anaphoric references in reading. *Journal of Verbal Learning and Verbal Behavior, 22,* 121–132.

Duffy, S. A. (1986). Role of expectations in sentence integration. *Journal of Experimental Psychology: Learning, Memory, and Cognition, 12,* 208–219.

Fletcher, C. R., & Bloom, C. P., (1988). Causal reasoning in the comprehension of simple narrative texts. *Journal of Memory and Language, 27,* 235–244.

Fletcher, C. R., van den Broek, P. W., & Arthur, E. J. (1996). A model of narrative comprehension and recall. In B. K. Britton and A. C. Graesser (Eds.), *Models of understanding text* (pp. 141–163). Hillsdale, NJ: Lawrence Erlbaum Associates.

Graesser, A. C., & Clark, L. F., (1985). *The structures and procedures of implicit knowledge.* Norwood, NJ: Ablex.

Halliday, M., & Hassan, R. (1976). *Cohesion in English.* London: Longman.

Haviland, S. E., & Clark, H. H. (1974). What's new? Acquiring new information as a process in comprehension. *Journal of Verbal Learning and Verbal Behavior, 13,* 512–521.

Husebye-Hartmann, E. (1992). *Causal elaborative inferences in text comprehension: Implications for psychology and education.* Unpublished doctoral dissertation, University of Minnesota.

Irwin, J. W. (1986). *Teaching reading comprehension processes.* Englewood Cliffs, NJ: Prentice-Hall.

Just, M. A., & Carpenter, P. A. (1987). *The psychology of reading and language comprehension.* Newton, MA: Allyn and Bacon.

Kahneman, D., & Treisman, A. (1984). Changing views of attention and automaticity. In R. Parasuraman and D. R. Davies (Eds.), *Varieties of attention* (pp. 29–61). New York: Academic Press.

Kintsch, W. A., & van Dijk, T. A. (1978). Toward a model of text comprehension and production. *Psychological Review, 85,* 363–394.

Lesgold, A. M., Roth, S. F., & Curtis, M. E. (1979). Foregrounding effects in discourse comprehension. *Journal of Verbal Learning and Verbal Behavior, 18,* 291–308.

Long, D. L., & Golding, J. M. (1993). Superordinate goal inferences: Are they automatically generated during comprehension? *Discourse Processes, 16,* 55–74.

Long, D. L., Golding, J. M., & Graesser, A. C. (1992). A test of the on-line status of goal related inferences. *Journal of Memory and Language, 31,* 634–647.

Long, D. L., Oppy, B. J., & Seely, M. R. (1994). Individual differences in the time course of inferential processing. *Journal of Experimental Psychology: Learning, Memory, and Cognition, 20,* 1456–1470.

Long, D. L., Seely, M. R., Oppy, B. J., & Golding, J. M. (1996). The role of inferential processing in reading ability. In B. K. Britton and A. C. Graesser (Eds.), *Models of understanding text* (pp. 189–214). Hillsdale, NJ: Lawrence Erlbaum Associates.

McKoon, G., & Ratcliff, R. (1992). Inference during reading. *Psychological Review, 99,* 440–466.

Miller, J. R., & Kintsch, W. (1980). Readability and recall of short prose passages: A theoretical analysis. *Journal of Experimental Psychology: Human Learning and Memory, 6,* 335–355.

Posner, M. I., & Snyder, C. R. R. (1975). Attention and cognitive control. In R. L. Solso (Ed.), *Information processing and cognition: The Loyola symposium* (pp. 55–85). Hillsdale, NJ: Lawrence Erlbaum Associates.

Schneider, W., Dumais, S. T., & Shiffrin, R. M. (1984). Automatic and control processing and attention. In R. Parasuraman and D. R. Davies (Eds.), *Varieties of attention* (pp. 1–27). New York: Academic Press.

Singer, M. (1988). Inferences in reading comprehension. In M. Daneman, G. MacKinnon, & T. Waller (Eds.), *Reading research: Advances in theory and practice* (Vol. 6, pp. 177–219). New York: Academic Press.

Thurlow R. (1991). *The inference of causal antecedents during the reading of narratives.* Unpublished doctoral dissertation, University of Minnesota.

Trabasso, T., Secco, T., & van den Broek, P. W. (1984). Causal cohesion and story coherence. In H. Mandl, N. L. Stein, & T. Trabasso (Ed.), *Learning and comprehension of text* (pp. 83–111). Hillsdale, NJ: Lawrence Erlbaum Associates.

van den Broek, P. W. (1989). The effects of causal structure on the comprehension of narratives: Implications for education. *Reading Psychology: An International Quarterly, 10,* 19–44.

van den Broek, P. W., Risden, K., & Husebye-Hartmann, E. (1995). Comprehension of narrative events: Maintaining sufficient explanation. In R. F. Lorch, Jr., & E. O'Brien (Eds.), *Sources of coherence in reading* (pp. 353–373). Hillsdale, NJ: Lawrence Erlbaum Associates.

van den Broek, P. W., & Thurlow, R. (1990, November). *Reinstatements and elaborative inferences during the reading of narratives.* Paper presented at the annual meeting of the Psychonomic Society, New Orleans, LA.

Vonk, W., & Noordman, L. G. (1990). On the control of inferences in text understanding. In D. A. Balota, G. B. Flores d'Arcais, & K. Rayner (Eds.), *Comprehension processes in reading* (pp. 447–463). Hillsdale, NJ: Lawrence Erlbaum Associates.

Warren, W. H., Nicholas, D. W., & Trabasso, T. (1979). Event chains and inferences in understanding narratives. In R. O. Freedle (Ed.), *New directions in discourse processing* (pp. 23–51). Norwood, NJ: Ablex.

Reading as a Gateway to Language Proficiency for Language-Minority Students in the Elementary Grades

Valerie Anderson
Centre for Applied Cognitive Studies
University of Toronto

Marsha Roit
SRA/McGraw-Hill

Many educators maintain that language-minority students must be fluent in oral English before they engage in learning to read in English (e.g., Wong, Fillmore, & Valadez, 1986). The practical result is that reading instruction is frequently delayed in favor of instructional efforts toward oral language proficiency. The long-range results among students are inequities that persist across the school years. In view of the increasing numbers of culturally diverse students in nonspecialized classrooms and the decreasing educational resources, even the possibility of such inequities necessitates pedagogical approaches that ensure some basic consistencies in instruction across students and grade levels.

From *Promoting Learning for Culturally and Linguistically Diverse Students: Classroom Applications from Contemporary Research,* 1998, Wadsworth, a division of Thomson Learning. The authors are grateful for the support of the Spencer Foundation in completing this work. Further thanks go to Elizabeth Lee for her helpful editorial assisstance with the manuscript.

In the past many bilingual classrooms consisted of students from one or two language groups—often primarily Hispanic. Now due to changing immigration patterns, there are an increasing number of classrooms in which most of the students do not share a common first language. In fact, in many schools the diversity is so great that neither bilingual programs or language assistants in the classroom are a feasible solution to the problem. This chapter is specifically intended to address reading instruction in English for the language-minority students in these multiethnic classrooms.

Delaying reading for language-minority students has been recognized as a problem for some time (Goodman, Goodman, & Flores, 1979), yet there is little in the literature on how to effectively teach such students to understand what they read (Grabe, 1991), particularly when compared with the wealth of research on how to teach them to understand and speak oral English (Weber, 1991). Goodman et al. (1979) argue that reading in English should start when students begin to show receptive understanding. Like many people learning a new language, students may be reticent to speak in a new language even though they have some understanding. Because students may be equally receptive to written English, it seems reasonable that instruction in reading English should start earlier than is currently found in practice.

The potential reciprocity between learning to read and reading to learn has strong implications for developing oral language in language-minority students. Barrera (1983) noted that children learn to read in their second language before oral fluency develops. She substantiated the relationship between reading and language by pointing out that students are not limited by their oral language and that it is likely they learn English by reading in context. Despite these observations, practitioners to date have not generally taken advantage of this important reciprocity (Weber, 1991).

For nearly 10 years, we have worked extensively in the United States and Canada in grade 1–8 classrooms with high percentages of language-minority students from more than 40 countries. Our efforts have focused on helping teachers provide students with reading comprehension strategies (Anderson, 1992; Anderson & Roit, 1990, December, 1993). A natural outcome has been the informal gathering of information concerning instructional issues related to teaching the students to read. From conversations with teachers and administrators, observations of literacy teaching, and videotaped teaching sessions, we have identified six issues related to reading comprehension and language development. We state these issues as competencies that, when developed, increase both understanding of text and oral language proficiency. The competencies are English language flexibility, use of basic vocabulary that is difficult to visualize (e.g., *of, not, to*), consideration of larger contexts, determination of importance and unimportance, elaborated responses, and engagement in natural conversations.

Teaching these competencies through text has advantages over dealing with them simply on an oral basis. Spoken language is fleeting and inconsistent over time. Text, by contrast, is stable and does not pass the learner by.

When text is used, the learner can reread, reflect on, and reconsider the material to be learned, in its original form.

We focus on reading comprehension as a gateway to language development, rather than on proficient language as a prerequisite to reading. Each competency is described in one of the sections that follow. They are discussed separately for purposes of clarity; we realize that they are interrelated. We have not dealt with decoding, because there is much information on how to teach it (Adams, 1991). As with any learners, some language-minority students have decoding difficulties, but comprehension difficulties have a more direct bearing on language development and are more widespread, severe, and difficult to deal with instructionally.

The issues are followed by 10 suggestions for teaching the competencies. No attempt has been made to precisely fit suggestions to individual competencies in the way one might treat isolated skills. To do so would be out of step with current conceptions of teaching and learning (Bereiter & Scardamalia, 1989; Brown & Campione, 1990; Foresee, 1991). We offer a variety of interrelated activities, each of which could help to meet the literacy needs of language-minority students.

INSTRUCTIONAL ISSUES

English Language Flexibility

Anyone learning a new language feels good when they figure out *one* way to say something. To say something in more than one way may be initially beyond the learner. Consequently, language-minority students may respond to questions with answers in English and verbatim from the text. They find text words that correspond to a question, because they can read some of the words, but they may not know what their answers mean. They also may have difficulty putting text in their own words, because they do not understand the material or are not yet able to generate alternative ways to express it. Language inflexibility may actually be fostered by teaching in which students are expected to respond only in English. Numerous researchers (e.g., Cummins, 1989; Moll, 1994) contend that allowing children to use their first, or heritage, language to respond enhances second language learning.

Use of Basic Vocabulary That Is Difficult to Visualize

Vocabulary problems contribute substantially to language-minority students' problems in learning to understand text (e.g., Garcia, 1991). Cummins (1994) makes an interesting distinction between knowledge of surface vocabulary and knowledge of the cognitive vocabulary required for school achievement. Many teachers stress surface aspects of language, such as high-frequency nouns, verbs, and adjectives, rather than the more basic, abstract, and conceptual type of vocabulary that carries the logic of the language (e.g., negatives, conjunctions, prepositions, and other abstract words). Often, students learn these as part of their sight vocabularies, but confusions about usage and meaning persist.

Consideration of Larger Contexts

Despite frequent calls for teaching word meanings in context, typical instruction often focuses on accumulating the meanings of isolated words. While students clearly need to know more words, a concentration primarily on individual words may have unfortunate consequences. In a typical reading session, the teacher stops students at a word, asks for meaning, tells the meaning if necessary, has students repeat the word, and goes on like this every few words throughout the text. Students soon learn to grind down mercilessly on words and lose all sense of the context (Lee, 1984), further application, and ownership of the words on which they have worked so hard. When an emphasis on ungeneralizable words is coupled with a neglect of the contexts in which they occur, students begin to concentrate on minutia and ignore text meaning as a whole.

Determination of Importance and Unimportance

Unless students consider the context of words, they are unlikely to recognize important aspects of text, a crucial reading strategy (Dole, Duffy, Roehler, & Pearson, 1991). Language-minority students are surrounded by a mass of information waiting to be learned, and all readers tend to focus on highly noticeable but trivial aspects of text (Hidi & Anderson, 1987). To motivate students to speak, teachers may inadvertently underemphasize importance. For example, in classes where we observed the reading of a passage on mummies, teachers encouraged discussions on Egyptian embalmers pulling a dead person's brains out through the nose, but initiated no discussions on the cultural significance of the mummification process featured in the text. With so much input and no model of what is more or less important, what students learn from reading is often scattered and of limited applicability.

Elaborated Responses

The problems described make it understandable that language-minority students tend to respond in very few words. When prompted to say more, they commonly add as little as possible, with resulting piecemeal responses. Students rarely put together all of what they have said, and they end up with mere fragments of ideas.

Engagement in Natural Conversations

There is little chance for language-minority students to converse in English in the classroom. Gunderson (1985) found that most teachers taught reading in conventional ways and did not restructure their usual instruction to meet the special needs of students. Reading instruction is usually controlled by the teacher through teacher-generated questions, which do not encourage real conversation. Allington (1994, May) pointed out that only in schools are people constantly required to answer questions to which the asker already knows the answers—an infrequent occurrence in actual conversations. Conversations in students' homes in a first and/or second language have been shown to support the learning of a new language (Delgado-Gaitan, 1990). Yet most teachers fail to capitalize on this and may even counteract the benefits of heritage languages by discouraging students from using their first language and neglecting to foster natural conversations. Although some teachers stage "typical" conversations, these attempts do not usually capture the spontaneous and unstilted nature of real talk.

INSTRUCTIONAL SUGGESTIONS

The issues just listed involve *teachable* competencies. The following suggestions offer ways to teach these competencies through reading. Many language-minority students receive their instruction from regular classroom teachers who have little background in teaching English as a second language (Spangenberg-Urbschat & Pritchard, 1994). It is hoped that the suggestions will be especially helpful to these teachers.

The activities share the characteristics of productive practices defined by Gersten and Jiménez (1994)—practices that (a) lead to high levels of student involvement, (b) foster higher-order cognitive processes, and (c) enable students to engage in extended discourse. The suggestions also can be applied across grade levels and types of text. Further, the activities allow students to take part in a variety of ways and with different levels of English language experience. For each suggestion, we specify those grade levels, from 1 to 8, for which it seems most appropriate.

Shared Reading

Shared reading involves a teacher reading and sharing a book with students. Variations on this procedure have research support with many language-minority populations (e.g., Heald-Taylor, 1986), as well as widespread support from reading practitioners.

We suggest the following procedure for shared reading: Read a selection to the students a day or so in advance of when they are to read it. During this reading, with the help of teacher modeling, students should be encouraged to react freely to the text and to clarify any problems. Later, when the students read the selection, they will be able to contribute to a discussion in more sophisticated ways. The focus on meaning will be easier because problems with vocabulary and unfamiliar concepts will have already been addressed. Also, students will be able to clarify any remaining problems, read with more fluency and expression, and discuss what made the text enjoyable or interesting.

Although shared reading is most appropriate and commonly practiced in grades K–2, widespread anecdotal reports indicate that students at all levels continue to enjoy being read to, particularly when combined with their spontaneous input.

Vocabulary Networking

Often called semantic webbing or mapping, vocabulary networking is a current, popular, and effective way to develop vocabulary. In a semantic web, students graphically organize vocabulary from texts or other sources into related groups of words. Unfortunately, however, the activity is often carried out as a one-shot collective activity to which students do not return, or it is done too infrequently to provide the needed consistency. Alternatively, we suggest that a variety of networks be kept on separate sheets in a central location so that all students can return to them, add to them, and refer to them over time. It is critical to set a regular time for networking, or it may be neglected. The vocabulary base of the activity could also be designed to better meet the needs of the students. At the top of each sheet could be a word that the students agree is difficult. Students could organize meanings, examples, relationships, text references, and impressions for each word, drawing from their experiences, conversations, and readings. This not only increases students' understanding of particularly difficult words but also provides a source of vocabulary ideas for writing.

Since the vocabulary mapping suggested here calls on organization abilities as well as an understanding of superordinate and subordinate concepts, it is most appropriate for students in grades 3–8.

Expanding Context

Several procedures can help students become more aware of contexts for words. After clarifying a word, students can discuss what it has to do with the text, other texts, or their own experiences. Students can then exchange ideas on how they use new words in writing. Illustrating vocabulary can also put words into a context and, at the same time, encourage imagery. The important learning goal is to move from learning words in isolation to learning them in meaningful contexts. Even very young children can participate in these sorts of activities with easy texts.

Expanding context, however, applies to more than words and is appropriate at all levels. For students beyond first grade, difficult sentences and paragraphs, once understood, need to be thought of in terms of the whole text. This might be accomplished by simply asking, "What does this have to do with the rest of the text?"

Predicting

This strategy requires a sense of expanded context and is particularly important when reading narrative texts, such as stories, biographies, histories, and factual narrative episodes. It is futile to simply hope that students will predict when reading something they do not understand, so it is important that students first talk about their understandings of the text before they try to predict. It is also important for students to revisit predictions to see if text bears them out. Predictions can be written down and/or paraphrased so that all students can understand them. Gersten and Jiménez (1994) document effective teaching that includes the use of such written cues. Making predictions can be begun with very young children, as is done by most teachers. Teachers should push toward having students decide when to predict and why they wish to predict, so that students become independent in this strategy.

Imagery

Imagery (i.e., creating a mental image of text) aids comprehension in students from grade 3 on (Tierney & Cunningham, 1984). One way to encourage imagery is to talk more about illustrations. Since these do not always accurately depict important text aspects, it is critical to select texts in which the illustrations are supportive of understanding (Allen, 1994). Students could be asked to produce pictures of what they read and then to compare them with the text. Later, students might compare a text with its author's illustrations and tell whether the text and pictures match. A more sophisticated application of imagery might be judging whether the illustrations convey a text's most important, interesting, or difficult ideas. Students can begin talking about texts with supportive illustrations as early as grade 1, with the more advanced approaches carried out in grades 3–8.

Text Structures

Text structures are organizational options that authors choose when producing texts. These structures govern content to the extent that it relates to the structure chosen, such as cause and effect, compare and contrast, or problem and solution. Some studies have shown that teaching text structures to language-minority students increases their comprehension (Hague, 1990). An interesting instructional procedure, shown to be effective with students starting in grade 4 (Anderson, Chan, & Henne, 1995; McLaren & Anderson, 1992), involves teaching a text structure, such as problem and solution, by having students ask a series of questions that correspond to the characteristics of the text's structure (e.g., "What is the problem?" "What is the cause of the problem?" "What will happen if the problem continues?" "How can the problem be solved?"). Students then generate writing topics to answer the questions on the basis of their prior knowledge and use their answers to write problem-and-solution texts. The questions are scaffolds (instructional supports) for writing (Bereiter & Scardamalia, 1987). Text structures can be introduced with simple text types (e.g., narratives) in grade 1. Later, more difficult text structures (e.g., opinion texts, explanations) can be introduced. Examining text structures teaches students to ask important questions, improves reading comprehension, enhances language, encourages discussion, and integrates reading and writing.

Questioning, Identifying Problems, and Sharing Strategies

A number of recent studies show that language-minority students benefit from learning cognitive strategies for solving reading problems (e.g., Coterall, 1990). All students need to feel free to ask questions, explain their problems, and exchange and evaluate ideas for solving them. Fluent English is not necessary for such discussions. With the help of teacher modeling, think-aloud procedures have been implemented even with first graders (Pressley et al., 1992). Jiménez, Garcia, and Pearson (1996) show that language-minority students are able to think aloud about the strategies used in reading. Anderson (1992) has capitalized on this ability with culturally diverse adolescents in an instructional approach called collaborative strategy instruction, in which students and teacher work in a small group to identify aspects that make a text difficult, then work on strategies for resolving those difficulties (Anderson & Roit, 1990, December, 1993).

One strategy language-minority readers use to comprehend text is to draw on related background knowledge (Jiménez et al., 1996). Language-minority students may lack the background knowledge needed to understand some English texts. With so much to know, providing enough of this background in enough time is impossible, and it is not surprising that educators cannot accomplish the task. A more efficient way to solve the problem may be to teach students to handle a crucial lack of knowledge like the rest of us do, by questioning, identifying the problems, and finding ways to fill gaps as we read.

The use of strategies can be introduced in grade 1. At higher levels, more complex uses and variations may be introduced. From grade 5 on, students should more and more be expected to generate their own strategies and problem-solving ideas.

Text Explaining

Teachers often attempt to check understanding by allowing students to simply retell a text verbatim. This may be helpful for English speakers who know what they are retelling, but it may simply be poor practice for others. While language-minority students are often good at retelling, they may have little understanding of what they have retold. Instead of asking students to retell, teachers can encourage students to try to explain what the text means and to compare explanations with other students. This can be accomplished in collaborative groups, with simple, consistent directives that facilitate text explaining, such as, "What does this mean?" and "Can you explain it in your own words?"

Text explaining not only improves comprehension but also increases verbal elaboration and language flexibility as students exchange ideas. Text explaining also provides the teacher with a powerful way to assess whether students have really understood what they have read and to discover the sources of confusion. For language-minority students in particular, for whom so many forms of assessment are considered culturally unfair, such informal assessment is needed (Garcia, 1991).

The activity can be made less difficult with the support of teacher modeling and smaller text segments, moving to independent text explaining and larger segments as students become more proficient in English. Simple explanations of difficult words and phrases may begin in grade 1, with a gradual extension of the amount of text to be explained. From grade 4 on, more abstract ideas within text, such as seasonal change, photosynthesis, or molecules, might be explained by the students. Although a teacher may at first specify what children explain, it is more powerful to teach *them* to recognize what they think needs explaining (Anderson & Roit, 1990, December).

Conversational Opportunities

When learning a new language, most people look forward to opportunities to practice conversationally with a native speaker. These are usually lively exchanges about social or other matters, in which the conversationalists feel no discomfort from interrupting the flow of talk with language-learning questions, such as, "How do you say . . . ?" or, "Do you mean . . . ?" The purpose is to exchange information and find out about language in a friendly, enjoyable, and unintimidating way. Unfortunately, schools do not provide these opportunities. Gallimore, Boggs, and Jordon (1974) found that language-minority children were competent at home, where learning took place through group conversation, but not competent in school, where the rules were clearly different. Many researchers (e.g., Moll, 1988) have described the nonconversational recitation approach used in most schools for all children. We have pointed out that the home culture and the use of heritage languages in school can enrich school learning. It is undoubtedly true that proficiency in a heritage language is largely built from natural home conversations (Goldenberg & Gallimore, 1991).

The kind of teacher-student collaborative reading sessions reported by Anderson and Roit (1993) encourage conversational opportunities. They move away from teacher-questioning sessions to sessions in which students read and ask each other general but critical questions that stimulate real conversation: "Why is this important?" "What did I like best about it, and why?" "What is most interesting?" In other words, students are engaging in the kinds of conversations that adults engage in about their reading experiences. An added advantage of these kinds of questions is that they can be applied consistently and effectively across any number of texts. As these questions move into the hands of the students, they lead to lively and realistic conversational practice about reading and language. The intention here is not to tell students what to say to each other, but to encourage natural conversations and allow them to happen.

Many conversations occur between two people, so there should be opportunities for pairs of students to converse. These conversations need not always be between a good and a poor English speaker. Two students with poorer English can benefit from English conversational practice in which they share problems and information, and they clearly teach each other because they know different aspects of English. The challenge of such conversational opportunities is to implement them without their degenerating into stilted, teacher-controlled, and preplanned conversations. In short, ideal conversational practice should be natural, open, and freewheeling.

Conversational opportunities must be supported at all levels. The students themselves will guide the teacher in the type and level of conversation.

Culturally Fair Informational Material

Researchers have shown the importance of integrating students' cultures into teaching at all levels (Au & Jordon, 1981; Goldenberg & Gallimore, 1991; Moll & Greenberg, 1990), and educators have begun to realize the need to consider it. Perhaps the most popular and well-researched approach to including culture is through the use of culturally familiar reading materials (e.g., Rigg, 1986; Steffenson, Joag-dev, & Anderson, 1979).

Care must be taken, however, in the selection of multicultural materials. School reading materials chosen specifically for ethnic representation often illustrate sophisticated aspects of a culture, with which students actually have had little experience. In other words, while these selections could inspire pride, they may not inspire understanding. We are not suggesting that such selections be excluded, but rather that students also be provided with a relatively large set of short, simple expository passages that provide some interesting and enlightening information about very common ethnic experiences (e.g., holidays, animals, and foods). Such texts can be drawn from children's encyclopedias, trade books, and magazines. Barrera's (1992) analysis of multicultural literature and Allen's (1994) suggestions for selecting materials for ESOL students offer ideas for further sources. The students choose from these texts, read them independently, and tell the class about what they found out and how it related to their own experiences. Later, students' experience-based writing on expository topics might be added to the set of materials. In this way, students become authors, and their works become part of the class collection of relevant informational materials.

This activity has several advantages. First, it provides some culturally familiar material that students choose based on their prior knowledge and interests. Second, it gives students a chance to demonstrate their intelligence by sharing their own experiences and providing new knowledge to their peers. Third, and most importantly, it allows students to provide models for other students of at least three important reading strategies—identifying with text, reacting to text, and connecting text with prior knowledge.

In sum, the purpose of this chapter has been a practical one. We urge practitioners to avoid withholding reading from some students, while promoting it with others. The chapter describes a number of issues regarding language-minority students, some of which you may have observed. It also attempts to provide some easy-to-implement suggestions for helping students to learn English. The emphases on using strategies and collaborating allow teachers to help students use their natural social and cognitive abilities for learning to use their new language as they learn to read. Our suggestions provide equitably for student differences, because they are approaches that place value on differentiated contributions from students and that can be readily implemented on a schoolwide basis. Surely, equity is more easily accomplished in an environment where educators and students share similar learning goals and work together to achieve them.

REFERENCES

Adams, M. J. (1991). *Beginning to read: Thinking and learning about print.* Cambridge, MA: MIT Press.

Allen, V. G. (1994). Selecting materials for the instruction of ESL children. In K. Spangenberg-Urbschat & R. Pritchard (Eds.), *Kids come in all languages: Reading instruction for ESL students* (pp. 108–131). Newark, DE: International Reading Association.

Allington, R. (1994, May). *Balancing "Once upon a time" and "Scientists say."* Paper presented at the meeting of the International Reading Association, Toronto, Ontario, Canada.

Anderson, V. (1992). A teacher development project in transactional strategy instruction for teachers of severely reading-disabled adolescents. *Teaching and Teacher Education, 8*(4), 391–403.

Anderson, V., Chan, C. K. K., & Henne, R. (1995). The effects of strategy instruction on the literacy models and performance of reading and writing delayed middle school students. In *Perspectives on literacy research and practice: Forty-fourth yearbook of the National Reading Conference* (pp. 180–189). Chicago: National Reading Conference.

Anderson, V., & Roit, M. L. (1990, December). *Developing active reading behaviors with disabled adolescent learners.* Paper presented at the National Reading Conference, Miami Beach, FL.

Anderson, V., & Roit, M. L. (1993). Planning and implementing collaborative strategy instruction with delayed readers in grades 6–10. *Elementary School Journal, 94*(2), 121–137.

Anyon, J. (1981). Social class and school knowledge. *Curriculum Inquiry, 11,* 3–42.

Au, K. H., & Jordon, C. (1981). Teaching reading to Hawaiian children: Finding a culturally appropriate solution. In H. Trueba, G. P. Guthrie, & K. H. Au (Eds.), *Culture and the bilingual classroom: Studies in ethnography.* Rowley, MA: Newbury House.

Barrera, R. (1983). Bilingual reading in the primary grades: Some questions about questionable views and practices. In T. H. Escobedo (Ed.), *Early childhood bilingual education: A Hispanic perspective* (pp. 164–183). New York: Teachers College Press.

Barrera, R. (1992). The literacy gap in literature-based literacy instruction. *Education and Urban Society, 24*(2), 227–243.

Bereiter, C., & Scardamalia, M. (1987). *The psychology of written composition.* New York: Erlbaum.

Bereiter, C., & Scardamalia, M. (1989). Intentional learning as a goal of instruction. In L. B. Resnick (Ed.), *Knowing, learning, and instruction: Essays in honor of Robert Glaser* (pp. 361–392). Hillsdale, NJ: Erlbaum.

Brown, A. L., & Campione, J. C. (1990). Communities of learning and thinking, or a context by any other name. In D. Kuhn (Ed.), *Contributions to human development: Vol.*

21, *Developmental perspectives on teaching and learning thinking skills* (pp. 108–126). Farmington, CT: Karger.

Coterall, S. (1990). Developing reading strategies through small-group interaction. *RELC Journal, 21,* 55–69.

Cummins, J. (1989). *Empowering minority students.* Sacramento, CA: California Association for Bilingual Education.

Cummins, J. (1994). The acquisition of English as a second language. In K. Spangenberg-Urbschat & R. Pritchard (Eds.), *Kids come in all languages: Reading instruction for ESL students* (pp. 32–62). Newark, DE: International Reading Association.

Delgado-Gaitan, C. (1990). *Literacy for empowerment: The role of parents in children's education.* New York: Falmer Press.

Dole, J. A., Duffy, G. G., Roehler, L. R., & Pearson, P. D. (1991). Moving from the old to the new: Research on reading comprehension instruction. *Review of Educational Research, 61,* 239–264.

Foresee, V. (1991). Whole language practice and theory. Boston: Allyn and Bacon.

Gallimore, R., Boggs, J. W., & Jordon, C. (1974). *Culture, behavior, and education: A study of Hawaiian-Americans.* Newbury Park, CA: Sage.

Garcia, G. E. (1991). Factors influencing the English reading test performance of Spanish-speaking Hispanic children. *Reading Research Quarterly, 26*(4), 371–392.

Gersten, R. M., & Jiménez, R. T. (1994). A delicate balance: Enhancing literacy instruction for students of English as a second language. *The Reading Teacher, 47*(6), 438–449.

Goldenberg, C., & Gallimore, R. (1991). Local knowledge, research knowledge, and educational change: A case study of early Spanish reading improvement. *Educational Researcher, 20*(8), 2–14.

Goodman, K., Goodman, Y., & Flores, B. (1979). *Reading in the bilingual classroom: Literacy and biliteracy.* Rosslyn, VA: National Clearinghouse for Bilingual Education.

Grabe, W. (1991). Current development in second language reading research. *TESOL Quarterly, 25,* 375–406.

Gunderson, L. (1985). A survey of L2 reading instruction in British Columbia. *Canadian Modern Language Review, 42,* 44–55.

Hague, S. (1990). Awareness of test construction: The question of transfer from L1 to L2. In *Cognitive and social perspectives for literacy research and instruction: Thirty-eighth yearbook of the National Reading Conference* (pp. 55–64). Chicago: National Reading Conference.

Heald-Taylor, G. (1986). *Whole language strategies for ESL students.* Toronto, Ontario, Canada: OISE Press.

Hidi, S., & Anderson, V. (1987). Producing written summaries: Task demands, cognitive operations, and implications for instruction. *Review of Educational Research, 56,* 473–493.

Jiménez, R. T., Garcia, G. E., & Pearson, P. D. (1996). The reading strategies of bilingual Latina/o students who are successful English readers: Opportunities and obstacles. *Reading Research Quarterly, 31*(1), 90–112.

Lee, Y. J. (1984). Contextual reading. In B. W. Kim (Ed.), *The first yearbook of literacy and language* (pp. 93–103). Seoul, Korea: Literacy and Language Arts in Asia.

McLaren, J., & Anderson, V. (1992, December). *Instruction in two text structures: Effects on understanding and written production of expository text by elementary school students.* Paper presented at the National Reading Conference, San Antonio, TX.

Moll, L. C. (1988). Some key issues in teaching Latino students. *Language Arts, 65*(5), 465–472.

Moll, L. C. (1994). Literacy research in community and classrooms: A sociocultural approach. In R. B. Ruddell, M. R. Ruddell, & H. Singer (Eds.), *Theoretical models and processes of reading* (pp. 179–207). Newark, DE: International Reading Association.

Moll, L. C., & Greenberg, J. K. (1990). Creating zones of possibilities: Combining social contexts for instruction. In L. C. Moll (Ed.), *Vygotsky and education* (pp. 319–438). New York: Cambridge University Press.

Pressley, M., El-Dinary, P. B., Gaskins, I., Schuder, T. L., Bergman, J., Almasi, J., & Brown, R. (1992). Beyond direct explanation: Transactional instruction of reading comprehension strategies. *Elementary School Journal, 92,* 513–556.

Rigg, P. (1986). Reading in ESL: Learning from kids. In P. Rigg & D. S. Enright (Eds.), *Children and ESL: Integrating perspectives* (pp. 57–91). Alexandria, VA: Teachers of English to Speakers of Other Languages.

Spangenberg-Urbschat, K., & Pritchard, R. (1994). Meeting the challenge of diversity. In K. Spangenberg-Urbschat & R. Pritchard (Eds.), *Kids come in all languages: Reading instruction for ESL students* (pp. 1–5). Newark, DE: International Reading Association.

Steffenson, M. S., Joag-dev, C., & Anderson, R. C. (1979). A cross-cultural perspective on reading comprehension. *Reading Research Quarterly, 15,* 10–29.

Tierney, R. J., & Cunningham, J. W. (1984). Research on teaching reading comprehension. In P. D. Pearson (Ed.), *Handbook of reading research* (pp. 609–656). New York: Longman.

Weber, R. M. (1991). Linguistic diversity and reading in American society. In R. Barr, M. L. Kamil, P. Mosenthal, P. D. Pearson (Eds.), *Handbook of reading research* (Vol. 2, pp. 97–119). New York: Longman.

Wong Fillmore, L., & Valadez, C. (1986). Teaching bilingual learners. In M. C. Wittrock (Ed.), *Handbook of research on teaching* (pp. 648–685). New York: Macmillan.

SECTION VIII

Reading and Responding

Getting at the Meaning: How to Help
Students Unpack Difficult Text

Literature Circles, Book Clubs, and Literature
Discussion Groups

GETTING AT THE MEANING

How To Help Students Unpack Difficult Text

BY ISABEL L. BECK, MARGARET G. MCKEOWN, REBECCA L. HAMILTON, AND LINDA KUCAN

A STUDY THAT we conducted in 1991 on students' history learning included interviewing eighth graders as they finished their study of early American history. A question about what happened in the Revolutionary War prompted the following response from Jennifer, one of the students:

> I don't really remember this too well; I don't know why. We always learn about this and I always forget. It's so important too. Something like one of the colonies was too strong and something happened and they got into a war over it, and it was going on for a while and that's just one of the things. I don't know why I don't remember this. It's pretty embarrassing. (Beck & McKeown, 1994)

How many teachers have heard or expressed a sentiment that reflects Jennifer's confusion: "I've spent all week teaching this chapter and the students just aren't getting it"? That students do not "get it" is a common concern among educators. Despite the best efforts of teachers and the seeming attentiveness of students, students often fail to understand the ideas presented in their textbooks. In particular, students often are unable to connect the ideas they have encountered to information that is presented later. As one teacher expressed with frustration, "Sometimes the kids learn something; they even seem to know it for the test, and then, a month later, it's like they've never even heard of it!"

P. David Pearson, a reading researcher and the former Dean of the College of Education at the University of Illinois, recently described his encounter with this problem (Pearson, 1996):

Isabel L. Beck is a professor of education and senior scientist at the Learning Research and Development Center at the University of Pittsburgh. Margaret G. McKeown is a research scientist at the same Center. Rebecca L. Hamilton is a special projects coordinator for the Pittsburgh Public Schools. Linda Kucan is an assistant professor of education at Bethany College in Bethany, West Virginia. This article is adapted from the authors' book, Questioning the Author, *copyright © 1997 by the International Reading Association, Inc. Reprinted with permission.* Questioning the Author *may be ordered directly from the IRA by calling 1-800-336-READ, ext. 266.*

...when I ask teachers about their most serious concerns in literacy instruction, they invariably say—and this is especially true if they teach fourth grade or higher—'Well, if you think my kids have trouble with stories, you should come and see what we do with our social studies and science class. That's where the real trouble begins.'

...If you look in middle school and high school classrooms to examine the role of expository text, you are virtually forced to conclude that it has none. Occasionally teachers assign expository texts for homework, but when students come to class the next day, clearly having avoided the assignment, teachers provide them with an oral version of what they would have gotten out of the text if they had bothered to read it. Most high school teachers have quite literally given up on the textbook for the communication of any important content. While understandable, this approach is, of course, ultimately counterproductive. There comes a time in the lives of students —either when they go to college or enter the world of work—when others expect them to read and understand informational text.

The concern about reading comprehension—particularly comprehension of expository, informational text—is clearly widespread. Students are simply not garnering much meaning from much of the expository text they confront. Why? Part of the answer, of course, is that the texts are often not well written. They assume background information that the students do not have; they give inadequate explanations of the information they present; they fail to show the connections from a cause to an event and from an event to a consequence; and so on.

Earlier in our research, we confronted this problem head on. That is, we examined the extent to which more coherent text presentations would facilitate students' understanding. We revised textbook passages, establishing textual coherence by clarifying, elaborating, explaining, and motivating important information and by making relationships explicit. To some extent, it worked. When the revised passages were presented to the students, they recalled significantly more of the text and answered more questions correctly (Beck, McKeown, Sinatra, & Loxterman, 1991).

But even if we could count on all expository texts being as student-friendly as the revised versions we worked so hard on—and we clearly *can't* count on that happening—it wouldn't be sufficient.

Reprinted with permission from the Spring/Summer 1998 issue of the *American Educator,* the quarterly journal of the American Federation of Teachers

Despite the advantages shown for readers of the revised passages, the results of our study indicated that readers still had considerable difficulty understanding the texts. The recalls of many students pointed to surface-level treatments of text information. Reading the recalls gave us the impression that students took what they could get in one swift pass through the words on a page, and then formed that into a shallow representation of the text. This kind of cursory use of the text suggests that students resist digging in and grappling with unfamiliar or difficult content.

At this point, our research interests shifted to exploring ways to get readers to engage with texts and to consider ideas deeply. Over time, this led us to develop an approach we call Questioning the Author (QtA), which is designed to get students to build understanding of text ideas by becoming actively involved as they read, by diving into difficult information and grappling to make sense of it.

QtA is an approach that can be used equally well with either expository or narrative (fictional) texts. In this article, we will draw our examples from expository texts only—the genre of content area textbooks—because many teachers feel this is the harder nut to crack, the place where students are most likely to glaze over, disconnecting themselves from any chance for meaningful learning.

BUILDING UNDERSTANDING is not a new idea, but the way understanding is built distinguishes Questioning the Author from other approaches. Ideas in a text are cumulative, so in order to build meaning along the way, text is dealt with "on-line," as ideas are initially encountered, rather than waiting until after reading has been completed.

In QtA, we teach students that readers must try to "take on" a text little by little, idea by idea, and try to understand while they are reading what ideas are there and how they might connect or relate those ideas. To understand this approach, consider what is often done in classrooms when teaching from a text. It is typical practice to assign material to be read and then to pose questions to evaluate student comprehension. This read-question-evaluate pattern is an "after-the-

fact" procedure. There are two problems with this approach. First, students may have questions as they read or may simply finish a text knowing only that they are lost but are not sure why. The questions posed by the teacher only serve to expose their embarrassment over their lack of understanding. Also, there is no way for teachers to know if some students have constructed misconceptions about the passage and think they have understood. Second, even though students hear right answers, they may never understand what makes them right.

In QtA, however, the goal is to assist students in their efforts to understand as they are reading for the first time. Not only is this orientation a better reflection of how a reader needs to address text content to build understanding, but it is also an opportunity for valuable teaching and learning experiences. First, it gives teachers repeated opportunities to facilitate student efforts as they are trying to understand what they are reading. Teachers can model confusion, identify problematic language and difficult ideas in text, and ask *Queries* that focus student thinking. All these actions can serve as comprehension strategies that students ultimately learn and use on their own. Second, grappling with ideas during reading gives students the opportunity to hear from one another, to question and consider alternative possibilities, and to test their own ideas in a safe environment. Everyone is grappling, everyone is engaged in constructing meaning, and everyone understands that the author, not the teacher, has presented them with this challenge. The chance for cumulative misconceptions diminishes, and the opportunity for meaningful discussion increases.

Constructing meaning during reading means going back and forth between reading relatively small segments of text and discussing the ideas encountered. This back and forth process requires decisions about where to stop reading a text and to begin discussion of ideas. It is the task of a teacher using the QtA approach to prepare for this construction of meaning by analyzing and identifying the important concepts of a text and making decisions about how much of the text needs to be read at once and why. Making decisions about how much text to read is referred to as *segment-*

ing text, that is, identifying starting and stopping points. Decisions about segmenting the text are made based on the text content and the ideas and information presented, not on the length of a page or the point at which a page or paragraph ends.

QUESTIONING THE Author incorporates three major strategies. The first is what we call *Queries*, which are the probes used to prompt discussion. The second strategy consists of discussion "moves," such as modeling, revoicing, and annotating, which are necessary if discussion is to become a real vehicle for grappling with ideas and building understanding. The third component of QtA is the careful teacher planning required to make *Queries* and discussion effective tools for digging into meaning. It is beyond the scope of this article to elaborate all that's involved in these three strategies. Rather, we will focus on *Queries*, the engine that drives QtA.

How *Queries* Differ from Some Traditional Questions

We begin by considering what *Queries* are and what appears to differentiate them from some traditional questions. The major points of comparison are summarized in Table 1. One difference between questions and *Queries* is that some questions are used to assess student comprehension of text information after reading. In contrast, *Queries* are designed to assist students in grappling with text ideas as they construct meaning.

Table 1
Characteristics of Some Traditional Questions and QtA *Queries*

Questions	Queries
1. assess student comprehension of text information after reading	1. assist students in grappling with text ideas to construct meaning
2. evaluate individual student responses to teacher's questions and prompt teacher-to-student interactions	2. facilitate group discussion about an author's ideas and prompt student-to-student interactions
3. are used before or after reading	3. are used during initial reading

Earlier, we referred to a typical pattern of instruction in which students read a passage, the teacher initiates a series of questions, students respond, and the teacher evaluates their responses. This pattern, which has been documented as a prevalent teaching practice, is referred to as the IRE pattern of instruction: Initiate, Respond, and Evaluate (Dillon, 1988; Mehan, 1979). The IRE pattern *assesses* comprehension; it does not *assist* the process of comprehending. Moreover, the IRE pattern of asking questions after the reading is completed tends to involve questions that are more effective in encouraging students to recall what they have read rather than in supporting students as they build an understanding of what they are reading.

Queries, in contrast, are less focused on assessing and evaluating student responses than on supporting students as they dig in to make sense of what they are reading. *Queries* focus attention on the quality and depth of the meaning that students are constructing rather than on the accuracy of the responses they give. As indicated in Table 1, another difference between questions and *Queries* is that the purpose of some traditional questions seems to be to evaluate individual student responses and to prompt teacher-to-student interactions. In contrast, *Queries* aim to facilitate group discussion about an author's ideas and tend to prompt student-to-student interactions.

Questions are often useful in giving teachers a quick idea of which students are comprehending text and which are not. However, what also tends to happen is that, although a question is directed to the entire class, only one student provides the answer. This individual assumes all the responsibility and releases the other students from any share in it. The action takes place between the teacher and one student, and the rest of the class is not involved. Students tend to compete for the chance to say the right answer, and the teacher lets students know when their answers are correct.

Queries, on the other hand, are designed to change the role of the teacher to a facilitator of discussion. A teacher who uses *Queries* evaluates student responses less often and focuses more on encouraging students to consider an author's ideas and to respond to one another's interpretations of those ideas. As a result, student-to-student and student-to-teacher interactions tend to increase, and the context for learning is a classroom of spirited learners grappling with an author's text and working together to understand it.

Our last point, as noted in the table, is that questions typically are used before or after reading. In contrast, *Queries* are used continually during the initial reading of a text. When teachers ask questions after reading, students may get messages that teachers may not intend. For example, students may assume that questioning is a different and perhaps unrelated exercise from reading. Right and wrong is the focus of attention for both teacher as evaluator and student as evaluatee. Are these the messages we want to convey to students? A more correct message is that readers are always questioning as they read. Questioning and reading are symbiotically related, enhancing each other in mutually beneficial ways.

When teachers use *Queries*, students are more likely to get the message that reading and trying to determine the author's intended meaning are aspects of the same process. The thinking elicited by *Queries* is part of the reading experience, not something that is separate from that experience. *Queries* supplement the text, helping students deal with what is there as well as with what is not there. The focus of *Queries* is on building understanding, not on checking understanding.

Comparing the Effects of Questions and *Queries*

To provide a better sense of the nature of *Queries*, what they are, what they accomplish, and how they differ from some traditional questions, we will consider an example of a question-driven lesson and an example of a *Query*-driven lesson. The first example is based on an excerpt from a social studies textbook about early Polynesians that was used in a fourth-grade class. We will look at a transcript of the lesson as it unfolded with the teacher's traditional questions driving the discussion. In the second example, we will show how the same text excerpt was handled one year later by the same teacher after she had learned about QtA and how *Queries* can be used to direct discussion. Finally, we will consider the difference in what students seem to understand as a result of a *Query*-driven lesson in contrast to a question-driven lesson.

Here is the excerpt about early Polynesians from a social studies textbook (Laidlaw, 1985, p. 148):

> When the Polynesians settled on the Hawaiian Islands, they began to raise plants that they had brought with them. One kind of plant that the Polynesians raised was the taro plant. This is a kind of plant raised in warm, wet lands, mostly for its roots. The early Hawaiians cooked the roots, and then they generally pounded them on a board to make a paste called poi. This was a favorite food of the early Hawaiians. Sweet potatoes, bananas, breadfruit, and coconuts were some of the other plants that the early Hawaiians raised for food. Animals raised by the early Hawaiians for food were chickens, pigs, and dogs.

In the first example, to start the lesson, the teacher asks the question, "What did the early Hawaiians eat?" As indicated below, the students answer by naming things they read in the text, and the teacher repeats what each student says, sometimes interjecting other questions.

RANIA: Sweet potatoes.
TEACHER: Sweet potatoes. Excellent. Brent?
BRENT: Breadfruit.
TEACHER: Breadfruit. What is breadfruit? What is it? Is it bread? No, what is it? Carmen?
CARMEN: A tree that has fruit.
TEACHER: Yes. It's a tree that has a fruit. And when you cook the fruit, it looks like...
JIM: Bread.
TEACHER: Bread. That's why we call it breadfruit, isn't it? And it has no seeds. Excellent. Good readers. Nakisha?
NAKISHA: Coconut.
TEACHER: Coconuts. Beth?
BETH: Bananas.
TEACHER: Bananas. John?
JOHN: Chicken.
TEACHER: Chicken.
NICOLE: Pigs.
TEACHER: OK.

As the lesson proceeds, the students offer more examples of foods eaten by the early Polynesians, such as seaweed and roots. Then, the teacher asks questions that lead students to describe poi, the Hawaiians' favorite food, again through single-word responses, breaking the pattern only to elicit more information:

JIM: Seaweed.
TEACHER: Seaweed. Kelvin?
KELVIN: Roots.
TEACHER: Roots? What do you call those roots?
KELVIN: Uh. Poi.
TEACHER: OK. What did we call the roots?
JIM: Taro.
TEACHER: Good. Now, what did they make out of taro?

JIM: Poi.
TEACHER: Poi. What's the Hawaiians' favorite food?
JIM: Poi.
TEACHER: And what does it look like? How can we describe it? What's the poi look like, Nakisha?
NAKISHA: Like paste.
TEACHER: Paste. It doesn't taste like paste, goodness no, but it looks like paste. It has the same consistency, and it is called poi, and that was their favorite food. Did we miss anything. Nicole?
Nicole: Seafood.
Teacher: Seafood. I think we have it all. John?
John: They said they ate a kind of seaweed.

After naming all the foods, it is not clear if the students have any understanding of what this information means or how it connects to an important idea. Additionally, the tone of this lesson is dull and uneventful. There is a kind of monotonous pendulum-like effect, with the teacher and students echoing one another in one-word exchanges.

Now, we will look at how the same text excerpt was handled a year later by the same teacher, using *Queries* instead of questions to drive the lesson. Recall that the first time the teacher taught this lesson, she had the students read the entire text excerpt and then answer her questions. One year later, the lesson begins as follows, after the class had read just the first sentence of the text excerpt: "When the Polynesians settled on the Hawaiian Islands, they began to raise plants that they had brought with them." Then the teacher begins the discussion as follows:

TEACHER: What does the author mean by just this one sentence?
ANTONIO: He means that they brought some of the food that they had there with them.

Antonio's response misses a key point that is essential to understanding the message of the paragraph: The Polynesians brought certain foods with them that they then began to raise in their new environment. The teacher's next *Query* emphasizes this point and leads to an important exchange with Temika:

TEACHER: Um-hmm, we decided that yesterday. But what does the author mean by they began to *raise* the plants they brought with them. Temika?
TEMIKA: Like the plants and stuff, they began to plant them.
TEACHER: They began to plant them, why?
TEMIKA: For their food!
TEACHER: Right! They can plant the things that they brought, then they're going to have their own crops in Hawaii. OK, good.

When the important concept about raising crops is brought out, notice how the QtA orientation of digging into text information produces a question from a student:

ALVIS: Why do they need to plant things when they already brought things over?

Alvis realizes that he does not understand the significance of the author's point. Notice that rather than answering the student herself, the teacher returns the responsibility for thinking and grappling with the issues to the students:

TEACHER: Who can answer Alvis's question? He said, they already had food, why did they have to plant the food? Roberta?

ROBERTA: Maybe because, like back then in the Hawaiian Islands ... probably, you couldn't drive to the store, like they do now.

TEACHER: OK, so Roberta's saying they couldn't get in their car and drive to the stores, but Alvis still has a point. Why not just eat the food they brought?

ALVIS: They could run out.

TEACHER: Oh, I think you just answered your own question. Alvis, say what you just said.

ALVIS: 'cause they'll run out of food.

Turning back the question to students gives them a chance to rediscover the idea that food eventually runs out and that to survive the Hawaiians needed to plant their own crops. Roberta's explanation helps Alvis realize that the food may have run out. Once the issue has been resolved, the teacher is ready to continue. This segment of the lesson transcript suggests that the combination of deliberate segmenting of text based on the ideas in the text and a sequence of carefully developed *Queries* make it possible for students to grapple with important ideas.

To capture some of the important differences between the two lessons about early Polynesians, a summary of some characteristics of the question-driven and the *Query*-driven discussions is presented in Table 2. First, the *Query*-driven discussion seemed to change student responses. In the question-driven discussion, students tended to respond in short, one-word answers, and they frequently used the author's language. In the *Query*-driven discussion, the students gave longer, more elaborate answers that reflected original thought and analysis expressed in the students' own language.

Second, the text orientation of the *Query*-driven discussion was different from the question-driven discussion. Students tended to use a text in the question-driven discussion as a resource for retrieving information, a place to check the facts against their own memories. The text was little more than a source for finding correct answers. In contrast, in the *Query*-driven discussion, the text seemed to take on a different role. It seemed to become a working reference for connecting ideas and analyzing an author's style and motivation. The text became an ally in constructing meaning.

Table 2
A Comparison of Question-Driven and *Query*-Driven Discussions about Early Polynesians

Question-Driven Discussions	*Query*-Driven Discussions
Student Responses	
■ one-word answers	■ longer, more elaborate answers
■ in author's language	■ in student's language
Text Orientation	
■ resource for retrieving information	■ reference for connecting ideas
■ source for finding correct answers	■ ally in constructing meaning
Discussion Dynamics	
■ teacher-to-student interactions	■ student-to-student interactions
■ dull pace: little student engagement	■ exciting pace: student engagement
■ product oriented	■ process oriented
■ all questions teacher initiated	■ some questions student initiated

Third, there were differences in the dynamics of the question-driven and the *Query*-driven discussions. Questions tend to promote teacher-to-student interactions with few opportunities for students to respond to one another or debate issues. As a result, question-driven lessons had a dull pace with little student engagement. The question-driven discussion was product oriented, and the product was what students remembered or what they could find in the text.

In contrast, the *Query*-driven discussion tended to promote student-to-student interactions as well as student-to-teacher exchanges, a more natural context for considering ideas. The *Query*-driven discussion seemed to have an exciting pace, with evidence of student engagement. In addition, the *Query*-driven discussion was process oriented. The goal was not focused completely on getting the right answer; rather, the goal was to get involved in the process of approaching a text in ways that encourage deep thinking.

Finally, in the question-driven discussion, almost all questions were teacher initiated. In the *Query*-driven discussion, at least some questions were student initiated.

Let's look at another text example. The following lesson transcript is from a social studies lesson about life in Siberia. The teacher begins by expressing concern about some sentences from the text and rereading those sentences:

TEACHER: Hold on. I'm concerned about these sentences: "During the summer months these people spent time preparing reindeer meat. They also made cheese from reindeer milk. These foods were then stored for the long winter months." What's the author trying to tell us here? "These foods were then stored for the long winter months." Charles?

Students begin to respond, focusing mainly on it being too cold in Siberia to gather food in the winter. The teacher persists in trying to get the students to go beyond the words in the text and reach for greater meaning:

CHARLES: They, they had to gather up food because they um, because they'd need food for the winter since it's so cold.

TEACHER: Oh, OK. Charles said 'cause it's so cold. I'm still a little confused. What do you think, Antonio?

ANTONIO: I think that the author thinks that during the summer months they had to go out and be gathering up the food 'cause it's not as cold but it's still cold. And then when it's winter, they don't have to worry about uh, trying to get their food.

TEACHER: I think we're all agreeing that in the wintertime, they're not gonna get anything to eat, but I'm not sure I understand why. What do you think, Alvis?

ALVIS: I think, I think they do it in the summer because in the winter it's too hard to find all the food, because there's a lot of snow. And the trees and the plants and everything are dead because it's too cold.

TAMMY: I think that they store all their food because the animals like, go away for the winter. They can't find animals to kill because it's too cold.

BETTY: I think that they do it in the summer because, I agree with Tammy, 'cause it's warmer so they can find animals.

The teacher then recaps the ideas students have suggested and points out that they—not the author—came up with the ideas:

TEACHER: Those are really good ideas. The author just told us, "These foods were then stored for the long winter months." But did he tell us why?

STUDENTS: No.

TEACHER: No. And Tammy thinks it's 'cause the reindeer kind of hibernate. Is that what you mean? And Alvis and Betty said it's because it's too cold for the hunters to hunt. And you know what? I don't really know the answer. But I think you have some good ideas that might possibly be why. And it's important that you were able to come up with those ideas.

Gradually, as the contributions of Antonio, Alvis, Tammy, and Betty are combined with the teacher's sum-

---

Examples of Queries

Initiating Queries
- What is the author trying to say here?
- What is the author's message?
- What is the author talking about?

Follow-up Queries
- What does the author mean here?
- Did the author explain this clearly?
- Does this make sense with what the author told us before?
- How does this connect with what the author has told us here?
- Does the author tell us why?
- Why do you think the author tells us this now?

---

marizing, the students build the understanding that climate affects behavior and motivates action, and that the author did not express this idea very clearly. We do not believe that these understandings would have been as likely to be constructed without the *Initiating Query* that began the discussion.

To summarize, we observed three specific effects of the *Initiating Query* in the "life in Siberia" lesson. First, students did the work of constructing meaning. The teacher asked students to do the thinking and started a discussion and set things in motion with a clear goal in mind. She guided the students to a realization about the text, but she did not tell them what the realization was.

Second, students discovered the difference between knowing what an author says and knowing what an author means. They also helped one another get the job done; they needed to combine ideas, and with prompting and encouragement, they dug into the text more than once to unravel the meaning.

Finally, the tone of the interactions was positive; there was evidence of engagement and personal investment in ideas and thought. The students were learning, and they were enjoying the activity.

Now, let's analyze one final example of how Questioning the Author can help students build meaning. This example is from a discussion about these two sentences in a social studies text (Laidlaw, 1985, p. 87): "There is no sunlight during most of the winter months in Antarctica. However, during the summer months, the sun shines twenty-four hours a day." The teacher begins with an *Initiating Query* that draws a response that does not address the issue represented by the text:

TEACHER: What's the author trying to tell us here?

ALETHA: The earth keeps on going around, keep on going around 24 hours a day.

The teacher then poses a *Follow-up Query* that directly addresses the difficulty: The author is presenting information that conflicts with what the students already understand about night and day.

TEACHER: Aletha says the earth keeps going around, twenty-four hours a day. So right now on one side of the earth it's daylight, and over here it's dark (pointing on a globe). So what does the author mean when he says there's no sunlight during most of the winter, and the sun shines twenty-four hours a day in the summer?

DARLEEN: Um, I think it's like, um, every time it goes around from the light to dark, every time it goes around it changes from light to dark, every twenty-four hours.

Darleen's response misses the point, so the teacher presses with another *Follow-up Query*. The *Query* urges students to put the pieces of information together, which the next student called on begins to do very nicely:

TEACHER: Well, I think Darleen's saying the same thing that a lot of you are saying, that the globe is turning around and when it's light on this side, it's dark over here. Does that make

HEIDI: sense with what the author just told us?

This part right here; it's summer now. And this part down here; it's winter, and it snows down here all the time 'cause there's no sun getting down there. Antarctica's right down here, and when the sun comes, Antarctica's getting sun and the sun's coming this way, and it's hitting Antarctica.

Building from Heidi's comment, the teacher recaps what the discussion has revealed so far and prompts students to consider if the author has explained why the sun works this way in Antarctica. The teacher then asks students to recall information that a student had mentioned in an earlier discussion:

TEACHER: Heidi's added some important things. She said that when the globe's going around when it's winter down here, Antarctica never gets any sun, and when it's summer, Antarctica does get sun. Now it seems like that is what the author's telling us. But does the author tell us why?

CLASS: No.

TEACHER: Think about this for a minute. There's something else that Amber said a little while back. She said there's something funny about the earth. It's not straight up and down.

The students begin to work out the explanation for Antarctica's pattern of sunshine and weather:

TAMMY: It's tilted.

TEACHER: It's tilted. Now how does that connect with what the author has told us here?

BRANDY: It doesn't get as much sun in the winter, 'cause the sun has to come up under but it's tilted the other way in the summertime.

THOMAS: I think he's saying, like Brandy said, it goes around for twenty-four hours a day and, here goes the sun, the sun shines on Antarctica, slanted, all the way around twenty-four hours a day.

SHANELLE: Um, um, I think I know what they're saying because when, when the Earth is going around and the sun is coming, it's hitting— the lower part of Antarctica is showing, 'cause it's tilting more. So then it has sunshine twenty-four hours.

As the teacher recaps student contributions, it seems clear that the students have indeed put all the information together; that is, that the tilt in the Earth's axis explains the 24 hours of light in Antarctica.

TEACHER: I think we've worked this out. What Shanelle and Thomas are saying is that because the Earth is tilted when it's going around the sun, we got twenty-four hours of sunlight in the summer, 'cause the sun keeps hitting and keeps hitting Antarctica, even though this part of the globe is in darkness.

There are several specific effects of the *Follow-up Queries* in the "climate of Antarctica" transcript. First, we can see that with the teacher's guidance, the students were able to link past knowledge with new information in the text. Second, as the discussion unfolded, students built on one another's comments to unravel important information: The author was alluding to a scientific concept they had to understand before they could understand the text. Finally, meanings and explanations emerged from several sources, not only from the students, teacher, or text, but also from a collaboration that involved all three.

* * *

Developing and sustaining an environment that encourages students to share their thinking about text ideas and to work toward building meaning is a highly complex task. As Cazden (1988) says, "It is easy to imagine talk in which ideas are explored rather than answers to teachers' test questions provided and evaluated.... Easy to imagine, but not easy to do."

In the course of developing Questioning the Author, we collaborated with fourteen teachers in four different schools, who taught third through eighth grades. And although QtA was "not easy to do," with support each of these teachers became to various degrees competent and comfortable with the orientation, and each of them incorporated their own "styles."

As for the effects on students, teachers often tell us they are surprised at the change that takes place. In a journal she kept during the time we worked together, Kelley Sweeney, one of our first collaborating teachers, described the impact QtA had in her class: "I was astonished at the responses and involvement in the discussion from some of my students who usually never participate. I cannot express my astonishment enough." In this regard, consider a story that Al Shanker used to tell. According to Shanker, if people from Mars came to earth and observed our ways, when they returned they would report that earthlings had a particularly peculiar custom in association with their children. That is, five days a week parents sent their children to a place where the children sat and watched an adult work.

In contrast to that scenario, consider a fifth-grade youngster, who when asked to say what he liked and disliked about QtA, responded, "What I like about QtA is that people let other people know what they're thinking. What I dislike is that it makes us work too hard! When we're done, it makes us feel like we're dead!" □

REFERENCES

Beck, I.L., & McKeown, M.G. (1994). Outcomes of history instruction: Paste-up accounts. In J.F. Voss & M. Carretero (Eds.), *Cognitive and instructional processes in history and the social sciences* (pp. 237-256). Hillsdale, NJ: Lawrence Erlbaum Associates.

Beck, I.L., McKeown, M.G., Sinatra, G.M., & Loxterman, J.A. (1991). Revising social studies text from a text-processing perspective: Evidence of improved comprehensibility. *Reading Research Quarterly, 26,* 251-276.

Cazden, C. (1988). *Classroom discourse: The language of teaching and learning.* Portsmouth, NH: Heinemann Educational Books, Inc.

Dillon, J.T. (1988). *Questioning and teaching: A manual of practice.* New York: Teachers College Press.

Laidlaw (1985). *Living in world regions.* River Forest, IL: Author.

Mehan, H. (1979). *Learning lessons: Social organization in the classroom.* Cambridge, MA: Harvard University Press.

Pearson, P.D. (1996). Reclaiming the center. In M.F. Graves, P. van den Broek, & B.M. Taylor (Eds.), *The first R: Every child's right to read.* New York, NY: Teachers College Press.

Literature Circles, Book Clubs, and Literature Discussion Groups

Some Talk about Book Talk

NANCY L. ROSER
University of Texas at Austin

SUSAN STRECKER
University of Texas at Austin

MIRIAM G. MARTINEZ
University of Texas at San Antonio

Our office shelves house a new (and seemingly, expanding) section of professional books. Straddling the space between the textbooks devoted to children's literature and those focused on teaching students to read and write sits a relatively new "genre": professional texts that examine and explain classroom book conversations. The growth of interest in students' talk about books has been both marked and continuous in recent years. Besides the spate of published texts, our professional journals, too, are replete with the discoveries and insights gained from observing, encouraging, planning for, and judging the effects of more and better classroom book conversations. Why this surge of interest, investigation, and teacher-to-teacher sharing about "book talk"? In this chapter, we offer four possible explanations.

From *Promoting Literacy in Grades 4–9: A Handbook for Teachers and Administrators* by K. D. Wood and T. S. Dickinson. Copyright © 2000 by Allyn & Bacon. Reprinted by permission.

Four Explanations for Interest in "Book Talk"

A portion of the current keen interest in what students have to say about books stems from the intense interest in text comprehension that took root in the 1970s, initiating a period of research that contributed to refined theories of how knowledge is accumulated, stored, and retrieved (Pearson, 1985). With better understanding of comprehension came the need to determine what students know and how they bring their experiences to texts. Investigators in this period often used prompts and questions to determine students' understandings, rather than encouraging responsive "book talk."

Perhaps a second explanation for heightened interest in what children have to say about texts is based on a "rediscovery" of sorts. In the 1930s, Rosenblatt (1938/1976), a professor of English education and a literary theorist, described her understanding of reading as a "two-way process" involving a reader and a text interacting in a particular time and circumstance, with both reader and text contributing to meaning. Students, she believed, should be given opportunities to approach literature personally, to reflect upon their responses to it, and then to understand *what* within the work and within themselves contributed to their responses (Farrell & Squire, 1990, Rosenblatt, 1938/1976). In many elementary and middle-grade classrooms, literature discussion groups have begun to do just that: give students opportunity and confidence to reflect upon, to express, and to support their responses to texts.

Still another possible contributor to interest in students' responses to reading may stem from the influence of Vygotsky (1978), who posited that learners, to make sense of their world, must act upon it, "constructing" the sense of it for themselves. Vygotsky considered the vital role that language plays in shaping and clarifying thought. Teachers and researchers who subscribe to a "constructivist" theory provide instructional opportunities that require learners to untangle complexities, problem solve, and hypothesize—that is, to "construct" meanings for themselves. One important "opportunity" teachers provide is good literature, which, by its nature, requires a great deal of "gap filling" (Iser, 1978). Students (sometimes with help) must build the images, patterns, categories, and hypotheses that make the text make sense. They become active, "constructive" readers. When readers act in concert—that is, when they talk over their reactions and interpretations with other readers—their responses can become thicker and richer and more meaningful. Their "socially" constructed meanings (Bakhtin, 1986) can represent the range of experiences, ideas, and backgrounds of the conversants within the conversational setting of book clubs, literature circles, or literature discussion groups.

A fourth explanation for keen interest in classroom book conversations could be a by-product of both the proliferation of fine, "chewable" literature for children and the influx of more "real books" into classrooms and curricula—books not just for literacy instruction but for content study as well. "Literature-based" curriculum, the 90,000 children's titles now in print, and the approximately 6,000 children's books published annually (Huck, Hepler, Hickman, & Kiefer, 1997) mean more impetus both inside and outside the classroom for reading (and talking) about literature.

As with any complex phenomenon, the causes and influences of increased interest in book conversations are no doubt multiple and related. Nevertheless, it seems that many kids in middle- and upper-grade classrooms are getting to say *what* they think about books and *why* they think what do.

Why Book Talk Is Important to Literacy and to the Study of Literature

Like the pioneering Rosenblatt, many teachers believe that literature is to be "explored." Given that metaphor, there must be room for both wandering and wondering through a variety of books throughout the classroom day. Even so (and again like Rosenblatt), many teachers also understand that literature has *both* shape and substance; thus, effective "book talk" must consider both the form of the literature as well as its content. To read and talk about a set of folktales without eventually recognizing some of their structural similarities is to miss an opportunity to focus on patterns that aid recognition, understanding, and appreciation. By contrast, to ask readers to notice motifs or to identify literary language without their first having had time to agonize over a character's losses or glory in her victories is to deny them participation in the story world. Classroom book talk *can,* however, move in both directions; it can yield thoughtful expressions of ideas and inquiries as well as in-depth "study" of literature in all its forms. For example, book talk can result in better understanding of informational texts by helping readers shape, confirm, and even modify their individual reactions.

Ensuring Better Book Talk

Whether conversations about books are called literature circles, book clubs, or literary discussion groups, the teachers that offer these special opportunities share some notions about how to best nurture insightful thought and talk in the classroom. See Table 20.1 for some comparisons of the terms.

Good Book Talk Requires a Good Book

Teachers and researchers who value book talk indicate that the better the book, the more gripping its plot, the more gray its choices, the more the ethical dilemmas pull the reader in, the better the book talk. Eeds and Wells (1989), for example, in their benchmark study of "grand conversations," discovered that fifth- and sixth-grade students, invited to talk about literature, had deeper and richer responses to Babbitt's (1985) *Tuck Everlasting* than to *Harriet the Spy* (Fitzhugh, 1964). *Tuck,* it seems, is the kind of book that demands discussion. There are many others: Lowry's (1993) *The Giver;* Paterson's (1994) *Flip-Flop Girl;* Spinelli's (1990) *Maniac McGee;* Taylor's (1976) *Roll of Thunder, Hear My Cry;* Avi's (1991) *Nothing But the Truth;* Fine's (1992) *Flour Babies;* Staples's (1989) *Shabanu: Daughter of the Wind;* Byar's (1977) *The Pinballs;*

TABLE 20.1 Learning about Conducting Literature Circles, Book Clubs, and Literature Discussion Groups

Terms for Book Conversation Groups	How Defined	Where to Read More
Literature Circles	"A curricular structure to support children in exploring their rough draft understanding of literature with other readers." Readers read independently and think collaboratively. Literature circles are primarily geared toward "encouraging children to become reflective and critical thinkers and readers." (Short, in Hill et al., pp. x–xi)	Hill, B.C., Johnson, N.J., & Schlick Noe, K.L. (1995). *Literature Circles and Response.* Norwood, MA: Christopher-Gordon. Daniels, H. (1994). *Literature Circles: Voice and Choice in the Student-Centered Classroom.* York, ME: Stenhouse. Hanssen, E. (1990). Planning for Literature Circles: Variations in Focus and Structure. In K.G Short & K.M. Pierce, (Eds.), *Talking about Books: Creating Literate Communities* (pp. 199–209). Portsmouth, NH: Heinemann.
Book Clubs	"A group of three to five students who meet to discuss a common reading, including specific chapters from longer books. They share personal responses, clarify confusing aspects of the reading, create interpretations, discuss authors' intent, etc." (McMahon & Raphael, 1997, p. xii)	McMahon, S.I., & Raphael, T.E. (Eds.). (1997). *The Book Club Connection: Literacy Learning and Classroom Talk.* New York: Teachers College Press. Paratore, J.R., & McCormack, R.L. (Eds.). (1997). *Peer Talk in the Classroom: Learning from Research.* Newark: DE: International Reading Association.
Literature Discussion Groups	"Emphasizes the reading and discussing of unabridged . . . literature in small, self-selected groups. It assumes comprehension and relies heavily on open-ended discussions." (Samway & Whang, p.14) Often teacher-guided, with planning for the kinds of literary insights or interpretations that the book provides for. (Eeds & Peterson, 1990)	Eeds, M.A., & Peterson, R. (1990). *Grand Conversations.* New York: Scholastic. Gambrell, L.B., & Almasi, J.F. (Eds.). (1996). *Lively Discussions!* Newark, DE: International Reading Association. Samway, K.D., & Whang, G. (1995). *Literature Study Circles in a Multicultural Classroom.* York, ME: Stenhouse.

Cormier's (1990) *Other Bells for Us to Ring;* Paterson's (1978) *The Great Gilly Hopkins;* and Fenner's (1995) *Yolanda's Genius.* The list is as limitless as the talk can be. Further, our own work has shown different types of books may well move talk in somewhat different directions (Martinez & Roser, 1995).

Good Book Talk Has Agreed-Upon Goals

The more agreed-upon the goals for book talk and the more its procedures are planned and practiced, the better the outcome. Hepler (1991) suggests that the primary goal of literature discussion is to create communities of readers. These communities

> have the advantage of giving children a chance to react to a book in the company of other similarly focused readers. The teacher provides the setting, and in some cases, the direction, and children talk their way through books. (p. 183)

McMahon and Raphael (1997) recommend that teachers and students generate these goals together. Depending on how book talk fits the curriculum—whether as a structure for literature study or as a launch for content units—book talk serves by helping students to think and speak (and even write) more clearly, listen more attentively and respectfully to others' ideas, take turns in conversation, use texts to support their ideas, appreciate the author's craft, and become more immersed in and attuned to the universal themes of literature. Ultimately, it is the teacher's stance toward literature and its centrality that most influences these goals.

Good Book Talk Means a Chance for *Each* Participant to Think and to Talk

Although group discussion can considerably enhance individual "gap filling" (Eeds & Wells, 1989, p. 22), some students may be unduly swayed by others' ideas before their own thoughts have had a chance to germinate. They may require the protective cocoon of a quiet time provided (after reading and prior to book talk) for responding in a reflection journal or literature log—a place to record an idea, a question, or a concern they would like to talk about before that idea is lost. Because students at any level can be silenced by more forceful peers, it is possible that not all novice book talkers will claim the floor unless the group is closely monitored. "Monitoring" may take the form of encouraging students to share from their literature logs—their "preserved" written reactions to the text—and of explicitly teaching roles and responsibilities of group membership, providing models of how to offer ideas, and having a daily group evaluation that includes reviewing each member's participation.

When serving as members of a book discussion group, teachers, too, work hard not to dominate the discussion. They realize that good book talk means judicious use of the imposed question, for example. Researchers who have considered the role of the question (and the questioner) tend to agree that ill-placed, scatter-shot, or rapid-fire questions can interfere with the genuine exchange of ideas that characterizes effective book conversations. Teachers who use fewer questions (Eeds & Wells, 1989), who work themselves to the periphery of the book discussion group (O'Flahavan, Stein, Wiencek, & Marks, 1992; Short & Kauffman, 1995), or who ensure that their contributions are those of a joint respondent support their students' participation in book talk. The teachers are also, however, the most knowledgeable "curator" of the art and the most careful reader of the book. Their contributions to conversations can help to refocus the students' ideas, reinforce and label their literary insights, and, like a curator (see Eeds & Peterson, 1991), help respondents see in new ways.

In the following example of fourth-grade students discussing *Make Way for Sam Houston* (Fritz, 1986), their teacher applied the language of literature study to an insight that Christopher had. Peterson and Eeds (1990) call it shooting "arrows of literary insight at appropriate moments" (p. 62).

> CHRISTOPHER: I think his (Sam Houston's) life is tied together in a big knot and he can't get it untied.
>
> TEACHER: That's a metaphor he just made. Did you hear? He said Sam Houston's life is tied in a knot. Life . . . with a knot. How does life compare with a knot?
>
> ABBY: You can't get out of it.
>
> ANTOINETTE: 'Cause you're in trouble and you can't solve it.
>
> TEACHER: What a struggle! You move a little way and you're back into it. What a lovely metaphor. Life . . . and a knot.

As the discussion of Sam Houston continued chapter by chapter over the days that followed, other children returned (in the pages of their journals) to Christopher's metaphor:

- I think his knot is almost undone.
- I think that Sam Houston has gotten half way through the knot in his life.
- I don't think his knot will ever come undone.
- His knot is unraveling.
- In the end, his knot unwravled (*sic*).
- I think his life was finnly (*sic*) out of his knot.

Good Book Talk Depends on a Conversational Setting

As simple as the idea seems, some classrooms are not arranged for good book talk. One teacher we know never asked her students to adjust their chairs or tables so that speakers faced one another for conversation. As a result, talk tended to ricochet for a few turns and then stop short. When she adjusted the classroom seating plan to provide for conversational groups (much like the seating arrangement at kitchen tables), the students adhered to the topic longer, built off others' comments, made eye contact, were more sensitive to dominating the talk, and evaluated the discussion as more effective.

What Good Book Talk Sounds Like

Good book talk is exciting, insightful, and honest exchange. It considers the text as a story world to be lived within, as an "object" that has been crafted by an author, and, often, as "messages" or themes of far-ranging import. It makes reference to the text to support its points. It demonstrates connection with the book experience and the world of literature beyond it.

Fourth-grade students in Ms. Frank's class were talking about *Castle in the Attic* (Winthrop, 1985) when they wondered about the ethics of William, the book's young protagonist, having used a magic charm to shrink his nanny, Miss Phillips, solely to keep her from leaving him:

C1:   I think that's kind of good and kind of bad in a way.

C2:   Not because of his shrinking, but about the way he felt about her.

C3:   She was getting ready to go home and everything.

C2:   And he shrinks her without her permission and everything.

C4:   And then Miss Phillips comes up with a very good idea.

C3:   "I'm not coming out of this room until you come in and get me."

C5:   He can't unless *he* is small.

C2:   I'm really glad because now he understands what he did to Miss Phillips and that wasn't right.

When Ms. Harp's class talked about Jean Fritz's (1986) *Make Way for Sam Houston* as a entrée into their social studies unit on Texas as a young republic, the talk was initially characterized by their involvement with the biography and linkage with Sam, but it moved to the foibles and motivations that were made visible through Fritz's close inspection of a larger-than-life Texas hero:

C1:   I wonder why Sam was so dedicated to doing big things.

C2:   How can he be so intelligent and foolhardy at the same time?

C3:   If Tiana's dead, who's taking care of their children?

C4:   I think Sam needs more . . . get some self control, and self-stopness.

Getting Started with Book Clubs, Literature Circles, or Discussion Groups

From the research on literature discussion groups and book clubs, it becomes clear that rich, cohesive, and insightful book conversations do not simply happen. They take good books (as noted above), and they require a great deal of "practice."

Modeling Book Talk

The best introduction to (and practice for) book conversations seems to occur when good books are read aloud in classrooms daily and teachers and students take time to mull over their reactions. Read-aloud time, then, is not finished with the last page of the day's chapter. That is when the second important phase of read-aloud begins: the talk-about. Whole group discussion, besides providing an open forum for students, permits teachers to model the stance of the questioning, responsive learner. More than one expert recommends that the teachers be thoroughly familiar with the text, open to its possibilities, sensitive to their own initial reactions to it (given they have read it more than once), and aware of the literary elements that can be pointed out or reinforced (such as mood, structure, symbol, theme, extended metaphor). Teachers, according to Peterson and Eeds (1990), float "literary balloons," only some of which are grabbed onto.

Book Selection and Fit

We (and others) have found important variables in the successful organization for book talk: (1) Students need to be given some choice or voice in the selection of the books to be discussed, and (2) the book must be within reach of their reading level. Besides adjusting the levels of books, we have used such "scaffolds" for struggling readers as audiotapes, paired reading, and printed discussion prompts.

Time Management and Class Organization

There is no one plan for organizing for book discussion groups. Smith (1990), for example, gives her fifth- and sixth-grade students approximately five days to read a chapter book such as *Dicey's Song* (Voigt, 1982). The literature group (about six students) meets with her three days the following week (for about 20 minutes each day) to discuss the selection. During the discussion sessions with one group, others are reading in preparation for their discussions (Eeds, Edelsky, Smith, Penka, & Love, n.d.). During the first session, students come together to freely share responses—their thoughts and feelings about the text. In this session, students are likely to skip from one topic to another, with topics not necessarily being explored in any depth. The session ends with students brainstorming topics they think might be interesting to explore in greater depth at subsequent meetings. The group then decides on one or two topics to talk about during the next sessions. With the assignments clarified (and sometimes expanded) by Karen, they delve into the book again in preparation for their discussions, gathering the evidence that supports their thinking. Over time, the discussion grows more connected, focused, and analytic. Karen models how literate readers make connections and offers the language of literature study embedded at relevant points. The third session ends with an evaluation of the discussion and each member's contributions to it.

Other teachers find a safe beginning for literature discussion by initially giving the whole class a copy of the same book and conducting a "giant-sized" book club so that procedures become clear. Still others use the same title, but they organize students into small, concurrent student-led groups (rather than a large teacher-led one). We have worked with three related books being discussed simultaneously in the same classroom (after students have become accustomed to expectations and procedures for book clubbers). Almasi (1995), in her comparison of teacher-led and student-led discussions, noted that students in peer-led groups tended to offer responses that were more elaborate and complex than student-responses in teacher-led discussions. Further, she found that the students explored issues that seemed important to them.

Roles of the Students

Using a nomenclature derived by our colleague, Jim Hoffman, we assigned rotating roles to students new to managing themselves in book clubs. The roles and their responsibilities are printed and passed out to the students each day. A discussion leader checks with each member to make certain the agreed-upon chapters have been read and that each discussant has brought a log to the group with at least one idea for talk. The orator sets the mood for the discussion by reading aloud from a selected passage and then telling why that passage is significant to him or her. The scribe keeps track of the group's important ideas, wonderings, or other notes on language charts. Members of the group are responsible for listening, contributing, and helping to evaluate the effectiveness of each session.

Roles of the Teacher

When teachers choose to provide the direction for book club, they have options. One is to be a guide on the side, to intervene when the talk seriously falters; another is to serve actively as participant, curator, guide, facilitator, interpreter, or literary critic. Rules of participation for teacher are the same as for the rest of the group: Receive each member's contributions, and, without a predetermined destination, entertain the possibilities the text offers.

Chambers (1996), in the book *Tell Me,* offers three easy-to-remember invitations to talk. Labeled as the "three sharings," the invitations are both open-ended and are likely to result in original and unpredictable insights. Students are invited to (1) share

TABLE 20.2   One Plan for Book Talk: The Three "Sharings"

The Sharing of Enthusiasms (enthusiasm for what was noticed in the story)	What did you notice? What parts did you like?
The Sharing of Puzzles (the speculation about meanings, wonderings)	What parts puzzled you?
The Sharing of Connections (the finding of patterns and connections that reflect the core of the book)	Did you notice any patterns? Are you reminded of any other books (or characters) that are similar to this one?

Source: Adapted from *Tell me: Children, reading, and talk,* by Aidan Chambers.

or recall what they most want to talk about, what they noticed or observed in the text; (2) tell what they are puzzled about or uncertain of in the story—their wonderings about the text; and (3) recall what (in the book) they connected with and what they were reminded of, either in their own experiences or in the experiences of other characters and books. Chambers' three invitations, presented in Table 20.2, have given us (and students) a simple, but useful, framework for launching book talk and keeping it afloat.

Good Book Talk Is for Everyone

In classrooms in which children's first language is not English, children become collaborative language learners and meaning makers through book conversations (Battle, 1995; Samway & Whang, 1995; Smith, 1990). In mainstream settings, children who have been referred for special education participate successfully in literature discussion (Goatley, Brock, & Raphael, 1995). Although Wollman-Bonilla (1994) found that struggling readers were so focused on text comprehension that they were hesitant to offer their own ideas for conversation, we have observed many struggling readers succeed in literary conversations when they are matched with appropriately leveled text, when expectations for interpretive thinking are clearly communicated and modeled, and when supported by audiotapes or read-aloud partners. In short, our own experiences with book talk have shown us that book talk works with all children. Christopher, for example, who made the insightful metaphor about Sam Houston, was a child who had been labeled "emotionally disturbed," who spent only a portion of his day in the regular classroom, much of that under his desk.

The books and articles on book talk that crowd our shelves have taught us a great deal. The teachers who provide books and time for thoughtful reading and discussion have taught us, too. Most of all, students have shown us that they are capable of powerful ideas about texts. Their ideas are made more powerful in the presence of others—supportive groups of idea sharers who posit, test, reflect, and often modify their thinking. When good books are made available to students, when the classroom organization provides for groups of book talkers, when literate models show how reflection and support look and sound, there is good reading, good talk, and good learning.

Good book talk is within hearing distance.

REFERENCES

Almasi, J. (1995). The nature of fourth graders' sociocognitive conflicts in peer-led and teacher-led discussions of literature. *Reading Research Quarterly, 30,* 314–351.

Bakhtin, M.M. (1986). *Speech genres and other late essays.* Austin: University of Texas Press.

Battle, J. (1995). Collaborative story talk in a bilingual kindergarten. In N.L. Roser & M.G. Martinez (Eds.), *Book talk and beyond: Children and teachers respond to literature* (pp. 157–167). Newark, DE: International Reading Association.

Chambers, A. (1996). *Tell me: Children, reading, and talk.* York, ME: Stenhouse.

Eeds, M., Edelsky, C., Smith, K., Penka, C., & Love, B. (n.d.). *Literature study: Karen Smith's classroom.* Tempe: Center for Establishing Dialogue in Teaching and Learning, Inc., Arizona State University.

Eeds, M., & Peterson, R. (1991). Teacher as curator:

Learning to talk about books. *The Reading Teacher, 45,* 118–126.

Eeds, M., & Wells, D. (1989). Grand conversations: An exploration of meaning construction in literature study groups. *Research in the Teaching of English, 23*(1) 4–29.

Farrell, E.J., & Squire, J.R. (Eds.). (1990). *Transactions with literature: A fifty-year perspective.* Urbana, IL: National Council of Teachers of English.

Goatley, V.J., Brock, C., & Raphael, T.E. (1995). Diverse learners participating in regular education book clubs. *Reading Research Quarterly, 30*(3), 352–380.

Hepler, S. (1991). Talking our way to literacy in the classroom community. *The New Advocate, 4,* 179–190.

Huck, C.S., Hepler, S.,Hickman, J., & Kiefer, B.Z. (1997). *Children's literature in the elementary school.* Madison, WI: Brown and Benchmark.

Iser, W. (1978). *The act of reading: A theory of aesthetic response.* Baltimore, MD: Johns Hopkins University Press.

Martinez, M., & Roser, N.L. (1995). The books make a difference in story talk. In N.L. Roser & M.G. Martinez (Eds.), *Book talk and beyond: Children and teachers respond to literature* (pp. 32–41). Newark, DE: International Reading Association.

McMahon, S.I., & Raphael, T.E. (1997). *The book club connection: Literacy learning and classroom talk.* New York: Teachers College Press.

O'Flahavan, J.F., Stein, C., Wiencek, J., & Marks, T. (1992, December). *Interpretive development in peer discussion about literature: An exploration of the teacher's role.* Paper presented at the 42nd annual meeting of the National Reading Conference, San Antonio, TX.

Paratore, J.R., & McCormack, R.L. (Eds.). (1997). *Peer talk in the classroom: Learning from research.* Newark, DE: International Reading Association.

Pearson, P.D. (1985). *The comprehension revolution: A twenty-year history of progress and practice related to reading comprehension.* Reading Education Report No. 57. Urbana-Champaign, IL: Center for the Study of Reading.

Peterson, R., & Eeds, M.A. (1990). *Grand conversations: Literature groups in action.* New York: Scholastic.

Rosenblatt, L.M. (1938/1976). *Literature as exploration.* New York: Modern Language Association.

Samway, K.D., & Whang, G. (Eds.). (1995). *Literature study circles in a multicultural classroom.* York, ME: Stenhouse.

Short, K.G., & Kauffman, G. (1995). So what do *I* do?: The role of the teacher in literature circles. In N.L. Roser & M.G. Martinez (Eds.), *Book talk and beyond: Children and teachers respond to literature* (pp. 140–149). Newark, DE: International Reading Association.

Smith, K. (1990). Entertaining a text: A reciprocal process. In K.G. Short and K.M. Pierce (Eds.), *Talking about books: Creating literate communities* (pp. 17–31). Portsmouth, NH: Heinemann.

Vygotsky, L.S. (1978). *Mind in society: The development of higher mental psychological processes.* Cambridge, MA: MIT Press.

Wollman-Bonilla, J.E. (1994). Why don't they "just speak"? Attempting literature discussion with more and less able readers. *Research in the Teaching of English, 28,* 231–258.

CHILDREN'S BOOKS CITED

Avi. (1991). *Nothing but the truth.* New York: Orchard.

Babbitt, Natalie. (1985). *Tuck everlasting.* New York: Farrar, Straus and Giroux.

Byars, Betsy. (1977). *The pinballs.* New York: Harper Trophy.

Cormier, Robert. *Other bells for us to ring.* (1990) New York: Dell Yearling

Fenner, Carol. (1995). *Yolanda's genius.* New York: Aladdin.

Fine, Anne. (1992). *Flour babies.* New York: Puffin.

Fitzhugh, Louise (1964). *Harriet the spy.* New York: Harper and Row.

Fritz, Jean. (1986). *Make way for Sam Houston.* New York: G. P. Putnam's.

Lowry, Lois. (1993). *The giver.* Boston: Houghton Mifflin.

Naylor, Phyllis. (1991). *Shiloh.* New York: Atheneum.

Paterson, Katherine. (1978). *The great Gilly Hopkins.* New York: Harper Trophy.

Paterson, Katherine. (1994). *Flip-flop girl.* New York: Lodestar.

Spinelli, Jerry. (1990). *Maniac Mcgee.* Boston: Little, Brown.

Staples, Suzanne Fisher. (1989). *Shabanu: Daughter of the wind.* New York: Knopf.

Taylor, Mildred D. (1976). *Roll of thunder, hear my cry.* New York: Bantam.

Voigt, Cynthia. (1982). *Dicey's song.* New York: Fawcett Juniper.

Winthrop, Elizabeth. (1985). *The castle in the attic.* New York: Bantam-Skylark.

Differentiated Instruction

Diverse Learners and the Tyranny of Time:
Don't Fix Blame; Fix the Leaky Roof

Effective Academic Interventions in the
United States: Evaluating and Enhancing the
Acquisition of Early Reading Skills

Diverse learners and the tyranny of time: Don't fix blame; fix the leaky roof

Kameenui is Associate Dean of the College of Education and Associate Director of the National Center to Improve the Tools of Educators at the University of Oregon, Eugene, Oregon. His research and writing have focused on instructional approaches for special education students and other diverse learners.

From *The Reading Teacher,* February 1993, Vol. 46, pp. 376–383

In this commentary, I argue against a single "right" method or approach to literacy instruction. I assert that such a search for the "right" approach to literacy instruction is misguided and takes its greatest toll on students who have diverse learning and curricular needs. Instead, I suggest that diverse learners face on a daily basis the tyranny of time, in which the educational clock is ticking while they remain at risk of falling further and further behind in their schooling. I maintain that we should not spend any more time and effort determining or assigning fault for why diverse youngsters are failing, or which approach is the "right" approach to literacy instruction. Rather, we ought to move forward by designing, implementing, and validating instructional programs and interventions for children with diverse learning and curricular needs. These programs and interventions should not be wedded to any single, "right" instructional method, but instead simply work. To achieve this end, I offer six general pedagogical principles that provide a conceptual framework for guiding educators in the development of literacy programs for diverse learners.

The right method myth

As reading professionals, we have imposed upon ourselves an untenable standard of always searching for the single right best method, process, or approach to literacy development and instruction, especially for children in the formative years of schooling. The search for "rightness" is not unique to reading, nor is it unique to reading educators. It seems to be a peculiar and persistent artifact of human beings, no matter what craft we profess or practice. According to literary folklore, Mark Twain once observed, "The difference between the almost right word and the right word is really a large matter—'tis the difference between the lightning bug and the lightning." In another attempt to discern the rightness of something, the noted physicist Wolfgang Pauli responded to a highly speculative proposal in physics by stating, "It's not even wrong" (Flanagan, 1988, p. 226).

Discerning what is *right*, what is *almost right*, and what's *not even wrong* is an especially troublesome task these days for educators, reading researchers, administrators, publishers, and the international reading community in general. The difficulty rests in part in responding to the unique and diverse needs of learners in the classroom. Evidence of this difficulty can be found in the current debates and discussions about definitions of literacy (Calfee, 1991; Goodman, 1990; McGill-Franzen & Allington, 1991; Rush, Moe, & Storlie, 1986; Venezky, 1990, 1992; Venezky, Wagner, & Ciliberti, 1990), literacy instruc-

tion (Fisher & Hiebert, 1990; Yatvin, 1991), whole language and direct instruction (Chall, 1992; Goodman, 1992; Kameenui, 1988; Liberman & Liberman, 1990; Mather, 1992), beginning reading (Adams, 1990, 1991; Bower, 1992; Chaney, 1991), and diverse learners (Garcia, Pearson, & Jimenez, 1990; Stein, Leinhardt, & Bickel, 1989).

Although such debates are intellectually stimulating, they are often based upon the premise that there is a right approach, philosophy, or method of literacy instruction, something that is unlikely to be empirically established anytime soon, and even less likely to be accepted by reading professionals who hold multiple perspectives and epistemologies. Further, the identification of children as diverse learners itself suggests that *multiple* perspectives and approaches will be necessary to accommodate the needs of children who possess differences in abilities and learning histories, and who will be schooled in various instructional contexts.

The realities of diversity

While many of these debates and discussions about the right approach to literacy development and instruction take place within the professional community of reading educators, they are often distant from the realities of the world outside the reading community.

The identification of children as diverse learners itself suggests that multiple *perspectives and approaches will be necessary to accommodate the needs of children who possess differences in abilities and learning histories, and who will be schooled in various instructional contexts.*

Some of these realities were made stark in a recent article by Hodgkinson (1991) entitled "Reform Versus Reality":

- Since 1987, one-fourth of all preschool children in the U.S. have been in poverty.

- Every year, about 350,000 children are born to mothers who are addicted to cocaine during pregnancy. Those who survive birth become children with strikingly short attention spans, poor coordination, and much worse. Of course, the schools will have to teach these children, and getting such children ready for kindergarten costs around $40,000 each—about the same as for children with fetal alcohol syndrome.
- On any given night, between 50,000 and 200,000 children have no home.
- The "Norman Rockwell" family—a working father, a housewife mother, and two children of school age—constitutes only 6% of U.S. households.
- About one-third of preschool children are destined for school failure because of poverty, neglect, sickness, handicapping conditions, and lack of adult protection and nurturance.
(Hodgkinson, 1991, p. 10)

These facts, according to Hodgkinson, are indicative of education's "leaky roof," a metaphor he uses "for the spectacular changes that have occurred in the nature of the children who come to school" (p. 10).

Hodgkinson's (1991) demographic analysis is reinforced by additional reports in the popular press documenting the plight of diverse learners. For example:

The child poverty rate rose by more than 11% during the 1980s, reaching 17.9% in 1989. Black children were the most likely to fall into this group. In 1989, a black child had a 39.8% chance of living in poverty, a Native American child a 38.8% chance and a Hispanic child a 32.2% chance. The figure for Asian children was 17.1% and for white children 12.5%. ("Poverty Rates Rise," 1992)

Similarly, an advertisement for the Children's Defense Fund reads:

Approximately 2.5 million American children were reported abused or neglected last year ....Fourteeen nations boast smarter 13-years-olds than the United States. ("Children's Defense Fund," 1992)

Hodgkinson (1991) concludes his analysis by offering a poignant soliloquy on the current slings and arrows of education's outrageous fortunes:

There is no point in trying to teach hungry or sick children. From this we can deduce one of the most important points in our attempts to deal with education: *educators can't fix the roof all by themselves.* It will require the efforts of many people and organizations—health and social welfare agencies, parents, business and political leaders—to even begin to repair this leaky roof. There is no time to waste in fixing blame; we need to act to fix the roof. And unless we start, the house will continue to deteriorate, and all Americans will pay the price. (p. 10)

The tyranny of time

Hodgkinson's assertion that *"there is no time to waste in fixing blame; we need to act to fix the roof"* is of particular significance to students who reside in the basement of the house with the leaky roof—children identified as poor readers, reading disabled, at-risk, low performers, mildly disabled, language delayed, and culturally disadvantaged, all of whom have diverse learning and curricular needs. Like literacy, the face of diversity is complex, and at this point, it defies a definition comprised of only the right words (Garcia et al., 1990).

Despite the differences that these children bring to school, what is profoundly and unequivocally the same about them is that they are behind in reading and language development. Moreover, they constantly face the tyranny of time in trying to catch up with their peers, who continue to advance in their literacy development. Simply keeping pace with their peers amounts to losing more and more ground for students who are behind. This predicament has been referred to as the "Matthew effect," a concept resurrected and insightfully applied to reading by Stanovich (1986). According to the Matthew effect, the literacy-rich get richer, and the literacy-poor get poorer in reading opportunities, vocabulary development, written language, general knowledge, and so on.

The pedagogical clock for students who are behind in reading and literacy development continues to tick mercilessly, and the opportunities for these students to advance or catch up diminish over time. Benjamin Bloom (1964) concurred with this general phenomenon almost 30 years ago when he observed that *"growth and development are not in equal units per unit of time"* (p. 204, emphasis added). In other words, not all human characteristics (e.g., height, intelligence, vocabulary) grow at the same rate over time; there are periods of rapid growth and periods of relatively slow growth. Bloom noted what we have now come to accept as a developmental and pedagogical truism: "Although it is not invariably true, the period of most rapid growth is likely to be in the early years and this is then followed by periods of less and less rapid growth" (p. 204).

Evidence of the critical importance of what Bloom (1964) referred to as "the early environment and experience" (p. 214) now appears overwhelming:

- According to a study by Juel (1988), the probability that a child who is a poor reader at the end of Grade 1 will remain a poor reader at the end of Grade 4 is .88. There is a near 90% chance of remaining a poor reader after 3 years of schooling. Juel noted, "Children who did not develop good word recognition skills in first grade began to dislike reading and read considerably less than good readers both in and out of school" (p. 27).

Hodgkinson's assertion that "there is no time to waste in fixing blame; we need to act to fix the roof" *is of particular significance to students who reside in the basement of the house with the leaky roof.*

- Allington's program of research (1980, 1983, 1984) on the opportunities children have to read reveals that the average skilled reader reads almost three times more words than the average less-skilled reader (Stanovich, 1986). Similarly, students identified as mildly handicapped appear to "spend significantly less time engaged in writing and silent reading, and more time passively attending, than do their nonhandicapped peers" (O'Sullivan, Ysseldyke, Christenson, & Thurlow, 1990, p. 143).
- Phonemic awareness and knowledge of letter names that prereaders have upon entering school appear to influence reading acquisition (Adams, 1990; Griffith & Olson, 1992; Stahl, 1992; Williams, 1984). As Adams (1990) states, "In the end, the great value of research on prereaders may lie in the clues it gives us toward determining what the less prepared prereaders need most to learn. For these children, we have not a classroom moment to waste. The evidence strongly suggests that we must help them develop their awareness of the phonemic composition of words" (p. 90).

- The amount of reading that children do outside of school appears to strongly influence reading proficiency (Anderson, Wilson, & Fielding, 1988). However, many children come from homes in which there is very little, if any, preschool language and literacy support (Heath, cited in Adams, 1990).
- Children in Grades 2 and 3 who lack decoding skills and a reasonable base of sight words "may be condemned to school careers marred by increasing distance between them and other children unless successful remediation occurs" (Byrne, Freebody, & Gates, 1992, p. 150).
- Matching classroom instruction with reading abilities appears to be difficult for teachers in general education kindergarten classrooms (Durkin, 1990). Durkin notes, "Use of whole class instruction was the practice even when differences in children's abilities were so great as to be obvious to anyone willing to take but a few minutes to observe. Such differences meant that some children kept hearing what they already knew; for others, the observed lesson was too difficult and proceeded too quickly" (p. 24).

Teacher uncertainty and experimentation in the face of diversity

When this evidence is considered in the context of education's leaky roof, it carries the potential for creating at least two serious problems for reading educators. The first is pedagogical paralysis, which is in part reflected in a teacher's lack of personal teaching efficacy (e.g., "What can I possibly do as one teacher to make a difference?") in the face of a "concentration of low-achieving students" in the classroom (Smylie, 1988, p. 23). In a study of teachers' teaching efficacy, Smylie observed, "The lower the achievement level of students in the class, the less likely teachers seem to be to believe that they can affect student learning, despite the level of confidence they may have in their knowledge and skills related to teaching" (p. 23). The characteristics of the classroom (e.g., class size) and heterogeneity of learners appear to affect teachers' beliefs about their ability to influence student learning (Chard & Kameenui, 1992).

Equally problematic, however, is the tendency for educators to engage in fashionable experimentation—experimentation that often draws on fad and fashion (Kameenui, 1991; Slavin, 1989)—rather than well-established and documented practice. This kind of experimentation often occurs when teachers are unsure of what to do with children who are behind. As a result, they experiment with practices that leave some children at risk of falling even further behind in their reading and language development. The experimentation reflects teachers' genuine desire to do the best for their children who, they believe, despite their diverse learning and curricular needs, should benefit from the same "literacy events" and reading activities provided more able readers. However, children who are behind because of language, learning, or reading problems *do* require substantially different kinds of *reading experiences*—ones that go beyond those typically provided more able readers (Mather, 1992).

Some have argued that the current emphasis on "whole language" approaches to beginning reading exacts its harshest consequence on students with learning and language difficulties (Liberman & Liberman, 1990; Mather, 1992). Others have called for striking a reasonable balance between whole language and direct instruction (Chall, 1992; Cunningham, 1991). Still others have argued for whole language only (Edelsky, 1990; Goodman, 1992). While the debates about how best to teach beginning reading are age-old, reaching back more than 100 years to the "beginning of pedagogy" (Bower, 1992, p. 138), the current context of education's leaky roof requires that we consider the purpose and consequences of these debates.

Although educators alone cannot fix education's leaky roof, the plight of today's children in society (Garcia et al., 1990; Hodgkinson, 1991) places an unusual burden on schools, teachers, and even professional organizations such as the International Reading Association to get their houses in order. The water from the leaky roof is rising in the basement, and its cost is greatest to students with diverse curricular, learning, and literacy needs. There is not time to waste in fixing blame; we need to act *now* to fix the roof.

Principles for guiding action

The realities that poor readers remain poor readers, that insufficient opportunities to read seriously deter reading progress, and that particular instructional arrangements (e.g., whole-class instruction) fail to promote adequate reading growth set the stage for the reading community to reconsider the needs of students who face pedagogy's ticking clock. The reading experiences required for these students can be derived and constructed from at least six general pedagogical principles (Dixon, Carnine, & Kameenui, 1992). These principles do not prescribe a single method and by no means represent an exhaustive list. Rather, they offer a conceptual framework for informing our decisions about how to develop the early reading and literacy experiences of these students:

1. *Instructional time is a precious commodity; do not lose it.* If a reading strategy, concept, or problem solving analysis can be taught two different ways and one is more efficient, use the more efficient way.

2. *Intervene and remediate early, strategically, and frequently.* The magnitude of growth in the early years for students who are behind is influenced substantially by what we teach and how we teach. As Stanovich (1986) argues, "Educational interventions that represent a *more of the same* approach will probably not be successful.... The remedy for the problem must be more of a *surgical strike*" (p. 393). The following applications should be considered:

- Provide children with more frequent opportunities to read.
- Promote instructional arrangements that allow children to actively participate in literacy activities, for example, small group story reading instead of one-to-one or whole-class instruction (Morrow & Smith, 1990).
- Help children develop phonemic awareness and knowledge of letter names early.

3. *Teach less more thoroughly.* The conventional wisdom in working with students who have diverse learning and curricular needs is to teach more in less time (Kameenui, 1990; Kameenui & Simmons, 1990). While the logic of this advice seems reasonable (i.e., children who are behind in conceptual knowledge and skills must be taught more in a shorter period of time in order to catch up), the actual practice of trying to teach more in less time simply ignores the constraints of

teaching. Instead, by selecting and teaching only those objectives that are essential, and by focusing instruction on the most important and most generalizable concepts or strategies (i.e., "big ideas," Calfee, Chambliss, & Beretz, 1991; Carnine & Kameenui, 1992), more can be learned more thoroughly in the limited time available.

4. *Communicate reading strategies in a clear and explicit manner, especially during initial phases of instruction.* For many students with learning problems, new concepts and strategies should be explained in clear, concise, and comprehensible language. Explicit instruction is still most effective for teaching concepts, principles, and strategies to at-risk students.

Children will not automatically bloom by being immersed in a literacy hothouse rich with literacy events and activities.

---

5. *Guide student learning through a strategic sequence of teacher-directed and student-centered activities.* Teacher-directed instruction is necessary if students are to catch up and advance with their able-reading peers. Children will not automatically bloom by being immersed in a literacy hothouse rich with literacy events and activities. While these activities enrich students' literacy development, they are not sufficient for children who are behind. Teacher-directed instruction need not preempt, minimize, or supplant child-directed activities to develop literacy (Yatvin, 1991). Both sets of activities have their place; however, reading instruction guided by an efficacious teacher is essential. The goal of reading and literacy instruction is to move from teacher-directed to student-centered activities.

6. *Examine the effectiveness of instruction and educational tools by formatively evaluating student progress.* In testimony given on March 18, 1992, to the Select Committee on Education, Kenneth Komoski, Director of the Education Products Information Exchange,

noted educational materials (e.g., print materials, computer software) are used during more than 90% of the 30 billion hours in which America's 40 million students are in school. In many cases, the efficacy of these materials is questionable, despite state laws (e.g., Florida statute 233.25) that require a learner verification and revision process to substantiate their "instructional effectiveness." Teachers must formatively evaluate the effectiveness of their instructional approaches and materials in order to adapt instruction to meet the needs of learners. As a guideline, current research suggests that measuring student performance twice per week provides an adequate basis for instructional decision making (Deno & Fuchs, 1987).

Conclusion

Human beings, like the words they use, are peculiar creatures, idiosyncratically possessive of their thoughts and words (Bryson, 1990). Even under ideal circumstances, finding the *right* words is indeed difficult. Unless you are part of Wolfgang Pauli's professional community of physics, selecting the right word in the Twain tradition is risky business. Paradoxically, it seems as though words have gotten in the way of our real goal. The standard of always searching for the single right best method for literacy development may be misguided. The search instead should be for multiple perspectives of rightness guided by the diverse needs of learners and sound instructional principles, practices, and craft knowledge.

Hodgkinson (1991) concludes his analysis of the realities in educational reform by posing two "high-priority" questions—"What can educators do to reduce the number of children 'at risk' in America and to get them achieving well in school settings? And how can educators collaborate more closely with other service providers so that we can all work together toward the urgent goal of providing services to the same client?" (p. 16). Before reading educators can begin to collaborate with "other service providers," they must first collaborate with one another. Our charge is clear, and because the rain won't cease, there is no time to waste; we need to act to fix education's leaky roof. These are the right words; anything less is not even wrong.

This article is based in part on a Visiting Minority Scholar lecture at the University of Wisconsin-Madison, March 19, 1992. The preparation of this paper was supported in part by the National Center to Improve the Tools of Educators (NCITE), Grant H180M10006 from the U.S. Department of Education, Office of Special Education Programs.

References

Adams, M. (1990). *Beginning to read: Thinking and learning about print.* Cambridge, MA: MIT Press.

Adams, M. (1991). Beginning to read: A critique by literacy professionals. *The Reading Teacher, 44,* 371-372.

Allington, R.L. (1980). Poor readers don't get to read much in reading groups. *Language Arts, 57,* 872-876.

Allington, R.L. (1983). The reading instruction provided readers of differing reading abilities. *The Elementary School Journal, 83,* 548-559.

Allington, R.L. (1984). Content coverage and contextual reading in reading groups. *Journal of Reading Behavior, 16,* 85-96.

Anderson, R.C., Wilson, P.T., & Fielding, L.G. (1988). Growth in reading and how children spend their time outside of school. *Reading Research Quarterly, 23,* 285-303.

Bloom, B.S. (1964). *Stability and change in human characteristics.* New York: Wiley.

Bower, B. (1992). Reading the code, reading the whole: Researchers wrangle over the nature and teaching of reading. *Science News, 141*(9), 138-141.

Bryson, B. (1990). *The mother tongue: English and how it got that way.* New York: Morrow.

Byrne, B., Freebody, P., & Gates, A. (1992). Longitudinal data on the relations of word-reading strategies to comprehension, reading time, and phonemic awareness. *Reading Research Quarterly, 27,* 141-151.

Calfee, R. (1991). What schools can do to improve literacy instruction. In B. Means, C. Chelemer, & M.S. Knapp (Eds.), *Teaching advanced skills to at-risk students* (pp. 176-203). San Francisco: Jossey-Bass.

Calfee, R.C., Chambliss, M.J., & Beretz, M.M. (1991). Organizing for comprehension and composition. In W. Ellis (Ed.), *All language and the creation of literacy.* Baltimore, MD: Orton Dyslexia Society, Inc.

Carnine, D., & Kameenui, E.J. (1992). *Higher order thinking: Designing curriculum for mainstreamed students.* Austin, TX: Pro-Ed.

Chall, J. (1992, May). *Whole language and direct instruction models: Implications for teaching reading in the schools.* Paper presented at the meeting of the International Reading Association, Orlando, FL.

Chaney, J.H. (1991). Beginning to read: A critique by literacy professionals. *The Reading Teacher, 44,* 374-375.

Chard, D.J., & Kameenui, E.J. (1992). *Instructional efficacy: Toward a specification of efficacy research.* Monograph Number 3, Project PREPARE. Eugene, OR: University of Oregon.

Children's Defense Fund. (1992, July). *SV Entertainment,* p. 13.

Cunningham, P. (1991). *What kind of phonics instruction will we have?* Paper presented at the National Reading Conference, Palm Springs, CA.

Deno, S., & Fuchs, L. (1987). Developing curriculum-based measurement systems for data-based special education problem solving. *Focus on Exceptional Children, 19*(8), 1-16.

Dixon, R., Carnine, D.W., & Kameenui, E.J. (1992). *Curriculum guidelines for diverse learners.* Monograph for National Center to Improve the Tools of Educators. Eugene, OR: University of Oregon.

Durkin, D. (1990). Matching classroom instruction with reading abilities: An unmet need. *Remedial and Special Education, 11*(3), 23-28.

Edelsky, C. (1990). Whose agenda is this anyway? A response to McKenna, Robinson, and Miller. *Educational Researcher, 19*(8), 7-11.

Fisher, C.W., & Hiebert, E.H. (1990). Characteristics of tasks in two approaches to literacy instruction. *The Elementary School Journal, 91*, 3-18.

Flanagan, D. (1988). *Flanagan's version: A spectator's guide to science on the eve of the 21st century.* New York: Vintage.

Garcia, G.E., Pearson, P.D., & Jimenez, R.T. (1990). *The at risk dilemma: A synthesis of reading research.* Champaign, IL: University of Illinois, Reading Research and Education Center.

Goodman, K. (May, 1992). *Whole language and direct instruction models: Implications for teaching reading in the schools.* Paper presented at the meeting of the International Reading Association, Orlando, FL.

Goodman, Y.M. (Ed.). (1990). *How children construct literacy.* Newark, DE: International Reading Association.

Griffith, P.L., & Olson, M.W. (1992). Phonemic awareness helps beginning readers break the code. *The Reading Teacher, 45*, 516-523.

Hodgkinson, H. (1991). Reform versus reality. *Phi Delta Kappan, 73*, 9-16.

Juel, C. (1988, April). *Learning to read and write: A longitudinal study of fifty-four children from first through fourth grade.* Paper presented at the annual meeting of the American Educational Research Association, New Orleans, LA.

Kameenui, E.J. (1988). Direct instruction and the Great Twitch: Why DI or di is not the issue. In J.R. Readence & S. Baldwin (Eds.), *Dialogues in literacy research: Thirty-seventh yearbook of the National Reading Conference* (pp. 39-45). Chicago, IL: National Reading Conference.

Kameenui, E.J. (1990). The language of the REI—Why it's hard to put into words: A response to Durkin and Miller. *Remedial and Special Education, 11*(3), 57-59.

Kameenui, E.J. (1991). Guarding against the false and fashionable. In J.F. Baumann & D.D. Johnson (Eds.), *Writing for publication in reading and language arts* (pp. 17-28). Newark, DE: International Reading Association.

Kameenui, E.J., & Simmons, D.C. (1990). *Designing instructional strategies: The prevention of academic learning problems.* Columbus, OH: Merrill.

Liberman, A., & Liberman, I. (1990). Whole language vs. code emphasis: Underlying assumptions and their implications for reading instruction. *Annals of Dyslexia, 40*, 52-76.

Mather, N. (1992). Whole language reading instruction for students with learning disabilities: Caught in the cross fire. *Learning Disabilities Research & Practice, 7*, 87-95.

McGill-Franzen, A., & Allington, R.L. (1991). Every child's right: Literacy. *The Reading Teacher, 45*, 86-90.

Morrow, L.M., & Smith, J.K. (1990). The effect of group size on interactive storybook reading. *Reading Research Quarterly, 25*, 213-231.

O'Sullivan, P.J., Ysseldyke, J.E., Christenson, S.L., & Thurlow, M.L. (1990). Mildly handicapped elementary students' opportunity to learn during reading instruction in mainstream and special education settings. *Reading Research Quarterly, 25*, 131-146.

Poverty rates rise. (1992, July). *Time*, p. 15.

Rush, R.T., Moe, A.J., & Storlie, R.L. (1986). *Occupational literacy education.* Newark, DE: International Reading Association.

Slavin, R. (1989). PET and the pendulum: Faddism in education and how to stop it. *Phi Delta Kappan, 90*, 750-758.

Smylie, M.A. (1988). The enhancement function of staff development: Organizational and psychological antecedents to individual teacher change. *American Educational Research Journal, 25*, 1-30.

Stahl, S.A. (1992). Saying the "p" word: Nine guidelines for exemplary phonics instruction. *The Reading Teacher, 45*, 618-625.

Stanovich, K.E. (1986). Matthew effects in reading: Some consequences of individual differences in the acquisition of literacy. *Reading Research Quarterly, 21*, 360-407.

Stein, M.K., Leinhardt, G., & Bickel, W. (1989). Instructional issues for teaching students at risk. In R.E. Slavin, N.L. Kesweit, & N.A. Madden (Eds.), *Effective programs for students at risk* (pp. 145-194). Boston: Allyn & Bacon.

Venezky, R.L. (1990). Definitions of literacy. In R.L. Venezky, D.A. Wagner, & B.S. Ciliberti (Eds.), *Toward defining literacy* (pp. 2-16). Newark, DE: International Reading Association.

Venezky, R.L. (1992, Summer). Matching literacy testing with social policy: What are the alternatives? *Connections.* Philadelphia, PA: National Center on Adult Literacy, University of Pennsylvania.

Venezky, R.L., Wagner, D.A., & Ciliberti, B.S. (Eds.). (1990). *Toward defining literacy.* Newark, DE: International Reading Association.

Williams, J.P. (1984). Phonemic analysis and how it relates to reading. *Journal of Learning Disabilities, 17*, 240-245.

Yatvin, J. (1991). *Developing a whole language program for a whole school.* Richmond, VA: Virginia State Reading Association.

Effective academic interventions in the United States: evaluating and enhancing the acquisition of early reading skills

Roland H. Good III, Deborah C. Simmons, and Sylvia B. Smith
University of Oregon

In grades one through three, the primary challenge facing general education teachers and students is the acquisition of basic reading skills. No educational yardstick is used more frequently to evaluate the efficacy of schooling than literacy built upon a firm foundation of basic reading skills. In addition, poor reading skills have been linked to the development or exacerbation of concomitant behavioral and/or emotional problems, including aggressive behavior, hyperactive behavior, patterns of poor effort, poor self-concept, and school dropout.

Professional educators and the public at large have long known that reading is an enabling process that spans academic disciplines and translates into meaningful personal, social, and economic outcomes for individuals. Reading is the fulcrum of academics, the pivotal process that stabilizes and leverages children's opportunities to succeed and to become reflective, independent learners. Despite society's recognition of the importance of successful reading, only recently have we begun to understand the profound and enduring consequences of not learning to read and the newly found evidence of the critical and short-lived period in which we can readily alter reading trajectories (Lyon & Chhabra, 1996).

The educational research program initiated by the National Institute of Child Health and Human Development (NICHHD) reported that "40 per cent of the US population have reading problems severe enough to hinder their enjoyment of reading" (Grossen, 1997, p.5).

National longitudinal studies indicate that more than one in six young children experience reading difficulties in grades one through three (Kameenui, 1996). Though considerable debate surrounds the issue of differentiating children who have "reading disabilities" from those who are poor readers, the reality that almost 20 per cent of all students have significant difficulty learning to read indicates that reading deficits are not specific to disability.

Regardless of disability, children who experience severe difficulty learning to read display two common characteristics that can guide assessment and intervention. A first common denominator among students who place in the lower quartile of the reading continuum is a trajectory of reading progress that diverges extremely early from their peers who are

From *Educational and Child Psychology*, 1998, Vol. 15, No. 1

learning to read successfully. It appears that initial differences in rate of reading acquisition establish a developmental reading trajectory that is resistant to change (e.g., Juel, 1988). The term "trajectory" refers to a relatively smooth and continuous curve of reading progress that extends through the elementary school years. The existence and stability of reading trajectories can be inferred from longitudinal data and observed directly using recent advances in reading measurement.

The second common characteristic of children who experience severe difficulty learning to read is their inability to use the phonologic structure of language to read and write in an alphabetic system. The phonologic deficit results in an inability to use the sound structure of language to learn written language. This deficit manifests itself in an array of phonologic-alphabetic tasks and reliably in the inability to segment words into phonemes and to decode nonsense words (Lyon & Chhabra, 1996). The phonologically based deficit of students with reading difficulties has garnered such empirical convergence that it has been deemed a "core deficit" (Stanovich, 1986; Torgesen & Hecht, 1996).

Differences in developmental reading trajectory

Longitudinal reading studies have examined reading acquisition by measuring reading skills at isolated points in time (e.g., Juel, 1988). One of the most replicated and disturbing conclusions from these studies is that students with poor reading skills initially are likely to have poor reading skills later. Stable reading trajectories can be inferred from the high correlation between reading performance in the early primary grades and reading skills later in school. For example, Juel (1988) found that the probability of a child who was a poor reader in first grade remaining a poor reader in fourth grade was .88.

Monitoring individual developmental reading trajectories

These longitudinal correlations may not communicate sufficiently the magnitude of the problem, and they do not provide a means to monitor individual student progress or to evaluate the effectiveness of interventions. Developmental reading trajectories can be examined directly using Curriculum-based measurement (CBM) in reading (see Shinn, 1989 for information on CBM). Reading CBM procedures are based on standardized, short duration, oral reading fluency tasks. Most frequently, students read from basal reading passages usually derived from their curriculum. For program evaluation purposes, students may read word lists that are developed to represent multiple years of a) curriculum. CBM reading measures have been shown to provide a valid and reliable measure of overall reading proficiency (e.g., Shinn, Good, Knutson, Tilly & Collins, 1992). Using CBM reading, it is possible to examine students' reading trajectories directly and evaluate their rate of progress (Good & Shinn, 1990; Shinn, Good & Stein, 1989).

The differences in reading trajectories for students are illustrated with CBM reading data from the St. Croix Education District in Minnesota. During the 1990-1991 school year, the reading progress of all students in Grades 1 through 5 from four schools was assessed monthly throughout the school year. Once per month, all students read orally for 1 minute a stratified random sample of words from the Harris-Jacobson word list, with equal numbers of words from grade levels 1-6 on each list. Students also read orally for 1 minute from a passage sampled randomly from their grade level of the curriculum. Complete data were available for 926 of the 984 students, 177 to 201 at each grade level.

The performance of the five, single-grade cohorts on the Harris-Jacobson word lists is presented in Figure 1. For each cohort, the 10th and 50th percentiles of student performance on each monthly assessment and on the first two months of the following year are graphed. Through most of first grade, the reading skills and rates of progress of middle (50th percentile) and low (10th percentile) readers are not distinguishable. However, by the end of first grade, distinct developmental reading trajectories are apparent with the discrepancy between middle and poor readers increasing with the passage of time.

Matthew Effects: reading problems get worse

The data displayed in Figure 1 provide direct evidence of what Stanovich (1986) called a "Matthew Effect" after the biblical passage in which the rich get richer and the poor get poorer. According to Stanovich (1986), a Matthew Effect occurs when differences in initial skills lead to faster rates of acquisition of subsequent skills for those students with high skills and slower acquisition for students with lower initial skills.

Differences in developmental reading trajectories can be explained, in part, by a predictable and consequential series of reading-related activities that begin with difficulty in foundational reading skills, progress to fewer encounters and exposure to print, and culminate in lowered motivation and desire to read (Stanovich, 1986). For example, Juel (1988) reported that, by the end of first grade, good readers in her study had seen an average of 18,681 words in running text in basal readers. In contrast, poor readers had been exposed to only 9,975 words, or about half as many words. Thus, the poor readers received half as much practice, half as much opportunity to learn, and were exposed to half as much vocabulary. As low reading trajectories become established, secondary problem behaviors can further impede effective instruction.

Both the early onset and the magnitude of the problem are illustrated by data from the St. Croix Education District. In Figure 2, the CBM reading scores on grade-level passages of second-grade students with poor reading skills (1st to 10th percentile) at the beginning of the year and middle reading skills (45th to 55th percentile) at the beginning of the year are plotted. Each line represents an individual student's developmental reading trajectory. Plotting the trajectories of the middle and low students in this way allows a visual comparison of (a) group performance, (b) the variability of individual performance within the group, and (c) the degree of overlap between groups. The progress of students with middle and low developmental reading trajectories are clearly distinct and nonoverlapping.

For these students, low reading skills that are discrepant from their peers appear to be an intractable problem. However, the problem is not a lack of progress. Students on the low trajectory are progressing. When comparing student performance at the beginning and ending of the second grade, students on the low trajectory gained 25 words per minute in oral reading fluency. The problem is not lack of service. Many students on the low trajectory receive additional educational services and support. Of the 19 students performing in the lowest 10% of second graders, 12 were receiving Chapter 1 services and four were receiving special education. Only three were not receiving additional reading instruction.

The problem of increasingly discrepant reading skills for students on a low developmental reading trajectory is twofold: they begin with lower scores, and they increase their skills at a slower rate.

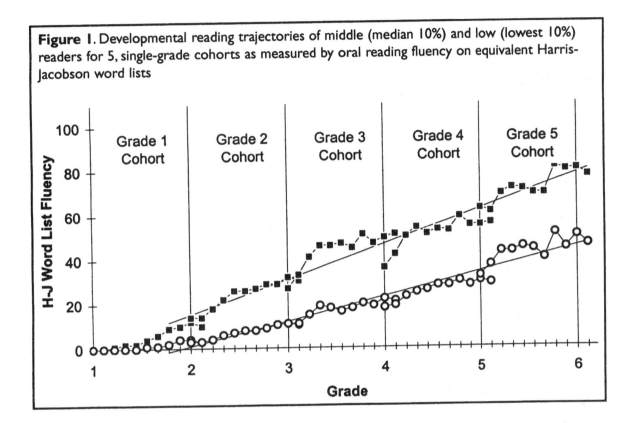

Figure I. Developmental reading trajectories of middle (median 10%) and low (lowest 10%) readers for 5, single-grade cohorts as measured by oral reading fluency on equivalent Harris-Jacobson word lists

The need for early intervention

Low initial skills and low slope combine to make "catching up" all but impossible for students on a low developmental reading trajectory. To "catch up" to students on the middle reading trajectory, students on the low trajectory must attain a reading proficiency of about 100 WCPM by the end of the year. To accomplish this goal, students on the low trajectory must increase their rate of progress from 2 WCPM per month to 10 WCPM per month. However, the mean slope of student progress for all second graders was an increase of about 5 WCPM per month (SD = 2.34). Consequently, students on the low trajectory must increase their rate of progress by 3.5 standard deviations and acquire reading skills twice as fast as the mean progress of their peers to achieve the same reading rate. The solution is to intervene early so that students have both adequate initial skills, and the necessary pre-skills to make adequate progress. With comparable initial skills, students need only to make progress at the same, not a faster, rate as their peers.

Early identification for early intervention

Early intervention requires accurate identification of children at risk for reading failure. In general, direct and frequent measures of reading skills such as CBM have been most accurate in identifying children with reading problems and providing a basis for evaluating interventions (Shinn, 1989). However, even direct measures such as reading CBM cannot identify children who will experience reading failure early enough to prevent the establishment of low reading trajectories. This problem is illustrated in Figure 3 in which individual reading trajectories on grade level passages are plotted for students whose reading skills at the end of first grade will be in the bottom 10%, or in the median 10%. It is not until the end

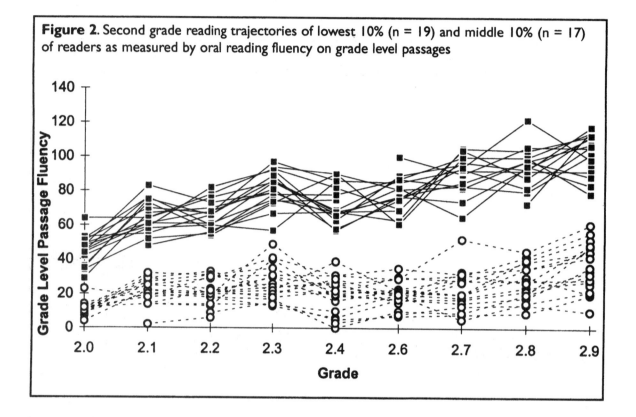

Figure 2. Second grade reading trajectories of lowest 10% (n = 19) and middle 10% (n = 17) of readers as measured by oral reading fluency on grade level passages

of first grade that the developmental reading trajectories are distinct and nonoverlapping. As we have just seen, however, by the end of first grade and beginning of second grade, students on low developmental reading trajectories face nearly insurmountable obstacles to catching up with their peers. The answer lies in the early identification of children with deficits in crucial early literacy skills and enhancing their acquisition of those skills.

Enhancing the acquisition of early reading skills

In the following section, we summarize the converging evidence in beginning reading regarding *what to teach* and *what to assess* to enhance the acquisition of early reading skills. Fortunately, an emerging body of intervention research demonstrates reliable parameters for determining the components of effective early reading instruction. Converging conclusions from multiple sources, including the National Center to Improve the Tools of Educators (NCITE; Kameenui, 1996), the National Institute on Child Health and Human Development (NICHHD; Grossen, 1997), and integrated research reviews (e.g., Adams, 1990; Chard, Simmons & Kameenui, in press; Smith, Simmons & Kameenui, in press; Torgesen & Hecht, 1996) are presented.

Area 1: phonological awareness

Fundamental to early reading success is a facility with the sound structure of our language. Phonological awareness as defined by Torgesen (Torgesen & Hecht, 1996) is "one's sensitivity to, or explicit awareness of, the phonological structure of words in one's language" (p. 136). Although research has not definitively concluded which dimensions of phonological awareness (e.g., segmentation, identity, blending) are obligatory for early reading, con-

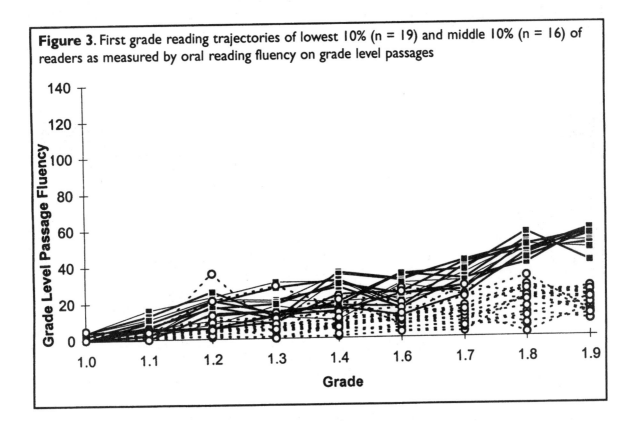

Figure 3. First grade reading trajectories of lowest 10% (n = 19) and middle 10% (n = 16) of readers as measured by oral reading fluency on grade level passages

verging evidence underscores the importance of explicit phonological awareness instruction prior to formal alphabetic awareness instruction, especially for children with deficits in this area (Smith *et al.*, in press). There is no question that students low in phonological awareness are at risk for reading failure and that phonological awareness instruction can ameliorate that risk. Smith's *et al.*, (in press) synthesis of phonological awareness research identified six prevailing findings:

1. Phonological processing explains significant differences between good and poor readers.
2. Phonological awareness may be a group of highly related, distinct phonological abilities or a general ability with multiple dimensions.
3. Phonological awareness has a reciprocal relation to reading acquisition.
4. Phonological awareness is necessary but not sufficient for reading acquisition.
5. Phonological awareness deficits and delays can be reliably identified in young children.
6. Phonological awareness is teachable and promoted by attention to instructional variables.

Area 2: alphabetic understanding

Alphabetic understanding is concerned with the "mapping of print to speech" and establishing a clear link between a letter and a sound. In her review of word recognition research, Juel (1991) cited eight studies that provide considerable evidence of the importance of alphabetic understanding in accounting for differences between good and poor readers. Reliable and efficient letter-sound or grapheme-phoneme correspondence is a critical building block for efficient word recognition (Chard *et al.*, in press).

Area 3: phonological recoding

Vandervelden & Siegel (1997) defined phonological recoding as "the use of systematic relationships between letters and phonemes to recognize the printed match of a spoken word or syllable, to retrieve the pronunciation of an unknown printed string, or to spell" (p. 64).

According to Vandervelden and Siegel, phonological recoding involves a developmental progression. Easiest in the progression is the speech-to-print task in which children hear a word, *frog*, and match it with one of three printed words (e.g., *sad, mitt, frog*). Later in the progression, children use letter-sound correspondences and their positions in sequences to spell and read words. In initial phonological recoding readers recode letter strings into their corresponding sounds and blend the stored sounds into words, overtly and slowly. As children learn to distinguish each sound, they begin, sometimes laboriously, to decode written words by attending to every letter. With redundancy and practice, word recognition efficiencies increase. Phonological recoding has an inverse relationship with the frequency of the words to be recognized in reading. When readers encounter unfamiliar words, they rely on the phonological properties to recognize the word. Familiar words are activated interactively through semantic, orthographic, and phonologic processors (Adams, 1990). It is in the presence of less familiar words that phonological recoding becomes of paramount importance (Chard *et al.*, in press).

A primary issue of current investigation is the level or unit of phonological recoding (i.e., sequential segmentation of each phoneme or a combination of phoneme and orthographic components like b–at). The effect of orthographic sensitivity to word parts upon word recognition speed has prompted considerable, yet somewhat divergent research findings (Chard *et al.*, in press). Ehri's (1991) review of 16 studies indicated that orthographic sensitivity follows automatic phonological recoding skill and repeated reading of phonologically regular and irregular words sharing the same patterns. Other studies show that skilled readers become sensitive to rule-governed word parts as opposed to word parts that occur frequently but do not adhere to alphabetic rules.

Area 4: accuracy and fluency with connected text

Not surprisingly, less skilled readers' comprehension continues to be highly dependent upon word recognition skills (Stanovich, 1991). Readers who are not yet facile at phonological recoding fail to recode words in meaningful groups and, therefore, are less likely to maintain the meaning of a clause or sentence in short-term memory (Adams, 1990). Thus, poor word recognition appears to limit (a) storage of and access to word meanings, and (b) ability to access or remember sequences of words (Chard *et al.*, in press).

A first step in enhancing early reading acquisition is identifying *what to teach*. The essential skills of phonological awareness, alphabetic understanding, phonological re-coding, and accuracy and fluency with connected text can be enhanced by making them instructional priorities in the early grades. To realize optimal benefit, however, these instructional priorities must be taught through validated methods. In the following section, we profile the interface of *what to teach* and *how to teach* using phonological awareness as the example focus area. We focus on phonological awareness for two reasons. First, phonological awareness assumes a pivotal role in establishing a developmental reading trajectory toward literacy. Second, the importance of phonological awareness in early literacy instruction is unequivocal, but underestimated by teachers and teacher trainers. In fact, phonological awareness has been referred to as the "missing foundation of teacher education" (Moats, 1995, p. 9).

Evaluating the acquisition of early reading skills: linking assessment to intervention to outcomes

The selection of phonological awareness programs that document effectiveness for most children or that meet the criteria drawn from phonological awareness intervention research provides an initial basis to guide program selection decisions. However, two problems remain. First, evidence for program effectiveness is essential for *each* program implementation. Local characteristics may vary, the programs may not be implemented with sufficient fidelity to attain desired outcomes, or the great ideas that work in controlled environments may not work in practice. The stakes are too high for educators to implement great ideas and hope for the desired outcomes. Wrong guesses can affect the learning, success, and life outcomes for our children. We need evidence to show our constituents and ourselves that what we are doing is having the desired effect. Second, we know that not all children with phonological awareness deficits benefit sufficiently, even from these research-based interventions (e.g., Blachman, 1994). However, these are the very children most in need of early effective intervention. "For these children, we have not a classroom moment to waste" (Adams, 1990, p. 90). We need direct measures of early literacy skills to assess student progress and make formative intervention decisions to ensure desired outcomes for all students.

Our thesis is that effective academic interventions are predicated on the linkage of assessment to intervention. However, many current assessment practices in the area of early literacy and readiness are not equal to the challenge because they (a) assess reading indirectly using latent constructs hypothesized to be related to reading, (b) assess performance infrequently, and (c) do not assess student progress. Instead, dynamic indicators of basic early literacy skills are needed to provide a basis for linking assessment with intervention to enhance outcomes.

Dynamic indicators of basic early literacy skills

Addressing the flaws in current assessment procedures for early identification and early intervention requires more than just a new test; it requires a different approach to assessment. In particular, assessment procedures are needed to (a) identify children early who are experiencing difficulty acquiring early literacy skills, (b) contribute to the effectiveness of interventions by providing ongoing feedback to teachers, parents, and students, (c) evaluate the effectiveness of interventions for individual students, (d) determine when student progress is adequate and further intervention is not necessary, (e) identify accurately children with serious learning problems, and (f) evaluate the overall effectiveness of early intervention efforts.

To accomplish these purposes, Dynamic Indicators of Basic Early Literacy Skills (DIBELS) have been developed by a team of researchers at the University of Oregon (Good & Kaminski, 1996; Kaminski & Good, 1996; Kaminski & Good, in press). The rationale, procedures, and criteria for developing DIBELS parallels that of curriculum-based measurement (CBM) (Deno, 1992), with some exceptions described in Kaminski & Good (in press). First, DIBELS measures should be *dynamic* allowing a continuing evaluation of students' literacy skills as they change with the passage of time. They also must be sensitive to changes in student performance as a result of effective interventions. Dynamic measures of student change must be easy to administer, capable of repeated and frequent administration, and time efficient and cost effective.

Second, DIBELS need to be *indicators* – representative of, or correlated with, important skill areas. Like CBM, DIBELS are intended to provide educators with "indicators of 'vital signs' of growth in basic skills comparable to the vital signs of health used by physicians" (Deno, 1992, p. 6). DIBELS are not intended to be exhaustive of all important skill areas for young children, but to provide a fast and efficient indication of the academic well-being of students with respect to important early literacy skills. Low performance on these measures would not be expected to identify all problem areas, but would indicate that educators should be concerned about the child's progress. As an indicator, DIBELS should be reliable and valid with respect to other measures of risk and early literacy.

Finally, DIBELS measures of *basic early literacy skills* are needed. Measures of basic early literacy skills need to satisfy two criteria. First, the measures should have predictive validity with respect to future reading performance. Second, and even more importantly, the measures should be functionally related to reading acquisition; instruction and acquisition of the skills should be causally related to success in early reading acquisition. While measures meeting both criteria are most desirable, measures that satisfy the first criterion only can still be helpful for some purposes. Phonological awareness measures, in particular, have emerged as strong predictors of later reading skills that are causally related to reading success. Two DIBELS measures of phonological awareness have been developed and validated for use with children in kindergarten and early first grade. For a discussion of other DIBELS measures and their relation to literacy acquisition, see Kaminski and Good (1996).

Phoneme Segmentation Fluency (PSF) is a DIBELS measure of phonological awareness intended for children in winter of kindergarten through fall of first grade. In PSF, children are asked to segment a spoken word into its component sounds. For example, if the spoken word was "fish," a child would say the sounds /f/ /i/ /sh/. The child receives credit for each correct sound segment of the word produced. Thus, if the child says /f/, he or she would receive credit for 1 correct sound segment. If the child says /f/ /ish/ they would receive credit for 2 correct sound segments. Complete segmentation would receive credit for 3 sound segments. The task is timed, and the number of correct sound segments per minute is computed.

A single PSF probe consists of 10 words and takes about 3 minutes to administer and score. A set of 20 probes is available, with each probe consisting of a random sample of 10 words from a pool of 2 and 3 phoneme words selected from early reading curricula and language word lists. A single probe has a reliability of .88, and the average of 3 probes has a reliability of .96. The one-year predictive validity with reading outcome measures ranges from .73 to .91 (Kaminski & Good, in press).

Onset Recognition Fluency (OnRF) is another DIBELS measure of phonological awareness intended for children in late preschool through the winter of kindergarten. A single OnRF probe consists of 16 items. A recognition response is required for 12 items, in which the child is presented with 4 pictures and asked, for example, "Which picture begins with /b/?" A production response is required for 4 items, with the child shown a picture of a hat, for example, and asked, "What sound does 'hat' begin with?" Again, 20 probes are available, each an alternate form constructed by random sampling from a pool of items. The reliability of a single probe is .65, and the reliability of the average of 5 probes is .90. The concurrent validity of OnRF with PSF ranges from .44 to .60 (Kaminski & Good, in press).

Evaluating student progress

Direct measures of the slope of student progress when provided with instruction are crucial in evaluating a child's risk for reading failure and for evaluating the effectiveness of early interventions. Using direct and frequent measures of early literacy skills, the extent to which a child's skills are changing can be examined. A child who is rapidly acquiring early literacy skills will exhibit a large positive slope. A child who is making little progress will display a slope near zero. Considering the slope of student progress is essential for evaluating the effectiveness of an intervention for an individual child: An intervention is effective if it results in an increase in the slope of student progress. Consequently, a measurement system that assess response to instruction must be used instead of static measures of what a student knows (Howell, 1986). No matter how great an intervention sounds, no matter how much it costs, no matter how much research has been published, and no matter how many criteria or belief systems it satisfies, if the intervention does not change the child's trajectory, then it is not effective for that child and a change is indicated.

Early, effective intervention is especially urgent for those children who experience difficulty acquiring early literacy skills like phonological awareness and letter-sound correspondence even with effective, research-based interventions. While some have termed these children "non-responders," or "treatment resistors" (e.g., Blachman, 1994) we prefer the term "children-for-whom-an-effective-intervention-has-not-yet-been-implemented," although it is a bit of a mouthful. A two-thirds response rate is not good enough: our goal is all. The consequences of reading failure are too serious, pervasive, and lifelong to settle for less. For children-for-whom-an-effective-intervention-has-not-yet-been-implemented, mobilizing sufficient instructional resources to identify, design, and implement an effective intervention is urgent. A problem-solving model of assessment for educational decisions based on the DIBELS measures is described elsewhere (Good & Kaminski, 1996).

Enhancing and evaluating early reading acquisition: the big ideas

While many children learn to read regardless of the instructional methods and procedures used by educators, many children will learn because of what and how we teach. As the number of learners with diverse needs continues to increase, we can expect the importance of instruction to increase as well. Kindergarten and first grade are times of unprecedented opportunity. If students can complete their first two years of school with adequate early reading skills, on a trajectory toward literacy, an important step toward a successful school experience will have been attained. Perhaps never before has the education profession had at its disposal such validated principles and practices to inform instructional decisions, alter achievement trajectories, and achieve this vision. In this article we have focused on some big ideas to help guide instruction and assessment:

1. Establish early reading acquisition as an urgent priority.
2. Target phonological awareness as a core component of early effective interventions.
3. Employ research-based principles as a guide to selecting instructional programs and interventions.
4. Establish an intervention/evidence feedback loop.
5. Expect intervention to change developmental reading trajectories.

The linkage of assessment and intervention is essential to accomplish this vision. The history of education is replete with examples of intuitively and theoretically appealing innovations that failed to achieve their espoused effects. Whether it is teaching to students' learning modalities (Kavale & Forness, 1987) or California's abandoning skills teaching in the late 1980s and embracing a whole language approach (Honig, 1996), adopting instructional methods and innovations that lack efficacy can have profound and enduring effects. No matter how great the idea or how compelling the research, if an intervention is not working, something must change. Theory and prior research are extremely valuable tools for selecting and designing interventions, but the empirical criterion is paramount.

References

Adams, M. J. (1990). *Beginning to read: Thinking and learning about print.* Cambridge, MA: The MIT Press.

Adams, M. J., Foorman, B. R., Lundberg, I. & Beeler, T. D. (1997). *Phonemic awareness in young children: A classroom curriculum.* Baltimore: Brookes.

Blachman, B. A. (1994). What we have learned from longitudinal studies of phonological processing and reading, and some unanswered questions: A response to Torgesen, Wagner, and Rashotte. *Journal of Learning Disabilities, 27,* 287-291.

Byrne, B. & Fielding-Barnsley, R. (1991). *Sound foundations: An introduction to prereading skills.* Sydney, Australia: Peter Leyden.

Chard, D. J., Simmons, D. C. & Kameenui, E. J. (in press). Word recognition: Research bases. In D. C. Simmons & E. J. Kameenui (Eds.), *What reading research tells us about children with diverse learning needs.* Mahwah, NJ: Erlbaum.

Deno, S. L. (1992). The nature and development of curriculum-based measurement. *Preventing School Failure, 36*(2), 5-10.

Good, R. H. & Kaminski, R. A. (1996). Assessment for instructional decisions: Toward a proactive/prevention model of decision making for early literacy skills. *School Psychology Quarterly, 11,* 326-336.

Good, R. H. & Shinn, M. R. (1990). Forecasting accuracy of slope estimates for reading curriculum-based measurement: Empirical evidence. *Behavioral Assessment, 12,* 179-193.

Grossen, B. (1997). *Thirty years of research: What we know about how children learn to read: A synthesis of research on reading from the National Institute of Child Health and Human Development.* Santa Cruz, CA: The Center for the Future of Teaching and Learning.

Honig, B. (1996). *Teaching our children to read: The role of skills in a comprehensive reading program.* Thousand Oaks, CA: Corwin.

Howell, K. (1986). Direct assessment of academic performance. *School Psychology Review, 15,* 324-335.

Juel, C. (1988). Learning to read and write: A longitudinal study of 54 children from first through fourth grades. *Journal of Educational Psychology, 80,* 437-447.

Juel, C. (1991). Beginning reading. In R. Barr, M. L. Kamil, P. B. Mosenthal & P. D. Pearson (Eds.), *Handbook of reading research* (Vol. 2, pp. 759-788). New York: Longman.

Kameenui, E. J. (Ed.). (1996). *Learning to read/reading to learn: Helping children with learning disabilities to succeed information kit. (Technical Report).* Eugene, OR: National Center to Improve the Tools of Educators.

Kaminski, R. A. & Good, R. H. (1996). Toward a technology for assessing basic early literacy skills. *School Psychology Review, 25,* 215-227.

Kaminski, R. A. & Good, R. H. (in press). Assessing early literacy skills in a problem-solving model: Dynamic indicators of basic early literacy skills. In M. R. Shinn (Ed.), *Advanced applications of Curriculum-based measurement.* New York: Guilford.

Kavale, K. A. & Forness, S. R. (1987). Substance over style: A quantitative synthesis assessing the efficacy of modality testing and teaching. *Exceptional Children, 54,* 228-234.

Lyon, G. R. (1995). Toward a definition of dyslexia. *Annals of Dyslexia, 45,* 3-27.

Lyon, G. R. & Chhabra, V. (1996). The current state of the science and the future of specific reading disability. *Mental Retardation and Developmental Disabilities Research Reviews, 2,* 2-9.

Moats, L. C. (1995). The missing foundation in teacher education. *American Educator, 19*(2), 9, 43-51.

O'Connor, R., Notari-Syverson, A. & Vadasy, P. F. (1998). *Ladders to literacy: An activity book for kindergarten children.* Baltimore: Brookes.

Shinn, M. R. (Ed.). (1989). *Curriculum-based measurement: Assessing special children.* New York: Guilford.

Shinn, M. R., Good, R. H., Knutson, N., Tilly, W. D. & Collins, V. L. (1992). Curriculum-based measurement reading fluency: A confirmatory analysis of its relation to reading. *School Psychology Review, 21,* 459-479.

Shinn, M. R., Good, R. H. & Stein, S. (1989). Summarizing trend in student achievement: A comparison of models. *School Psychology Review, 18,* 356-370.

Smith, S. B., Simmons, D. C. & Kameenui, E. J. (in press). Phonological awareness: Research bases. In D. C. Simmons & E. J. Kameenui (Eds.), *What reading research tells us about children with diverse learning needs.* Mahwah, NJ: Erlbaum.

Stanovich, K. E. (1986). Matthew effects in reading: Some consequences of individual differences in the acquisition of literacy. *Reading Research Quarterly, 21,* 360-406.

Stanovich, K. E. (1991). Word recognition: Changing perspectives. In R. Barr, M. L. Kamil, P. B. Mosenthal & P. D. Pearson (Eds.), *Handbook of reading research* (Vol. 2, pp. 418-452). New York: Longman.

Torgesen, J. K. & Bryant, P. (1994). *Phonological awareness training for reading.* Austin, Texas: PRO-ED.

Torgesen, J. K. & Davis, C. (1996). Individual difference variables that predict response to training in phonological awareness. *Journal of Experimental Child Psychology, 63,* 1-21.

Torgesen, J. K. & Hecht, S. A. (1996). Preventing and remediating reading disabilities: Instructional variables that make a difference for special students. In M. F. Graves, P. van den Broek & B. M. Taylor (Eds.), *The first R: Every child's right to read* (pp. 133-159). New York: Teachers College Press.

Vandervelden, M. C. & Siegel, L. S. (1995). Phonological recoding and phoneme awareness in early literacy: A developmental approach. *Reading Research Quarterly, 30,* 854-873.

Vandervelden, M. C. & Siegel, L. S. (1997). Teaching phonological processing skills in early literacy: A developmental approach. *Learning Disability Quarterly, 20,* 63-81.

The authors express their appreciation to Gary Germann and the faculty, students, and administrators of St. Croix Education District in Pine County, Minnesota, for the use of their progress data. This research was supported, in part, by the Early Childhood Research Institute on Program Performance Measures: A Growth and Development Approach (H024360010) and by the National Center to Improve the Tools of Educators (H180M10006) funded by the U.S. Department of Education, Office of Special Education Programs.

Address all correspondence concerning this article to Roland H. Good III, School Psychology Program, DABCS College of Education, 5208 University of Oregon, Eugene, OR 97403-5208, roland_good@ccmail.uoregon.edu.

(Acknowledgments, continued from page 2)

Association. All rights reserved. Dowhower, S. L. (1999) "Supporting a Strategic Stance in the Classroom: A Comprehension Framework for Helping Teachers Help Students to Be Strategic." *The Reading Teacher, 52*, 672–683. Reprinted with permission of Sarah Lynn Dowhower and the International Reading Association. All rights reserved. Kameenui, E. J. (1993, February). "Diverse Learners and the Tyranny of Time: Don't Fix Blame; Fix the Leaky Roof." *The Reading Teacher, 46*(5), 376–383. Reprinted with permission of Edward J. Kameenui and the International Reading Association. All rights reserved. Nagy, W. E. (1988). *Teaching Vocabulary to Improve Reading Comprehension* (pp. 1–24). Newark, DE: International Reading Association. Reprinted with permission of William E. Nagy and the International Reading Association. All rights reserved. Rasinski, T. V. (1989). "Fluency for Everyone: Incorporating Fluency Instruction in the Classroom." *The Reading Teacher, 42*, 690–693. Reprinted with permission of Timothy V. Rasinski and the International Reading Association. All rights reserved. Templeton, S. and Morris, D. (1999) "Questions Teachers Ask About Spelling." *Reading Research Quarterly, 34*, 102–112. Reprinted with permission of Shane Templeton and the International Reading Association. All rights reserved.

Stephen Krensky: "The History of the English Language" by Stephen Krensky. Copyright ©1996 by Stephen Krensky. No part of this material may be reproduced in whole or part without the express written permission of the author or his agent. Stephen Krensky is the author of over fifty books for children. For more information on the author and his books, please visit www.stephenkrensky.com.

Lawrence Erlbaum Associates, Inc.: Excerpted from "Emergent Literacy: Research Bases" by Barbara K. Gunn, Deborah C. Simmons, and Edward J. Kameenui. In *What Reading Research Tells Us About Children With Diverse Learning Needs,* edited by Deborah C. Simmons and Edward J. Kameenui. Mahwah, NJ: Lawrence Erlbaum Associates, Inc., 1998. Used by permission of the publisher.

Louisa Cook Moats: "Spelling: The Difference Instruction Makes" by Louisa Cook Moats. In *The California Reader,* Summer 1997. Used by permission of Louisa Cook Moats.

The Ohio State University, College of Education: "Repeated Reading: A Strategy for Enhancing Fluency and Fostering Expertise" by Irene H. Blum and Patricia S. Koskinen. In *Theory Into Practice,* Summer 1991, Vol. 30, No. 3. Copyright © 1991 by the College of Education, The Ohio State University. Reprinted with permission of the authors and The Ohio State University.

Taylor and Francis: Adapted from "The Multisyllabic Word Dilemma: Helping Students Build Meaning, Spell, and Read 'Big' Words" by Patricia M. Cunningham. In *Reading and Writing Quarterly: Overcoming Learning Difficulties,* 1998, Vol. 14, No. 2, pp. 189–218, Taylor & Francis, Philadelphia, PA. Reproduced with permission. All rights reserved. Copyright 1997, "Automaticity and Inference Generation During Reading Comprehension" by Richard Thurlow and Paul van den Broek, *Reading and Writing Quarterly: Overcoming Learning Difficulties,* Vol. 13, No. 2, pp. 165–181. Reproduced by permission of Taylor & Francis, Inc./Routledge, Inc., http: www.routledge-ny.com.

Joseph K. Torgesen and Patricia Mathes: "What Every Teacher Should Know About Phonological Awareness" by Joseph K. Torgesen and Patricia Mathes. Used by permission of the authors.

Wadsworth Publishing, a division of Thomson Learning: "Reading as a Gateway to Language Proficiency for Language-Minority Students in the Elementary Grades" by Valerie Anderson and Marsha Roit. In *Promoting Learning for Culturally and Linguistically Diverse Students: Classroom Applications from Contemporary Research, 1st edition,* by R. M. Gersten and R. T. Jiménez. Copyright © 1998. Reprinted with permission of Wadsworth, a division of Thomson Learning. Fax 800-730-2215.